HIT AND MISS

THE STORY OF THE JOHN BARRY SEVEN

HIT AND MISS

THE STORY OF THE JOHN BARRY SEVEN

Geoff Leonard · Pete Walker

First published in 2018 by Redcliffe Press Ltd.,
81g Pembroke Road, Bristol BS8 3EA

© Geoff Leonard and Pete Walker
www.johnbarry.org.uk

British Library Cataloguing in Publication Data.
A catalogue record for this book is available from The British Library

ISBN 978-1-911408-39-0

Design and cover design: Ruud Rozemeijer

Printed and bound in the Czech Republic via Akcent Media

CONTENTS

Acknowledgements   vi
Picture Sources   vii
Preface   ix
Authors' Note   x

1   We All Love To Rock   11

2   The Bee's Knees   46

3   Beat for Beat Girl   80

4   Hit and Hits   110

5   The Magnificent Seven   153

6   I'm Movin' On   195

7   Seven (New) Faces   227

8   The Party's Over   259

    Postscript: Life after 'The Seven' – What Happened Next   302

    Group Members Included   318

    Awards   318

    Selected Diary of Events   319

    Selected TV and Radio Appearances   325

    Selected Discography   338

    Selected Bibliography   342

    Index   344

ACKNOWLEDGEMENTS

This book would not have been possible without the help of a large number of people. We received magnificent support from all the former members of The John Barry Seven, but special mention must be given to: Alan Bown, Vic Flick, Jimmy Stead, Ray Russell, Terry Childs, Mike Peters, Stan Haldane, Bob Downes, Jeff Bannister, Mike Cox, Ken Golder, Keith Kelly, Ray Stiles, Ronald Arghyrou, Dave Elvin, Dave Richmond, Les Reed OBE, Brian Hazelby, Bobby Graham, Dougie Wright, Ray Cooper and John Barry OBE.

We also gratefully thank: Timothy Ades, Rachel Bell, David Boocock, Bill Boston, Gareth Bramley, Joe Brown, Dave Bryceson, John Burgess, Dave Burke, Jon Burlingame, Ruth Caleb OBE, James Carr, Jackie Dennis, Maureen Evans, Ann Golder, Aedín Gormley, John Hutchinson, Bob Kingston, Jeffrey Kruger MBE, Spencer Leigh, Emma Lloyd-Jones, Cormac Loane, Donald MacLean, Brian Matthew, Alan More, Garth Newton, Jess O'Neill, Liza Page, Julie Rayne, Ian & Claire Salmon, John Scott, Julie Smith, Peter Stanhope, Alan Taylor, David Toop, Ken Townsend MBE, Eric Tring, Peter Varley, Julian Ward-Davies, Pip Wedge, Brian Willey, Marty Wilde MBE.

The following organisations also provided valuable assistance:

BBC Written Archives
EMI Archives
The Press, York
Bristol Central Library
Stonnall History Group
Chatteris Community Archive
The Stage
New Musical Express
Disc
Melody Maker
Record Mirror
Pipeline Magazine
British Newspaper Library

PICTURE SOURCES

Pages 39 (bottom) 41 (bottom), 198 & 199 – V & A Museum; 41 (top), 77 (top), 103 (bottom), 147 (bottom), 309 (top) & 314 (top) – Mirrorpix; 44 (bottom) – The Press, York; 187 (bottom) – Getty Images; 191 (bottom) & back cover – Rex Features; 264 (top) & 306 (bottom) – Gered Mankowitz.

We are also grateful to the following for the use of their photographs: Jeff Bannister, Norman Fowler, Stan Haldane, Mike Peters, Jimmy Stead, Ken Golder, Vic Flick, Pip Wedge, Alan Bown, Bobby Graham, Emma Lloyd-Jones, and Peter Varley.

Whereas every effort has been made to supply the book with pristine photographic images throughout, there have been occasions on which this has not been possible. Of those featured with any imperfections, they were identified as being far too relevant and/or rare to have warranted rejection solely on the grounds of quality.

FROM THE SAME AUTHORS

Books:

John Barry: A Life In Music
John Barry – The Man with the Midas Touch

CDs:

Beat Girl/Stringbeat
John Barry – The Hits & the Misses
John Barry – The Early Years

The web:

johnbarry.org.uk

ohboy.org.uk

johnbarry.org.uk/adamfaith/

ohboy.org.uk/thank-your-lucky-stars/

Facebook: The John Barry Seven Appreciation Society

PREFACE

Hit and Miss: The Story of The John Barry Seven has been on the table for a long while now. For me, the lengthy gestation period can be traced as far back as a wet winter's day in 1982 when I entered the cramped confines of the *NME* offices in Carnaby Street with a view to working through back copies dating from 1957 onwards. The aim was relatively small-scale: to lay the groundwork towards a planned article for *Record Collector* magazine.

Although ultimately rejected, it sowed the seed of an even grander project, for little did I know at the time, elsewhere, another budding writer, Geoff Leonard – a first-generation JB7 admirer – shared similar aspirations. However, his loftier ambition stretched to publishing a fully-fledged biography. *John Barry: The Man With The Midas Touch* was the summation of further extensive research, a great deal more legwork, access to an array of primary sources plus invaluable discussions with some of the main players; among them John Barry, himself, with whom Geoff struck up a genuine rapport over a number of years. Many a transatlantic telephone call was made between their homes in Bristol and Oyster Bay (New York) during that period.

Being a book designed primarily to encapsulate Barry's entire career meant that a delicate balance needed to be maintained, much to the detriment of a good deal of what had been gleaned about the earlier years. In fact, so much was omitted that it was always our intention to publish a companion volume designed to concentrate solely on The JB7's colourful history, the culmination of which is the tome you are now reading.

Since *'Midas Touch'* was published in 2008, we have been able to build upon our initial findings considerably, to the point where the text now bears little resemblance to what was first drafted. We have since spoken to and corresponded with many more significant contributors to the story – in particular, past band members – each and every one of them most helpful and cooperative in providing further insights, thereby enabling us to flesh out events with greater detail and accuracy.

As a result, we have managed to explode a few myths along the way and, indeed, have even come to contradict our own previously held assumptions at times. Therefore, if you do come across a piece of information that appears to be at variance with what you may have first read in *'Midas Touch'*, then it is because we have been stood corrected either by the sheer weight of evidence presented to us or through conversations with one or more of the protagonists.

There are many people deserving of our thanks and gratitude and, as such, they are acknowledged above. If we have missed anyone who should have been included, then we can only apologise in advance. Sadly, a good few of those named are no longer with us, which makes it all the more poignant for us knowing full well that they will have never seen the finished article. Nevertheless, their contributions proved invaluable and were always greatly appreciated. Hopefully, their part in the story will live on via the book.

We are pleased with the outcome; we only hope you will be too.

Pete Walker, September 2018

AUTHORS' NOTE:

Sales figures listed in the text pertaining to John Barry Seven vinyl releases were obtained from EMI Archives (Hayes, Middlesex) and apply to total UK sales up to the end of April 1963 (unless otherwise stated).

Comparative prices and values were derived from a number of sources including the 'moneysorter' website; both volumes of David Kynaston's *Modernity Britain* (see bibliography) and *The Daily Mail*'s 'Weekend' supplement (18/11/2017).

1

WE ALL LOVE TO ROCK

FEBRUARY – DECEMBER 1957

This was a very rough rock and roll group. The size was large for this sort of music – the arrangements very poor. The intonation in the band was very bad and there were no good soloists. The Band was built around one singer – the leader, John Barry. He had not much drive or personality in his voice. No!

– the verdict of Jimmy Grant (BBC Light Programme Producer)
on The Seven's first radio audition

*When he (Barry) made up his mind to do something,
woe betide you if you tried to make him change!*

– June Lloyd-Jones (Barry's sister)

The circuitous route taken by John Barry in becoming Britain's pre-eminent and most decorated film composer of all time was an extraordinary one that was comprehensibly covered in our companion volume: *John Barry - The Man With The Midas Touch.* One significant by-product of his steely ambition was in the formation of the ensemble that gave him a firm grounding in the music business *per se*, The John Barry Seven.

In many a potted pen-picture of John Barry posted on the internet or printed in music encyclopaedia these days, The John Barry Seven are represented, more often than not, as a mere footnote to a dazzling career festooned with Oscars, Grammys and BAFTAs. However, were it not for the existence of The Seven in its various incarnations, John Barry's own path towards 'cinematic immortality' may have been seriously derailed or, worse still, permanently stymied. The purpose of this book is in redressing the balance somewhat by explaining the importance of The John Barry Seven to Barry, himself, and also by giving prominence to a talented group of musicians who created a niche of their own on the British music scene from 1957 to 1965. In doing so, we shall illustrate just how well received and hard-working an act they were.

In the annual music polls conducted immediately prior to the Liverpool 'beat group' explosion, The John Barry Seven were second only to The Shadows in terms of popularity. They packed out auditoriums night after night; appeared on TV and radio regularly; sold thousands of records, and even had a fan club set up in their name.

Out of The John Barry Seven, many fine musicians emerged – some drifted out of the music business, while others forged successful careers from within it. This book is their chance to claim a moment in the sun, although throughout the text, the shadow of illustrious leader, John Barry, looms large and is never that far away from shaping events. It is probably fair to say that once he decided to relinquish his role as a 'hands-on' touring member of the band, they began to lead increasingly separate existences, parallel lives even, and would eventually drift apart. Nonetheless, Barry's looming presence was never far from the band while it remained viable.

What you will discover throughout the book is just how industrious the life of a jobbing musician was during the period under discussion and, allied to that, just how precarious a career in the music industry can be. This is a story that will be viewed through the lens of the 'spit and sawdust', 'bed and breakfast', 'blue collar' end of the show business telescope with only the odd glimpse of London Palladium-like glamour and ostentation surfacing.

Why The John Barry Seven failed to enter pop folklore in quite the same way as The Shadows have done is a difficult one to fathom, given that, in Vic Flick, they possessed a lead guitarist as distinctive and as versatile as Hank B. Marvin. The reasons are in all likelihood due to the rationale behind their formations together with the rapidly changing musical climates during these periods, barely two years separating them.

The John Barry Seven was formed to further John Barry's musical aspirations and structured from the outset on an established 'jazz band' model, with a dominant leader fronting his hirelings (including brass, rhythm and woodwind sections) in keeping with many a dance or big band line-up emanating from the 1920s onwards. This just so happened to have occurred at the very point at which a major new musical trend had begun to emerge, which left those 'big band/ dance band' ensembles struggling to survive. Barry jumped ship to keep up with the prevailing fashion, but kept the same structure in place. In an attempt to capture the best of both worlds, he experimented with vocals before settling on an instrumental format. That way the band were playing to their strengths, but in doing so and by dint of the type of work they were chasing, found themselves backing dozens of artists rather than concentrating solely on their own material. This became a bone of contention among some members of the band and was why Barry, himself, eventually left, so that he could concentrate on his own music.

The Shadows, on the other hand, emerged directly out of the shadows of Cliff

Richard, solely to back him on stage and on record. These young musicians were unashamed first generation 'skifflers-come-rock 'n' rollers' with a more democratic outlook, who had not been subjected to a hierarchic, disciplined National Service experience. What's more, the 'big band' model was almost extinct by then in any case. Had The John Barry Seven emerged at that exact time and had been exclusively aligned to Adam Faith (who, like Cliff, was also weaned on skiffle and rock 'n' roll); had they been called 'The Rialtos', 'The Farragos' or 'The Rodeos', say, rather than being stuck with a 'big band' moniker, then they might well have enjoyed equal prominence and respect.

This is all conjecture admittedly, but it does explain why the individual members of The John Barry Seven very rarely attracted any publicity of note. The band was always John Barry's baby. He was the figurehead and leader, and as a result, the first port of call for any quote, interview and soundbite. After all, this was the vehicle he had built primarily to make himself known.

Nevertheless, the dynamic of The John Barry Seven changed considerably as Barry was pulled further and further away from the pop mainstream once other extra-curricular musical activities began to dominate his working life. His name may have remained over the shop door (as it were), but he was no longer serving the customers. Vic Flick took the helm, Bobby Graham and Alan Bown followed. The band played on. This book is aimed at raising the profile of all those members who played on and who made a contribution throughout the band's lifespan. For many years, especially during the eighties and nineties, the name of John Barry meant very little in the UK, having once been on everybody's lips during the sixties. Spending much of his time in the US from the mid-seventies onwards, including a period of self-imposed exile, didn't help his cause, but a return to the London concert hall platform in the late nineties, some big-selling albums, a TV special, and, notably, no less than three books written about his life and career, significantly redressed the balance.

However, one injustice continued seemingly in perpetuity. The group that originally made John Barry a household name and was instrumental in assisting his entrée into the film business remained largely anonymous. The John Barry Seven may have changed personnel on a number of occasions throughout its eight-year existence, but from start to finish, it was always a combo comprising of exceptionally gifted musicians.

Hopefully this book will redress the balance by affording prominence to the history of the group and the array of talent passing through its ranks, thereby drawing attention to why they were so important to John Barry, and how, with a little more luck and guidance, could easily have measured up to The Shadows as the UK's most famous and distinguished instrumental group.

For John Barry the band always existed as a means to a specific end, even if initially this might not have been quite so cut and dried; for a good while there was every need for him to hedge his bets. Covering all options was a sensible and pragmatic approach at a time when there was no guarantee a life in the film

industry was beckoning. This is why it was highly unlikely that any member of the band anticipated him ever pulling the plug completely on the Seven whilst he was still feeling his way as a film music composer. Nevertheless, what became increasingly apparent even at the very early stages of his career was just how insistent he would be on being in the spotlight at all times to the point of keeping the rest of the band firmly in the background particularly when it came to handling the press and publicity. He was always the spokesperson, even after Vic Flick had become the on-stage leader, and if a photograph was required it was nearly always one of Barry rather than the Seven!

There is no escaping the fact, therefore, that no matter how one looks at it, The JB7 was formed in the image of its leader without whom it would never have emerged and, for that reason alone, it is Barry to whom we must first turn when relating the band's origin.

⧗

Born in York on 3rd November, 1933, John Barry Prendergast could claim the cinema as his second home from the moment he set foot in the world by virtue of the nature of the family business, since father Jack Xavier (or 'JX' as he was commonly known) was the owner of a small chain of 'picture palaces' – eight in all – scattered around the North of England. His name was legendary locally for running the pre-eminent and iconic cinema/concert venue, The Rialto, in the heart of Fishergate, York.

The Prendergast family – father JX, mother Doris and three children (elder son Patrick, daughter June and the youngest John) – lived in a semi-detached house in Hull Road until John was aged fourteen at which point they moved to Fulford House, which has since become The Pavilion Hotel (York).

Barry's earliest childhood recollection was, appropriately enough, a cinematic one; being carried into the huge purpose-built York Rialto auditorium by his father, and then confronted by a giant black and white mouse moving across a large white screen. In an interview with the local press in York, Barry's older sister June revealed how music became an all-consuming passion for her little brother. Even at an early age, the staging of grand battles, enacted with Dinky toys, was accompanied by a suitably stirring classical music soundtrack blaring out from the family gramophone. The dramatic possibilities of a background score were already informing young John's imagination. By the time he was in his teens, he would spend what any money he had on records, sheet music and music theory books. "Every day he went into York, and came back with more things to do with music. It sent my dad mad!" June recalled.

Formal education at the Bar Convent Junior School and then St. Peter's Public School as a day pupil was not an overwhelming success on account of Barry's single-minded interest in all things music. He was considered somewhat of a daydreamer in class. Even before he started learning the piano he had already

made his mind up as to where his career path would take him. At the age of fifteen, piano lessons were jettisoned in preference for the trumpet once he had discovered the thrill of jazz courtesy of elder brother Pat.

At around the same time, while avoiding school as often as he could, Barry was also immersing himself in the 'bread and butter' aspects of family life by becoming a highly proficient film projectionist, box office clerk, programme seller and limelights operative. He vividly remembered the 1945 film, *A Song To Remember* (a biopic depicting the life of Chopin with Paul Muni in the lead role) as his first great inspiration towards composing music for films.

JX was soon to realize that a stubborn streak so typical of Yorkshire folk appeared to be integral to his son's DNA too; therefore, he decided to bite the bullet and help nurture John's musical ambition by formally approaching Dr Francis Jackson, then Master of Music at York Minster, to take on the task of tutoring and mentoring him. A well respected teacher and highly accomplished musician in his own right, Dr Jackson knew Jack Prendergast in his capacity as a concert promoter, and, as such, attended a number of his post concert soirées when the Hallé Orchestra was in town. On agreeing a programme of study, Dr Jackson was to teach Barry the rudiments of harmony and counterpoint, together with a lifelong appreciation of choral music.

With formal schooling consigned to the past (much to his relief), Barry began working full time for his father, whilst also playing third trumpet most evenings semi-professionally in a local jazz band, Johnny Sutton's Modernaires. Sister June was instrumental in getting him this gig, by dint of her friendship with the band's front man. According to life-long friend, Pete Varley, Johnny Sutton and Francis Jackson were the two most important formative influences on his musical education. Both would push Barry like no others, and would instil in him a drive towards constant self-improvement that would stand him in good stead for the rest of his life.

As a way of getting what he wanted (i.e. a thorough musical grounding), Barry circumvented compulsory National Service by signing up as an army regular for three years instead. By doing so, he was able to pick and choose the direction of his military experience, which is why he joined The Green Howards as a bandsman during August 1953. As Barry would later comment during many a subsequent interview, he learned much in the army, because he was able to make mistakes without anyone noticing. Pete Varley confirmed as much. This is where he and Barry first met, hitting it off from-the-off. He recalled Barry first playing cornet for The Howard's before moving on to trumpet, during which time he would also run the dance band and supply all of the arrangements thereof. At the same time, he was also able to start taking an invaluable correspondence course in 'Composition and Orchestration for the Jazz Orchestra' tutored by Bill Russo, who at the time was writing highly innovative arrangements for the Stan Kenton Orchestra.

On returning to York following his demobilisation, he soon began to pick up from where he left off three years earlier by immersing himself in the local music scene. Although a peripheral presence in and around the nascent Skiffle movement, he found the energy it generated captivating and liberating and would soon apply these positive attributes to his own band. Watching from the wings, he became friendly with members of Johnnie Newcombe's Wabash Four (including lead singer Dave Garlick) with whom he would later share a stage at the Rialto (and at other venues) once the Seven were up and running. Barry was by now also writing increasingly challenging jazz arrangements. Influenced by Kenton, Gerry Mulligan, Chet Baker, etc., he sent the best of them to Johnny Dankworth, Ted Heath and Jack Parnell, as he had done in his pre-army days. He clearly believed in learning from the best. What was clearly changing, however, was the musical landscape.

Two pieces of astute advice from Parnell were to prove invaluable, both of which would eventually shape Barry's destiny. Firstly, he suggested that Barry should form a band of his own, whilst at the same time warning him of the harsh economic realities facing a big band in the latter part of the 1950s. Even paired down to sixteen members, Parnell was finding it increasingly difficult to meet the wage bill. Barry took notice, not only of the waning appeal of such large and unwieldy ensembles, but also of the emergence of a new music sweeping America that would conveniently mean having to down-size operations. Secondly, he advised Barry not to be afraid to take the popular route. Find your audience first, he argued, and then by taking them with you, this will allow for experimentation at a later date.

There is little doubt that Barry would have been all too aware of the impact being made by the onset of rock 'n' roll, and most likely, in his capacity of cinema projectionist, would have witnessed first hand the pandemonium caused by the film *Rock Around the Clock* when it opened in the UK during July 1956. The Rialto was no different to any other picture house in the country, and one suspects that a keen-eyed Barry would have also kept a keen ear on the music, which was causing audiences throughout the nation to go wild in the aisles. Whether this was an epiphany or not, here was a clear message being projected directly from the big screen that there was something in the air about to be unleashed with the power to blow the roof off the house of conformity... and Barry was clearly taking note of the fact. Quick off the mark to absorb the latest trends and new influences, he astutely saw the potential in fashioning his own take on rock 'n' roll, Yorkshire-style, for the British teenager.

Among the acts featured in the film was one in particular whom he thought he could emulate domestically. As he was to admit in later life, Freddie Bell and the Bell Boys became the blueprint for the type of ensemble that was fermenting in his mind. In many ways, they were the perfect hybrid: a six-piece serving up a 'big band' version of rock 'n' roll, highly influenced by the swing-inflected jump blues of Louis Jordan. Now this style may not have been Barry's own artistic preference, but he knew how to write and arrange it and, what's more, fraternised with local musicians who were more than capable of playing it. He just had to convince them that playing jazz – his (and their) first love – was no longer the way forward anymore.

With rock 'n' roll sweeping across the Atlantic, Barry clearly took Parnell's words to heart, by pragmatically hitching a ride on the back of a homespun anglicised version. As well as working up a considerable head of steam, it was also conveniently cheaper to manage. Therefore, during one particular night following a stint with the Modernaires, he took the plunge and followed such sage advice. He gathered some ex-army colleagues together with other local musicians to form the John Barry Seven. For some of them, abandoning their beloved modern jazz path was entirely unexpected and not easy to take in at first.

Among the former was Mike Cox, who first encountered Barry when they played together in the Green Howards' army band, and although on demob there was vague talk of keeping the muse going in the form of some kind of band, he was definitely among those completely taken aback when Barry asked him to join one that would be playing rock 'n' roll rather than jazz. To many purists, this was akin to dumbing down big time.

Another ex-Green Howards bandsman, Derek Myers, was also brought on board. Growing up, he had been taught saxophone by a blind musician in Wakefield by the name of Francis Walker, who would later also teach future member, Jimmy Stead.

Scarborough born Ken Richards started playing the guitar at the age of fifteen from which he graduated to playing professionally with Geoff Laycock's Orchestra at Scarborough Spa as well as a number of other local groups. He also taught at Hull College and owned a smallholding in East Ayton (a nearby village sitting on the bank of the River Derwent) on which he kept chickens.

For Fred Kirk, his musical career began eight years earlier when he started playing the E flat bass in the Sherburn Brass Band. By 1950 he had joined the R.A.F. on a five-year engagement and after being stationed for a time at Linton-on-Ouse, was posted to Malta during December 1951. It was while serving at Luqa as an engine fitter where he began playing the string bass. On leaving the R.A.F. in 1955 he became a welder at Sherburn, whilst also playing with Geoff Laycock's Orchestra at Scarborough Spa and with Charles Riches at Scarborough's Olympia.

By the time he was sixteen, Ken Golder knew what he wanted: to become a professional drummer. Born in St Helen's Square Scarborough and educated at Gladstone Road School, then at technical college, Ken began training as an apprentice joiner at an antique repair firm in the town, but the lure of a music career was where his heart lay and he was soon having drumming lessons, much to the dismay of his parents. "When I listened to music" he recounted, "it was always the percussion that I liked to listen to. I decided that that was what I wanted to do as a hobby and so started having lessons. My parents thought it was terrible because I was making a lot of noise."

As an eighteen year old, he succeeded in nailing his first chance at drumming in a band by successfully auditioning for the Blue Mariners band at Scarborough Spa. "It was great," he recalls. "I was absolutely delighted to be picked at such a young age, and it was there I met all the name band drummers; legends like Jack Parnell, Eric Delaney and Ronnie Verrell."

By 1952, Golder was already an experienced twenty-one year-old. When called up for military service, he sensibly joined the East Yorkshire Military Band in order to continue playing drums and tympani. After six months in Berlin, he spent two years in Singapore, whereupon he played in orchestras accompanying film stars making personal appearances, among them Abbe Lane (with orchestra leader Xavier Cugat) and Ava Gardner. He also played in a band that made weekly radio broadcasts. An impressive 'CV' was already emerging.

This was enhanced on returning to Scarborough in 1955. Despite working as a joiner at Shephard's Builders and later Plaxtons, he still found time to sit in on the Leslie Thorpe Orchestra in Aberdeen. A further six weeks was spent the following year playing with George Crow and his Blue Mariners at Scarborough Spa before he joined Harry Leader's Orchestra at Bridlington Spa.

Golder vividly remembers his introduction to his new band mates at a time when he was playing drums with the Blue Mariners, alongside two friends – guitarist Ken Richards and bassist Fred Kirk. At that time, Barry would often attend dances at the Spa with his girlfriend Barbara Pickard, who knew the band. As a result, they all became acquainted and would regularly chat during intervals. Shared experiences in the army together with a mutual love of modern jazz meant that they quickly bonded. Eventually Barry asked all three of them whether they would be prepared to break from the Mariners in order to form a band with him alongside two saxophonists from Leeds, Derek Myers and Mike Cox; the intention being to rehearse on Sunday mornings at the Rialto.

Recalling this initial approach, Golder's overriding memory was being taken by surprise: "I remember when playing at the Spa with the Mariners during 1957, John Barry – or John Prendergast as he then was – would often come in dancing on a Saturday night. On one particular occasion as I came off the stage and was walking across the ballroom, he approached me and said 'Would you be interested in playing and starting a group?' I was so taken aback that I asked two other lads, Fred Kirk and Ken Richards (who were also from Scarborough) what they thought. We decided to give it a go and we went to one of John's father's cinemas, the Rialto, in York. We came out and played and it sounded all right and we were quite pleased with the sound that we got."

Local singer and guitarist Keith Kelly became the final piece in the jigsaw. He and Barry were already good friends, often cycling around York together, visiting coffee shops, and at one point were even considering buying scooters in order to tour Europe. He introduced John to Barbara Pickard, Barry's future wife, at the De Grey Rooms. At that time she was working as a shop assistant at Cussins and Lights Ltd., York's premier electrical retailer based in King's Square (York). With the Suez crisis then at its height, both Barry and Kelly were suddenly called up from the reserves, to the point of even embarking upon a farewell dinner together on the eve of being posted. In the end, however, the UN initiated cease-fire in November '56 that stopped the Anglo-French alliance in its tracks put pay to either of them ever having to make the journey abroad, although Kelly seems to recall Barry getting as far as Southampton.

Born in Selby, Yorkshire, during December 1934, Kelly spent three years in the Royal Air Force. He was posted to Egypt, then to Cyprus, and it was during one night in a Cyprus nightclub when a group of friends persuaded him to do a cabaret turn on the mouth organ. The manager was so pleased with Keith's efforts that he asked him to play there regularly, and not long after, he was being offered work to play with the resident band at the Acropole Hotel in his spare time. On returning to Britain in August 1955, he began learning the guitar after a friend had given him one.

While living at 51 Leaside, Dringhouses, he became well known in York by dint of his singing engagements for Johnny Sutton at the De Grey Rooms on dance nights. During one night early in 1957, while Barry was sitting in on trumpet with Johnny Sutton's Modernaires, he unexpectedly caught Keith taking the lead vocal on a number of songs at Sutton's behest. What normally happened was that Keith would simply guest on mouth organ, but having recently heard him sing off-stage, Sutton saw some genuine vocal potential there and decided to throw him in at the deep end. He sounded okay to all those present, John Barry included.

Like many a teenager, Kelly had giddy aspirations of making a name for himself in the music business, but his feet were kept firmly on the ground, in his case literally, since his day job saw him selling shoes in his capacity as assistant manager at the local branch of Saxone; a well-established, national chain that sold footwear produced in Kilmarnock. He would never forget the day when JB came bounding into the shop with the big news that not only was he was forming his own group, but he also wanted his mate to be a part of it as a vocalist/rhythm guitarist. Since he was the kind of guy who tended to go with the flow, he agreed without hesitation, despite not knowing any of the other personnel whom Barry had earmarked for inclusion.

The Seven's first full line-up was now in place and read as follows: **John Barry (vocals and trumpet), Mike Cox (tenor-sax), Derek Myers (alto-sax), Ken Golder (drums), Fred Kirk (bass guitar), Ken Richards (lead guitar/vocals) and Keith Kelly (rhythm guitar/vocals).**

At this juncture, it would be remiss of us to ignore the role played by Barry's father, Jack, in furthering his youngest son's ambitions. Certainly, one could never have described him as a cuddly or fluffy father figure, who was prone to shower bucket loads of affection on his children; on the contrary, he could be a 'difficult to please', hard taskmaster around whom fools would fear to tread, yet at the same time, he was an encouraging presence and astute enabler, who instilled a sense of self-belief and a rigorous work ethic into his offspring. In his own way, JX was just as influential in informing Barry's music career as Dr. Francis Jackson, Johnny Sutton and Bill Russo, albeit from a practical, financial and theatrical perspective. For a start, he was incredibly well connected and was a concert promoter, *par excellence*. Yes, JX knew the right people and, just as importantly, knew how to put on a show. For any aspiring young Yorkshire-based musician wanting to gain entry into the world of entertainment, there was no better 'go to' guy.

In many ways, Jack Prendergast MBE was Yorkshire's 'Mr. Showbiz' throughout the 1940s and 50s, with the Rialto – a splendid art deco designed cinema he completely rebuilt in 1935 following a disastrous fire that gutted the original building – his crowning glory. It was at this venue where the great and the good could be seen performing on a regular basis. Doubling up as a cinema and concert hall, the Rialto became synonymous with attracting the biggest acts not only from the UK, but also from across the Atlantic. For Barry, this was the perfect opportunity to witness the cream of the entertainment industry plying their trade at close proximity. There was nowhere else in the North able to present such diverse talent as the likes of Count Basie, Lonnie Donegan, Sarah Vaughan, Duke Ellington, Lionel Hampton, Billy Cotton, Dickie Valentine, The Hallé Orchestra, Sidney Bechet, Nat 'King' Cole and Stan Kenton all under the same roof. JXs' organisational prowess was second to none, and it was this down-to-earth pragmatism that clearly rubbed off on young John in addition to the drive and determination requisite to make that happen. To fulfil any dream, hard graft was a given; combining that with the entrepreneurial spirit instilled into Barry's psyche by his father, here were two pivotal attributes that would ultimately pay dividends.

Keith Kelly, who witnessed JX's 'larger than life' personality first hand, remembered him with a great deal of affection. "He was a perpetual snuff-taker, who always had a silk handkerchief on display, and was a huge fan of actor Jack Buchanan," he recalled fondly. Indeed, JX was a natty dresser, replete in trademark trilby, who did model his appearance on this major Scottish star of stage and screen; in his day, Buchanan was *the* archetypal debonair 'man-about-town'. In fact, the two Jacks would eventually become firm friends.

The group's historic first rehearsal took place on 17th February at The Rialto. Further ones were also held in an 18th century barn situated in the grounds of Fulford House, the Prendergast family home. This was the perfect bolthole for maintaining privacy and for not upsetting the neighbours. According to Barry's niece, Emma Lloyd Jones, this was one of a number of out buildings situated on the estate, and one which also doubled up as a means of accommodating another of JX's business sidelines, cinema screen manufacturing. The Sunday morning session soon became a regular part of their lives, as did rehearsals arranged upstairs at the Clifton Ballroom (also owned by JX). During Rialto ones, JX would often observe from a seat in the stalls. In fact, according to Golder, whenever he was impressed, he would throw his trilby in the air and jump up and down excitedly.

JX was evidently a champion of the band right from its inception, but it went much further than simply moral support.

Not only was he able to offer the band their first professional engagements at the Rialto (as if that was ever in doubt), but he also agreed to lend his son the considerable sum of £5,000 to enable him to move operations to London – the epicentre of the music industry in 1950s Britain. Bearing in mind that the average house would have cost in the region of £2,000 in 1957, you can gauge the full extent of JXs' commitment to his son's future. He even sourced and secured the BOAC travel bus that was to serve as The Seven's first bandwagon. Kelly alluded to a communal atmosphere emerging during the early interactions between group members, but it was Barry who soon became the dominant voice, which was not in the least bit surprising. From the very moment JX provided such substantial financial investment (worth £84,285.71 as calculated in 2018), The JB7 was never going to run along democratic lines. The band and brand leader was, for all intents and purposes, rolled into one. In fact, Barry was soon to tie up each member to individual contracts as employees. Yes, this was always going to be Barry's vehicle for self-promotion. He was firmly entrenched in the front seat and, from the outset, determining its direction and, as will be illustrated later, he was still in control of the 'sat nav', even when he became a backseat driver, as it were. Tellingly, Kelly was soon advised to drop the calypsos he had originally brought to the table. "You don't want to sing that nonsense!" retorted Barry.

Nevertheless, he did sing the very first two John Barry compositions that were recorded on acetate to illustrate the band's potential; presumably the two songs Barry later sang himself and sent to TV producer Jack Good.

Another asset JX passed on to his son was an appreciation of and an ability to work the media. As a cinema owner and concert promoter, forging links with local journalists and networking with the city's dignitaries was vital for raising the profile of his business empire. Barry soon learned the value of a good publicist when he was entrusted with that role while working for his father, and in light of the experience, it didn't take him long to realise that this was one aspect sorely lacking as far as the group's chances of success was concerned. As a result, he decided to draw upon the know-how of a contact he had made via concerts at the Rialto – a local journalist working for the *York Evening Press* by the name of Stacey Brewer.

Stacey Brewer MBE was to become one of the senior journalists for the *Evening Press* in a distinguished career that lasted over forty years, but in 1957, his role was a more modest one; the paper's designated feature writer on television and showbiz matters. He was soon to become an essential cog in the wheel by acting as the group's unofficial publicist, moonlighting in the role while continuing the day job as an up-and-coming reporter. For Brewer, who wrote a weekly column featuring Yorkshire bands, receiving regular unsolicited letters and phone calls from aspiring musicians was part and parcel of the job. There was nothing to suggest any different when he received a bell from yet another, one day during the May of that year.

"My name is Barry Prendergast. I've got a band and I'd like you to hear it and give me your opinion," said the voice on the phone. As good as his word, Brewer arranged to drop in on a rehearsal at the Rialto Cinema (based as it was locally in the Fishergate area of York). He sat in the empty stalls as he heard the band rip through the big rock 'n' roll hits of the time including 'Rock Around the Clock' and 'Giddy-Up-a-Ding Dong' (the film *Rock Around the Clock* had clearly made a profound impression)... but it was the inclusion of 'Blue Moon' that made Brewer prick up his ears, sit up and take notice. Completely taken by surprise, his reaction was as follows: "That was a classic ballad. No rock band would dream of playing that. And no other rock band could have played it, the way I was hearing it. Lush deep chords, warm cross-harmonies; almost a full orchestral sound, from only seven musicians – three guitars, two saxophones, one trumpet and drums. It was amazing".

Brewer wanted to know immediately who had actually written the arrangement and when Barry revealed it was all his own doing, he was a picture of self-satisfaction. "It didn't take a genius to see that he (Barry) possessed a unique talent," Brewer added. "I quickly arranged a picture-call with an *Evening Press* photographer, and the next day, the Press carried the photograph with my story about this exciting new home-grown group."

The picture caption had originally referred to the group leader as Barry Prendergast – his real name (since family and friends always referred to him as Barry). However, according to Brewer, at the last minute on the morning of publication, this was changed. The rather cumbersome surname was dropped in favour of his two forenames; here was the moment when the moniker John Barry – musician, arranger and composer – became set in stone. For the group, The John Barry Seven's first-ever publicity promotion, courtesy of the *Evening Press*, was another milestone reached.

≈

The launch of The John Barry Seven was carried out with such military-like precision that very little was left to chance. Every aspect was planned meticulously, all facets considered, be it instrumentation, presentation, publicity, photographs, representation, dress code, transport, dance instruction right down to the personalised notepaper. Even the name of the band was the subject of a family brainstorming session. Emma Lloyd Jones remembers her mother (June) telling her that it was she who threw the name 'John Barry Seven' into the ring during that particular discussion. Hence, the name of the band and the stage name of its leader, though ultimately one and the same, seemingly came to being by way of a different set of circumstances.

≈

The success of the first major provincial article to feature the band proved to be the start of a close relationship between Brewer and Barry that was to take the journalist up and down the country over the next two-and-a-half years, writing slick Press and promotional material in a determined effort to 'launch' and establish this new group. For Brewer, it was tough going, working for the *Evening Press* all week, then spending weekends and days off in London, doing the rounds of show business magazines and writers; having to knock out press releases on a portable typewriter in theatre dressing rooms, from Blackpool to the Glasgow Empire.

Brewer recalled Barry establishing roots in the Capital. "His first London address was a small 'pad' in the heart of Soho, not far from Landseer's studios, where his first glossy Hollywood-style portraits were shot. Later, when things improved, he occupied a first-floor flat at 39, Redcliffe Gardens, near Earl's Court. As the band became better-known, he traded-in his grey Triumph Mayflower car for a huge American automobile, a gold-coloured Chevrolet Impala. We didn't half turn some heads the first time he drove it along Coney Street! Sometimes we used to meet to plan publicity at a Stonegate coffee bar on the corner where Mulberry Hall now stands."

One of Brewer's most successful publicity stories, concerning the band, was in persuading the *Sunday Mirror* to run a bizarre story about a £10,000 insurance policy taken out against any of the musicians (all bachelors at the time) getting married within a year. According to Brewer, the *Sunday Mirror* lawyers ran the rule over the policy and after finding it all in order, carried the story alongside a big picture of the band. What they didn't know, was that although the policy was genuine, any claim would have been deemed null and void on account of no premiums ever having been paid. Clearly, the old adage, 'any publicity is better than no publicity', was never better illustrated than on this occasion.

Rewinding back to March 1957, The Seven may have been busily ensconced on the Fulford estate determined to make full use of the rent-free accommodation and unlimited rehearsal time available to them to fine-tune the musicianship... but it wasn't only the music that was being honed to perfection. Barry was as fastidious about the band's visual image as he was about the sound they were making. Light grey suits now became obligatory and a choreographer was brought in to teach basic dance steps – the kind eventually made famous by The Shadows, then ultimately ridiculed by The Beatles.

However, their first public appearance came as a surprise to everybody – none more so than the group! After one rehearsal at the Rialto Cinema had gone particularly well and evidently impressed by the progress being made by his boy's new charges, JX decided to give them a snap tryout between films on the following Sunday night. History was in the process of being made, when on the 10th March 1957 the band stood before a paying audience for the very first time. Initially intending to play just three numbers, they were so well received that they carried on playing for a full thirty minutes adding six more to the set.

Barry handled most of the vocals, doubling on trumpet when commencing with 'Rock Around the Clock', with Ken Richards and Keith Kelly also contributing a vocal each, the latter singing the contentious calypso that would eventually be dropped.

Writing in volume two of her detailed history of York's popular music scene, *Something in the Air*, Van Wilson was able to relive that triumphant debut, recalling how the audience "yelled out for more and more" so vociferously that the band was in no position to suddenly stop dead in their tracks; egged on by the audience they eventually played as many as nine! Sister June was able to concur in describing the ensuing reception as "unbelievable", a night she would never forget.

The success of this venture so delighted JX that he immediately signed them up officially to support Mitchell Torok and Cy Laurie's Jazz Band, who were appearing at the Rialto the following Sunday. Featured on this occasion were 'Rock Around the Clock', 'Rip it Up' and 'Giddy Up a Ding-Dong' with Barry on vocals; 'R.O.C.K', featuring Richards, and Kelly's 'Marianne', the soon to be jettisoned calypso. The runaway train was rapidly picking up pace. During the following month – on 7th April to be precise – the band were sandwiched on a bill between Vic Lewis and His Orchestra and one of the biggest live draws of the era, Johnnie Ray, whose latest single, 'Yes Tonight Josephine' was on the cusp of being released to provide him with his third UK chart topper.

Exposure in York was all very well and good, but Barry knew that the band could not rely on the local scene alone to provide them with sufficient live experience. What's more, they needed to spread their wings further afield were they ever to stand a chance of becoming a recognised household name. Once again, he could rely on his father's network of names to find the right contact – enter Harold Fielding.

Woking-born Fielding, who first tasted show business himself as a child violinist, was a master of publicity and a hugely successful concert promoter long before he became one of the UK's leading theatre impresarios. Able to straddle the pop and classical spheres with ease, he also presented variety bills, which toured the length and breadth of Britain, some under the banner 'Music for the Millions'. Conscious of the fact that 'Theatreland' *per se* traditionally observed the Sabbath by closing its doors on that day, he pioneered the idea of lighting up these 'dark' nights with the introduction of the evening Sunday concert. This caught on so well that he would eventually produce as many as a thousand such events every year all over the country. Such was his powers of persuasion that, in 1950, he even managed to convince Frank Sinatra, on his first UK visit, to play the New Opera House in Blackpool when he only ever intended to play the London Palladium.

JX would have had frequent dealings with Fielding given their mutual interest in attracting the cream of the entertainment industry to the North of England. For example, Gracie Fields' Winter tour of 1952 included a date at the Rialto on 7th November, one of many concerts which would have necessitated dialogue between the two Northern theatre industry moguls. In 1957, Fielding (alongside Harold Davison) arranged Count Basie's first-ever British tour. One can imagine JX putting in a good word with Fielding on his son's behalf when he was tying up the contract for Basie's date at the Rialto on Good Friday, 17th April – a mere twelve days on from the success of the Johnnie Ray concert.

Whatever was said worked a treat, because not long after, Harold Fielding agreed to act as the band's agent after they had successfully auditioned for him in Blackpool and in no time at all, he was telephoning the *New Musical Express* personally with a glowing reference on behalf of his latest discovery after securing a number of dates for them on the Northern cinema circuit. On Sunday 5th May, The JB7 played The Crescent Cinema in Pontefract, billed as 'The Boys with Rhythm With 'Em!'

Fielding's show business credentials were impeccable and his experience vast. There is no doubt that he would have been able to circumvent The JB7 having to rise up the variety ladder, like most acts had to do back then, on account of his close relationship with Val Parnell, Managing Director of Moss Empires, the company that controlled the London Palladium, the Prince of Wales Theatre and the extensive provincial Hippodrome circuit – the biggest chain of theatres in the country. There existed at the time an unspoken, established hierarchy among variety theatres (deemed levels one, two and three in importance) of which Moss Empires were universally ranked one – the undisputed *crème de la crème* of auditoriums. Such was his clout that Fielding was able to ensure his boys a billing somewhere on the top tier.

Moreover, he would have also known how best to please Parnell's formidable and fearsome Artistes Booking Controller, Cissie Williams, whose overpowering influence could make or break an act on her say-so alone. Her regular Monday morning auditions held at the Finsbury Park Empire were legendary. She vetted every act that treaded the Moss Empire boards and was known to have rejected any hopeful simply for having poorly polished shoes, irrespective of talent. Fielding would have insisted on The Seven looking the part for this reason alone; hence, the smart suits and clean cut look.

While Fielding and Brewer were working busily behind the scenes, Barry took it upon himself to write personally to the BBC on behalf of the band, knowing full well that the only way to maximise exposure was to curry favour with what was then the most influential and dominant force in British broadcasting. He was only too aware of the instant impact that was being made by the introduction of *Six-Five Special* by BBC Television since it first blazed across the small screen on 16th February of that year. This ground-breaking, nationwide weekly programme was the first attempt of its kind to cater for the musical tastes of a younger teenage audience, and was precisely where any up-and-coming act needed to be if they wanted to grab a piece of the action.

Once again, JX laid down the groundwork by putting out the necessary feelers – this time with producer Jack Good – in order to ascertain his son's band's chances of appearing in the show. Barry was best advised to supply some tangible evidence of the band's prowess, which seemed fair enough. Therefore, on 8th May he wrote to the young co-producer, enclosing local press-cuttings together with a demo recording made by The Seven of two songs he had written for them; 'We All Love to Rock' and 'Rock-a-Billy-Boogie'. Despite being impressed, Good told a disappointed Barry that he would not be able to include The JB7 among his roster of hopefuls, simply because they sounded too familiar to his semi-regular house band, Don Lang and His Frantic Five. Mind you, this was hardly surprising, since there were very few role models available for any aspiring rock 'n' roll act in the UK at the time. Every band invariably used Bill Haley's or Freddie Bell's sound as its blueprint.

Undeterred, the band played on.

JX, too, continued to call in favours, this time by targeting the national music press. His friendship with Isidore Green, the editor of *Record Mirror*, inspired a lengthy article to help ignite the publicity machine. Under the heading: 'Theatre owner's son heads John Barry Seven', it featured a discussion with JX about John, "I know a good act when I see one, and I won't be influenced by a relationship. I'm convinced my boy is leading a first rate outfit, and I'm sure he'll get along on merit, without any push from me." At pains in pointing out how his enthusiasm was in no way borne out of flagrant nepotism, he stressed that he would never have even bothered with the band had it not been so good and professional.

Meanwhile, elsewhere in the country, the UK's biggest teenage pop star of the day, Tommy Steele (with his group The Steelmen) was topping the bill alongside Freddie Bell and The Bellboys in a sell-out variety package tour, organised by Fielding, that also included, among others, Mike and Bernie Winters, and French harmonica group, The Trio Raisner. Throughout May, a week-long residency took place in Liverpool, Cardiff, London and Glasgow consecutively. However, with Freddie Bell and the Bellboys unable to continue thereafter – having already been signed up for a series of headlining one-nighters of their own – a similarly primed act was needed to replace them later that July for a four-week summer engagement at the Blackpool Palace Theatre. – and who better to fill those shoes than the UK's own variant, the rapidly emerging John Barry Seven.

Such a fantastic opportunity as this one was – undoubtedly their biggest break so far – could have done well without a major hiccup along the way, but in time-honoured tradition, one managed to arrive just on cue. Following another appearance at the Rialto on 19th May, Ken Golder was reminded by George Crow of an outstanding commitment that he had already made with his band The Blue Mariners at the Spa (Scarborough) for a ten-week summer season, and with contracts already signed, there was no way of him getting out of it. With The JB7's most prestigious and lucrative engagement yet only weeks away, Barry was now left scratching his head for the name of a new drummer. Fortunately, he managed to secure the services of a stand-in, Don Martin (from Torquay), who was available to join the rest of the band in time for the start of the Steele shows due to commence on the 22nd July on a bill shared with The Ken-Tones, Desmond Lane and compère Reg Thompson, all three of whom the Seven backed. Whilst in Blackpool, classes were also pencilled in for the band to attend a dance school set up specifically for the showbiz fraternity in a bid to hone the act.

An enthusiastic reporter from *The Stage* reacted as follows: "Harold Fielding, who presents the show, has heard, seen, and experienced more acts than he cares to remember and he rarely enthuses, but he has expressed the opinion that The John Barry Seven, headed by ace-trumpeter Barry, will prove the British equivalent of the States' Bell Boys. And from what I saw of The Seven's performance on Monday and the way the audience accepted it, he could be right."

The Tommy Steele experience proved to be such a resounding triumph that in no time at all, The JB7 were being offered further summer season stints, this time with Frankie Vaughan in Bournemouth and Torquay, on weeks commencing 19th August and 2nd September respectively. Not only that but equally significant was a successful audition for ITV's popular *Jack Hylton's Music Box* series that resulted in The JB7's television debut on Friday 30th August. Such was the success of this broadcast that it persuaded Jack Good to seriously think again about hiring the band; three weeks later, they were making their *Six-Five Special* debut on a bill which also included Ted Heath and His Music, Larry Adler, Eve Boswell and Dennis Lotis. This was the first of many appearances for The JB7; some of them, ironically, on the same bill as the very act whose presence wrecked that first approach, Don Lang and His Frantic Five! – more of which will be discussed below.

Shortly before this, however, towards the end of the Torquay week, 'The John Barry Seven' suddenly and unexpectedly became 'John Barry and The Seven', when John E. Aris (a 22 year-old Brixham-born vibes player), was asked to join. Aris had first met Barry when they were both serving with the Army in the Middle East, but after 'demob' had invariably lost touch; that was, until Aris dropped in to talk about old times at one of the Frankie Vaughan shows. The reunion ended with him being offered a place in The Seven, after he had appeared initially as a 'guest artist' with the group during their two final shows in Torquay.

The true acid test for Aris was how he performed the following day at the band's most prestigious concert to date. It was to be quite some baptism of fire, since The Top 20 Hit Parade All-Star Show, as it was promoted, was The JB7's début appearance at London's Royal Albert Hall alongside some illustrious company. Also on the bill were headliner Lonnie Donegan, Bob Cort, Russ Conway, Nancy Whiskey, Russ Hamilton and The King Brothers; indeed, a fair cross-section of British pop talent in 1957. Donegan was at the time the undisputed 'King of Skiffle' and at the peak of his popularity having already topped the charts twice during the year with 'Cumberland Gap' and 'Gambling Man'/'Putting On the Style'. Nancy Whiskey and the Chas McDevitt group had occupied the Top Twenty for months with 'Freight Train', while on the weekend of the show, Russ Hamilton was in the top ten courtesy of his massive hit 'We Will Make Love'.

The King Brothers were also riding high on the back of their biggest hit, 'A White Sports Coat'. Compères were actor John Fraser and Radio Luxembourg DJ Keith Fordyce. What is quite remarkable about this concert from The JB7's perspective was the fact that at the time, they did not have a record contract let alone a hit, so an appearance on a bill representing the current cream of British chart acts was both a canny piece of promotion and a huge vote of confidence. Aris, incidentally, must have impressed, for he joined the band on a full-time basis immediately afterwards.

New Musical Express, co-promoters of The All-Star Show, gave the band a ringing endorsement. In the vernacular of the day, they reported that 'another solid rock success was The John Barry Seven. Reminiscent of Freddie Bell and the Bellboys, this British unit certainly had the vast hall jumpin' with some all-out beat music, spiced with vocals and precision movements. John Barry himself proved a true leader and shone in solo work, climaxing with 'Three Little Fishes'.'

Now free to return to active band duty, Ken Golder resumed his rightful place behind the drum kit, thereby replacing Don Martin, just in time for the band's *Six-Five Special* BBC TV debut on 21st September and with Aris now in tow, it looked on the surface as if two new members were being introduced. On this first appearance, The JB7 performed two vocals, Barry's tried and trusted 'We All Love to Rock' plus 'Every Which Way', which was eventually to become the band's second single. Between them, the group made £35 for the live performance (the equivalent of £590.00 in 2018) plus a further £14.70 for Friday and Saturday rehearsals (equating to another £245.00), out of which commission had to be deducted to pay agent Harold Fielding his fee. Nevertheless, given that the average weekly wage was in the region of £7 10s (£7.50) per week in the UK throughout 1957, the band were already beginning to earn good money, and with their feet now firmly in the door, this was to become the first of a long string of contracts for BBC Television.

Keith Kelly was neither overawed nor impressed by his experience on *Six-Five Special*, astonished as he was by the ramshackle nature of the programme. He described the production values as "very amateurish", instantly recalling one occasion when a certain member of The Mudlarks was seen on camera picking his nose while waiting to sing! Co-producers Josephine Douglas and Jack Good must have been suitably impressed with The JB7's contribution, because they would return on a number of other subsequent occasions.

A variety bill supporting skiffle queen Nancy Whiskey, which toured the country playing weekly at venues such as The Metropolitan and Chiswick Empire in London, Edinburgh Empire and Chester Royalty, maintained the band's upward trajectory with the songs 'We All Love to Rock', 'Every Which Way' and 'Three Little Fishes' all becoming staple features of the act. More importantly, the national music press was beginning to take serious notice. Taking the *Record Mirror's* 28th September review as a prime example, it is clear that The JB7 were considered a cut above the rest in spite of its rather patronising tone: "The first half of the show is closed by The JB7, who are mainly on a rock kick, but if you can stand that, then the act is excellent. They are faultlessly turned-out, perform with slickness, precision and abandon. An act produced with professional thoroughness, an object lesson to other youngsters in the business." *The Stage*, albeit a tad confused, also admired the performance: "Then there was The John Barry Singers *(sic)* – a combination of two saxes, xylophone, drums, trumpets and three guitars – that made more noise but to better purpose than anything like it seen before."

What is most noticeable, above all, is the condescending language prevailing within the media towards anything connected with the burgeoning youth culture at the time. Make no mistake about it, 'rock 'n' roll', through its association with teenage delinquency (real or imagined), was viewed with a great deal of suspicion and derision throughout this period.

～

For one early convert – eleven-year-old Roger McDermaid – catching the Seven live on two separate occasions at the Edinburgh Empire during 1957 would make a lasting impression. This was due entirely to his Aunt Peggy, who as a shop owner was able to obtain free tickets in the front stalls on Monday nights in exchange for displaying the theatre's latest billboard outside her premises. Roger was so bowled over by both performances that he became a life-long devotee. He takes up the story as follows: "This was in the heyday of variety when John and his boys were the first act up once the opening dancing girl chorus left the stage. On the first occasion I saw them, they were on with Terry Wayne, on the second with the Chas McDevitt Skiffle Group. I thought they were terrific. They were a much more rockier outfit back then, and sounded far more brassy. John played the trumpet alongside a torrent of saxes, a double bass and drums. Being sat at the front, I got a real good view of the band. Each member wore a light turquoise/blue suit while John's was a much darker midnight blue. One tune I particularly liked was 'Every Which Way' sung by John. I thought then it was real hip – such happy memories from a distant childhood."

～

Even though a major breakthrough was achieved in winning over the television wing of the BBC, it was the radio network that remained the dominant force during 1957 (TV was considered its infant sibling back then). Securing airtime on the Light Programme was still considered to be the best way of capturing the ears of the nation. The main priority now was in engineering this much-needed radio breakthrough. It proved harder than Harold Fielding could ever have imagined, even after he had successfully arranged an audition for them on writing to the BBC's head of variety, Jim Davidson. This was arranged for 18th September 1957, just days before their first TV appearance on *Six-Five Special*. Although producer

Jimmy Grant was left in charge of this audition, he received strict instructions from Fielding as to how best to make use of the facilities and set up The Seven's instruments, which was to also include a vibraphone for John Aris.

Two weeks later, however, came the most disappointing, discouraging and disparaging of responses in the form of a terse, flat rejection. An internal memo written by Donald Maclean, BBC Radio's Head of Popular Music, pulled no punches in stating that he had no option but to turn down the band, reasoning that "reports on the audition recording indicate that they are not acceptable for broadcasting." He went on to add, "The solos were sub-standard by any criterion. Main fault is that the voice is unexciting – the only thing a 'R&R' singer mustn't be". Such a dogmatic and entrenched viewpoint was to last for another couple of years. Radio would prove to be a tough nut to crack.

On the positive side, rock 'n' roll was now beginning to gain a toehold on British popular culture in 1957. Up to this point, all package tours were still modelled largely on traditional music hall variety shows, which would feature a range of specialist 'turns' and novelty acts. Therefore, a popular crooner could be sharing the stage with a comedian, magician, conjurer, contortionist, drag act, or even a performing dog, all featured on the same bill. Still construed by many of the old guard on the theatre circuit as a mere passing fad – just as skiffle was – John Barry and The Seven were, by dint of their slick presentation, traversing uncharted territory and attracting a great deal of attention in the process. Reviews were encouraging, bookings increasing. In hindsight, their sound was little more than a pale pastiche of American counterparts; nevertheless they were addressing a gap in the market, were better than any of their local rivals and were clearly offering something fresh and vibrant otherwise lacking elsewhere on the British music scene. Barry had now repeated what he had first achieved in the army by successfully harnessing the collective talents of a well-disciplined band. All that was lacking at this stage, radio approval notwithstanding, was a *bona fide* recording contract.

All this was about to change, however. The band had suddenly become hot property largely on the back of those rave notices emanating from the Royal Albert Hall concert. *New Musical Express* jumped the gun somewhat embarrassingly by erroneously revealing that Philips had already secured the band's services as part of its attempt to capture the appeal of what they termed a "teen-age audience." According to its sources, Philips had beaten off overtures from two other interested labels just prior to their first appearance on *Six-Five Special*. The *New Musical Express* had clearly backed the wrong horse. What can't be disputed, however, is that a fierce bidding war did ensue with Harold Fielding in the thick of the negotiations, but it was Decca and Philips who ultimately lost out, outmanoeuvred by an offer from EMI. Perhaps Barry was won over by the promise of inclusion on a forthcoming *Six-Five Special* LP (in addition to the obligatory single releases); whatever the reason, John Barry and The Seven joined the Parlophone stable during October 1957.

In fact, their first recordings – made on 20th October – were indeed those contributions earmarked for Parlophone's *Six-Five Special* tie-in that was scheduled for release in December. Barry's self-penned, 'Let's Have a Wonderful Time' (actually a re-write of 'We All Love to Rock') and 'Rock-a-Billy-Boogie' together with Mel Tormé's 'Every Which Way' (all of which featured Barry, himself, on lead vocals) were the tracks selected for the LP. However, it was the two cuts recorded a few days later ('Zip Zip' and 'Three Little Fishes') that were actually chosen to form both sides of the debut single for Parlophone. Three weeks later three more were in the can – an alternative version of 'Three Little Fishes' in addition to 'Every Which Way' and 'You've Gotta Way' (the brace that would become the second single).

~

Barry, incidentally, was not the first member of the Prendergast family whose name adorned a record label. That honour belonged to JX in his capacity as mentor and sponsor of York's most popular dance band, 'The Rialtonians'. He took them to London to record three 78s for Octocross Records during August 1934, on which they were billed as 'J Prendergast and The Rialtonians'; Barry was not yet twelve months old at the time. The Rialtonians were the only dance band from York ever to record commercially.

~

Quite why a cover version of a recent Diamonds track ('Zip Zip' being the B-side of their most recent 45, 'Oh How I Wish') was picked out for launching The JB7's career was never made clear, although it was consistent with the policy at that time of replicating American originals. It was not a resounding success by any stretch of the imagination save some sizeable sales in Barry's home city of York. Neither was it any better than The Diamonds' version. If you can imagine a gruff Yorkshire baritone singing in a faux American accent backed by The Comets, then you will have some idea of just what the record sounded like. By his own admission Barry was never going to win any talent contests as a vocalist. He has often quoted one reviewer, who described his vocal style as sounding like a 45 played at 33 ⅓, in many a latter-day interview to emphasise just how bad he thought he was.

Barry's reluctance to sing was pushed aside on account of being the group's figurehead, since he felt a sense of responsibility for taking the lead. Unfortunately he lacked the necessary skills and charisma to carry it off. Moreover, he wasn't even the best vocalist in the band! And as we shall learn later, this became ever more evident a few years down the line when Keith Kelly demonstrated his singing credentials on embarking on a solo career.

What was so surprising was that it took another vocal-oriented single, the aforementioned 'Every Which Way', for Parlophone to finally get the message.

Not that Barry minded. The JB7 were now genuine recording artists and, more importantly, he had placed himself in an ideal position to learn how a recording studio operated.

Even though the record may not have set the UK into euphoric raptures, the *Record Mirror* disc reviewer thought it showed promise, albeit grudgingly: " 'Zip Zip' will either die quickly or zip zip to the top – it's that kind of song. Set at a furious pace, John Barry sings in an almost monotone fashion, while the musicians twang its beat behind him. Frankly, I can't tell whether it will sell or not and I'm not sticking my neck out either way. It's not outstanding but it's certainly got the commercial flavour about it somewhere." Hardly a ringing endorsement, but it could have been worse.

~

Renowned recording engineer, Ken Townsend MBE, who first joined EMI on the 1st November 1950 at the age of seventeen and who would eventually become General Manager of Abbey Road Studios, kindly talked the authors through the rigid organisational structure that existed there during the time when The JB7 were regular visitors. Each recording session followed uniformly laid down guidelines under a hierarchical framework within which roles were strictly defined, and according to Townsend, it ran like clockwork.

As such, the following procedure would apply to any particular session irrespective of the artist or content. It would start with the A&R manager (later termed the 'producer') establishing the availability of a studio by consulting with booking coordinator, Vera Samwell, who strictly controlled the diaries and allocated time slots accordingly. Only a producer was allowed to book sessions and only after completing a statutory red form, a copy of which would be sent to the accounts department, since session fees would have to be agreed in advance.

Every Friday, five or six sheets would be posted for display on notice boards detailing exactly which producers and engineers would be required in each studio for the week ahead. This could be revised and updated on a daily basis. Samwell (and later Colette Barber) were the only ones allowed access to the booking logs between 1943 and 2016.

Any recording session necessitated the presence of three participants: a balance engineer, a technical (maintenance) engineer, and a tape operator ('button pusher' or 'assistant engineer'). The producer very often phoned the balance engineer in advance for a prior discussion about what equipment was required.

It was the balance engineer's role to produce a diagram mapping out the precise studio layout expected for each specific session and, in all likelihood, this would have involved discussing the minutiae beforehand with the maintenance engineer (e.g. the exact placement of microphones and so on). All of the heavy lifting involved in moving the studio equipment was the exclusive domain of the porters/janitors, who were distinguishable by the brown coats they wore, but it was the maintenance engineers (replete in white laboratory coats) who were solely responsible for such tasks as positioning the mics, changing the cabling and altering signal routings, for these were the acknowledged technical boffins.

Requisite checks were often made before commencing a given session so that the balance engineer simply had to open the faders in order to start promptly. Standard session times were 10a.m. to 1p.m.; 2.30p.m. to 5.30p.m., and 7p.m. to 10p.m., as agreed with the Musicians Union. Overtime of half-an-hour was permitted on occasions, but anything more was frowned upon in light of the expense.

The JB7's early sessions were engineered either by Stuart Eltham or Peter Bown, with Norman Newell producing; from 1959 onwards, newcomer Malcolm Addey and John Burgess would have taken on the respective engineering and production roles, more often than not.

~

When John Barry and The Seven made a return to *Six-Five Special* on the 23rd November (in a cast that also included Chris Barber and His Jazz Band, Jim Dale, Sheila Buxton and Don Lang and His Frantic Five), it proved to be the final appearance of John Aris as a member of the band, after having decided to put the course of true love before a career as a professional musician. Without actually ever been given an ultimatum as such, Aris's then girlfriend (and future wife) Vilma, explained that this difficult decision arose from having to reconcile divided loyalties. According to Vilma, Barry had told her to back off seeing Aris so that he could free himself up to concentrate fully on a music career. Evidently, Barry did not like the prospect of marriage interfering with the running of the band. However, for Aris, it was not quite as clear-cut as that. Such inner turmoil reached its zenith on Paddington Station just as Vilma was about to take the next train back home to Torquay not long after having participated as one of the audience on the show. For Aris, saying goodbye to Vilma there and then was simply too much to bear; instead he made an immediate about-turn, jumped on board the train and accompanied Vilma home, never to be part of the band again. Torn between the two passions in his life, he chose Vilma. As she so succinctly put it, "He gave up everything for me."

Aris's departure, note, meant that the band reverted back to being a seven-piece unit once again, which explains why the 'John Barry and The Seven' moniker was no longer appropriate for any record releases after 'Zip Zip'.

Despite this unexpected casualty, the band's fortunes took yet another mighty leap forward, when they were chosen to provide the backing for Paul Anka throughout his UK tour in December. At that precise juncture, there was no hotter property on the pop scene than this Canadian born sixteen-year-old, whose debut UK 45 (the self-penned 'Diana') was all set to become the biggest selling single of 1957. Ken Golder recalls the band auditioning for Anka and his management in a deserted Soho nightclub one Sunday morning, when the usually bustling area was eerily quiet. What Anka wanted was a tight, reliable, versatile combo, and after coping with 'Diana' (alongside other material chosen for them to play), The JB7 got the gig. Anka was delighted with them. "That's the band I want; they're just the job for me", he enthused. The sixteen-date tour (including six consecutive nights at the Liverpool Empire) was a significant challenge, for not only were they expected to back Anka throughout his act, but they were also contracted to open both halves of the show in their own right. The bill also included singer Billie Anthony, whose pianist Michael Austin became a temporary addition to the band during Anka's set. One reviewer noted that their best work as Anka's accompaniment was on 'Down by the Riverside' and 'Shake, Baby, Shake'. *The Stage*, on reviewing the performance at Kilburn Gaumont on 8th December, described The JB7 as "lively and well presented."

Also on the bill during that tour was an act The Seven had previously met at the Royal Albert Hall, the Bob Cort Skiffle Group, in whose ranks was a dazzling new guitarist by the name of Vic Flick. Barry and Flick hit it off straight away, and often found themselves eating, drinking and talking music together on the tour. Vic Flick was very much John Barry's type, combining showmanship with technical brilliance and musical flair. Barry was to remember him later when it became clear that changes were necessary in The Seven.

A New Year's Eve charity ball at the London's Dorchester Hotel aside, the triumphant Anka tour, which climaxed at The Regal, Edmonton on the 22nd December, was a fitting way to end what was an astonishing year for the group.

The year 1957 was one marked out by considerable change, not only in the UK but also worldwide. This was the year in which Harold Macmillan succeeded Anthony Eden as Prime Minister following the Suez debacle; the year his often quoted "you've never had it so good" speech was made, even if his actual words were "let us be frank about it, most of our people have never had it so good". Indeed, Britain was at last starting to feel a good deal better about itself now that it was beginning to witness some chinks of light emerging out of the dark days of post-war austerity, fuelled by the great engine of consumerism revving itself up into a roar. Petrol rationing, for example, had finally ended, while white goods and labour-saving devices, such as toasters, food-mixers, and vacuum cleaners, were starting to flood the market. Also that year, the Cavern Club first opened its doors in Liverpool; John Lennon met Paul McCartney; the Soviet Union launched the first space satellite, Sputnik 1, then sent a dog in space via Sputnik 2; Britain first tested the H-Bomb; *The Sky At Night* and *Emergency-Ward 10* made their television debuts; national premium bonds were being introduced; the consumer protection magazine, *Which?*, was launched; the Queen's first ever Christmas television address was made from Sandringham; a direct causal link between tobacco smoking and lung cancer was initially identified; the 'Best Foreign Film' category was first introduced at the Oscars (won by Fellini's *La Strada*), while *The King and I* won Best Music Score. Yes, these were giddy times.

For John Barry, personally, the year 1957 had been a stratospheric one. A band that had started in January as no more than a fanciful idea fermenting away in his fevered imagination was by December a hard-working, eye-catching and increasingly sought-after reality. The John Barry Seven was going places and, much like the Super Powers, would soon be reaching for the moon.

Fulford House, Main Street, Fulford, York, the home of the Prendergast family from the 1940s onwards.

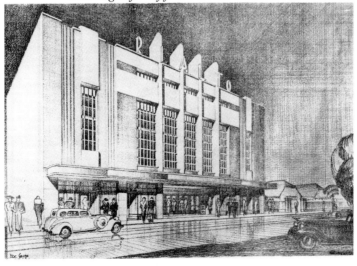

The Rialto Cinema, Fishergate, York, owned and managed by Jack Prendergast.

Bill Russo's advert in Downbeat magazine in 1955.

Jack and Doris Prendergast.

John Barry, far right, on trumpet in Johnny Sutton's Modernaires, c. 1956.

The first line-up, from left: Derek Myers, Mike Cox, Fred Kirk,
Ken Golder, John Barry, Ken Richards, Keith Kelly.

*John Barry and The Seven at The NME's Top 20 Hit-parade All Star show
at the Royal Albert Hall, on 8th September 1957.*

Paul Anka rehearses with The JB7 before his appearance at The London Palladium – 6th December 1957.

EMI Chairman Sir Joseph Lockwood presents Paul Anka with a gold disc for sales of "Diana", with several members of The JB7 looking on, including the unusual sight of Fred Kirk playing stand-up bass.

SEVEN BACHELORS .... WORTH £10,000 EACH ! !

Dynamic new beat-group JOHN BARRY AND THE SEVEN are single men without a thought ... of marriage! Or that's the way it's got to be for the next 12 months. For 23-year-old JOHN BARRY (himself a bachelor) has taken out an insurance policy -- with the approval of the SEVEN -- under which he will be paid the sum of £10,000 .... "in the event of any member of the SEVEN entering into a state of matrimony." This is to sustain the group's teen-age appeal, and to prevent the rigours of touring causing domestic disharmony -- and possibly leading to some member leaving the SEVEN as a result.

Bachelors with the £10,000 price on their heads are:

Mike Cox (tenor-sax), Derek Myers (baritone and alto-sax), John B. Aris (vibes), Ken Richards (solo guitar), Fred Kirk (electric bass), Ken Golder (drums) and Keith Kelly (rhythm guitar).

And what about JOHN BARRY ? ...... "I guess the boys in the group will see to it that I stay single, too!"

HEAR THE "BEAT BOYS'" NEW HIT DISC:

JOHN BARRY AND THE SEVEN

Zip; Zip / Three Little Fishes

PARLOPHONE R4363

THE PALACE THEATRE — BLACKPOOL

Licensee: Wm. H. H. Smith   Entertainments Executive Manager: Kathleen Williams   House Manager: R. G. Wood

Monday 22nd July 1957 for Four Weeks (Mondays to Saturdays)
Each Afternoon at 2.30 p.m.

HAROLD FIELDING presents

THE TOMMY STEELE AFTERNOON SHOW

Programme

1. THE JOHN BARRY SEVEN —
Derek Myers (baritone and alto sax), Mike Cox (tenor sax)
Don Martin (drums), Fred Kirk (electric bass)
Ken Richards (solo guitar, vocals), Keith Kelly (rhythm guitar, vocals)
and JOHN BARRY (trumpet)

2. Introducing your Compere —
REG THOMPSON

3. Famous Harmony Group —
THE KEN-TONES

4. Penny Whistle Boogie Man —
DESMOND LANE

INTERVAL

5. THE JOHN BARRY SEVEN —

6. Britain's Teenage Idol —

TOMMY STEELE

and

THE STEELMEN

Presentation under the Personal Supervision of HAROLD FIELDING
Decor designed and painted by Edward Delany
Venetian Blind built by J. Avery & Co. (Est. 1854) Ltd.
Tommy Steele and the Steelmen's clothes designed and executed by Teddy Tinling
Rock 'n Roll Shoes by E. K. Coles Ltd.
Ken-Tones clothes designed by Alec Shanks and executed by (disco) Alec Shanks and (suits) Morris Angel
Programme produced by the Harold Fielding Organisation, Fielding House, Haymarket, London, S.W.1
and printed by Claridge, Lewis & Jordan Ltd., 56-70 Wardour Street, London, W.1.
Production Manager }
Stage Manager } for HAROLD FIELDING   Ray Gammond   Brian Penders

John Barry and The Seven with their new "chaperone", Amy Rosser, 19th October 1957.

Billie Anthony, Paul Anka, Bob Cort and John Barry backstage after a concert.

The Boys With Rhythm With'em

THE JOHN BARRY 7

Fulford House
15 Fulford
York

Tel. 77331.

Wednesday - May 8th.57.

Mr. Jack Good,
"6-5 Special"
B.B.C. T.V.Centre,
Wood Lane,
London, W.12.

Dear Mr.Wood,

I understood that my father spoke to you on the 'phone the other day with regards to an appearance on your "6-5 Special" programme. I enclose photographs, press cuttings, programmes etc.

Also enclosed you will find a record we made of two original numbers I have written. They are called "We All Love To Rock" and "Rock-a-Billy Boogie".

They leave much to be desired by modern recording studio standards, but they will give you a rough idea. The group sounds a great deal fuller and "living" than on these recordings.

Looking forward to hearing from you in the near future.

Yours truly,
John Barry

Thanks — very good enclosed, but Dev Lang & Frankie Fur Booked as regular feature for this sort of band

---

HAROLD FIELDING

AGENCY DIVISION

(Licences normally by the London County Council)

Telegrams: Concerts, Lesquare, London
Cables: Concerts, London
Telephone: Whitehall 4041 (ten lines)

FIELDING HOUSE
53-54 HAYMARKET
LONDON, S.W.1

11th September 1957

J. L. Davidson Esq.,
Assistant Head of Variety Production,
British Broadcasting Corporation,
Aeolian Hall,
New Bond Street,
London, W.1.

Dear Jim,

Confirming my telephone conversation with you yesterday, I would be very happy if an audition could be arranged for THE JOHN BARRY 7.

This is a new combination which we launched with great success in "The Tommy Steele Show" at Blackpool during the summer season. The instrumentation is two saxophones, one trumpet, drums, bass and two guitars.

They have already appeared on Commercial Television, and are appearing on B.B.C. Television in the "Six-five Special" on September 21st.

The unit is based on York, and as they are coming to London next week for their Television show, it would be ideal if a Radio audition could be arranged for them on either Wednesday, the 18th, or Thursday, the 19th of September.

With kindest regards,

Yours sincerely,
Ian Bevan
HAROLD FIELDING AGENCY DIVISION

IB/MS

Landseer Studio publicity photo for John Barry and The Seven, September 1957.

1. THE JOHN BARRY SEVEN
   The Boys with rhythm with 'em

2. DICKIE DAWSON
   Canada's good humour man

3. THE GITSOM SISTERS
   Glamour in harmony

4. BOB CORT SKIFFLE

5. Intermission

6. THE JOHN BARRY SEVEN

7. BILLIE ANTHONY
   The atomic blonde

8. DICKIE DAWSON
   With more humour

9. From America . . .

the sensational young Singing Star

PAUL ANKA

Hit recorder of " Diana," etc.

❀ ❀ ❀ ❀ ❀

PAUL ANKA, the handsome young 16-year-older whose initial recording on the Columbia label of " Diana " (written by himself) catapulted him into the national spotlight, has been in great demand for personal appearances and television guest shots. Besides being the composer of " Diana," Paul has also written songs for other record stars—Andy Williams, Johnny Nash, Micki Marlo and Dick Roman. Paul Anka was born in Ottawa, Canada, on July 30th, 1941. Of Syrian ancestry, Paul is the oldest of a family of three and he has been singing in public since he was 10, making his first night club appearance at the age of 12 at Ocean Beach, Mass., where he impersonated Johnnie Ray and others and so captivated a tough night club audience they threw money on the stage ; when collected there was $35. Prior to his hit record, Paul used to hang around the night clubs in Ottawa talking to all the stars. He's eternally grateful for the very helpful advice given to him by such top groups as the Four Lads, the Diamonds, the Rover Boys and the Crew Cuts on how to rise to the top in the entertainment field. He then formed his own vocal group called " The Bobbysoxers." Paul Anka wrote " Diana " for his girlfriend, Diana.

ICE CREAM, SOFT DRINKS AND NUTS ARE AVAILABLE FROM THE ATTENDANTS DURING THE INTERVAL.
THE FOYER KIOSK IS OPEN WITH A WIDE SELECTION OF CONFECTIONERY AND CIGARETTES.

Journalist Stacey Brewer with his wife, Jean,
after receiving the MBE in 1989.

JOHNNIE RAY

THE PHENOMENON OF SHOW BUSINESS

VIC LEWIS
AND HIS ORCHESTRA

1. Intermission Rock - - - BAND
2. Everything Happens To Me - JOE McINTYRE
3. Banana Boat Song - - - CLAYTERS
4. Trumpet Rock - - - TRUMPET SECTION
5. Two Different Worlds - - IRMA LOGAN
6. This Can't Be Love - - ART ELLEFSON
7. My Old Flame - - - ART ELLEFSON
8. Love, Love, Love - - VIC LEWIS
9. Natal - - - - ANDY WHITE
10. Julie - - - - COLIN BRADFIELD
11. Rose Room - - - COLIN BRADFIELD
12. It Happened In Monterey - VIC LEWIS
13. All Of You - - - IRMA LOGAN
14. In The Mood Rock - - BAND

15. THE JOHN BARRY SEVEN
THE BOYS WITH A RHYTHM WITH 'EM

Looking from left to right, as they appear on stage, the boys are:

Derek Myers (alto-sax). He's 22, comes from Carlton, near Wakefield. Worked as a grocery assistant in Lofthouse, but threw it over in favour of music. Was a corner-man with Edgar Jackson and His Music at Castleford.

Mike Cox (tenor-sax). From Bardley, near Leeds, Mike is 21. He started off playing clarinet, but switched to saxophone five years ago. Mike worked as a clerk in Leeds; has also played with Edgar Jackson and His Music.

John Barry (vocals and trumpet). Leader of the group, he's 23. John met Derek and Mike when they were all in the Regimental Band of the Green Howards, in Egypt and Cyprus. He is studying advanced orchestration and composition under Bill Russo, one-time arranger for Stan Kenton.

Ken Golder (drums). At 16 started playing drums and had his own group. In the Far East he played with bands accompanying visiting American film stars, including Abbe Lane, Xavier Cugat and Ava Gardner. Has drummed for George Crow and Harry Leader.

Fred Kirk (electric bass). Joined a brass band eight years ago and developed an interest in music. Took up playing string bass while serving in Malta, in the R.A.F. Has played in bands at Scarborough Spa and Olympia.

Ken Richards (solo guitar). Started playing guitar at 15. During the war had his own jazz group, which included Bobbie Pratt (now high-note trumpet man with Ted Heath) and Bill LeSage (well-known pianist with Johnny Dankworth).

Keith Kelly (rhythm guitar). Originally played a mouth organ. During R.A.F. service in Cyprus he did cabaret turns at local hotels. Used to sing at a York dance hall, and began playing guitar after a friend had given him one. He's 22.

16. Peanut Vendor

INTERVAL.

1. Zing Went The Strings
THE WORLD'S GREATEST RECORDING STAR

JOHNNIE RAY

SATURDAY, 4th MAY   6-15 and 8-30 p.m.
Direct from America—

THE SENSATIONAL

GERRY MULLIGAN QUARTET
and
"JAZZ TODAY"—Ten British Jazz Stars

Prices: 10/6, 8/6, 7/6, 5/-, 3/6
Organise Your Party for a Great Show

6th MAY — ALL WEEK
Twice Nightly at 6-20 and 8-35 p.m.

THE THRILLING VOICE OF

DAVID WHITFIELD
and All-Star Variety Show

NO INCREASE IN PRICES

Tickets: 6/-, 4/6, 3/6, 2/6 (unreserved) — All Seats Bookable
Booking Plan Open Now, 12-0 noon to 8-0 p.m. — Write! Call! Phone! Tel. 22119

2

THE BEE'S KNEES

JANUARY – DECEMBER 1958

In those early days, even though Norman Newell was my A&R man and John Burgess, his assistant, it was me who actually called the shots because I was the one who had written and played on the records. Take 'Rodeo' as an example – the odd combination of baritone sax with twangy guitar created a strange kind of effect. It was me in charge of those fresh approaches at that time.

– John Barry

One very important aspect to understand was that The John Barry Seven was NEVER a co-operative. We were paid for each engagement; I had a contract of employment with John Barry, which was carefully managed by his then wife, Barbara.

– Jimmy Stead (baritone sax).

In a 1985 interview with music writer, David Toop, Barry admitted to deliberately jumping on the 'rock 'n' roll' bandwagon in the belief it would prove the quickest and most direct way of gaining prominence within the music business. Putting this down to the impatience and impetuousness of youth, he said that he couldn't get there fast enough and, judging by the events of 1958, the momentum was undoubtedly accelerating. What also convinced Barry he was moving in the right direction was the way in which this 'new music' was more prepared to embrace any technological innovation, to wit he was able to boast leading the first British group to incorporate an electric bass guitar (manufactured by the German company, Hofner) together with amplification capable of drowning out a sixteen-piece big band!

The choice of 'Every Which Way' as the band's second single (released in January) may not have been that difficult to comprehend given the knowledge that The JB7 were about to be filmed performing the song in the forthcoming big screen version of *Six-Five Special*. The film, itself, may not have been scheduled for general release until April, but by that time, the 45 would have already been made available in the shops and secured some radio airplay. Both sides of the single had been recorded at Abbey Road much earlier on 14th November, alongside a Barry original, 'Little Old-Fashioned Love', which, to this day, remains in the EMI archives. This latter track was also intended for inclusion in the film, but much like the master tape of the song, was confined to the cutting room floor. As for the film sequences themselves, the group travelled overnight from York to the Alliance Studios in Twickenham during January, to complete them.

Surviving members of this JB7 line-up have only vague recollections of appearing in the film. Mike Cox recalled spotting a huge ship in a field adjoining the studio, which turned out to be a partial replica of the RMS Titanic as used in the film *A Night To Remember*, and while he also remembered his wife receiving the sum of ten shillings (£0.50) for taking part as one of the dancers in the studio, Keith Kelly could only recall the innumerable hours spent in make-up! – so much for the razzamatazz and glamour of showbiz.

The JB7's appearance in the film seems all the more remarkable for the following reasons: not only were they still relatively unknown (outside of York), but they had also yet to register any semblance of a hit record. Therefore, by being seen amongst such exalted company as Dickie Valentine, Jim Dale, Petula Clark, Joan Regan, Johnny Dankworth and Lonnie Donegan (all big-selling artistes), there really was no better way of raising one's profile in 1958.

As for the single, it received a favourable review in the 18th January edition of *Record Mirror* albeit in the rather condescending language of the time, "The disc is good stuff for the kids who like to dance to their discs," exclaimed the reviewer, adding further that the saxes "produce a noise which ought to sell quite a few copies." In reference to the flip side, "The Seven and her singer (surely a mistake here) rough it up... and make the most of a muzzy noise." Quite so.

Meanwhile, the ever-restless Jack Good was becoming increasingly disenchanted with the way in which the TV version was evolving, and as a result was now in the midst of hatching a plan to take *Six-Five Special* on the road around the provinces for a series of music-dominated presentations. This was more in keeping with his own vision of the show, since his aim was always to push its spontaneity, drive and dynamism to the very limit, much preferring to concentrate on the energy created by the musical content rather than the more sedate educational and human-interest items that also peppered the broadcast. Evidently, the BBC thought otherwise, and, once made aware of this out-of-hours touring edition, promptly decided not to renew his contract, much to Good's own bewilderment.

Nevertheless, the stage version did go ahead as planned with The JB7 very much to the fore (alongside regular presenters Pete Murray, Josephine Douglas and Freddie Mills). Promoted by Harold Fielding, these shows hit the road over two consecutive mid-weeks (Tuesdays and Wednesdays) starting on 7th January in Leicester, then moving on to Hull, Newcastle and Sheffield respectively.

Although not a runaway success as was hoped (one suspects as a result of the rather unpromising mid-week scheduling), it was responsible for two significant developments. Firstly, it instilled in Good a taste for presenting live music in a theatre setting and, secondly, it initiated the first meeting of two men who would bring a new sound to British pop before the decade was out, John Barry and a teenage newcomer being tried out by Good on the tour, Adam Faith. For the Seven, sandwiched in between these dates was another *Six-Five Special* appearance on 11th January; an edition that also included Don Lang, Rosemary Squires plus Marty Wilde and His Wildcats.

With bookings somewhat spasmodic around this period, Barry was free to attend the film premiere of *Six Five Special* at the Dominion Theatre, Tottenham Court Road, on 30th March and was better placed to concentrate his fullest attention on the contents of and arrangements for the third Parlophone single, 'Big Guitar/Rodeo', the recording of which went ahead on 6th March.

Recording a guitar-led instrumental was not exactly the most obvious course of action to take for an act seeking its first hit during the spring of 1958. Whether borne out of intuition, calculation or desperation, Barry's decision to ditch vocals *per se* in favour of this approach proved to be the most pivotal of them all throughout the entire lifespan of the group. It was, to use modern parlance, *the* game-changer, for it put The JB7 at the vanguard of an emerging trend a good two years before its 'golden era' when the sound of a guitar-driven instrumental became a dominant presence in the pop firmament.

There is no doubt, however, that Barry would have taken note of the huge commercial success currently being enjoyed by Bill Justis's 'Raunchy' when weighing up his options at the time. This, the first instrumental of its ilk to ever make a significant impact on the UK charts, was soon followed into the top thirty by a British cover version courtesy of Ken Mackintosh and His Orchestra. The combination of electric guitar, saxophone and piano was precisely the type of juxtaposition that would perfectly play to the strengths of The JB7. Clearly, Barry was now on the lookout for something similar – a pounding guitar-laden piece enveloped by a brass section – and as was the general practice of that era, he took his lead from what was making waves across the Atlantic with a view to making a creditable British-made alternative, He found it in the form of the brooding 'Big Guitar', which was originally recorded by Frank De Rosa and His D Men, but became a huge hit for the Owen Bradley Quintet in the USA.

With time of the essence, it was imperative to record a creditable anglophile version as soon as possible, not only before the original recordings surfaced in the UK, but also before other local talent followed suit. As it turned out, Irving Ashby and Johnnie (The Gash) Gray both had the same idea, which meant that no fewer than five versions were competing in the same market, which inevitably split sales. Not for the first time in this era of the 'cover version', a plurality of alternatives prevented one act from securing the hit. Barry, however, shrewdly continued his policy of writing the B-side, on this occasion 'Rodeo', which was the clearest sign yet of what was to come. Tucked away unobtrusively, this western-tinged theme (Barry's first recorded instrumental composition) did not go under the radar of bandleader Frank Chacksfield, who deemed it good enough for releasing as a single under his own name. Thus, ironically, 'Rodeo' (the flip side of a cover version) became the first commercially recorded John Barry cover version.

The band were able to plug the new single during another appearance on *Six-Five Special* on 5th April, which was broadcast from Edinburgh, while 'Rodeo' was selected by 'disc arranger' Ker Robertson and played by presenter Kent Walton during an edition of *Cool for Cats* on 2nd April.

Despite the protestations of the musical establishment, 'youth music' was not going away; in fact, on the contrary, it was growing in strength and now also gaining popularity throughout the length and breadth of Europe. However, writing in the *Melody Maker* in June 1958, vociferous critic Steve Race – who first wrote in 1956 that "the current craze for 'rock 'n' roll' is one of the most terrifying things ever to have happened to popular music" – was now offering a simpler two word obituary for its inevitable death, "Good riddance", while Billy Cotton on his BBC Saturday night variety show observed archly that 'skiffle' rhymed with 'piffle'. There was no denying that the new generation was ruffling the old order, and that the premature demise of 'rock 'n' roll' was merely wishful thinking, given that elsewhere at around the same time, George Harrison was passing his audition as lead guitarist of The Beatles by performing a flawless rendition of 'Raunchy', while Mick Jagger was in awe as he watched Buddy Holly perform 'Not Fade Away' at The Woolwich Granada. The horse had long since bolted.

John Barry was of an age where he saw no dichotomy in acknowledging the best of both generations: being able to appreciate the past whilst looking eagerly ahead. It also helped having an agent as powerful as Harold Fielding on one's side. By April 1958, Tommy Steele (whom Fielding mentored almost like a son) was at the peak of his popularity as a pop star to the point where his fame had now spread way beyond the British Isles. After receiving a rapturous reception wherever he went throughout a tour of South Africa earlier in the year, his sights were next set on a comprehensive tour of Scandinavia with the aim also of promoting his latest film *The Duke Wore Jeans*. Thanks entirely to their mutual representation, together with previous experience of working alongside one another, The JB7 was booked as part of this prestigious package starting in Denmark on 14th April. After first stopping off in Copenhagen, the tour took in Aarhus, Stockholm, Eskilstuna, Orebro, Linkoping, Jonkoping, Aalborg and Odense. What the band was about to witness was the utter hysteria and pandemonium caused by a teenage pop sensation at the height of his fame.

Initially, Steele was unable to travel with the group after having being involved in a minor car accident on his way to the airport thereby missing the scheduled flight. Instead, he had to charter a private aircraft in order to arrive on time for the first show, but he was soon to experience the type of mass adoration that was to follow him throughout Denmark and Sweden. For example, nearly 2,000 fans waited at Bromma Airport for a glimpse of their idol, some of them after having queued up to eight hours. In Stockholm alone, an audience of eight thousand turned up to see the show in the city's largest stadium – the Royal Lawn Tennis Hall – each night. *Melody Maker*'s Scandinavian correspondent, Sven Winquist, reported that as many as thirty policemen had been recruited to keep the fans at bay, but despite this, one of them still managed to invade the stage with the sole intention of kissing the singer. As for the concert, he found the constant screaming so incredibly deafening that it was practically impossible to make out what Steele was singing nor what The JB7 were playing, although that did not appear to detract from the audience's enjoyment of the occasion from what he could observe.

Ken Golder, who had nothing but fond memories of the entire experience, was able to witness from the wings the electric atmosphere generated by Steele's exuberant following. "Every night there were hundreds of kids outside the theatres screaming for him," he recalled. As for Steele, "He was a lovely bloke who used to come for a drink with the lads after the show." From Golder's perspective, he felt privileged to have been among one of the instigators of a nascent British music scene. On the Scandinavian trip, he added, "We had a great time, and I've got a lot of good memories from when I was with the band." He sensed also that The JB7 were breaking new ground: "We felt like pioneers of rock and roll, because the whole popular music scene was just starting to take off. There weren't many bands going around playing that kind of thing." In acknowledging Barry's insistence on a strict dress code, he added, "We always dressed smartly, because they used to like that on TV."

Not for the first time was the fate of The JB7 inextricably linked with the career of Tommy Steele, and sure enough, this was about to happen yet again; only on this occasion it was all connected with the singer being laid out of action for a short while. On returning from Europe, Steele and The Steelmen immediately set off on what was to be yet another lengthy concert and variety tour of the UK, with The JB7 once again in support, except that this time it didn't get any further than the first date at Dundee's Caird Hall on 30th April. It was at this venue where Steele fainted in his dressing room after having been injured and traumatised by besieging fans storming the stage in attempts to get a piece of their hero. In the resulting mayhem, his right arm was badly hurt, chunks of his hair were pulled out and his shirt ripped off. According to *The Scotsman*, the next thing he knew was on being woken at the Edinburgh Royal Infirmary nursing a wounded shoulder. Being incapable of resuming the tour on doctor's orders, the latest teen sensation – fifteen-year-old Scot, Jackie Dennis – was hastily drafted in to replace him for certain dates while others had to be cancelled.

Mike Cox recalled being particularly annoyed at missing out on such a potentially well-paid tour, even more so when rumours began circulating to the effect that the incident had been deliberately blown up out of all proportion by Steele's management solely for publicity purposes. Subsequent photographs surfacing in the press of Steele cradling his right arm in a sling did nothing to dispel the theory. "Admittedly this was mere speculation, but we were a bit miffed as it cost us a few quid!" – obviously, not good news at all for The Seven, which was further compounded on finding themselves squeezed out of the revised tour schedule entirely, with Dennis now accompanied by The Steelmen and apparently no room for the Barry boys in any capacity whatsoever. However, Dennis made such a good job of deputising that he was rewarded with a headline tour of his own, which proved fortuitous for The JB7, for on this occasion they were part of the package, both as his backing group and as an act in their own right.

Hence, throughout the months of May and June, The JB7 were back on the road alongside yet another up-and-coming 'teenybopper'. Dubbed 'the lilt with the kilt' by his manager Eve Taylor (who, herself, would soon become a prominent player in Barry's own professional life), Dennis was discovered performing at Prestwick Airport (then a US air base) by comedy duo, Mike and Bernie Winters. The archetypal overnight sensation, Dennis enjoyed two sizeable hit records, the biggest of which was 'La Dee Dah', and for a brief period was reputedly earning as much as £1,000 per week! Also on the bill were trumpeter, Kenny Baker; comedy double act, Joe Baker and Jack Douglas; close-harmony group, The Kordites; American comedian, Don Hooton and ventriloquist, Fred Lovelle.

The tour began on 2nd June at The Empire, Nottingham, followed by further weekly residences in theatres at Nottingham, Birmingham, Bournemouth and London (Chiswick). A brief mention in *The Stage* commended The JB7 on looking smart and playing "good and loud", adding "Featuring three electric guitars, two saxophones, drums and trumpet / vocals, the band gave stage backing to Master Jackie Dennis in addition to their own successful spot in the show."

As for Jackie Dennis, he was living the dream on this tour, which explains why he always looks back on those times with a great deal of affection, enthusing "I had a £50,000 contract with Harold Fielding for a year, and that included a tour of Moss Empire theatres. John Barry was brilliant and did all my arrangements, while The JB7 was a great band providing wonderful accompaniment for both myself and The Liddell Triplets, who were also behind me." What stood out for Dennis was just how appropriate The JB7's backing was for his smattering of celebrity impersonations, among them Jerry Lewis, Dean Martin and Johnnie Ray. "I loved the way Ken Golder's drum-beat accompanied me across the stage; it was dead on the money as I took on Jerry Lewis' funny walk," he added. "I got on well with them all, especially Keith Kelly."

During the tour, The JB7 managed to fit in what turned out to be their last ever appearance on *Six-Five Special* on 31st May, performing on an episode alongside Marion Ryan, The Dallas Boys, The Mudlarks, The Cockatoos, and Eric Delaney and His Band. This edition gave them the ideal opportunity for promoting the forthcoming single, 'Pancho/Hideaway', which was recorded a few days earlier on the 23rd May. Again, in search of that elusive first hit, Barry fixed both ears firmly on the latest musical trend, and with The Champs' Latin-infused 'rock 'n' roll' instrumental, 'Tequila', hurtling up the hit parade, this seemed a valid genre to explore as well as a good way of widening the band's musical palette. What's more, it provided Barry with the opportunity of putting two of his own compositions on the table, buoyed by the attention and encouragement he was receiving from A&R man, Norman Newell. On vinyl at any rate, the band was still trying to its find its true identity.

One quite unexpected event worthy of mentioning occurred during the residency at the Chiswick Empire. On the Thursday of that week (12th June), Barry arrived for the evening's performance, as per usual, only to announce to his band-mates that he had spent the afternoon at Caxton Hall getting married to his long-time girlfriend, Barbara! It proved to be a good story for *The Daily Herald*, since it made front-page news the following day with particular reference given to the group's 'no marriage insurance policy' publicity stunt from the previous year. Barry confessed to having only proposed five days earlier on the Saturday (the 7th), with Barbara informing her parents a mere twenty four hours before the ceremony.

Reaction to the new single proved encouraging on two fronts. Firstly, the record was beginning to make an impression on the local charts, which was an indication that the band was developing a fan base. Back in 1958, *Record Mirror* printed weekly lists of 'Top Tens' representing sales at selected shops throughout the UK, albeit primarily in the London area. More often than not, a band that had recently played live in a particular locality was bound to make a greater impact. 'Pancho' registered in a few of these charts, without hitting the all-important national listing, but it was a huge shot in the arm and one that would have registered favourably with the number-crunchers at Parlophone.

Secondly, a lengthy four-star review in *Record Mirror* on 5th July was positively glowing in its praise. 'Hideaway', in particular, was singled out by dint of its affecting melody and use of harmonica. Barry was lauded for his boldness and originality in bringing together the nostalgic air of a harmonica with the bold percussion indicative of a Latin American accompaniment, while the use of flute to compliment the tenor sax on 'Pancho' was also applauded. "I was most surprised when I put these two sides on the turntable. One expects purely rock 'n' roll when the name John Barry comes up on the label, but not so here. Both are excellent Latin-American sides composed by Mr. Barry," enthused the reviewer. Here were two early examples of Barry delivering the unexpected.

Jack Good's defection to the world of commercial television was always likely to be a far better fit for someone with his dynamism; a maverick producer hell-bent on adding the vitality of youth into the weekend schedules. Having become increasingly frustrated by the BBC's preference for toning down the spontaneity, energy and pace of his original blueprint for *Six-Five Special*, when ABC Television offered him the opportunity of producing two trial live broadcasts in accordance with his own vision of what a youth-oriented music show should look like, he jumped at the chance. Already convinced live transmissions were the way forward following his experience on the *Six-Five Special* tour, he was to hire the Hackney Empire in East London as a venue for his half-hour blast of non-stop live music. *Oh Boy!*, a more cutting-edge and less antiseptic antidote to the BBC's flagship, was about to be born.

Had it not been for the fact that The JB7 were busily touring Scandinavia with Tommy Steele, they may well have been initially chosen to form the resident house band, since Good was known to be a great admirer of both leader and band. Instead, he turned to Harry Robinson, whose Lord Rockingham's XI would soon enjoy great success of their own on the back of fulfilling these duties. Not that The JB7 were completely ignored, however. As soon as they were back in Blighty, they were snapped up for both pilot shows not only as a performing outfit in their own right but also as a supplementary resident house band to accompany other artists.

The first of the pilots was broadcast on Sunday 15th June, the second a fortnight later. Each one was shown very late at night and only in the London and Midlands regions. The casts were as follows:

Pilot One: The Dallas Boys; The John Barry Seven; Lord Rockingham's XI; Ronnie Carroll; Bertice Reading; Marty Wilde; Cherry Wainer; Red Price; Neville Taylor and the Cutters; Dudley Heslop; Kerry Martin and The Vernons Girls

Pilot Two: The Dallas Boys; The John Barry Seven; Jackie Dennis; Lord Rockingham's XI; Bertice Reading; Marty Wilde; Cherry Wainer; Red Price; Neville Taylor and the Cutters and The Vernons Girls

In spite of such a limited audience, both editions of the embryonic *Oh Boy!* were so well received that it wasn't long before Good was promised a fully syndicated nationwide series later in the year. *Six-Five Special* was about to be usurped.

Curiously, when The Seven returned home to The Rialto in between pilots on 22nd June, appearing on the same bill as Sarah Vaughan (clearly a highly prestigious engagement), they were billed as 'from the TV show, Oh Boy!'; this, despite the fact that none of the audience could have possibly seen the show living in and around York. The Sarah Vaughan show provided a glimpse into the band's then-current repertoire, which was an eclectic mix of standards, originals, vocals and instrumentals: 'Get Happy'; 'Wonderful Time Up There'; 'Rodeo'; 'Blue Moon'; 'Pancho'; 'Every Which Way'; 'You've Gotta Way'; 'Hideaway'; 'Festival' and 'Up Above My Head', five of which were Barry compositions (including the unrecorded 'Festival').

※

The life of a working musician is a notoriously precarious and insecure one at the best of times. The money may well have been above the average weekly wage on the upper echelons of the ballroom and variety theatre circuits during 1958, but if the work wasn't constant and regular enough, then it became increasingly difficult to make end's meet. What's more, incessant daily travelling, combined with working anti-social hours, was not everyone's preferred lifestyle choice, and when families were involved, this could strain the most rock-solid of relationships. The JB7 was no different from any other touring entourage reliant on a constant stream of engagements during the middle of 1958 and, as a result, was susceptible to all of the above pressure points. A combination of these factors was about, therefore, to herald the first significant changes in the line-up of the band.

Certainly, a gruelling touring schedule, scattered seemingly haphazardly from one end of the UK to the other and then back again, created such strain and tension that eventually morale did become severely affected with cracks forming among band mates. Disagreements started to surface. Fatigue bred discontent. Some resentment towards Barry also simmered to the boil, on account of him not having to appear in the line-up when accompanying other artists on the bill. Add the homesickness caused by being constantly on the road to the list of grievances and it became quite obvious that all was not well. To compound this further, during periods of inactivity (and there were a number of those during the first half of 1958), certain members of the band would make a point of returning home to Yorkshire for some respite, only to find as soon as they were feeling settled, Barry (who by this time was entirely London based) recalling them south again for a few more dates. Not before long, serious hard choices needed to be made.

As a consequence, when Derek Myers received an offer to join a big band in Scotland on a permanent basis, with regular work guaranteed, it was an offer he could hardly refuse. A week of almost constant bickering made up his mind for him. He was replaced by Jimmy Stead, who arrived in time to make his band debut at the Sheffield Empire as part of the Jackie Dennis package tour. Next to depart was trained aircraft fitter Fred Kirk; putting job security above all other considerations, he spotted and landed a job in aviation. Mike Peters took over on bass guitar, after having been recommended by newest member, Stead.

While all this was going on, Barry was unveiling his own plans for the future, via an article in *The Stage*, that involved augmenting The Seven with an additional member, valve-trombonist and pianist, Stuart Atkins. In partnership with Larry Parnes and John Kennedy (joint-managers for Tommy Steele and Marty Wilde), this was all part of an all-encompassing project aimed at placing The Seven at the forefront of British light entertainment with a view to shoring up every conceivable live outlet: variety, TV, concert theatres and, now, the ballroom circuit also. One suspects that this latter move influenced the musical direction of the Latin-tinged, newly released single, and indeed, the one thereafter.

Commenting on the new line-up at the time, Barry said: "I shall now have a front-line sound of trumpet, valve-trombone, tenor sax doubling flute, alto sax doubling baritone. I am also using my solo guitar as a front-line instrument. The rhythm section — amplified bass, guitar and drums — will be arranged to provide what I think will be one of the most danceable beats ever heard in Britain's ballrooms". (Note, even at this stage, how Barry was already envisaging a time when the electric guitar would take centre stage and become the dominant instrument within the structure of the band).

There was, however, one major flaw in this grand design, which in all likelihood thwarted the scheme before it had truly got off the ground, and which resulted in Stuart Atkins never actually joining the group after all. Quite simply, the entire fabric of Britain's variety theatre tradition *per se* was in such steep decline by this time that it was starting to haemorrhage alarmingly towards extinction. Taking London alone as an example (itself, a microcosm of the country writ large), there were twenty-one thriving variety theatres doing good business at the start of 1951, whereas by the end of the decade, there were only four remaining. What with the Portsmouth Empire, Camberwell Palace and Woolwich Empire all closing down during 1958 (along with many others changing usage or mysteriously burning down), the plan proposed by this triumvirate of like minds, one envisages, was quietly dropped against such a discouraging backdrop.

On the other hand, for new boy, Jimmy Stead, joining The JB7 was a godsend, since this was a difficult period for any aspiring jazz musician seeking work, with the big band era also nose-diving into oblivion. Jack Parnell's earlier, prescient forebodings were being felt sharply at the coalface, about which Stead was acutely aware. No one was going to turn down the potential for a constant flow of work in such a climate, not least this young saxophonist, as he would later attest: "I, for one, was over the moon at being in The Seven. Rock 'n' roll put many big band musicians out of work. Archer Street in London's West End was where many of us met to chat and hopefully get a gig. The saxophone soon became an instrument of the past once the guitar rose to the top where it remains to this day." Ironically, it was nearly-man, Stuart Atkins, who recommended Stead to Barry.

As for Stead's background, he was taught saxophone from the age of eight by Francis Walker, a blind multi-instrumentalist based in Wakefield. Often left in awe by his tutor's adeptness at accompanying himself on piano with his left hand whilst simultaneously playing the harmonica with his right, Stead remembers fondly travelling by bus from his home in Ossett to Wakefield for his weekly alto lesson. He was later to learn that Walker had also taught his predecessor, Derek Myers.

For Stead, a career in music was always his life-long ambition; in fact, such was his unbridled enthusiasm that he was playing semi-professionally as early as ten years of age, supported and encouraged all the way by his parents. Therefore, making the leap from being a semi-pro at the Wakefield Embassy Ballroom (eventually deputising for the regular alto player six nights a week) to becoming a full-time member of an emerging rock 'n' roll band without a hit to its name (and thereby forsaking the security of a day job with the National Coal Board) was not, from Stead's viewpoint, the kind of gamble it may have seemed on the surface. As he would point out, "I was already used to earning more money from being a musician as a semi-pro than from my job at the NCB".

As far as he was concerned, this was his big break. "I was over the moon, bought myself a baritone sax and took to my new job with gusto; in fact, like a duck to water." He was soon to be further encouraged by the support and camaraderie from his new workmates. "My second week with The Seven was at the famous Glasgow Empire, one of the larger Moss Empires. Next to the stage door was a great pub, The Empire Bar, which sold Carlsberg Special Brew, not available then in England. Keith Kelly asked if I wanted to pop to the pub; being sociable I said great, so off we went and he ordered a couple of these specials, then another round before returning to resume our spot. I didn't usually drink beer, lager or anything else as it used to go straight to my head. The upshot of it all was that our usual closing thirty minutes act seemed to be over in a flash. To this day I never knew whether Keith had a similar hangover! I enjoyed every minute of my time with The John Barry Seven," he concluded.

Mike Peters had much to thank his pal for, since it was Stead who was instrumental in pushing his name forward when the vacancy arose for a bass player. Peters was something of a precocious talent as a child, having mastered the violin and oboe at school. By the time he became friends with Stead, he, too, was working in a band at the Embassy Ballroom in Wakefield – his first professional job straight out of the army after having served three years as a bandsman playing trumpet, oboe and double bass stationed in Germany (alongside future JB7 recruit, Dennis King). Peters takes up the story: "When Jim got the job in The Seven, I mentioned to his girlfriend that if ever John Barry needed a bass player, I would be more than interested. Next thing I knew, I was talking to John on the phone asking me whether I would join the band in Edinburgh the following week."

For Peters, he was very soon in the throes of negotiating the steepest of learning curves, as this was the first time he had ever set eyes on an electric bass guitar let alone actually played one. So there he was, standing in the wings with his trusty double bass working out precisely what Fred Kirk was playing (since the music wasn't written down) in order to be able to transfer the notes afterwards from his own acoustic to the unfamiliar electric variant. "I went on stage one Wednesday night during the first house as a trial, and no sooner had I come off stage, there was Fred packing his things, ready to go. John said he could go, as I had played okay." Such was the speed of the transition that Peters barely said a word to Kirk. Peters would later describe his time with The JB7 as the most hectic five years of his life.

Throughout the 1950s, Britain remained rigidly defined by its class structure and, as such, upward social mobility continued to be strictly limited. In 1960, for example, only 2.5% of 18-year-olds from working class backgrounds went to university. For anyone with a modicum of talent, therefore, the entertainment industry was one of few genuine outlets offering the means of escaping what would have been in all likelihood a life of drudgery in unskilled and semi-skilled occupations. The worlds of football, boxing, the stage and music provided the less privileged with an opportunity of earning above the national average wage and of seeing the world outside one's birth place. Jimmy Stead and Mike Peters were both prime examples of the musically gifted taking full advantage of such acumen to widen their horizons.

While new boys Stead and Peters were cutting their teeth on the Jackie Dennis tour, Jack Good was busy plotting the first series of *Oh Boy!* after having successfully convinced his new bosses at ABC of its merits following the pilot shows transmitted earlier in the year. Set up in 1956, Associated British Cinemas (Television) Ltd. (hence, ABC for short) was awarded the commercial television weekend franchises for the Midlands and the North. However, the company's intention for *Oh Boy!* was by no means regional, but a fully syndicated nationwide series, set up in direct competition to BBC's *Six-Five Special* and scheduled for broadcast at the same time.

With live variety seriously on the wane and experiencing severe financial hardship, a number of theatres were now being sold off and taken over by television companies to avoid closure (and, ultimately, demolition). In early 1956, ATV (Associated TeleVision Ltd) took out a lease on the Hackney Empire and, in doing so, hired out the venue to ABC for the live editions of *Oh Boy!*. By setting out to produce a frenetic half-hour, non-stop, live (and in the main) 'rock 'n' roll' music show, Good was aiming to make his last project look positively quaint and genteel in comparison. He succeeded, for within six weeks, the audience had doubled in size, with *Six-Five Special* looking decidedly passé.

The JB7 were hired for that first networked edition, which was broadcast live to the nation at 6p.m. on 13th September. On the bill with them were many artists who would become regulars (some, household names even): Bertice Reading, Marty Wilde, Ronnie Carroll, The Dallas Boys, Cherry Wainer, Lord Rockingham's XI, Neville Taylor and the Cutters, The Vernons Girls, Red Price, and Cliff Richard and The Drifters. Such was its massive impact that *Oh Boy!* could be justifiably credited for launching the UK's first wave of credible, home-grown rock 'n' roll stars – Cliff Richard, The Shadows, Marty Wilde and Billy Fury. In fact, Cliff was offered his first national tour supporting the Kalin Twins on the strength of only two appearances on the show. Indeed, the phenomenal speed of his overnight success made The JB7 look like old stagers in comparison despite only being in the business, themselves, just over eighteen months.

What this undoubtedly did prove, however, was that The JB7 were, once again, in the right place at the right time. Not only were they about to be directly associated with yet another groundbreaking popular music-oriented TV show, but it also enabled the band to forge friendships amongst the latest crop of emerging artists, most notably with Marty Wilde (and manager, Larry Parnes), whom they would have met during the pilot editions ... and with Wilde all set to headline seven dates across the country playing leading Essoldo cinemas (in a tour dubbed 'Extravaganza!'), The JB7 found themselves joining him as the main support act in a bill that also included Vince Eager, The Sophisticats and Pat Laurence.

From the 'Extravaganza!' tour onwards, a steady stream of work was to ensue throughout the remaining months of the year deriving from a combination of high profile outlets, whether this was from music tours/variety bills (backing Jackie Dennis or Marty Wilde); television work (mainly via *Oh Boy!*) or recording commitments (through Parlophone). Evidently, all this legwork was beginning to pay off, for when the *New Musical Express* revealed its 1958 Readers' Poll, The JB7 finished an impressive third behind Lonnie Donegan and Chris Barber. This was a staggering achievement for a band yet to register a hit record at that stage, and who were still learning the ropes of the music industry.

For a very brief period from the late fifties through to the early sixties, variety and rock 'n' roll became curious bedfellows. The JB7 found themselves on the same bills as a plethora of very different turns, observing the conventions of a theatre tradition that had lasted for over a century. However, this particular marriage was borne out of mutual convenience rather than any sense of compatibility, and as a result, it was not to last long once the wilder and more exuberant teenage element drove out the family audiences upon which variety had always previously thrived and relied. Whilst the former were there to demonstrably witness their idols in the flesh, the latter were paying for an older, far more traditional and diverse array of acts. Something had to give, and it was variety that was eventually to pay the price. The inclusion of rock 'n' roll turned out to be but a short-lived solution for an ailing theatrical model in terminal decline.

Nevertheless, Jimmy Stead, to this day, views those variety tours with great fondness. "I loved Variety," he said, reminiscing. "A new town or city every week and a great deal of fun with different members of the show." From a practical point of view, he was grateful to the infrastructure created by the variety circuit for introducing him (and the rest of the band) to the best theatrical digs in the land, thereby enabling him to plan ahead and book in advance. Bearing in mind that each group member had to pay for accommodation out of his own pay packet, this was invaluable information. "We even got passes from all the local cinemas," Stead recalled ruefully, "So sad that variety died."

Ken Golder was another who loved the colourful characters he encountered among the Variety community. He particularly recalls befriending comedian Larry Grayson, who would accompany the band on shopping expeditions around the big cities. On one occasion, he remembered him emerging from a changing room in one outfitters dressed in a slinky dress, "We used to have a real good laugh," he concluded, "but that's show-business!"

After making their second appearance on *Oh Boy!* on 27th September (alongside Marty Wilde, Ronnie Carroll, Lorrie Mann, Red Price, Lord Rockingham's XI, Cherry Wainer, Neville Taylor and The Cutters, and The Vernons Girls), the Marty Wilde tour continued unabated.

The Birkenhead date at the Essoldo (Ritz) on Wednesday 1st October turned out to be a landmark for one shy young hopeful eager to impress 'Mr Parnes, Shillings and Pence' (as Larry Parnes was being dubbed by the press back then, such was his reputation for grooming young stars of the future). Following a letter from his mother, Parnes had agreed to meet eighteen-year-old Ronald Wycherley backstage before the Wilde concert. Armed with his guitar, he played the impresario a selection of songs he had recently written, which he thought suitable for Marty Wilde to record. Unbeknown to him, Parnes had decided to put him on stage immediately after the interval. The petrified youth, with knees knocking and hands trembling, went on to perform three of his own songs (Margo, Don't Knock Upon My Door and Maybe Tomorrow), and in doing so, not only wowed the audience, but also became a permanent fixture on the rest of the tour as a result. Yes, that was the night Billy Fury was born.

Backing Marty Wilde and performing in their own right during a week's engagement at the Chiswick Empire (w/c 6th October) garnered another positive response for The JB7 from a reviewer writing in *The Stage* and also demonstrated just how radical their stage act was viewed at the time. Much was made of the high decibel levels emanating from their set. Now this may not have been quite as ear splitting as The Who in their pomp, but it was enough to elicit a mild rebuke: "Although the powerful amplification of electric guitars in The John Barry Seven makes heavy demands on ear-drums, the group is most entertaining and musically satisfying. Intelligence and a sense of humour enhance their presentation."

~

Comic set pieces were to become a deliberate part of the set, as Jimmy Stead would later confirm. He distinctly recalls enacting one pre-planned ploy at the point of the show when he would start to play a melody based on the 'My Fair Lady' tune, 'Wouldn't It Be Loverly?'. In that instance, he would move towards the centre stage mic whilst pretending to experience difficulties in finding the next note, succeeding only once Barry had pulled out a succession of socks and clothing from his baritone sax. He also remembered how one particular flute solo would also bring the house down. This was due to the way centre stage mics operated in all of the Moss Empire theatres. They were usually hidden beneath the stage, unless in use, and therefore relied upon a trap door to secure their concealment. Hence, during one particular flute solo, the said mic would be slowly lowered down with beleaguered flautist (Stead) forced to follow it until it disappeared completely. "The first time this happened I just fell about laughing and the audience also loved it – so we kept it in the act."

~

Stead recalls Marty Wilde's take on Peggy Lee's then-current hit, 'Fever', being particularly well received on the tour.

A week later saw the band back in the studio recording their latest single, 'Farrago'/'Bee's Knees'. For Jimmy Stead, this was his first exposure to working at EMI/Abbey Road, and although his recollections are somewhat vague now, he can distinctly recall feeling apprehensive allied with a sense of excitement.

Thereafter, it was anything but daunting – more routine, just a musician doing his job. What he was pains to point out was that he was never actually involved in any of the creative discussions circulating from inside the control room (this was more Barry's domain). He was there simply to play what was written for him, and if anything, was more akin to a hired hand. This was how he described a typical session: "We seldom spoke to anyone in the EMI studio other than to Barry. We arrived, set up, Barry dished out the charts and off we went with one or two run-throughs, after which Barry would then confer with either Norman Newell or John Burgess and the engineers. If all was well, he would return to the studio floor for a take – on reflection, rather impersonal, but I guess we were just session musicians who happened to be members of a group called The John Barry Seven." If anything, what gave him far more anxiety above all else was in trying to find a parking space outside the studio!

'Farrago' was the second successive Latin-influenced A-side recorded by the Seven, the style of which *Record Mirror*, on awarding it three stars, was keen to point out: "The repeated theme is quite attractive and the success of this side will be in direct ratio to the degree of interest the public holds for the cha-cha." One can't help concluding that, Barry, ever the pragmatist, was once again anticipating the latest fad, for on the very day 'Farrago' was recorded, the Tommy Dorsey Orchestra's version of 'Tea for Two' (arguably *the* archetypal cha-cha) entered the hit parade. By the time 'Farrago' had been released on November 7th, Dorsey's single was No. 12 in the charts and still climbing. Unfortunately, The JB7's take on this particular dance craze (which was being foisted on the general public by all the major record companies) proved nowhere near as popular as Dorsey's.

Incidentally, 'Farrago' was the last track on which Barry would play the trumpet on any JB7 recording, and in keeping with the Latin flavour of the new single, it was around this time that Mike Peters can clearly remember Barry having the band do the cha-cha on stage when they played it live, "long before The Shadows ever started to do their dance steps," he would add. Only one rival cover version emerged at the time, and even this one, released a month earlier by the Ted Taylor Four was relegated to B-side status.

As for The JB7's own flip, the guitar-led 'Bee's Knees', this was a striking Barry original that was a clear precursor of the style of instrumental that the band was later to record for Columbia; here was 'Beat Girl's and 'The James Bond Theme's elder sibling no less. It was thus called in jest, as an in-joke reference to Barry's pet name for wife Barbara, Bee.

With the fifth single now in the can, the band returned to the Empire Theatre the next evening for the sixth edition of *Oh Boy!*, and, exactly a year to the day since the *Six-Five Special* LP was recorded, were back at Abbey Road as one of several acts invited to contribute to a similarly-themed 'live' *Oh Boy!* album, which featured those from EMI's roster who had already featured in the show. The entire LP was recorded at that one session in a bid to replicate the frenetic pace indicative thereof, with Jack Good present to make sure that that happened (acting as co-producer with Norman Newell). Good would regard the finished product as a far more professional and streamlined one compared to its predecessor. The JB7 cut versions of their current single, 'Pancho', together with their regular show closer, 'When the Saints Go Marching In', for inclusion on the LP.

Disharmony in the ranks, though, continued to prevail and no sooner had Derek Myers and Fred Kirk left, than three more originals – Mike Cox, Ken Richards and Ken Golder – opted to part company. Mike Cox attributed his disenchantment primarily to lack of regular gigs, caused in no small measure, according to Cox, to Barry's unwillingness to set foot outside the capital. "John Barry did not want to leave London," he explained. "Touring the provinces at Moss Empires did not appeal to him at all, so consequently we weren't earning any money." Now this may have been a valid point leading up to his date of departure, given the number of fallow weeks evident throughout 1958, but future tour itineraries would indicate otherwise. Barry was more than happy to work the provinces and frequent Moss Empire theatres right up to and until he relinquished leadership of the band. The JB7's heyday was still some way off in any case.

The most significant aspect of this change in personnel from Mike Peters' perspective, more than anything else, was in losing access to Richards' Bedford minibus, which was an invaluable addition to the pool of transportation available at the time. Mind you, he wasn't about to miss the exorbitant mileage rate the guitarist would charge them all. "If, like me, you were awake most of the time, you would notice that Ken took the van out of gear to go downhill; thus, getting more miles per gallon. I'm sure if he was still around, he would be laughing about it now!" Richards decided to retire his electric guitar in order to resume poultry farming.

Once again the 'old boys' network came to the rescue for finding suitable replacements, this time courtesy of Mike Peters, who immediately identified his ex-army buddy, Dennis King, as an ideal candidate for replacing Cox, having known King well from when the two of them were playing in the 4th/7th Royal Dragoon Guards. Born and educated in Harlesden (London), King left school in order to take up an apprenticeship in the printing industry, during which time he bought his first saxophone from a fellow workmate. He soon began to realise that his heart would never lie in printing, at which juncture he decided instead to follow his muse as a musician. So at the age of seventeen, he signed on for three years in an army band where he was able to hone his talent to a professional standard. Peters also recommended guitarist Jack Oliver, with whom he had previously worked back in Leeds, to take over from Ken Richards; a far cry, indeed, from the retail establishment where they first met.

After learning of Richards' decision to return to Scarborough, Golder felt the urge to do likewise, not wishing to be the only one of the original big-band trio remaining. He was also becoming tired of the rhythm section devoting far too much time to accompanying other artists rather than refining their own act. This was not what he wanted to concentrate on, and, as a consequence, he believed that The JB7 'sound' was becoming compromised. "After three years (*sic*), I'd had enough of getting on and off a bus and touring around. I was ready for a change," he later said. To this day he maintains that the original band would have lasted much longer had they not been called upon to do the additional work on touring shows. Some of the artists they backed, he insisted, were so unnecessarily fussy, that they would often spend rehearsal time perfecting other people's material when they really should have been fine-tuning their own. Mike Peters would later echo these sentiments. Not being paid for rehearsing these other acts was his main bugbear.

The 1st November edition of *Oh Boy!* (on a bill shared with Cliff Richard and The Drifters, Peter Elliot, Bill Forbes, Cherry Wainer, Red Price, Lord Rockingham's XI and The Vernons Girls) was to be the trio's swansong. Also working on the show was callboy Jeremy Hoare, who was given permission by Jack Good to film the rehearsals with his 8mm camera. The footage which he has subsequently placed on YouTube shows brief glimpses of what was the last ever performance of the Barry/Stead/Cox/Golder/Richards/Kelly/Peters line-up.

∾

Sadly, Ken Golder's departure was not the most amicable of partings. Among his artefacts remains a copy of an original formal 'service' contract' between him and Barry that was neatly typed on personalised 'John Barry and his Seven' notepaper. Short and to the point, it confirms Golder's engagement as a member of the band from the date of 15th August 1958 for a period of one year subject to two weeks' notice on either side, signed by both parties. Scribbled underneath, however, is a terse message that underlined a seething discontent; "Finished Sat 1st Nov 1958 Good Riddance JB." There was evidently no love lost at the time, with emotions still very raw.

∾

Dougie Wright was drafted in post haste as replacement for Golder, following a recommendation from Jimmy Stead, who had played alongside the drummer in the Leeds-based, Bill Marsden Big Band. Stead, on confirming the connection, said, "When I was playing in Bill Marsden's Orchestra, we won our local heat in the Musician Union's Big Band competition only to come second or third at regional level... guess who was the drummer? Yes, Dougie Wright."

Wright came from a musical background on his mother's side; it was this, which nurtured his own interest. His maternal grandfather worked at Leeds Empire as a musician, while his mother played piano, thereby inspiring him to do the same for a couple of years or so whilst at school. He distinctly remembered often being paraded around for his keyboard prowess by his then-music teacher. After leaving school at the age of fifteen in 1952, he took up routine factory work cutting ladies costumes. He may have been there a good six years, but his true obsession lay in trad jazz. The recent revival of the 1920's, American jazz scene, as championed by young British players, had captivated the impressionable Wright to the point where he attended as many concerts as he could. These venues would act as his training ground. "Most trad bands – like Chris Barber's – were seven piece ones. I used to watch them and educate myself that way," he would recall.

After studying many of the best-known drummers in a live setting, he became convinced that he could emulate them. In order to do so, he started off by purchasing a second-hand snare drum for 30/ – (£1.50), which at the time was the equivalent of a week's wages! Not long afterwards, he was investing 3/6 (17.5p) in a pair of brushes and sticks from Boosey and Hawkes (London) by post. Now equipped, he was able to take up drum lessons from Alick Sidebottom, which lasted around eighteen months, ably assisted by Buddy Rich's teaching manual. He practiced religiously in the attic of his home for hours on end, luckily not to have met any resistance from his tolerant neighbours.

By 1956 Wright had secured his first position behind the drum kit with Frank Young and his Music, a dance band, but this was a short-lived affair, for he was soon asked to leave on account of being too modern! A longer lasting and more satisfying tenure was with The Bill Marsden Band, a big band hugely influenced by Stan Kenton's stylistically more modern arrangements, and so he happily resided with them from 1957 right through till mid-1958. Any drummer with a leaning towards Stan Kenton's brand of jazz was going to fit in with a band led by John Barry. Jimmy Stead was about to become the facilitator.

Dougie Wright vividly remembers that moment: "A phone call came through one morning to the factory office from Jimmy Stead, who asked me if I wanted to join The John Barry Seven. The JB7 was an all-Yorkshire Band of note, so I said yes immediately. John Barry was changing the band little by little, because the original band before 1958 weren't good sight-readers. He was getting a lot of backing work so he wanted readers."

Conceivably, the sight-reading issue was likely to have been all part of Barry's sales pitch rather than being entirely accurate given that the ex-bandsmen amongst the first generation were, by dint of their military training, all expert readers. As Ken Golder would later reminisce, "We (the original line-up) were a polished band that could read music really well. We used to look at the music, have a tinkle and then we would be off." The guitarists amongst that incarnation, however, may not have been quite of the same calibre, which was more likely what Barry was actually alluding to when confiding in Wright, since he had already put a contingency measure in place for recording purposes by drafting in Bob Rogers to augment The Seven in order to rectify any apparent deficiencies. This he had done right from the outset on 'Zip Zip' and would continue to do so up to 1959's 'Long John'. Rogers was Don Lang and His Frantic Five's lead guitarist, and, with a proven session pedigree, was as good an insurance policy as any. The sonic similarities to Lang's outfit, therefore, were not just coincidence. Even then one can see that Barry had no qualms whatsoever in rocking the boat if it meant furthering the band's prospects, however unpopular that might have been.

Mike Peters has since also alluded to the difficulties faced by Ken Richards, albeit this time on the set of *Oh Boy!*, where – under the watchful eye of taskmaster, Jack Good – he struggled to grasp his parts at the first time of asking. He was exceptionally gifted at playing by ear, but needing time to learn a piece in the wake of such a fast-paced show was a luxury Jack Good was unlikely to have tolerated, and according to Peters, this may have resulted in the band not always being asked to appear, what with Bob Rogers on duties elsewhere, often with the Frantic Five. Vic Flick's later testimony would appear to back this up.

Dougie Wright was thrown in at the deep end, not only in having to learn The JB7's extensive repertoire, but also Marty Wilde's full set-list. "When I joined", he explained, "we were backing people like Marty Wilde. In the Empire days, Marty had his own band, the Wildcats, but we were soon to take over as his backing band." He added, "We were with Marty for about three months doing regular jobs each in different places including Norwich Theatre Royal, Cardiff New Theatre, Sunderland Empire, and the Metropolitan Theatre (London). Marty had a good quality voice, and was a real nut case as a character, but then we were all barmy!" Evidently, it didn't take long for Wright to fit in. "When seven guys (and all their kit) travel around non-stop in a Dormobile they soon get to know each other," he explained.

The departures occurred just at the point when The JB7 were resuming a series of dates with Marty Wilde and Nancy Whiskey after having completed their final two weeks on the variety circuit with Jackie Dennis (consecutive one-week residencies at Finsbury Park and Liverpool Empire respectively on w/c 13th and w/c 20th October). On Monday 3rd November the band began a week at The Theatre Royal in Norwich, which heralded debuts for Dennis King, Jack Oliver and Dougie Wright.

Alas, for Jack Oliver, this was to be one of the briefest careers imaginable, as Mike Peters remembers: "The show went well until Wednesday when Jack told both John and I that he was finding it difficult being out front as the lead instrument, so he agreed to finish the week off and go back to his job and family in Leeds."

Marty Wilde fondly remembers working with The JB7 on that tour, and above all the amount of laughter generated by the good-natured repartee. His impression of Barry was that of a softly spoken, laid-back kind of guy, who was very easy to get on with. One event, in particular, would lodge in his mind forever, for he would never forget the novel way in which Barry dealt with a rather irritating chambermaid at their Norwich hotel. "Every morning one of the staff in our cheap hotel would knock on our bedroom doors, and then just barge in with some excuse or other without knocking. John promised to sort this out pronto, and so the very next morning, an almighty scream could be heard throughout the entire building let out by this young chambermaid. What had happened was that John had pulled the bed sheets down and exposed his bare bottom to the poor lass as soon as she entered the room. Needless to say, we were never bothered again by the red-faced lady of Norwich."

What also struck Wilde on this tour was just how studious Barry was in between gigs. "While I would be reading magazines, there he was, with his wife sitting beside him, pouring over big band scores, often studying Stan Kenton's musical parts. When I come to think of it, you can hear the Kenton influence in those early James Bond films, so I guess the time he spent with me wasn't wasted at all," adding, "He was a lovely man and a great composer; it was my pleasure to have known and worked with him."

Jack Oliver's swift exit meant that Barry was now in urgent need of finding a guitarist able to handle the stage work. It was Vic Flick, then still working with Bob Cort, to whom he would turn for digging him out of this particular hole. Much to Barry's relief, he jumped at the chance and arrived in time to rehearse for the next tour venue, The Metropolitan in Edgware Road, the following Monday.

Vic Flick's interest in music started in his early teens, when he joined a band led by his piano-playing father, a band that also included his brother on saxophone and a neighbour on violin. Although he could already read music and play the piano, he felt the band was missing one vital ingredient, a guitar, and so he decided to take up the instrument. Flick only had four lessons, but with the added benefit of many hours of listening to records and practicing, he soon became good enough to take his place alongside his father and brother in their band. His first attempt at a professional career saw him with Les Clarke and his Musical Maniacs at a Butlin's Holiday Camp in Skegness. After a winter's worth of unemployment − interrupted only by a sporadic gig or two − he decided to link up again with his brother Alan. They agreed to form The Vic Alan Quintet, and successfully auditioned for a summer season at another Butlin's, this time in Clacton. The resident bandleader was a big name, Eric Winstone, and at the auditions he quickly realised that Flick was a rare bird indeed, a young musician who could actually read music.

Before long, Flick found himself working, not only with his own Quintet, but also with Winstone's band throughout the entire engagement at Butlin's. So impressed was Winstone with Flick, that he offered him more work afterwards on gigs and broadcasts for BBC radio. Flick's name soon became synonymous with a certain slick professionalism, technical expertise and an easy-going nature, and it must have come as no surprise in the business when he was asked to join the Bob Cort Skiffle group, as a replacement for Ken Sykora on guitar. When the Cort group got a good break as a support act on Paul Anka's JB7-backed, nationwide, UK tour during the winter of 1957, the meeting of two musical minds was inevitable. Eight months down the line, Barry's phone call to Flick was to change his life forever. It was the classic offer he couldn't refuse, and almost before he had put pen to paper, he was deep in rehearsals for that 20-minute spot at The

Metropolitan. Five days after what was a successful debut, Flick was making his first appearance on *Oh Boy!* as a fully fledged member of the band.

Flick's own recollections are worth quoting verbatim: "Having studied the piano from the age of six and having transferred at the age of fourteen to the guitar, reading music was no problem. My first pro job on guitar was at a summer camp with a group of forward looking musicians led by a musical maniac. To this man's credit, if you suggested a crazy idea for a treatment of a song he'd let you go ahead. So in 1955 we were playing titles like 'My Bonnie Lies Over the Ocean Rock' – and the kids loved it!

After playing freelance for a while I joined a folk group called Bob Cort Skiffle. Bob had a couple of hits and was cashing in – he was actually an advertising executive. While I was with Bob, the group did Paul Anka's first tour of the UK. On the tour was The John Barry Seven – a rock instrumental band who were backing Paul Anka. John Barry and I got on well and used to enjoy hunting for Chinese restaurants in the northern towns of Great Britain, a daunting task in the late fifties. The tour ended and we all went our separate ways. A few months later I received a call from John Barry asking me to join his group and audition for a TV show. He'd lost one TV series because his guitar players couldn't read and he didn't want to lose another. So, in I went."

Flick would have been no doubt acutely aware of the fact that by November 1958, the skiffle craze was already looking to have burned itself out into a frazzle. He would have clearly seen which way the wind was blowing. The ever-fickle world of pop was moving on at a furious pace with rock 'n' roll the latest brand leader: more raucous, more exciting and, above all, more electric. The previous year's 'movers and shakers', who were flying the flag for the skiffle boom, such as Johnny Duncan and The Blue Grass Boys, the Chas McDevitt Skiffle Group featuring Nancy Whiskey, and The Vipers, couldn't buy a hit in 1958. Even Lonnie Donegan, 'the King' himself, was struggling to make as big an impact on the charts. The writing was indelibly inked on the wall when BBC Radio's flagship youth programme, *Saturday Skiffle Club*, was renamed *Saturday Club* on 4th October. Flick was about to make a very astute move.

At The Metropolitan, The Seven was contracted to perform a 20-minute act as well as backing Marty Wilde and Nancy Whiskey. The line-up now read: **John Barry (trumpet), Vic Flick (lead guitar), Mike Peters (bass guitar), Keith Kelly (rhythm guitar), Jimmy Stead (baritone sax), Dennis King (tenor sax) and Dougie Wright (drums).**

Vic vividly recalls his debut with the group: "The John Barry Seven was first on after the interval so there was plenty of time to set up on stage behind the curtain. There was also plenty of time to get good and nervous. Every note that I had committed to memory had vaporised from my mind. As the house lights dimmed and the stage-hands busied themselves taking their places to walk the curtain back, I heard an echo-like, 'Ladies and Gentlemen. The John Barry Seven.' Those words seemed to float around in my head as the curtains parted and the expectant applause rose from the darkness. Two incredibly bright spotlights played on the stage, semi-blinding me. Suddenly John's voice cut through the haze with, 'One. Two. One. Two. Three. Four.' My fingers clasped the guitar neck and somehow the opening chords of 'Bee's Knees' resounded from my amplifier. It was a struggle to keep moving about, smiling and remembering the music and my performance wasn't, to me, note perfect but at the end John congratulated us all. I had just entered a new phase of my life."

The congratulations were well-deserved, according to the reviewer from *The Stage*, who was impressed by the overall quality of the show: "Nobody is likely to mistake The John Barry Seven for anything but the most modern of musical combinations. and although Nancy Whiskey's singing has a quality of plaintive timelessness, she, too, has deserted the folk songs which she formerly included in her act and gone one hundred per cent into the contemporary camp. Personally, I think this is unfortunate, because she loses thereby a touch of distinction, but the fringe of dreamy-eyed but very vocal teenagers attracted to the Met by this bill, approve beyond doubt. They approved, too, of Marty Wilde, a young man whose recordings sit pretty consistently among the top ten. I must say that, not for the first time, I agree with them. Young Mr. Wilde has a wonderful confidence, a voice adequate to his purpose, and an air of moody, melancholic majesty that is certainly worth the entrance money. Splendidly backed by The John Barry Seven, he puts in a long arduous session that is excitement all the way. The remainder of the show is noted for the pretty idiocy of Kelty and Delta's clever satire of the conventional balancing and acrobatic act; Earl and Elgar bringing the colour of the circus to their musical clowning; Roy Lance quipping as he cartoons; Billy Livingstone providing a rather lightweight interlude of comedy, and the Horler Twins cheerfully opening both halves of the show with some gay concerted dancing." Encouraging words indeed for a genuine variety bill that would soon become a thing of the past.

Flick's triumphant debut was quickly followed by his (as well as Wright's and King's) first television appearance (on the 15th November edition of *Oh, Boy!*), and then by a succession of concerts throughout the North of England. All part of the Marty Wilde package tour, these combined one-night stands (in places such as Workshop, Scunthorpe, York and Burnley) with full weekly residencies (at Sunderland Empire and Cardiff New Theatre), and in doing so, provided both Wright and Flick with the perfect platform for bedding themselves in good and proper.

One particular date still causes Flick much merriment to this day. It concerned Barry's hometown concert back at the Rialto on 22nd November. JX, still keenly cheer-leading his son's career, had arranged for posters advertising The Seven's latest 45 to be plastered liberally all over the city and surrounding villages. The pity being that whereas the record was actually called 'Farrago', the posters were getting very excited about something called 'Farrango'. It was not the first time JX had got his wires crossed. On the night of that famous visit to York Rialto of the American bandleader Stan Kenton, he was so excited to have finally booked the great man that he announced him as 'Ken Stanton'!

With 1958 drawing to a close, you may well have thought that integrating five new members into the line-up would have been more than enough to worry about, but not so, Barry. During late November, he made the surprising decision to introduce a female singer into the act, which was duly noted in that week's edition of *The Stage*: "On 8th December, the group starts rehearsals in London with glamorous eighteen-year-old Lisa Page, younger sister of Jill Day, who is joining The Seven on that date, as its first featured female vocalist. Leader John Barry is currently busy on tour writing special arrangements for the group, which is to undertake a number of ballroom engagements in the New Year."

The rationale behind this move may have been motivated by the ballroom plan Barry was hatching with the Parnes/Kennedy partnership, but the idea of introducing a featured vocalist as an adjunct to the band (in much the same way Stan Kenton did with Anita O'Day and June Christy, and Ted Heath likewise with Lita Roza) seemed to be a strangely, anachronistic development even by 1958's standards. Barry appeared to be hoping to revive the big band model albeit on a smaller scale, but as has already been discussed, this *modus operandi* really was fast approaching its sell-by date. Joe Loss was one of the few bandleaders still making this option pay, but by this time, he was hardly cutting edge.

What Lisa Page's introduction did prove, however, was that Barry had far from abandoned the idea of retaining a vocalist as an integral part of the band. Born and bred in Brighton (the youngest child of William and Phyllis Page), Lisa made her solo stage debut as a four-year-old at the local Labour Club in Lewes Road. Throughout her childhood she won many talent contests and appeared in several Vera Gazbert productions held at Brighton's Regent Ballroom. From the age of fifteen, she began to undertake formal singing lessons from Professor George Lunnellie, as well as speech and drama coaching with Flossie Freedman, which necessitated her having to travel to London and back five times a week by train on the 'Brighton Belle'.

After making her first television appearance on Dickie Leeman's 'Christmas Show' a mere nine months later, the seventeen-year-old songstress then decided to move to London in order to further her singing ambitions. Six months down the line, she was being asked to join The JB7, after Barry had seen her singing in a hotel bar accompanied by the pianist Bill McGuffie. The aim to unveil her as their latest recruit during the band's next television appearance on the 17th December edition of *The Jack Jackson Show* was derailed when they were unexpectedly only allotted one slot, rather than two. Given the significance of such exposure, this left Barry with little choice but to promote the new single, 'Farrago', which was in need of a sales lift. Also appearing on the show were Dickie Valentine and Russ Hamilton.

So as 1958 drew to a close, it was clear that The JB7 had made significant strides at establishing footholds in every aspect of the music business (national radio notwithstanding) and what's more, as a means of maintaining them, were evolving musically as rapidly as the social landscape. In a year packed with incident and innovation – the Munich Air Disaster; the Jerry Lee Lewis marriage scandal; the first disposable biro; first stereo hi-fi; first 'Carry On' film; first televised state opening of parliament; first publication of *Saturday Night and Sunday Morning*; first performance of *A Taste of Honey*; first showings of *Grandstand* and *Blue Peter*; the Aldermaston CND marches; the introduction of the first personal bank loan and Green Shield Stamps; the Notting Hill riots; the great London bus strike and so forth – the line-up of The John Barry Seven (Mark II) was emerging and nigh on complete, with only John Barry and Keith Kelly remaining from the original line-up.

Jackie Dennis, who toured extensively with The JB7 throughout 1958.

On the Six-Five Special film set in February 1958.

Jimmy Stead, front centre, and Dougie Wright, drums, in The Bill Marsden Orchestra in 1958.

TOMMY STEELE SCANDINAVIAN TOUR, 1958

Outward flight:

Monday, April 14 — BEA 220, leaving London Airport at 10.25 a.m.
Bus leaves West London air terminal in Cromwell
Road, S.W.5., at 9.20 a.m. artists should be at
the air terminal not later than 9 a.m.

All artists arriving at the airport will be driven direct to the
concert hall for a fit-up and rehearsal; then taken to their hotel for a rest
before the first concert. Lunch will be served on the 'plane going to
Copenhagen.

Homeward flight:

Monday, April 28 — BEA 221, leaving Copenhagen Airport at 15.10 p.m.
Bus leaves Copenhagen air terminal at 14.15 p.m.
Arrives London Airport 16.50 p.m.

Transport in Scandinavia: Will be arranged throughout by the managements.

Itinerary:

April 14/15/16 — Copenhagen
April 17 — Aarhus (Denmark)
April 18 — Travel to Sweden
April 19/20 — Stockholm
April 21 — Eskilstuna
April 22 — Örebro
April 23 — Linköping
April 24 — Jönköping
April 25 — Return to Denmark
April 26 — Aalborg (Denmark)
April 27 — Odense
April 28 — Return to Copenhagen; fly to London

Management:

In Copenhagen, rooms have been reserved at the Hotel Mercur.

In Denmark, the tour is under the management of

Messrs. Engstrom and Sødring,
Palaegade 6,
Copenhagen K.

'Phone: Central 3228

In Sweden, the tour is under the management of

Mr. E. Eckert-Lundin,
Barzelii Park 9,
Stockholm 1.

'Phone: 108100

Accommodation:

Has been reserved throughout by the managements, but artists are
individually responsible for paying their own bills.

---

38 Old Compton Street,
London W.1.

19th March 1958

Dear

We are going to Scandinavia on April 14th for
two weeks; same kick as the Blackpool show, Des,
Kentones etc.

Would you please send me by return of post the
following details with regards to your Passport.

NAME, real and professional
ADDRESS
DATE OF BIRTH
OCCUPATION
DATE OF ISSUE OF PASSPORT
NO. OF PASSPORT
WHERE PASSPORT WAS ISSUED

I have fixed a "6-5 Special" for Saturday April 5th
which will be transmitted from Edinburgh; it is a number
one plug for our disc. Kerr Roberts is playing, "RODEO"
on T.V.'s "COOL FOR CATS" about April 2nd. I have also
fixed another top T.V. record plug, but I cannot say anything about this yet.

The Juke Box companies are also going to give it the
works; a trade paper called The Worlds Fair, which has the
biggest solo influence on juke box plugs, is giving the
disc a big push next week.

Parlophone are taking a big advertisement in Disc the
same weekend as we do it on "6-5 Special". Disc has already
got the biggest circulation of any musical paper, over a
hundred thousand.

With additional sound radio plugs to the above mentioned,
I think things should start moving; everyone seems quite
excited about it down here.

The enclosed £4 is for the extra days shooting for the
film. I have seen the film, by the way, and it has come off
good for us. I should have some news about our T.V. show
later on today or tomorrow.

THE WINTER GARDENS — MARGATE

Entertainments Manager: Percy Rowland

Week commencing Monday 7th July 1958 for Six Days

1. Overture —
   LESLIE WHEELER
   and the WINTER GARDENS ORCHESTRA

2. Pert and Petite —
   THE LANE TWINS

3. The Acrobatic Humorist —
   TED DURANTE

4. Novelty and Originality —
   LOS BRAZILIANOS

5. With 'Willie Heckle' and 'Canasta' —
   ROGER CARNE

6. The New Recording Star —
   JACKIE DENNIS

   INTERVAL

7. Reintroducing —
   THE LANE TWINS

8. Presenting —
   THE JOHN BARRY SEVEN

9. Juggling Equilibrist —
   ALAIN DIAGORA

10. Television Recording Artists —
    KENNETH EARLE and MALCOLM VAUGHAN

Music for the Millions
is Produced and Presented
by

HAROLD FIELDING
FIELDING HOUSE — HAYMARKET
LONDON — S.W.1

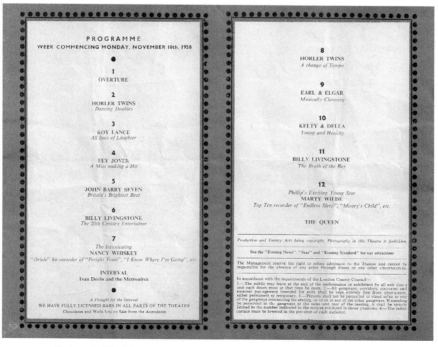

PROGRAMME
WEEK COMMENCING MONDAY, NOVEMBER 10th, 1958

1
OVERTURE

2
HORLER TWINS
Dancing Doubles

3
ROY LANCE
All lines of Laughter

4
FEY JOVER
A Miss making a Hit

5
JOHN BARRY SEVEN
Britain's Brightest Beat

6
BILLY LIVINGSTONE
The 20th Century Entertainer

7
The Intoxicating
NANCY WHISKEY
"Oriole" hit recorder of "Freight Train", "I Know Where I'm Going", etc.

INTERVAL
Ivan Dorin and the Metroaires

A Thought for the Interval
WE HAVE FULLY LICENSED BARS IN ALL PARTS OF THE THEATRE
Chocolates and Walls Ices on Sale from the Attendants

8
HORLER TWINS
A change of Tempo

9
EARL & ELGAR
Musically Clowning

10
KELTY & DELIA
Young and Healthy

11
BILLY LIVINGSTONE
The Broth of the Boy

12
Phillip's Exciting Young Star
MARTY WILDE
Top Ten recorder of "Endless Sleep", "Misery's Child", etc.

THE QUEEN

Production and Variety Acts being copyright. Photography in this Theatre is forbidden.

See the "Evening News", "Star" and "Evening Standard" for our attractions

The Management reserve the right to refuse admission to the Theatre and cannot be responsible for the absence of any artist through illness or any other circumstances.

In accordance with the requirements of the London County Council—
1.—The public may leave at the end of the performance or exhibition by all exit doors and each doors must at that time be open. 2.—All gangways, corridors, staircases and external passageways intended for exits shall be kept entirely free from obstruction, either permanent or temporary. 3.—Persons shall not be permitted to stand or sit in any of the gangways intersecting the seating, or to sit in any of the other gangways. If standing be permitted in the gangways at the sides and rear of the seating, it shall be strictly limited to the number indicated in the notices exhibited in those positions. 4.—The safety curtain must be lowered in the presence of each audience.

Debut for Vic Flick at the Metropolitan, Edgware Road, London.

71

PROGRAMME

Week commencing MONDAY, AUGUST 11th, 1958

1 OVERTURE ... The Empire Orchestra

2 EMERSON & JAYNE ... "Going East"

3 TWO PIRATES ... ... Oh Yes There Isn't

4 HANS BELA & MARY Luminous Jugglers

5 WALLY McKINLEY ... Modern Comedy

6 THE JOHN BARRY SEVEN
Parlophone Recording Group

INTERMISSION
THE EMPIRE ORCHESTRA
under the direction of GORDON L. ROLFE

Programme continued overleaf

FULLY LICENSED BARS ... ... TS OF THE THEATRE

PROGRAMME
Continued

7 EMERSON & JAYNE ... ... "Sailorstrip"

8 THE TUNEFUL LIDDELL TRIPLETS
Songs in Harmony

9 RONDART & JEAN Champion Dart Blower

10 LARRY GRAYSON ... He's Priceless

11 Decca's Fifteen Year Old Teenage Star
JACKIE DENNIS
The Lilt of the Kilt

The Management reserves the right to refuse admission to this theatre, and to change, vary or omit, without previous notice, any item of the programme.

PLEASE NOTE—PHOTOGRAPHING IN THE THEATRE IS FORBIDDEN

MANCHESTER HIPPODROME

Advance Booking Office: ARDwick 4161-2
Chairman ... PRINCE LITTLER
Manager ... FRED C. BROOKS
Assistant Manager: D. J. NISBET Stage Manager: F. STEARN

WEEK COMMENCING MONDAY, JULY 21st, 1958

6.25 TWICE NIGHTLY 8.40

1. ANN & VAL SHELLEY ... Youth in Springtime
2. THE TWO PIRATES ... Comedy Burlesque Acrobatics
3. THE CARALS ... The Sensational Continental Jugglers
4. LARRY GRAYSON ... He's Priceless
5. THE JOHN BARRY SEVEN
6. INTERMISSION
Selection from "Lisbon Story"
Manchester Hippodrome Orchestra under the direction of Jimmy Carroll
7. ANN & VAL SHELLEY ... Top of the Bill
8. WINSTON FOXWELL ... Giving Vent to Juggling
9. THE TWO TREVALS ... Thrills in the Air
10. LARRY GRAYSON

MANCHESTER HIPPODROME

11. The Lilt of the Kilt

Scotland's 15 year old
Teenage Star

JACKIE
DENNIS

Hit Recorder of "La Dee Dah"
"My Dream" and
The "Purplepeopleeater"

The MANAGEMENT reserve the right to vary or omit any part of the programme without previous notice

Postal and Party Bookings now accepted for
EMILE LITTLER'S GREAT LAUGHTER PANTOMIME

DICK WHITTINGTON

A RIOT OF MERRIMENT WITH

KEN ★ NAT ★ MARGARET
PLATT JACKLEY BURTON

Commencing TUESDAY, 23rd DECEMBER, 1958
Evenings at 7 p.m. Matinees Daily at 2 p.m. from Boxing Day

john barry and his seven — britain's freshest music makers

Fulford House,
Fulford,
York.

SERVICE CONTRACT BETWEEN JOHN BARRY AND KEN GOLDER.

This is to confirm your engagement as musician in the combination known as the John Barry Seven commencing on August 15th, 1958 for a period of one year. Such engagement to be subject to two weeks notice in writing on either side.

FINISED SAT 1st NOV 1958
GOOD RIDDENCE JB

signed...John Barry...

...Ken Golder...

t.v. — records — radio — variety — ballrooms — concerts

john barry and his seven — britain's freshest music makers

Fulford House,
Fulford,
York.

10th September, 1958.

Dear Ken,

Just a reminder that the "Oh! Boy" rehearsal commences at 8. 30 am. on Saturday morning at Hackney Empire. If you would get there at about 8. 15 it will give us time to set up before the recording.

If you don't know where the Hackney Empire is, 'phone the A. B. C. television office, Gerrard 7808 on Friday when you arrive, they are open until 5-o-clock.

Best Wishes,

Barry

t.v. — records — radio — variety — ballrooms — concerts

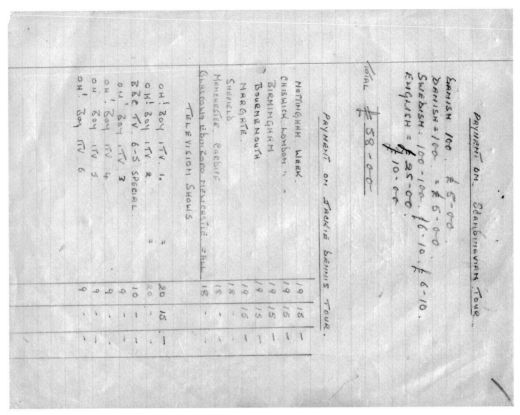

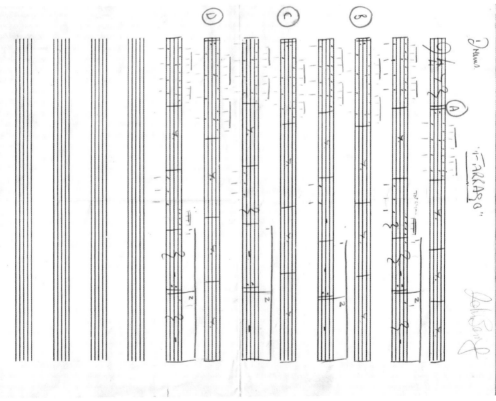

Ken Golder's drum part for Farrago and a page from his account book for 1958.

PROGRAMME
SARAH VAUGHAN
Selection of Songs

1. "If This Isn't Love"
2. "How High The Moon"
3. "Tenderly"
4. "Outside, Lookin' In"
5. "Poor Butterfly"
6. "It's Wonderful"
7. "Cherokee"
8. "I'll Never Smile Again"
9. "Summertime"
10. "Perdido"
11. "Gone Again"
12. "Stairway to Paradise"
13. "Body and Soul"
14. "Sometimes I'm Happy"
15. "Lover Man"

JOHNNY DUNCAN and his
BLUE GRASS BOYS

1. "Freight Train Blues"
2. "Frankie & Johnny"
3. "Mind Your Own Business"
4. "Goodnight Irene"
5. "Salty Dog"
6. "Crazy Arms"
7. "Just A Little Loving"
8. "If You Love Me Baby"
9. "Itching For My Baby"
10. "Press On"
11. "Ella Speed"
12. "Where Could I Go"
13. "My Rockabilly Baby"
14. "Last Train to San Fernando"
15. "Cindy"
16. "Footprints In The Snow"
17. "More And More"
18. "I Heard A Bluebird Singing"

JOHN BARRY SEVEN

1. "Get Happy"
2. "Wonderful Time Up There"
3. "Rodeo"
4. "Blue Moon"
5. "Pancho"
6. "Every Which Way"
7. "You've Gotta Way"
8. "Hideaway"
9. "Festival"
10. "Up Above My Head"

John Barry caught on camera off-duty by a fan during the late fifties.

*John and Barbara at Chiswick Empire,
London, after their wedding,
on 12th June 1958.*

Jimmy Stead and Mike Peters, far right both rows, in their first JB7 photo, August 1958.

Les Reed and Vic Flick at Clacton in July 1958.

Rehearsing for the first episode of Oh Boy! in September 1958.

The band pictured with their new vocalist, Lisa Page, in December 1958.

Des Lane, the Penny Whistle man.

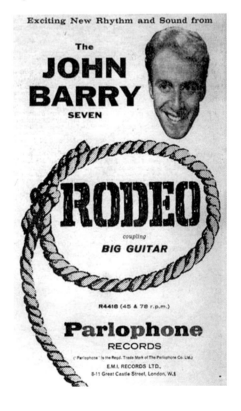

3

BEAT FOR BEAT GIRL

JANUARY – DECEMBER 1959

Like in all groups starting out, there are bound to be personality crises. One major one occurred when the likes of Vic Flick on guitar, Dougie Wright on drums and Les Reed on piano were drafted in – this was the nucleus of the group that started to go places.

– John Barry

I remember doing the soundtrack for Beat Girl; our remit was to marry the written music to the film, but on occasions where nothing was actually written down, we were expected to adlib some blues... and so that we could cope with every conceivable mood presented to us on screen, Barry augmented The Seven with other soloists.

– Mike Peters (bass guitar – describing recording sessions held at the Beaconsfield Film Studios).

For The JB7, the year 1959 was to be one of steady consolidation, during which time the band finally made its long overdue breakthrough on British national radio via the BBC Light Programme. After an aborted vocal experiment and yet another change in personnel, they were about to enter a far more settled phase, for this was the period when what is now considered the 'classic' JB7 line-up finally took shape. A change of management was also pivotal for steering The JB7 on to the next level of success.

On 13th November 1958, during the very week Vic Flick entered JB7 folklore, John Barry made one of the most significant moves of his formative career when he informed the BBC of his decision to appoint Evelyn Taylor, then working for the Will Collins Agency, as his new agent. By the time he confirmed her appointment in another letter to the same organisation some four months later, she had left Collins' and was now trading independently under the name of the

'Starcast Agency' having already taken a number of her existing clients with her.

Now Elvis Presley may well have had Colonel Tom Parker to catapult his career into the stratosphere, but no less hard nosed and demanding was the diminutive figure of straight-talking, chain-smoking Eve Taylor, who by dint of her forceful and forthright personality, was able to transform the most meagre of talents into box office gold. She was already representing the likes of penny whistle man Des Lane, comedians Mike and Bernie Winters, singers The Lana Sisters and Jackie Dennis (amongst others) by the time Barry joined her ranks, and was later to cement her fearsome reputation with the way in which she guided the careers of Adam Faith, Chris Andrews, Jackie Trent, Val Doonican and Sandie Shaw.

Steeped in show business herself (as part of a comedy/tap dancing variety act during the 1930s), she was also able to observe her impresario father at close quarters in her youth. As a consequence, she became fiercely protective of all her clients and was well known for driving the hardest of bargains on their behalf often with a combative and confrontational feistiness that belied her physical stature. From their perspective, she was a straight-talking, no-nonsense operator *par excellence*, but for those on the other side of the negotiating table, she was more than likely to have been viewed as the proverbial 'agent from hell'.

Even the mildest mannered of broadcasters, such as Brian Matthew, baulked at Eve Taylor's stubborn resolve and formidable presence, describing her in his autobiography, *This Is Where I Came In*, as "a tough old harridan." No doubt Barry, himself a child of the entertainment industry and not one for suffering fools gladly, would have seen some of his own steely determination and single-mindedness in Taylor's brash, intransigent approach, and was thereby quite happy to entrust his bidding to her shoulders. Most importantly, this freed up time for him to concentrate on the music.

Although the New Year began positively enough with tour dates arranged in Preston and Tooting, a much more prestigious date saw The JB7 make the line-up for the *New Musical Express*'s annual Poll-Winners' Concert at The Royal Albert Hall on the 11th January. These events, which began in 1953 just after the journal itself had first made the newsstands, acted as a significant barometer of an act's current standing in the industry, since participants were traditionally those artists who had figured prominently in the yearly *New Musical Express* polls.

On this occasion, The JB7 benefited from a lucky break. Although not originally chosen to appear, in spite of having finished a creditable third behind Lonnie Donegan and Chris Barber in the 'small group' section, they were brought in at short notice to replace trumpeter Eddie Calvert. For an act still in search of its first hit record, third place was a particularly remarkable achievement. In fact, The JB7, who opened proceedings, received a ringing endorsement from the *New Musical Express*'s James Wynn who warmed to their "torrid playing". He picked out "a big beat" version of 'When the Saints' as the highlight, which "got the show off to a good start." No sooner had the band left the stage of The Royal Albert

Hall during the afternoon, than they were packing up all their gear *post haste* for an evening gig in Edmonton on the other side of London. There was no time at all for any backstage celebrations.

In the capital at any rate, interest in the new single appeared to be growing. According to *Record Mirror*, 'Farrago' was placed at No. 4 and No. 7, respectively, in two of the participating chart-return record shops based in London, while the cast album of *Oh Boy!* was already well positioned at No. 4 in the national LP charts. To be seen making a significant contribution to such a healthy seller was important not only for raising the profile of the band, but also for keeping everyone at EMI onside and for sending out the right signals for the industry as a whole.

During February, the band undertook a short tour of selected Northern cinemas. Topping the bill were The King Brothers, who were supported by Russ Conway and The JB7 (together with new vocalist, Lisa Page). This set of dates took on greater significance when they turned out to be among Keith Kelly's final appearances as a member. Unlike the previous departures from the band, there was no trace of rancour or bitterness on Kelly's part, on account of the fact that he opted out on his own volition solely to try his luck as a singer in his own right. Given that The JB7's repertoire at the time only allowed for one singer, and what with Lisa Page now firmly *in situ*, he felt he would have better opportunity going solo.

Because of his long-standing friendship with Barry, Kelly never had any intention of being party to the previous year's mass exodus. This may have been borne out of a sense of loyalty to some extent, but it is also true to say that there was no alternative job on offer elsewhere nor handsomely paid trade to fall back on. In any case, he clearly enjoyed being based in and around the epicentre of the UK's music business capital. What he enjoyed most of all was working an audience, which after all, was how he got hooked in the first place: entertaining his RAF buddies by blowing his battered old harmonica whilst off duty.

When Kelly finally decided to take the plunge to pursue a solo career, it was fellow band mate, Mike Peters, who managed to secure an audition for him at the legendary 2i's coffee bar, simply because he was too shy to ask himself. In order to supplement his income, he also started working as a film extra and appeared in such films as *World By Night* (in which he proved expert at jiving) and *The Concrete Jungle* (in which he played a convict). He was also developing his talent as a songwriter, which would prove useful after eventually being spotted at the 2i's by representatives from Parlophone, who subsequently signed him to the label on the strength of his performances there. Indeed, both sides of his debut 45 ('(Must You Always) Tease Me'/'Ooh-La-La') – which was to become a Top Thirty hit – were self-penned.

However, that success occurred during May 1960, which is jumping the gun somewhat. Rewinding back fifteen months, you will find John Barry warming to the idea of introducing a keyboard player into the band, the speed of which was hastened by the prospect of an audition that Eve Taylor was setting up for the band with Stewart Morris, the appointed producer of BBC TV's next pop music vehicle, *Drumbeat*, who was on the look-out for a resident act. A pianist, Barry believed, would be a valuable asset when accompanying other artists performing on the show. Now with Kelly's departure, this conveniently crystallised his thinking, by providing him with an immediate opportunity of turning theory into practice, and what's more, Vic Flick knew a musician with the perfect credentials: his flat mate, Les Reed. After watching him in action at The Lido nightclub in the West End, Reed was duly given the nod by Barry. What no one would have envisaged at the time was that the final piece of the 'classic' jigsaw was destined to become one of Britain's most successful and celebrated songwriters of all time.

It is probably fair to say that Les Reed's father had the most influence on shaping his son's eventual career destination, in instilling into him the valuable lesson that if you wanted something badly enough, then you had to work hard for it. Reed Snr. ran a semi-pro troupe called The Westfield Kids, which numbered tap and ballet dancers, singers, and musicians amongst its ranks. As a result, the infant Les, already quite proficient on accordion, soon found himself booked on the same circuit of clubs and halls as the troupe; an experience he found exhausting for a lad of such tender years. To this day he has a strong aversion to the very thought of a coach journey, attributing this to a hangover resulting from those childhood days when he was booked as the travelling artiste for the Sunday coach trips to Brighton, Bournemouth and other nearby coastal resorts. "They used to have to stop the coach half way every time so I could get out to be sick!", he would painfully recall. On the plus side, however, the inevitable pub stop on the way home would prove rather lucrative for the youngster, since the more receptive, alcohol-fuelled among the party (not long after being freshly intoxicated) would generously cough up a tidy windfall in tossed coins of between £8 to £9, which was a small fortune back then.

Aside from this early apprenticeship as a performer, Les's father also studied music seriously and he expected his son to follow suit. When he was posted away in the army, for example, he would even send Les theoretical exercises to complete and expect them returned by post error-free. "Heaven help me had I got any of them wrong when he next came home!" Les would later remark. He would laugh about it now, but at the time he felt that he was always studying at a time when most of his contemporaries were out in the fields playing football. Not that he begrudges it now. On the contrary, he remains thoroughly appreciative of his father's efforts, encouragement and enthusiasm, which he admits lit the blue touch paper that fired his own life-long love affair with music.

Maybe his father thought he had spawned the next Mozart given that Les Reed became the proud possessor of his first piano as early as the age of five, but his precocious talent justified the purchase, for he passed all his London College of Music Examinations by the time he was fourteen, after which he formed a band, The Willis Reed Group, with jazz accordionist Peter Willis. Following four years spent touring around the country with the band, he was called up for National Service, spending the first year learning how to fire mortars and to become a physical training instructor, until he took up a one-year stint on piano and clarinet with the Royal East Kent Military Band. "The clarinet was more or less obligatory," he would later joke. "After all, it's a bit of an outsize feat to march a piano around a parade ground!" On completion of his call up, Reed turned fully professional by working as the featured pianist with many of Britain's top outfits. He became the resident player in various London nightclubs, among them The Lido (where he first caught Barry's eye). Developing into a fine jazz stylist, he also played with such stalwarts as saxophonist Tony Coe, as well as the acclaimed American trumpeter Dizzy Reece.

Vic Flick first came into Reed's life during 1957 when Reed was part of the resident house band at the Blackamore Hotel in Chessington. Flick recalls in his autobiography *Guitarman* that this particular venue attracted a sizeable crowd on account of not only staging jazz nights every Sunday, but also open mic singing sessions during the morning. Accordingly, would-be Sinatras throughout the area would make a beeline there. He observed time and time again just how well Reed, as resident accompanist, would accommodate the ropiest of singers by dint of his perfect pitch and transposition skills. As a consequence, these amateur crooners would readily return because he made them sound so good. It soon became obvious to Flick that Reed was just the musician he needed when his own combo, The Vic Alan Quintet, was offered a summer season at the Butlin's Holiday Camp in Clacton. When Reed readily agreed to join him, this set into motion the chain of events that led him to the path of The JB7. Right from the outset, theirs was an instant rapport based on mutual respect, and it was one which would blossom into a life-long friendship

Just prior to Reed's arrival, on 4th February, The JB7 were back beavering away in Abbey Road Studio 2 recording two tracks that would form both sides of the next single: 'Long John' and 'Snap 'n' Whistle'. However, that much-coveted breakthrough hit remained elusive, as it did throughout The JB7's stint with Parlophone, despite being extensively promoted on television and the nation's pop weeklies. The newest of them, *Disc*, together with *The Record & Show Mirror* and *New Musical Express*, expected great things of this single, but in keeping with previous releases they were proven wrong. The fact that Parlophone was still prepared to spend heavily on promoting the group's records, even after five previous disappointments, provided further evidence as to just how highly they were being regarded. Unfortunately, the band was unable, at this point, to translate their popular appeal as a live act into sizeable vinyl sales. All this would change in due course, but Barry was taking no chances. He readily accepted any extra-curricular studio experience on offer through keeping his options open by willingly moonlighting as an arranger for other labels under the pseudonym, Johnny Prendy. As well as expanding his ever-growing list of contacts, this accelerated his grasp of the recording process.

Like all of the major record companies in the late fifties, Parlophone's antennae were finely attuned to whatever was currently selling. This was, after all, a notoriously cut-throat business. Each major's *modus operandi* was predicated on trying to outdo its rivals in the quest to mould the public's musical tastes. Therefore, whenever one of them appeared to have 'hit the jackpot' by finding that latest winning formula, the others would invariably jump on said bandwagon. Add the fact that Barry's own thinking was influenced by Jack Parnell's 'mission statement' of "first taking the popular route", then the sound of the new 'A'-side should not have come as a complete surprise, for 'Long John' bore a striking resemblance to Lord Rockingham XI's Decca release, 'Hoots Mon', which had become the UK's biggest selling instrumental of 1958. In fact, it had topped the charts during November and December of that year. Here then was The JB7's attempt at replicating that success; the problem being that the record-buying public neither wanted nor needed another variant of 'Hoots Mon' (aside, that is, from the 11,643 of them who actually bought the record).

It was good job that no one could lay claim to a 19th-century sea shanty either, given that, melodically, 'Long John' (attributed to 'Farrago' writer and music publisher Bob Kingston under the pseudonym Barry White) was a virtual carbon copy of 'What Shall We Do with the Drunken Sailor?' – a fact that was immediately picked up on by reviewers in both the *New Musical Express* and *Disc*. Each gave favourable responses to the record, although one would not have expected anything less from friend and associate, Jack Good, who in writing for *Disc* in his role as regular columnist described both sides as the group's best yet. Like Good, the *New Musical Express* also made the connection with Lord Rockingham and the sea shanty in describing 'Long John' as "a lively, driving, ripalong (*sic*) piece of 1959 rock." Much praise was lavished on the flip side too, 'Snap 'n' Whistle', which was a Barry original. "It's different and it's good," claimed the *New Musical Express*. Both papers anticipated chart action, but it was not to be (well, not for now at any rate). The single was released on 27th February.

Lisa Page's tenure as the vocal focal point of The JB7 proved to be a short-lived flirtation that was abandoned just prior to the band's debut as the regular presence on BBC's latest venture into pop music, *Drumbeat*. There have been a number of reasons posited for why this didn't quite take off as planned, but Page is convinced that sexual politics was at the heart of her departure, blaming producer Stewart Morris's infatuation for and attraction to Sylvia Sands (whom he would later marry) as the principal cause. There was never going to be any room for two resident female singers on the show and Sands would have always been in poll position given her romantic entanglement with the producer.

From Vic Flick's perspective, there was trouble in paradise much earlier than this, citing Page's difficulties in bonding with the band as a contributing factor. There didn't appear to be any chemistry between them right from the start, and an unwillingness to 'muck in' didn't help nurture any camaraderie. He remembered one occasion on which Mike Peters was rebuked for asking her to help carry a box of cables. "I'm the singer, not a dogsbody," was the curt response, which was hardly the ideal way of bridge building. Jimmy Stead believed that she simply didn't enjoy the travelling involved between venues and a distinct lack of rapport on the road did little to endear her to the rest of the troupe. To be fair to Page, however, she may not have been entirely comfortable adjusting to a male-dominated environment, laced as it was with barrack-room humour, even though she was later to admit to finding touring a good experience. She certainly struck up a close friendship with Barbara Barry and even visited the Barrys when they were residing at the family home in Fulford.

There is no doubt that the announcement of Lisa Page's addition to the line-up came completely out of the blue at the time, particularly as Barry had regularly dismissed any idea of recruiting a singer on many an occasion in the past, even when it had been suggested by individual members of the band, who were keen to add greater versatility to the stage show. Given that this unilateral decision completely contradicted Barry's previous stance on the matter, it suggests the emerging influence of Eve Taylor may have been at work. Nevertheless, this was one innovation that didn't quite live up to expectations despite the best of intentions. Page revealed to the authors that she never truly felt at ease with the type of material that she was being expected to deliver, and as such, her vocal performances failed to capture her at her best. Barry, years after the event, concurred with that view in admitting that his arrangements for her had been "dreadful".

Life on the road as a professional musician during the late fifties was never quite as glamorous as it might have appeared in the pop weeklies and glossy teen magazines of the day. Most of the time was spent having to negotiate lengthy arduous journeys on Britain's antiquated and inadequate transport network consisting of poorly lit A, B and C roads. In 1959, there was no such thing as an integrated motorway traffic system to rely on. In fact, the first stretch of what would eventually become the M6, the 8.5 mile Preston Bypass, had only recently been opened by Prime Minister Harold Macmillan during the previous December (on the 5th). Admittedly, there were fewer cars around *per se*, but they were basic by today's standards and by no means as comfortable, devoid of any air conditioning, adequate heating and with very little suspension to speak of.

Shared 'harum-scarum' escapades on the road were, therefore, a regular hazard of the job. One such episode occurred at the unearthly hour of 2 a.m. in Bawtry (South Yorkshire) when Vic Flick, at the helm of his Rover 16, hit a nasty patch of black ice on the way back to London, which caused the car to career uncontrollably and dangerously in all directions. This 'heart in mouth' experience may have induced mass panic and irregular heart palpitations at the time, but it also had the positive side effect of bringing all band members present closer together. Bonds of friendship are often cemented during moments of crisis and this was one such example. A close-knit 'band of brothers' was now emerging, generating a team spirit that would stand them in good stead over the coming months.

Gaining exposure on national television was so prized that the band would often interrupt a series of dates for the golden opportunity of a short slot on a prime time show. During the King Brothers/Conway tour, for example, The JB7 recorded an appearance on ATV's *Music Shop*, which was presented by Teddy Johnson (of Pearl Carr and Teddy Johnson fame), and no sooner had the tour finished on 4th March than they were back in a TV studio as guests on another ATV production, *The Jack Jackson Show*. Lining up with them on that occasion was Cliff Richard and The Lana Sisters (who at the time had Mary O'Brien – *aka* Dusty Springfield – amongst their personnel). Jimmy Stead's recollections were fond ones: "Those Jack Jackson Shows were arguably the first of a breed of totally mimed ones. The studio was so extremely small that the dancers would sometimes run into each other – such a wonderful experience." Vic Flick would concur almost verbatim: "The show took place in a very cramped basement with people, cameras, cables, singers all under each other's feet. We seemed to be on that show a lot – a great show with Glen Mason sharing the hosting."

Even though The JB7, as a collective, had not appeared on *Oh Boy!* since the previous December, during March a number of the band made three more unexpected cameos in an errand of mercy (plus the prospect of a nice fat fee). This happened as a result of an ongoing dispute between Jack Good and Harry Robinson over the rights to the name Lord Rockingham's XI, who were the show's house ensemble. During the ensuing stand-off, each member of the band took sides, which left the line-up considerably depleted. Hence, Dougie Wright, Mike Peters and Vic Flick were all parachuted in to appear on those episodes broadcast on 14th, 21st and 28th March. As Wright succinctly put it, "Live TV needed 'deps' as a matter of urgency, and so the three of us from The JB7 were drafted in to play because we could literally read fly shit. So for a week or two, we became part of Lord Rockingham's XI." At one point, it was mooted that Barry would deputise as a replacement MD (alternating with Bill Shepherd), but this did not transpire, since moves were already afoot for a prolonged stint over on the other channel.

Lisa Page's 'farewell' tour, as it were, turned out to be a one-week set of engagements based at various Granada cinemas during the last week of March on a bill that included The Marino Marini Quartet and The Hedley Ward Trio; a show compèred by an up-and-coming comedian, Des O'Connor. The Italian-based quartet achieved much acclaim for their innovative use of an echo chamber in their live appearances – probably the first musicians to do so. Amongst The JB7's set list around this time were 'Farrago', 'Bee's Knees', 'Rodeo', 'When the Saints', 'Blue Room' and 'Flippin'. Big things may have been in the air for the band, but as documented, Lisa Page would no longer be part of the plan.

Quite simply, *Drumbeat* was potentially such a hugely significant stepping stone in The JB7's upward career trajectory, that it was one gig they could ill afford to miss out on. If the singer was the stumbling block, then she just had to go. Jettisoning Page so swiftly after only recently shoe-horning her into the group was a clear indication of just how ruthless Barry could be in furthering his (and The Seven's) ambitions. No matter how hard she pleaded with him to fight her case with Stewart Morris, Barry was not going to jeopardise the prospect of six months solid work performing live on national television in front of an ever-growing weekly audience. What's more, Morris wanted The Seven to back other acts on the show, which would have made Page's presence all the more superfluous. This was one battle that was not worth fighting and, in any case, it was one Barry knew he was likely to lose given Morris's clear preference for Sylvia Sands. When Page protested that she had spent the last four months on the road working towards this, her big chance, Barry countered with the argument that the band, themselves, had already put in several years of hard graft before reaching this point. No way was he going to throw away such a big break; hence, the parting of the ways for singer and group. In spite of what must have been a huge disappointment, Lisa Page remained friends and maintained contact with Barry throughout the years that followed. Had the *Drumbeat* offer not come up, one suspects Barry most likely would have kept her on.

The 'classic' JB7 line-up was now firmly in place and comprised the following: **John Barry (trumpet), Jimmy Stead (baritone sax), Dennis King (tenor sax), Vic Flick (electric guitar), Mike Peters (bass), Les Reed (piano) and Dougie Wright (drums).**

What marked this band out in comparison to the first incarnation was twofold: firstly, its pedigree (this time *every* member could read music) and, secondly, they were all based in London. This was a matter of necessity, given that the UK music business was so capital-centric at the time; every conceivable outlet thereof – the mass media, the music publishers, the major record companies *etc* – operated from London. In much the same way Brian Epstein and The Beatles were forced to abandon their Liverpool roots in 1963, so were The JB7 in having to say *au revoir* to York in 1959. Hence, Jimmy Stead, Dennis King, Dougie Wright and Mike Peters all pitched in to rent a newly available ground floor flat in Redcliffe Square (Earl's Court), while Vic Flick and Les Reed were already sharing a flat in Notting Hill Gate (with drummer Dick Harwood). No longer for them the need to rely on those theatrical digs in Old Compton Street, Soho, anymore.

By the middle of 1959, two thirds of all households in the UK now owned a television set with sales having doubled during the first six months of that year alone. What with Bush in the throes of launching its push button model and the 21-inch screen soon expected to supersede the 17-inch version, the acquisition of a television was an integral part of the consumer durables revolution. Consequently, viewing figures were rapidly escalating; therefore, to grab centre stage in a long-running music show like *Drumbeat* was clearly a much-coveted prize, which was why Eve Taylor made a big play of selling The JB7 on the strength of having what no other act had at the time – 'a new sound'. The JB7 had been initially recommended to Morris by Bob Kingston as a result of his involvement on *Oh Boy!*, but this was then subject to them having to pass an audition in Morris's presence, which was arranged at a pub near to the BBC Centre in Shepherds'

Bush. What intrigued him most of all was the 'new sound' that had been pitched so convincingly by Taylor.

The hyperbole attached to this claim certainly did its job in securing the audition, but the 'new sound' turned out to be anything but, and nothing more than the 'Piano Pick Up', Jennings Music's latest technological advance, which simply amplified the sound of an acoustic piano. In other words, by fitting a contact microphone inside a small block of wood strategically attached to the sounding board of a piano, once connected to an amplifier, the volume and sound could then be altered dramatically, and with a tremolo effect added to the output, hey presto!, a 'new sound' was born. Obviously, what was needed was for the band's latest recruit to demonstrate this innovative device in order to win favour; the only problem was that Les Reed was nowhere to be seen at the very moment Stewart Morris and his assistant Yvonne Littlewood burst into the rehearsal room on the day of the audition.

Flat mate Vic Flick had already left for the pub venue by car, well in advance, in order to transport and set up all their gear, knowing full well that Reed was still in a state of slumber after having finished a late night gig in the wee small hours of that very morning. He was to follow on later, only he overslept, causing him to be embarrassingly late for such an important date. With Morris such a stickler for punctuality, it couldn't have got much worse for the new boy, for this was not exactly the ideal way of making a good first impression. Fortunately, what might have been a tense, embarrassing and calamitous few moments in the band's entire lifespan was eased by a light-hearted response by Flick to Morris's initial greeting. "Hello, and where's this bloody 'new sound', then?" he asked. "I think it's still in bed!" was Flick's sharp reply – a jocular comment, which eased the mounting tension and lessened any negativity deriving from Reed's eventual arrival. After a profuse apology, his impressive playing and demonstration of the pick up managed to assuage the irritated producer. According to Flick, when the audition was over, Morris stood up from where he was seated, approached the band, and said, "Good, see you on the set." The 'new sound' had won the day!

In a bid to emulate *Oh Boy!*'s success at creating its own in house protégé (*a la* Cliff Richard), Morris was very keen to hire another unknown, yet up-and-coming, young singer to give *Drumbeat* a fresh look. He had no one in particular in mind at the time, until he asked Barry, who recalled working with Adam Faith on that ill-fated Jack Good stage version of *Six-Five Special*. After some initial difficulty in tracking him down (for Faith had reverted back to his real name of Terry Nelhams on resuming work as a film cutter at The National Studios, Elstree), Barry managed to arrange a successful audition. However, Faith was not as eager to accept the job as Barry had anticipated, after having already had his fingers severely burned once by the industry. His was a classic case of 'once bitten, twice shy', for he insisted on keeping his day job until he knew for certain whether *Drumbeat* would provide him with a solid enough base for a second stab at a full-time showbiz career. He need not have worried. Despite unfavourable comparisons with *Oh Boy!* from some critics, *Drumbeat* turned out be a significant landmark for both Faith and Barry. It was on the set of this programme where they met future collaborator Johnny Worth, then a member of The Raindrops vocal group.

Drumbeat was duly launched at 6.30 p.m. on Saturday 4th April with a line-up comprising of Bob Miller and The Millermen, The John Barry Seven, Russ Conway, The Kingpins, The Three Barry Sisters, Vince Eager, Roy Young, Sylvia Sands, Adam Faith, Dennis Lotis and compère Gus Goodwin (who was replaced by Trevor Peacock after just six editions). The theme tune – Barry's first – was the recently released B-side 'Bee's Knees', and on the show The JB7 also performed 'Long John', 'When the Saints Go Marching In' and 'Jumping with Symphony Sid' on which they were joined by The Millermen. The band also accompanied Vince Eager, The Barry Sisters, Roy Young, Adam Faith and guest star, Russ Conway, which was to be the way of things throughout the remaining twenty-one editions. This was a frenetically, urgent, fast-paced show that relied on precision and professionalism to pull it all together.

Rehearsals normally took place at either the Carlton Ballroom or the Riverside Studios, the latter the venue for the live broadcast. All but one of the editions were live, the exception being the 18th July transmission, which was 'telerecorded' (i.e. pre-recorded) on close circuit two days earlier – a show that also included Bob Miller and The Millermen, Vince Eager, Sylvia Sands, Adam Faith, The Raindrops, Danny Williams, The Poni-Tails, Derry Hart and Trevor Peacock (compère). During *Drumbeat*'s run, the terms of their contract prevented the Seven from appearing on ITV.

∾

The Drumbeat experience still makes Jimmy Stead smile to this day, although not necessarily because of the programme, itself, but on account of its fringe benefits, for not far from The Carlton Ballroom was a café regularly patronised by the band that served a particular delicacy and favourite of theirs: 'Baby's Head and Chips' (i.e. steamed meat and kidney pudding). "Now that could put lead in your pencil as you could well imagine!" was how he best summed it up, all part of those "Happy, happy days with lots of laughs."

∾

As the series went on, Barry became so deeply involved in the arrangements that he was able to negotiate himself an additional payment every four weeks. This extra work meant that he was forced to bring in outside help to produce enough copies of band parts, so he would send out the arrangements to a copier and then put in the bill direct to the BBC each month. It seems that after each performance Barry was in the habit of keeping all these parts for his own future use, but the BBC rapidly caught on to this. After three such bills they politely suggested that in future they would deal direct with the copyist, and keep the parts themselves.

As a result of these additional responsibilities, Barbara Barry soon found herself assuming the role of band secretary, office clerk, gofer and chief bottle washer rolled into one. When it came to organising payroll and itineraries; issuing wages and expenses; liaising with sheet music copyists (outside of the BBC) and dealing with day-to-day correspondence and general admin, Mrs Barry became the vital cog that kept The JB7 machinery ticking like clockwork. And to cap it all, when husband John decided to exploit the band's growing popularity by starting an official JB7 fan club, it was left to Barbara to see the job through. Accordingly, an advert was placed in the *New Musical Express* encouraging those interested to send a SAE to 39, Redcliffe Gardens, London SW10 – the Barry's own home address.

Vic Flick described *Drumbeat* as the most innovative and exciting TV series he ever worked on, as exhilarating as it was nerve-wracking. He found the heat in the studios at Riverside almost unbearable at times, not helped by having to wear sweltering matching pink suits, despite the fact that the show was shown in 'black and white' (colour television didn't emerge in the UK until 1967). With each show transmitted 'live', there was no margin for error, although one could never legislate for technical gremlins emerging. He recalled having to dodge runaway cameras and straying cables amidst the pressure of performing on cue and to split-second timing. A version of 'Guitar Boogie Shuffle', he remembers, once caused absolute pandemonium in the studio, because he played it at a far quicker tempo than the band and crew had anticipated; in fact, twice as fast! The reason was simply because he had been placed so far centre stage (on his own in isolation), that the backing behind him, which was situated some sixty feet nearer the studio wall, sounded to him completely out of sync. Flick later described this incident as one of the longest two minutes of his life. "The number collapsed to a crumbling finish," he added. However, he needn't have worried, since this embarrassing and scary *faux pas* turned out to be widely applauded by the general public, impressed as they were by his lightning-quick fretwork.

Despite endless arrangements played by The Seven, often at short notice, not to mention their own spots, Flick can recall only one other major hitch, which occurred when he was playing the Barry composition 'Little John'. Momentarily he lost his place after having gone completely blank, which in turn threw the cameraman, who up to that point had been following a strict order of shots. With some furious and frantic prompting from the others Flick managed to recover his place and finish the number reasonably successfully with a safe long shot covering up for the bungled continuity. This unusual lapse of concentration may have passed off unnoticed by the TV audience, but Morris was not impressed and he stormed down from the control room at the end of the show shouting, "This must never happen again." It didn't. Flick attributed this rare aberration to fatigue given the amount of work the band was being expected to do, which was compounded by the fact that every number seemed to incorporate a guitar solo on which the spotlight fell on the lead axe man.

Certainly, Flick had a point. No one worked harder on the series than The JB7. Each week involved knocking their own solo spot into shape, rehearsing material as backing group for the guest artists as well as being rigidly choreographed by the production and camera staff. As a result, a rigorous rehearsal schedule was put into place during the week of a show, which occupied Thursdays and Fridays (11 a.m. – 1 p.m. & 2 p.m. – 5 p.m.) and Saturday (10.30 a.m. – 1 p.m. & 2 p.m. – 3 p.m.). According to Jimmy Stead, the Saturday sessions were more of a technical nature involving camera shots, as opposed to the weekday's onus on the musical content.

By having to back such a wide variety of acts, The JB7 quickly became adept at adapting to and accommodating the individual quirks and characteristics of each artist with whom they were expected to work. Take Russ Conway, for example. Vic Flick considered him one of the nicest guys ever to appear on *Drumbeat*, but he was blighted throughout his career by crippling nerves. So deep were his insecurities that a contingency plan had to be devised in case his anxieties got the better of him during the live broadcast. This involved Les Reed having to play the same piece in perfect synchronization during transmission, off camera, just in case a panic attack stopped Conway playing momentarily. The cameras were ready to cut away to a long shot should that have happened with Reed's piano continuing in the background. Fortunately, the worst-case scenario did not occur on this occasion, but nothing was left to chance.

Roy Young was another such artist who needed to be micro-managed. He was an accomplished singer/pianist with an affinity for covering Little Richard and Jerry Lee Lewis songs. So keen was he to emulate their stage dynamism that this caused no end of problems within the confines of a television studio. To the band's dismay, Young's stage act was so excessively enthusiastic and gung ho that he had to be positioned at a considerable distance away from the backing; so far away, in fact, that he was virtually impossible to keep up with. Bearing in mind that these broadcasts were made long before the days when musicians could listen through their own personal headsets, accompanying a performer as erratic as Roy Young, with a penchant to improvise, was a particularly hazardous occupation. To quote Flick, "This didn't always make for a roaring, stomping Jerry Lee type performance but at least it was marginally musically correct."

Dougie Wright's own fond recollections of working on the series echo Flick's account wholeheartedly. "*Drumbeat* began in April, live, and went on for nearly six months right throughout the summer. The red lights would suddenly come on and, there we were, with millions of people looking at us on their TV screens, and with no room for mistakes. The adrenaline was pumping," he enthused. He was also at pains to point out that despite the obvious rivalry between *Drumbeat* and *Oh Boy!*, theirs was always a friendly one, since many of the guests would often appear on either channel.

In between regular transmissions and rehearsals, recording sessions continued in earnest. Just before the fourth episode on 23rd April, The Seven returned to the EMI studios in Abbey Road to record the two cuts that would form the seventh Parlophone single, 'Little John'/'For Pete's Sake'. These were the first tracks to feature Vic Flick and Les Reed. Now if their presence did not radically alter the overall sound as heard on the A-side, which, if anything, followed precisely the same formula that characterised 'Long John' only this time showcasing a brand new Barry composition, then the B-side was a different matter altogether. Reed's virtuoso lead on the 'Skip to My Lou'-like melody of 'For Pete's Sake' illustrated what he was able to bring to the table, demonstrating just what a keyboard component could add to the dynamics of the band. As usual, both sides were given regular airings on TV and radio as well as in their stage act, but the hit parade was proving an incredibly stubborn animal. Reviewed by *New Musical Express* on its release date, 19th June, 'Little John' was described as "a robust rocker", while Reed's playing was singled out for giving 'For Pete's Sake' "extra appeal".

With *Drumbeat* already proving popular, Norman Newell at EMI was not slow in picking up on the potential for recording an all-star replica of the show for vinyl release just as he had done so successfully before with *Six-Five Special* and, more recently, *Oh, Boy!*. Therefore, on Sunday 10th May, after a mere six episodes into the series, The Seven reported back to Abbey Road and recorded 'Bee's Knees'; 'Little John'; 'Rebel Rouser'; 'Mad Mab', and 'Good Rockin' Tonight' before a loud and enthusiastic audience of teenagers. In addition, they also accompanied Adam Faith, Vince Eager and Sylvia Sands on selected tracks. Dougie Wright recalled the thrill of recording an entire album in one day. As it transpired, The JB7 was the only act ever to appear on all three of these cast LPs, which illustrates just how ubiquitous they had become on British TV in such a relatively short space of time.

Not content to rely solely on Abbey Road for gaining valuable studio experience, Barry was now beginning to step up his freelance work markedly, never better illustrated than by his attempt at launching fellow *Drumbeat* artist, Adam Faith, into the charts. Once Barry had persuaded Eve Taylor to add Faith to her roster of clients, she immediately set about changing his image and appearance as well as teaching him stagecraft, before securing for him another stab at recording a single, this time with Top Rank. Two previous attempts via HMV had died the proverbial death, but it was hoped that on the strength of his growing following through *Drumbeat* and with Barry at the helm, his luck would turn. Unfortunately, the Barry-arranged A-side, 'Ah, Poor Little Baby' (recorded in May and released on 6th June), failed to reverse Faith's fortunes. Certainly, a national printing strike didn't help the cause by scuppering any planned publicity, but at least a promising working relationship in the recording studio between Barry and Faith had been forged. Clearly, what Barry saw was obvious teen potential; someone whom he could nurture into the charts.

Precisely how that could be achieved, however, wasn't immediately apparent, but was inadvertently helped by Cliff Richard (of all people) after he (with The Drifters) appeared on *Drumbeat* some weeks later on the 4th July edition singing his latest and biggest hit single to date, Lionel Bart's 'Living Doll', which had been radically slowed down from how it originally appeared in the film *Serious Charge*. The instrumentation was now much sparser, the vocal delivery far gentler and restrained.

With the song well on its way to hogging the No. 1 position throughout the whole of August, there was no getting away from it, so in recognition of its enormous popularity, Faith was asked to perform his own interpretation on the 15th August edition himself. This went down so well with the audience that it became transparently obvious to Barry that a softer, more delicate delivery, virtually *sotto voce* in style, was the best way of presenting Faith's voice on record in future, as opposed to the distinctly harsher sound emanating from his treatment of out-and-out rockers. This was Barry's Eureka moment. He suddenly recognised an alternative way forward.

Up to that point, Faith, like so many of his contemporaries, had been transfixed firmly under the spell of American rock 'n' roll and was masquerading as Acton's very own version of Elvis Presley. 'Ah, Poor Little Baby' was a case in point, as was much of the material he was performing on *Drumbeat* (e.g. 'C'mon Everybody' and 'I Vibrate'). As far as Barry was concerned, he believed that despite Faith's vocal limitations, these were more than compensated by the strength of his charismatic stage presence and engaging personality, which Barry was able to witness at close quarters on the *Drumbeat* set. He was convinced that with the right song and appropriate delivery, here was a genuine rival to Cliff in the making. The hunt was now on for a suitable song for him to record… and when it finally did arrive, it came from a source unexpectedly close to home.

With Faith placed firmly in the shop window, as it were, each week on *Drumbeat*, this succeeded in attracting the attention of film producer, George Willoughby, who was casting the net for someone to play a suitably surly teenage pop singer amidst London's Beatnik community in his forthcoming film, *Beat Girl*, then in pre-production stage. Following an enthusiastic tip-off from his besotted teenage daughter, who was struck by Faith's dynamic stage persona, he signed him on the strength of what he had witnessed on the small screen. By then Eve Taylor was promoting Faith's thespian ambitions as insurance against another failed attempt at pop stardom in any case, and since the script called for Faith to sing at least a couple of songs in the film, Taylor did what she always did when she sensed the whiff of an opportunity for her clients by tossing Barry's name in the frame as his musical director. Her pitch worked a treat, because not only was Barry assigned the songs, but he was also entrusted to write the entire score, which was, in effect, his entry into the world of film music composition.

What is probably not so widely known, however, is that Barry may well have made his film music debut some months earlier, when work began on the title song and caption sequence for a vehicle earmarked for Lonnie Donegan, entitled *The Hellion*, in which he was all set to star as a skiffle-playing 'bad guy' alongside James Kenney, who had recently starred as Bongo Herbert in the stage version of *Expresso Bongo*. Vic Flick clearly remembered recording music for this film at the Olympic Studios. What stuck in his mind was producer Hughie Green's 'hands on' approach. "He was in close attendance all the time, had much to say about the music, and entered into deep discussions with John Barry over what was needed," he recalled. However, nothing would ever emanate from these sessions, which meant that Barry's first stab at the genre would be lost forever. Ultimately, Donegan rejected the script anyway, and when subsequent re-writes also failed to satisfy him, the film was never completed.

Knowing that *Drumbeat*'s lengthy 22-week run was coming to an end on 29th August, Barry booked studio time at Abbey Road on the Wednesday before to record The JB7's next single with the idea of exclusively previewing it to a wide audience on that final show. That way, both titles would already be in the can and available for rush releasing. As an example of fine forward planning that cannot be faulted, but quite why 'Twelfth Street Rag' was chosen as the A-side is far more difficult to fathom, given that it had been recorded so many times in the past, and arguably on many an occasion far better. It seemed to be a perplexing decision to release something quite so unimaginative at that point in The JB7's career. Perhaps it was a 'contractual obligation' release, bearing in mind that Eve Taylor was by then in the throes of re-negotiating Barry's deal with EMI.

What it did point towards, however, was the future direction of the band, for 'Twelfth Street Rag' was the first of many singles on which the distinctive sound of Vic Flick's lead guitar would become the prominent focal point, although on this particular cut (which is arguably one of the shortest singles ever released) Les Reed, too, was given a brief solo. On the flip side, 'Christella', Reed's lounge piano dominates a classy slice of smooth George Shearing-esque cocktail jazz; the first recorded Barry composition written in his favourite style. The title has since been attributed to the name of a Cypriot shopkeeper's daughter with whom Barry became romantically embroiled whilst out-stationed there during his army days. Keith Fordyce, on reviewing it in the *New Musical Express*, almost unwittingly picked up on what inspired the track. "'Christella' is striking, attractive and unusual; the appeal is that of the often imagined and exotic far-off place," he enthused. *Disc* also gave the B-side its seal of approval in describing it as "different enough to take people's fancy", but it wasn't too keen on the main cut; "all right but not one of the best," was the curt verdict. The public's subsequent apathy towards the single on release suggests they must have agreed.

Working frantically behind the scenes on behalf of Adam Faith at around the same time was Eve Taylor, who was determined to hammer out a new recording contract for him after his one-disc deal with Top Rank came to nothing. On the back of regular, prime-time exposure via *Drumbeat* (which was as good a deal-breaker as any), allied to Norman Newell recognising a notable improvement in his vocal craft, she was able to sign Faith to EMI's Parlophone label; this, only a few months after he had been dropped by HMV – another EMI label, ironically enough. Job done, the hunt for the right song, in the meantime, continued in earnest.

It arrived courtesy of *Drumbeat* regular Johnny Worth (a member of the vocal quartet The Raindrops), who offered one of his unpublished songs to Faith on the set of the series; neither of them at the time could have possibly imagined just what was about to be unleashed as a consequence of this brief conversation. Up to that point, aspiring songwriter Worth had been met with complete indifference from every publisher he had approached in his attempts to sell the three songs he had so far written. When John Barry first heard the demo of one of them that he had put together with the help of Les Reed (entitled 'What Do You Want?'), the response was far more receptive, for this was precisely the type of material Barry thought would suit Faith's singing voice.

Suitably enthused, Barry then set about trying to persuade Norman Newell, his and Faith's A&R manager, to entrust him with the responsibility of arranging and recording the song. After much badgering, Newell relented, but because he was unable to oversee the production on account of being out in America watching Elvis live in concert, he allowed his assistant John Burgess (much younger and more attuned to teenage tastes) to take charge of proceedings, which he was to do for the remainder of Faith's EMI career. 'What Do You Want?' backed by 'From Now Until Forever' was recorded at Abbey Road on 25th September with an augmented John Barry Seven. Barry surprised everyone when he disclosed what lay behind his orchestral backing: just four strings, with two saxes replicating the sound of a cello. Who would have thought it: Dennis King and Jimmy Stead, the string section!

It has since been well documented just how much Newell absolutely detested the finished article when Barry first presented it to him to hear. Had it not been for the relentless hard-nosing emanating from Eve Taylor's 'never take no for an answer' attitude, he would not have sanctioned the song's release at all, but he was eventually made to eat humble pie when the single first hit the charts on 14th November. By the time it had reached No. 1 in the *New Musical Express* on 3rd December, no longer was 'What Do You Want?' the worst record Newell had ever heard. For Johnny Worth, now writing under the pseudonym Les Vandyke, this was the first of many hit compositions.

Scenting success in response to positive reviews in both the *New Musical Express* and *Disc*, EMI finally woke up smelling the roses by putting into motion a strong advertising campaign, promoting the single far more vigorously than either of Faith's first two HMV releases. Chart prospects were increased further when BBC TV's *Juke Box Jury* voted the track a unanimous hit, and also when Faith was asked to sing it live on an edition of ATV's *Boy Meets Girls*.

Barry would later reveal precisely how despondent he and Faith had become following previous commercial failures. This is why they were determined to impose their own personal tastes far more emphatically than they had done previously, a decision that clearly worked. In hindsight, this was a gamble that could easily have backfired, since no one else within EMI appeared to have much faith in Faith. What proved to be Barry's trump card was that, by this time, he had learned how to get the best out of Faith's light timbre in the recording studio. Rather than over-orchestrate, thereby swamping the vocal, he had chosen a more delicate and gentler backing, the effect of which was to bring out the singer's youthful charm. 'What Do You Want?' was the most parochial sounding of pop records at a time when America dominated the charts. Though a world away from The Beatles, Faith was staking a claim in the Top Twenty for a distinctive, unassuming archetypal British sound three years before 'Love Me Do'.

In light of 'What Do You Want?'s runaway success, it came as no surprise to find Norman Newell rapidly changing his assessment of Barry's capabilities as an arranger/conductor/producer, and as a consequence, he was rewarded with more of the same. Other EMI producers – and, indeed, other record company producers – jumped on the 'Barry bandwagon' culminating in a very busy period of recording activity. Over the next four years, Barry handled hundreds of sessions by a whole range of artists, although it is accurate to point out that of these, only Adam Faith made any lasting impact. A few came very close, while some were given their first taste of the recording industry before finding fame elsewhere. Anita Harris, Gerry Dorsey (aka Engelbert Humperdinck) and Peter Gordeno, in particular, eventually made their mark. Johnny De Little and Dick Kallman were not quite so lucky.

For 'Team Barry', life was beginning to look a lot rosier. All that groundwork was starting to pay off. Not only was Faith able to capitalise on his success on *Drumbeat*, so too was the band. In effect, The JB7 was diversifying like never before, and was soon branching out across the entire spectrum of the media to the point where even BBC Radio finally caught up with them, not wishing to miss out on an act in the ascendancy. After all, come October they would be placed joint second in the 'small group' section of the *New Musical Express's* 8th annual music poll (alongside Chris Barber and behind Lonnie Donegan). As previously documented, The JB7 failed their initial audition in 1957, when cited at the time as being 'unacceptable' to listeners of the Light Programme. With two years of solid touring behind them, together with a complete overhaul of personnel, that all changed when given the 'green light' to appear on Brian Matthew's *Saturday Club* on 3rd October 1959, which ironically was produced by the very person who oversaw that inauspicious first encounter, Jimmy Grant. This was to be the first of many appearances for the organisation that originally shunned them. The fee for their debut was £47, which was increased the following year to £59 to account for two 'specials' transmitted direct from the Royal Albert Hall.

Matthew was able to recall just how hard Barry worked in attempting to accurately reproduce the sound he was able to achieve at Abbey Road in the BBC's more primitive studio facilities at Aeolian Hall (New Bond Street). With equipment woefully behind the times, it immediately became apparent just how difficult it was to balance the sound, and without the luxury of multi-tracking, it was absolutely imperative to get this right since an entire performance was expected to be recorded in one, or at the most, two takes. Recreating Adam Faith's hits proved particularly irksome, inasmuch as it necessitated juxtaposing the sound of a delicate string quartet with that of a less subtle seven-piece rock 'n' roll band. What invariably happened was for the pizzicato effect to become completely swamped to the point of inaudible by the drum sound. The problem appeared insurmountable until the violins were placed inside a small narrator's booth situated next door, to where the rhythm section was fed through speakers.

Regular radio appearances aside, the band's staple diet of concert tours, recording and TV work continued unabated. For example, on one day alone, 18th October, The Seven made an appearance at the 35th Annual Concert for Claxton Convalescent Homes (alongside Adam Faith, Sylvia Sands, Jackie Dennis and Des Lane) at the Princes Theatre, London, before having to rush off at speed to fulfil another TV engagement, this a return to ATV's *Music Box* (with Ray Ellington and Jo Shelton). Likewise, in a single day during November (the 21st), following yet another *Saturday Club* appearance, the band headed off to the Brighton Pavilion for a performance on a bill that included Liza Rota, The Three Barry Sisters and American comedian Alan King. This involved having to rehearse the singing acts, each one of whom they were also backing, in addition to playing the opening set.

As it transpired, two poorly attended houses seemed scant reward for all the time and effort that was involved. Such was the theatre's sparsity that Alan King, on turning to The JB7 stationed behind him, joked, "Don't go away just yet, lads, it'll be terribly lonely if you do." Mike Peters clearly remembered that particular show: "We had to stay on stage for Alan King's entire spot, but I'm glad I did, as he turned out to be the best act I had ever seen up till then." Witnessing the event, the *Record & Show Mirror* was most impressed with the way in which The Seven "got the show off to a typical swinging start by way of 'Peter Gunn', 'Long John' and 'Farrago'." These were heady days indeed with Barry busily holed up in hotel rooms writing his score for *Beat Girl* between shows.

As the year began to draw to a close, however, it was the recording of *Beat Girl* that would preoccupy much of the band's time, firstly over at Beaconsfield Film Studios (Buckinghamshire) for the completion of the film soundtrack in its entirety and then at Abbey Road Studios for a far more satisfactory re-recording which was being earmarked by EMI for a stand-alone LP release. Aside from those engagements mentioned above, the other main diversions at that time were as follows: two TV appearances (on ATV's *Music Shop* and ABC's *Sunday Break* in October and November respectively); two editions of *Saturday Club* (the aforementioned 3rd October and 21st November ones), and a rare Sunday concert appearance backing Anthony Newley at the Newcastle City Hall on 20th December.

Vic Flick has vivid recollections of recording at Beaconsfield, but not necessarily for the best of reasons. This was mainly to do with the difficult conditions under which the band was expected to work. The sound stage, for a start, was far too vast and spacious for recording purposes. This was no Abbey Road. Microphones were dangled so far away from each instrument that delivering a tightly knit group sound was nigh on impossible. "The drums sounded like they were in the next county. My guitar had lost all its energy and depth. The overall ambiance was disastrous," Flick recalled. When the group made overtures about the poor microphone placement, they were politely yet firmly told to simply mind their own business. It was not until everyone had gathered together in the control room for the first playback that the issue was finally addressed for the better. Only after a long and tense moment of embarrassing silence when Barry assertively and bluntly declared, "We'll have to make some changes here," was anything done; after that, everything changed. Microphones were positioned closer, perspectives altered until a sound with some authentic dynamic punch was created. Needless to say, any cordial relations that might have existed between the band and the team of sound engineers (thoroughly miffed and chastened by the fallout) ceased to exist, but at least the film now stood some chance of being supplied with a half-decent sounding score.

Meanwhile, back at Abbey Road on 16th December, Adam Faith was busily recording two of his vocal contributions to the film. Word had circulated on the grapevine of a precocious teenager new to the circuit, by the name of Joe Brown, possessed of a guitar technique way beyond his years. Always on the alert for fresh talent, Barry was quick to draft him in to provide the lead guitar lick for 'Made You'. Brown had already come a long way in such a short space of time on the day he first entered Studio Two "with tousled hair and ever present smile" (as Vic Flick fondly remembered). Only a few months earlier, the young eighteen-year-old had been performing regularly as part of the summer season at the Butlin's holiday camp in Filey (North Yorkshire), until he decided to drop out when he became fed up of being part of a running gimmick that necessitated him having to shave his head like Yul Brynner. At that point he fled back home to Plaistow (London) to tread the pubs and bars there, which eventually brought him to the attention of Jack Good and a recording contract with Decca.

Although these days Brown remains vague as to precisely how he got this particular job, what he vividly recalls is his uncertainty as to what was expected of him when presented with the task at hand. The frantic, fiery fretwork that resulted was a consequence of him letting rip and hoping for the best, which, as it happened, proved very popular. "I just went crazy over the track and everyone seemed to like it," he recently recalled. Given that Vic Flick was in the band, Brown wasn't entirely sure why he was given the nod in preference. "Maybe John Barry just wanted a nut case on Adam's track," was his typically modest explanation. Many years later, on bumping into Flick at the bar of a Las Vegas venue following a gig, Brown was left almost speechless when Flick jokingly piped up, "You bastard, I've got a bone to pick with you." Sensing Brown had been taken aback by this comment, Flick quickly added with a wry smile, "After all this time and I'm still having to tell people that it wasn't me playing on 'Made You'!" For Brown, this was a humbling moment. "By this time, I'd totally forgotten this session, but it's nice to think that other people haven't," he reflected.

At the time, Mike Peters was immediately struck by Brown's natural talent, as well as his relaxed, laid-back demeanour. Even so, both Peters and Flick recall the studio engineers having to make allowances for Brown's inability to read music throughout that session. Peters' recollections read as follows: "Although we all had sheet music parts, Joe was simply told to fill in the last four bars, since he couldn't actually read the notes. He looked at Dougie Wright and asked how long were four bars to which Dougie replied by simply stretching his arms out wide and saying, "about that long!" Yes, it was that sort of session." Flick added that, as a precautionary measure, Brown's amplifier had to placed in an isolation booth, and thereby separated from the rest of the band, so that had he erred in any way, either by coming in at the wrong time or by playing too long, his sound would have been easily adjusted from the control room. As far as he was aware, there was never any need to apply these fixes at any stage of the recording.

On the meteorological and political landscapes respectively, 1959 would best be remembered for a swelteringly long hot summer and a Conservative 100-seat majority in October's landslide General Election. This was also the year in which a number of icons and symbols associated with the 1960s were being put into place. On 26th August, priced at £496 (including purchase tax), the Morris Mini Minor and Austin Seven Mini were launched by BMC to an eagerly expectant public. Earlier in March, American toy manufacturer, Mattel, introduced the Barbie doll to the world, while The National Radio and Television Exhibition at Earl's Court in August announced the portable transistor radio as the next technological breakthrough. Nothing symbolised the emerging dominance of television over radio than the final radio broadcast of Tony Hancock's *Hancock's Half Hour* over the Christmas holiday. From here on in, he would become a legend of the small screen.

With the old decade now rapidly coming to an end, work was already underway at Abbey Road Studios on setting the new one alight. There, on 30th December, Adam Faith, John Barry and The JB7 were busily putting together Faith's follow-up single to 'What Do You Want?'. The song in question, 'Poor Me', again written by Johnny Worth, was about to cement Faith's position as the UK's hottest new kid on the pop block and the only serious contender in 1960 to challenge Cliff Richard's position at the top of the tree. The future was, indeed, looking bright.

Autographed publicity photo of John Barry.

PROGRAMME

THE JOHN BARRY SEVEN

FROM I.T.V.'s "OH BOY" SHOW

★

DES O'CONNOR

★

THE HEDLEY WARD TRIO

IN SELECTIONS FROM :—

The greatest feeling in the world

That's the way love goes

Who's sorry now?

My baby's got such lovin' ways

Steamboat rock

Big ears

INTERMISSION

MARINO MARINI

QUARTET

★

TOTO .... the electric Guitar
RUGGERO ... the Singing Bass player
ANGELO .... Drummer
MARINO MARINI .... Pianoforte

★

Ciao, Ciao Bambina

Lo Sono il Vento

Volare

Come Prima

Bebe'

Capriccioxa

Marena

I could have danced all night

THIS PROGRAMME IS SUBJECT TO ALTERATION AT THE DISCRETION OF THE MANAGEMENT

102

★★★★★ (border)

POLL-WINNERS' CONCERT PROGRAMME ☆

Items to be selected from the following, but subject to alteration.

The John Barry Seven
Rodeo   Rebel Rouser

★

The King Brothers
Dennis King (piano/vocal), Mike King (guitar/vocal), Tony King (bass/vocal).

Leaning on a Lamp-post   Wake Up, Little Susie
Underneath The Arches   Put A Light In The Window

Petula Clark
Lucky Day   Baby Lover   Devotion

★

Joe Henderson
Trudie   Sing It With Joe   Mandy

★

Marty Wilde
Rockin' Robin   Fire Of Love
I Can't Give You Anything But Love

★

The Mudlarks
When   Book Of Love
Lollipop   The Love Game

★

Cliff Richard
Move It   Heartbreak Hotel
High Class Baby   Livin' Lovin' Doll

Compere : PETE MURRAY   ☆

The Chris Barber Jazz Band
Featuring Ottilie Patterson.

Chris Barber (leader/trombone), Pat Halcox (trumpet), Monty Sunshine (clarinet), Dick Smith (bass), Eddie Smith (banjo), Graham Burbidge (drums), Ottilie Patterson (vocals).

Bourbon Street Parade   When You And I Were Young Maggie
Maryland My Maryland   Strange Things Happening Everyday
Beale Street Blues

★

Alma Cogan
Love Makes The World Go Round   Tea For Two Cha Cha
Last Night On The Back Porch   Comes Love

★

Lonnie Donegan and his Skiffle Group
Lonnie Donegan (leader/guitar/banjo/vocals), Les Bennett (guitar), Peter Huggett (bass), Nick Nicholls (drums).

Tom Dooley   Cumberland Gap   Puttin' On The Style
My Dixie Darlin'   Long Summer Day   Lonesome Traveller

★

Frankie Vaughan
Am I Wasting My Time   Happy-Go-Lucky
Kisses Sweeter Than Wine   Garden Of Eden
Green Door

PRESENTATION OF AWARDS

Ted Heath and his Music
Ted Heath (leader), Bobby Pratt, Bert Ezard, Duncan Campbell, Eddie Blair (trumpets); Don Lusher, Wally Smith, Keith Christie, Jimmy Coombes (trombones); Leslie Gilbert, Ronnie Chamberlain, Henry Mackenzie, Bob Efford, Ken Kiddier (saxes), Stan Tracy (piano), Johnny Hawksworth (bass), Ronnie Verrell (drums).

Roll Call   Curly-headed Baby Cha Cha   Manhattan
That's A Plenty   Exactly Like You   Mah Jong

RONNIE ALDRICH AND THE SQUADRONAIRES

Page Six   Page Seven

★ ★ ★ ★ PROGRAMME ★ ★ ★ ★

THE 'TOP ALL-STAR POP' SHOW

COMPERED BY
REG THOMPSON
Direct from the Tommy Steele Show

THE GORGEOUS LOVELIES
MARGO and JUNE

LAUGHS GALORE WITH YOUR COMPERE
REG THOMPSON

STARS of COOL FOR CATS and the JACK JACKSON SHOW
THE AVON SISTERS
Songs will include their hits—Jerry Lee and Baby Oh

BRITAIN'S SENSATIONAL "ROCKIN" MEN
THE JOHN BARRY SEVEN
with LISA PAGE
Numbers selected from—Farrago   Bee's Knees   Rodeo   Saints
Blue Room   Flippin and many other great hits

— INTERVAL —

NOW ENJOY THE WONDERFUL FIVE-STAR SALES SERVICE
ICE CREAM   FRUIT DRINKS   POP-CORN   NUTS
and a wonderful selection of Confectionery and Cigarettes at the Kiosk

★

MARGO and JUNE

DYNAMIC SINGING STAR OF THE 6-5 SPECIAL
DON RENNIE
Songs will include—Rock Baby Rock   Volare   Rock-A-Bye
Day That The Rains Came

THE KING OF THE KEYBOARD, STAR OF RECORDS AND T.V.
RUSS CONWAY
Playing selections from—Pal Joey   South Pacific   Party Pops
Blues Medley   World Outside
and many other all time hits

BRITAIN'S FABULOUS TOP TUNE TRIO
THE KING BROTHERS
Selected from—Wake Up Little Susie   Oh Babe   Torero
Thank Heaven For Little Girls   Aint Misbehavin'
Leanin' On A Lampost   and many more top tunes

SENSATIONAL FINALE

GOD SAVE THE QUEEN

REG THOMPSON WILL CONDUCT THE GRAND DRAW FOR THE DREAM HOLIDAY
Look at your Programme Number on Page 3, your chance for a FREE HOLIDAY on the Cornish Riviera at the fabulous
KENEGIE HOLIDAY HOTEL (AND COUNTRY CLUB) GULVAL, PENZANCE

Keith Kelly (far right) in a last publicity photo before leaving for a solo career in March 1959.

Rehearsing on 3rd April 1959 at Riverside Studios before the first broadcast of Drumbeat, left to right: Jimmy Stead, Dennis King, Dougie Wright, John Barry, Mike Peters, Vic Flick and Les Reed.

104

Johnny Worth.

From left to right: Danny Williams, Bob Miller, Adam Faith, The Poni-Tails, Sylvia Sands, Vince Eager, John Barry, Stewart Morris.

Members of The JB7 and The Millermen meet The Poni-Tails at London Airport.

TELEVISION (C.S.)

THE BRITISH BROADCASTING CORPORATION

Head Office . BROADCASTING HOUSE, LONDON, W.I

TELEVISION CENTRE, WOOD LANE, LONDON, W.12

TELEPHONE : SHEPHERDS BUSH 8030   TELEGRAMS : BROADCASTS, TELEX, LONDON

Our Reference.......35/JM............   ....28th May, 1959............(Date)

DEAR SIR/~~MADAM~~.

We offer you an engagement to perform for broadcasting or recording for subsequent reproduction in the B.B.C. Television Service :—

DATE .....4th July, 1959.

PLACE .....Riverside Studios.
(or such other place as the Corporation may direct)

TIME .....7.30 – 8.00 p.m.,

PROGRAMME ....."DRUMBEAT"

FEE I.   Broadcast performance(s) or Recording Session(s) in substitution for Broadcast performance(s):
(See Clause 21 (c) overleaf.)

£241.10.0. for the services of the John Barry
Seven.   Fee made up as follows:—
Basic 5 hour period 3.00 – 8.00 p.m.
7 musicians @ £6 each   42.0.0.
Extra rehearsals: 7 @ £13.10.0.ea.   94.10.0
J.Barry's fee as Musical director   52.10.0
J.Barry's fee for arrangements.   52.10.0
                                             £241.10.0

FEE 2.   Mechanical Reproduction in the B.B.C. Television Service:
(See Clause 21 (d) overleaf.)
£21. 0. 0.

(Payable in respect of each such reproduction.)
N.B.—Fees under 2 above are payable only if a broadcast reproduction is given

FEE 3.   Other reproductions:
(See Clause 21 (e) overleaf.)
£42. 0. 0.

REHEARSALS

2 & 3rd July,
11.00 – 1.00 p.m.
2.00 – 5.00 p.m.,
Carlton Ballroom.

4th July,
10.30 – 1.00 p.m.,
2.00 – 3.00 p.m.,
3.00 – 8.00 p.m.,
Riverside Studios.

It is agreed that the Artists will
not appear for any other Television
Service from 27th June – 4th July,
inclusive, as per our letter dated
28th May, 1959.

All monies to be made payable to:
M. C. A. (England) Ltd.,

Artist's signature...................

Producer: Stewart Morris.

The above offer is contingent on your compliance with the conditions below and overleaf :—

1.   That your signed acceptance, together with all necessary particulars, is in our hands by return.

2.   That full programme particulars in accordance with the attached Programme Form are supplied. In this connection we must particularly stress the necessity for the accurate timing of each item and for the supply of composers', arrangers', and publishers' name in every case.

3.   That you and/or the Orchestra shall attend all rehearsals and performances as provided above.

4.   That if any members of your combination are in H.M. Forces they have obtained the permission of their Commanding Officer to accept this engagement at the fee offered.

Yours faithfully,
THE BRITISH BROADCASTING CORPORATION,

Name   The John Barry Seven,
c/o M.C.A. (England) Ltd.,
139, Piccadilly,
Address W.1.

Television Booking Manager.

Roy Young and Vince Eager on the Drumbeat set.

Terry Dene rehearsing for Drumbeat, with Dougie Wright,
Vic Flick and Les Reed at The Carlton Ballroom, London.

DRUMBEAT – SATURDAY 18th JULY 1959

18.29.58-18.58.40

A Telerecording of the programme recorded on closed circuit on 16.7.59.
Telerecording No.Ampex/6269

Duration: 28 mins 42 secs

Taking part:

Orchestra Director: Bob Miller
Orchestra: The Millermen
Group Leader: John Barry
Instrumental Group: John Barry Seven
Vocal Group: The Ponitails
Vocal Group: The Raindrops
Vocalists: Sylvia Sands
Adam Faith
Vince Eager
Danny Williams
Derry Hart

Compère: Trevor Peacock

Film Sequences Used:
BBC Specially Shot Film:
Footage: 17' Silent

MUSIC PLAYED 'LIVE'

VINCE EAGER & JOHN BARRY SEVEN
Party

VINCE EAGER & JOHN BARRY SEVEN
Cuckoo Girl

MILLERMEN
Wow

MILLERMEN
Hunt For Trumpet

ADAM FAITH & JOHN BARRY SEVEN
I Beg Of You

SYLVIA SANDS & MILLERMEN
I've Got My Love To Keep Me Warm

DERRY HEART & JOHN BARRY SEVEN
Come On Baby

ADAM FAITH & JOHN BARRY SEVEN
I Vibrate

RAINDROPS & MILLERMEN
There'll Never Be Anyone Else But You

DANNY WILLIAMS & MILLERMEN
Like Someone In Love

JOHN BARRY SEVEN
Teenage Guitar

PONITAILS & MILLERMEN
Come Dance With Me Joey

DANNY WILLIAMS & JOHN BARRY
SEVEN
Dixieland Rock

JOHN BARRY SEVEN
Flippin' In

PONITAILS & MILLERMEN
Moody

VINCE EAGER & COMPANY
Open Up Dem Pearly Gates

PRODUCED BY STEWART MORRIS

108

— john barry seven — britain's freshest music makers

39, Redcliffe Gardens,
London S.W.10.

27th November, 1959.

Contracts Dept.,
B.B.C.,
Broadcasting House,
Portland Place,
London W.1.

Dear Sirs,

The John Barry Seven are now solely represented by

Starcast,
14, Great Russell Mansions,
60, Great Russell Street,
London W.C.1.

c/o. Miss Evelyn Taylor.

All future negotiations for the Group should be directed to them.

Yours faithfully,

JOHN BARRY.

— john barry seven — britain's freshest music makers

FLAxman 1778.

Redcliffe Gardens,
London, S.W.10

13th November, 1959.

Bob Rogers,
Forest Hill,
London, S.E.23.

Recording music for the film "BEAT GIRL".

27.10.59	9 - 1 and 2 - 7	18. 10. 0
	Porterage	10. 0
29.10.59	2.30 - 6.30	8. 0. 0
	Porterage	10. 0
		£27. 10. 0

I'm sorry about the delay. Kindest regards.

Yours sincerely,

Barbara Barry

P.P. JOHN BARRY.

tv. —— records —— radio —— variety —— ballrooms —— concerts

PROGRAMME

SAMMY BROWNE
and the Escorts

★

Your Compere
ALAN CLIVE
T.V.'s Tall Host of Fun

★

A 1960 Star
LANCE FORTUNE
Signed by Pye Nixa for a big future

★

The one and only
MORTON FRAZER'S
HARMONICA GANG
A Riot of Fun and Music

Interval

Britain's Leading Musical Modernists
THE JOHN BARRY SEVEN
"6.5. Special," "Oh Boy" and "Drumbeat" Stars

★

Parlophone's Recording Star
ADAM FAITH
From T.V.'s "Drumbeat"

★

The Poll Winners
THE FIVE DALLAS BOYS
The Sensational Vocal Group

God Save The Queen

THIS PROGRAMME IS SUBJECT TO ALTERATION AT THE DISCRETION OF THE MANAGEMENT

THE JOHN BARRY SEVEN

The Band

JIMMY STEAD	-	Baritone Sax
DENNIS KING	-	Tenor Sax
DOUGY WRIGHT	-	Drums
MIKE PETERS	-	Electric Bass
VIC FLICK	-	Solo Guitar
LES REED	-	Piano

Recorded on Parlophone

Twelth Street Rag/Christella	R4582
Little John/For Pete's Sake	R4560
Long John/Snap 'n' Whistle	R4530
Farago/Bee's Knees	R4488
Pancho/Hideaway	R4453
Rodeo/Big Guitar	R4418
The Big Beat	E.P. GEP8737

The Twentieth Century Show of Youth produced by Jack Prendergast at The Rialto, York.

4

HIT AND HITS

JANUARY – DECEMBER 1960

*Working with The JB7 was a positive experience. Not only were they
a pleasure to be around, they were also skilled
and very professional musicians.*

– Julie Rayne (singer)

*I actually played 'stand up bass' on the records since electric models
were unable to replicate the sound of a true string bass at the time
due to the primitive amps of the day. Therefore, if you listen to most
of the early recordings, you will hear the sound of me playing the
Double Bass. No bass guitar could match that sound back then.*

– Mike Peters (bass guitar)

In literacy circles, the year 1960 was being heralded as 'The Year of the North'
in the wake of the publication of first David Storey's *This Sporting Life*, and
then Stan Barstow's *A Kind Of Loving*. Both highly regarded, these novels in
their strikingly different ways unashamedly portrayed Northern working-class
life in the raw through what later became generically known as kitchen-sink
social realism. Northern dialects were at last finding a voice in the arts, and
this was not confined solely to the realms of English literature. On the stage,
Salford-born Albert Finney was bringing Keith Waterhouse's creation, Yorkshire
lad Billy Fisher, to life in the West End production of *Billy Liar,* whilst doing
a similar job in the cinema through his portrayal of anti-hero Arthur Seaton
in the film adaptation of Alan Sillitoe's *Saturday Night and Sunday Morning*.
Perhaps, even more significantly, television was also muscling in on the trend,
when, in December, *Coronation Street* – a twice-weekly soap opera set in the
fictional Lancashire town of Weatherfield – was launched.

Even within the narrow confines of the capital-centred music business, the North was set to make a splash. One notable act originating from York, The John Barry Seven, was about to finally make its breakthrough on the national pop charts, which up to that point had seemed impervious to its charms. 1960 was to prove to be the band's *annus mirabilis,* a year in which they would sell more records than at any other stage in their entire existence, were invited to appear on *The Royal Variety Show* and would provide the live backing for the UK's hottest new teen idol, Adam Faith. Not only that, but John Barry, himself, was soon to become the most feted up-and-coming arranger to emerge on the British music scene.

Nothing at the start of the year, however, gave any indication as to what was to come with The JB7 busily ensconced in the studio on New Year's Day finishing off the *Beat Girl* album. No sooner had they completed that task, than they were reunited the following week with Brian Matthew, presenter of BBC's *Saturday Club.* Charged by head of popular music, Jim Davidson, with devising a similar but shorter version of *Saturday Club* for broadcast on Sundays, after some trial and error (including a pilot show called *Rumpus Room*), *Easy Beat* was the eventual chosen title of his conception. According to Matthew, "The plan was to have a resident band playing its own numbers and also accompanying guest soloists, augmented by a guest jazz band and either a folk or rock group. We were also to feature a teenage panel in a sort of *Juke Box Jury* spot whereby they gave the thumbs up or down to new releases." Matthew was to present and produce the show, himself, and given how impressed he had been by Barry's resourcefulness and endeavours on *Saturday Club*, he lost no time in engaging The JB7 as *Easy Beat*'s resident band. "What a talented group they were," he enthused, reflecting back on the show many years later. It was an opinion shared by singer Maureen Evans who would be accompanied by the band on the show for the next six months.

Still a teenager and living at home in Cardiff at the time, Evans was recommended to Matthew by her A&R manager, which meant her having to make weekly journeys to London by train for the recording in front of a packed audience at The Playhouse Theatre, near Charing Cross Station. Admitting to being painfully shy at the time, she was relieved not only to have been backed by a highly professional band, but also in having John Barry's arrangements ready for her each week. This was a luxury she was not normally accustomed to, as on most other occasions, it was left to her to search around various music shops for something appropriate in her key. Her memories of recording the shows remain fond ones; the way she managed to overcome her shyness the moment she stepped onto the stage was an abiding one with John Barry being quiet and unassuming but very kind towards her. Less memorable were those weekly train journeys between the two capitals, which often involved 'Sleepers' or 'Milk Trains', and so even though she loved doing the show, she just couldn't wait to get back home to Cardiff.

Usually, she was allocated two songs per show, which might include her latest Oriole single (like 'The Big Hurt'), a standard or a cover of a recent chart hit (such as 'Why?', 'Starry Eyed' or 'Do You Mind?'). Singing cover versions was something in which she was well versed having begun her recording career doing precisely that for Woolworth's Embassy label. As for the widely circulated rumour that her take on 'Stupid Cupid'/'Carolina Moon' actually outsold Connie Francis's original in the UK, she quipped that this was probably all down to her mother who worked on the record counter at Woolworth's in Cardiff at the time. She would do anything to give her daughter a plug!

Due to scheduling difficulties, *Easy Beat* actually began life on Saturday evenings before switching to a regular Sunday morning slot at 10.30 after a few weeks. The switch also saw a subtle change in the backing whereupon The JB7 added four violins to the line-up for their own spot and for accompanying Evans. On these occasions, Barry received £73 19s 6d per show, which had to be shared between the eleven musicians. On top of that, Barry received an extra £5 for himself as reward for his additional responsibilities. Not only was he expected to front the house band on the show (ostensibly The JB7), but also to write the arrangements for and to accompany the guest solo singers featured each week.

The JB7 performed much of its own repertoire on *Easy Beat* together with an eclectic range of cover versions. If 'Peter Gunn' and 'Rebel Rouser' represented prime examples of contemporary hits, what was more surprising was the inclusion of a number of standards played as instrumentals. Among these were 'What is this Thing Called Love?', 'I Remember You', 'Easy to Love', 'How High the Moon' and 'Black Bottom'. Barry also composed the *Easy Beat* signature tune, which was later recorded by guitarist Bert Weedon, who would eventually take over from The Seven when they were prised away for a summer season with Adam Faith in Blackpool. The group's run on the show lasted from January to June 1960, although Maureen Evans would continue as a regular for another year, accompanied by Weedon's band. Even after that she still made the occasional appearance; something The JB7, curiously, did not manage to do.

What struck Matthew most of all was Barry's ability to handle intense pressure with such cool aplomb; considering that the show was recorded as a live theatre performance before a large audience in London's Playhouse Theatre, this was no mean achievement. According to Matthew, "He [Barry] regularly just made deadlines, turning up at the theatre in time for rehearsal with only some of the parts written, while the rest were being delivered from the copyists as we went along. He always appeared to be calm and unruffled, although there must have been moments when his stomach was churning." Wife Barbara, it must be said, was instrumental in ensuring that the paperwork tallied and that deadlines were met, however tight.

The 'bread and butter' live work continued apace during January with a series of Sunday concerts at Edmonton (Regal), Derby, Cheltenham and Lewisham (Gaumont) alongside a diverse bunch of musical acts: Craig Douglas, Adam

Faith, The Five Dallas Boys, and Chris Williams and His Monsters. The show was compèred by Dickie Richards.

Occurring that same month, and arguably of far greater significance, was a label switch from within the confines of EMI. After eight unsuccessful attempts at cracking the charts at Parlophone, a decision was taken to release further records by The JB7 under the Columbia imprint. Although the authors could not find one definitive reason to account for this development, there are a number of scenarios that point towards this being a logical step. Firstly, for any artist closely connected with Norman Newell (and Newell was Barry's recording manager), the Columbia label – of which Newell was the head – was undoubtedly that artist's natural home. After all, Newell's recording assistant, John Burgess, had already been entrusted with producing Barry's recordings. Barry, himself, was always Newell's protégée rather than George Martin's anyway. Secondly, Eve Taylor was in the process of re-negotiating Barry's contract (about which more is discussed later). Suffice to say that Taylor had big plans for Barry that involved him becoming more than simply a recording artist *per se*. Thirdly, it is possible that EMI wanted to keep Adam Faith's and The JB7's recordings completely separate in the public eye (although that was never the case for Cliff Richard and The Shadows) and fourthly, the change may have been the result of nothing more than a mundane, internal, organisational reshuffle. According to Ken Townsend, who spent virtually his entire career working for EMI at Abbey Road Studios, he would not have been the least bit surprised to attribute the transfer to the budgetary constraints of the time as a way of shifting resources from one label to another in order to balance the books. Perhaps the signing of Faith to Parlophone necessitated The JB7's move to Columbia. Whatever the reason or combination of reasons, this change was soon to reap dividends for both label and band alike.

Meanwhile, appearing on *Saturday Club* remained an important part of The JB7's itinerary. On 16th January, they shared a bill with Adam Faith, The Lana Sisters, Al Saxon, Mike Shaun, Elaine Delmar, The Mike McKenzie Quartet, The Ken Jones Five and The Malcolm Mitchell Trio, while on the 30th, they were asked to appear on an even more prestigious production from the BBC Light Programme's *Saturday Club* team entitled 'Jazz & Rock Night', which was being held at the Royal Albert Hall. Brian Matthew introduced the following mixture of trad jazz pioneers (now suddenly in vogue) and current pop favourites: Mr. Acker Bilk's Paramount Jazz Band, Terry Lightfoot's New Orleans Jazzmen, The John Barry Seven, Adam Faith, Al Saxon, Craig Douglas, Cuddly Duddly, Betty Smith, The Five Dallas Boys, The Lana Sisters, Miki and Griff, Diz Disley, Clinton Ford, George Chisholm, Bert Weedon, Dill Jones, Eric Silk, Ike Isaacs, Sylvia Sands and Ken Jones.

February 1960 emerged as a landmark month in The JB7's career, marking as it did the band's arrival, at last, as a fully-fledged chart act. 'Hit and Miss', the debut Columbia 45, recorded on 14th January, joined Faith in the Top Ten, thanks immeasurably to being chosen as the brand new theme tune to *Juke Box*

Jury, which since its launch on 1st June 1959 had become the BBC's pre-eminent pop programme. Evidently, some very astute backstairs manoeuvring must have helped secure this vital leg-up. By now Barry had developed a solid relationship with the BBC to the point where his musical prowess had become widely noticed amongst the production staff of both radio and television wings.

When *Juke Box Jury* producer Russell Turner proposed to freshen up the opening sequence at the start of the year by replacing the existing theme, Ozzie Warlock and The Wizards' rendition of Tony Osborne's 'Juke Box Fury', with something more contemporary (i.e. electric guitar led), he took it upon himself to approach Barry (and/or his management) to pitch in with a suitable idea. Even if this decision had been partly spurred on by a dispute involving composer Osborne over a personal matter, it set off a fortuitous chain reaction benefiting the Seven no end. What better way of promoting the next single than by having it played each week at the start of a prime-time Saturday night music show that at the time was commanding audience figures of up to 9 million (and which in its heyday would rise as high as 12 million; even a staggering 23 million when The Beatles appeared). The ensuing title 'Hit and Miss', whereby deciding either of these two outcomes encapsulated the entire premise of the show, was therefore no coincidence, after having already been intentionally preconceived as a front for the show – a version of events that appears to have been borne out by Barry's decision during the 1990s to give a co-composer credit for 'Hit and Miss' to both Turner and music publisher Freddie Poser (then general manager of Mills Music) in due recognition of their contributions towards making a success of it all.

As a means of introducing the intended new theme to the viewer, the decision was made to include it as one of the new releases featured on the 6th February edition with Barry himself occupying the dreaded hot seat from behind the curtain awaiting the panel's critical dissection. Not surprisingly, 'Hit and Miss' was voted a unanimous hit and, a week later, was unveiled as the programme's resident theme tune where it was to remain throughout the series' original incarnation up to 27th December 1967 (although a 1965 cover version by 'Ted Heath and His Music' would eventually replace The JB7's during its final run). Note that subsequent remakes of the show in 1979 and 1989 continued to use the theme albeit in various stylistic guises that reflected the times.

There is little doubt that Barry's appearance on *Juke Box Jury* was a vital and priceless window of opportunity for the band at a time when media exposure of this nature was essential for them attaining the next level of success. A hit single was always a significant barometer of achievement; another failure was, therefore, unthinkable. Barry's cameo on the programme was one example of how much he tended to hog the spotlight at the expense of the other members of the band. While leader and troupe were all pulling in the same direction, this didn't seem to matter so much in 1960, but would in time cause much disgruntlement amongst some of its ranks. No one at that juncture could complain about the impact a weekly soundbite could have on the single's sales potential, however. 'Hit and

Miss' entered the UK chart on 10th March, would go on to sell 125,452 copies eventually peaking at No. 10. After three years of tireless striving, The JB7 had finally arrived.

The recording of both sides of The JB7's debut hit was notable for it being the first occasion on which Barry tailored the personnel to fit the requirements of the arrangement. This was the way in which he would operate throughout this period on Columbia, signalling the onset of a much freer reign. In other words, The JB7 became a more fluid entity; at times the core 'Seven' alone were required, but that was not always necessarily the case. For example, the 7 – 9p.m. recording session that produced both 'Hit and Miss' and its flip side, 'Rockin' Already', employed ten musicians, plus 'The Rita Williams Singers' who provided the female vocal backing to the latter. Augmenting both sides were four session-violinists supplying pizzicato backing: Bernard Monshin, Sid Margo, Charlie Katz and Alec Firman (Margo was later to act as Barry's 'fixer', the musician entrusted to supply ensembles for film music recording sessions). Hence, on release the record was attributed to 'The John Barry Seven plus Four'. Incidentally, all ten musicians received an extra £1 fee on account of the session going into overtime!

'Rockin' Already' was Barry's take on the traditional African song, 'Wimoweh', which pre-dated the two most successful vocal versions, from the Tokens and Karl Denver respectively, by over eighteen months. The track 'Hit and Miss' was to epitomise what was fast becoming Barry's trademark 'stringbeat' approach better than just about any other he ever recorded, and heralded, alongside Faith's early recordings, a key sound associated with the more innocent pre-Beatles era of British pop. It was also marked by a lengthy, slick improvised guitar solo from Vic Flick – the first of many indications throughout the year of the electric guitar becoming *the* instrument that would define the decade.

Keith Fordyce was quick to identify this 'signature' sound in his *New Musical Express* review of the single, whilst also accurately predicting its chart potential. "Could be a big seller," was his verdict. "This interesting John Barry composition combines some of the plucked string sounds that he has supplied to Adam Faith with the slower guitar that has been a feature of many driving rock instrumentals." The *Disc* reviewer wrongly attributed 'Rockin' Already' as the A-side, but nonetheless gave both cuts good reviews. "Guitar and sax noise is dead right for the jukes together with some girl voices," was the take on the perceived lead track, while 'Hit and Miss' was described as a "toe-tappy melody with a beat, blending front guitar with plucking strings." Such was the depth of analysis in the pop press at the time.

After the demise of *Drumbeat*, The Seven tried to fit in as many guest slots for the BBC as was feasible, including an appearance on *The Ted Ray Show*. This did not necessarily apply to commercial channels, however. During February, Eve Taylor rejected an offer from Jack Good for The Seven and Adam Faith to appear in a new nine-week ABC series entitled *Wham!*, although this was most likely to have been the result of a busy touring schedule in and around the

North of England. This tour began at Sheffield City Hall and included visits to York Rialto, Newcastle, Manchester and Worksop Regal, whereupon the band combined its own slot alongside accompanying Faith, who shared top billing with Emile Ford, with Mike Preston also appearing.

Jimmy Stead was able to vividly capture the flavour of life on the road in an era when the road traffic system and weather conditions combined to make travelling far more hazardous then it ever is today, despite fewer cars on the road: "February in Yorkshire during the 1960s could be rather foggy especially after dark. As I recall, Barry was driving an American left-hand drive at that time, while Dennis, Dougie and myself were travelling in the Ford off-set band wagon. One particular 'pea-souper' of a night on our way to the gig in Worksop left us with hardly any visibility at all. Once the car in front of us turned off our road, leaving us entirely on our own, we began to make even slower progress. This enabled Barry to catch up with us (in his sleeker vehicle) and slowly overtake us, gesturing at the same time that our rear taillight was very dim. As he slowly disappeared into the foggy haze, we pulled the van to the side in order to examine the rear light. As we were fixing it, we heard this motorbike coming towards us from out of the gloom. There we all were shouting at the rider to stop with Dougie taking off his hat and madly waving it, but to no avail. Unfortunately the motorcyclist didn't see us until it was too late. He couldn't stop and, as if time was standing still, hit the back of the van. Having picked him up and dusted him down, we checked to see if he and the bike were okay. Both appeared to be fine, so we were able to leave him to his own devices and resume driving through the gloom. And, yes, we managed to arrive at the show on time and, as usual, wowed the audience," With tongue firmly in cheek, he added, "Such a tough life, eh?"

Looking back at the transport and travelling arrangements at that time, Jimmy Stead had this to say: "The Ford off-set model we had the use of was a two door van finished in grey primer, but at a push, only three of us could be accommodated at any one time. We paid for the running of it out of our own pockets together with tea, coffee, digs, transport cafe meals *etc*. Barry wasn't exactly what you could call one of 'the big spenders'!"

On 21st February, The Seven were once again allocated a slot on the bill of the *New Musical Express* Poll-Winners' Concert now held at the Empire Pool, Wembley. The poll covering 1959 saw them fare one better than the previous year, this time finishing second to Lonnie Donegan. Invited to participate as due reward, they were joined by Adam Faith, who was booked as a late replacement for Alma Cogan. There, the band accompanied him singing his two chart-toppers, 'What Do You Want?' and 'Poor Me'. The concert venue had been switched to the vast Wembley Empire Pool, simply because it could seat 10,000 and therefore better equipped to meet public demand. The *New Musical Express*'s Keith Goodwin was impressed by The JB7. "When it comes to beat music", he noted, "The JB7 is unrivalled in Britain, and the outfit's own driving performance – including 'The

Saints' and John's latest composition 'Hit And Miss' – told us why this band is held so high in the estimation of fans."

On the very same evening of that concert, The Seven were kicking off the first of a series of one-nighters located at various Granada cinemas across the country (Aylesbury, Bedford, Dartford, Harrow, Kettering and Rugby among them). Joining them on stage in Kingston-upon-Thames that night and throughout the tour were Adam Faith, Little Tony, The Liddell Triplets, Julie Rayne and compère Mike Martin, but no sooner had they fulfilled this contract than they found themselves holed up again in Abbey Road cramming in a recording session for EMI's *Fings Ain't What They Used To Be* LP, accompanying Adam Faith on 'Carve Up' and 'Big Time'. This was the kind of hectic and gruelling day-to-day schedule that would seem unheard of these days, but was commonplace back then when a pop act's projected lifespan at the top was seen solely in the short term. Longevity was not construed as an option; therefore, a 'make hay while the sun shines' mentality was indicative of the industry.

This was one major reason why record companies were ever keen to issue follow-up singles long before the current hit had completed its chart run. A rapid turnover of releases was crucial for keeping that artist in the public gaze, and more importantly, for maximising sales. Maintaining the momentum was the key, for no one knew when the hits would dry up. As if to emphasise the point, on the very week 'Hit and Miss' entered the *New Musical Express* charts at No. 24, The JB7 were back in Studio Two recording both sides of what would become the next single, 'Beat For Beatniks/Big Fella'. This pressure to quickly consolidate also explained why record companies would play safe, more often than not, when choosing subsequent material. Hence, another Adam Faith session in March spawned an archetypal 'stringbeat' arrangement for another song from the Johnny Worth stable, 'Someone Else's Baby' (co-written with Perry Ford). Barry was never likely to tamper with a winning formula after registering two consecutive chart toppers, even if he was more akin to taking greater risks with his own material.

For singer Julie Rayne, her experience of touring with The JB7 was memorable for a number of reasons, but above all, for the way in which they helped her out of a potentially tricky problem. The difficulty arose from the failure of her musical arrangements to arrive in time for the tour thereby leaving her with no charts to give to the musicians backing her. When she asked Eve Taylor (Rayne's agent also) to explain this difficulty to the boys, they steadfastly refused to agree to play without the music, but she soon found out that this was a deliberate wind-up solely to put Taylor's nose out of joint. In truth, they were all too willing to come to her rescue and did so without any ado throughout the tour. Rayne would later discover an ulterior motive lay behind such acquiescence: "Les Reed recently admitted that this was because they all fancied me; mind you, they were a pretty cute bunch of guys themselves," she revealed.

That series of Granada concerts, incidentally, would later become collectively known as the notorious 'Water Pistol Tour', as Rayne would remember only too well, simply because she was indirectly responsible for starting it all off. She thought it would be a good idea to use said pistols as a means of harmlessly deterring over-enthusiastic youngsters from scaling the theatre drainpipes in order to get a sneaky peak at their heroes. Once Adam Faith liked the idea, it quickly caught on. "At first, we squirted these kids from the dressing room but once we took the pistols on stage with us, we started on each other during performances, and it all escalated from there as the tour progressed." She recalled one occasion when Faith exacted his own method of revenge on The JB7 after having been completely drenched by their onslaught mid-song. On introducing each individual member of The Seven to the packed audience, he asked them to stand up so as to milk the applause. Unbeknown to them, at that precise moment, he pulled out two water pistols and reeked havoc on them! "The Granada management were not amused one bit and threatened to sack us all were it to continue," she added.

Apparently, no one was spared a thorough soaking, and that included compère/comedian Don Arrol, who Vic Flick remembered coming off stage with water literally pouring off his shirt. In fact Arrol was the recipient of another example of their high jinks albeit one that didn't necessitate water. This involved Faith sitting on top of the cinema organ and then pressing the rise button halfway through Arrol's turn. According to Jimmy Stead, "The audience went mad as Adam suddenly rose like a phoenix from the ashes, and then turned to face them. Don – ever the trooper – just couldn't stop laughing, and yet he still managed to carry on with his act."

To a generation weaned on emails, Facebook, Instagram, YouTube, online games, Skype, laptops, WhatsApp and so on, such juvenile japes may now appear somewhat puerile in nature, but these pranks managed to allay the sheer tedium borne out of endless days travelling from gig to gig. There were simply no distractions of the kind taken for granted today. A mobile phone was nothing but an invention of science fiction back in 1960. Entertainment often took the form of practical jokes and jocular banter as a means of letting off steam (child's play, admittedly, in comparison to the type of anarchic behaviour later deployed by the likes of Ozzy Osbourne and Pete Townshend). Some of these ruses were even built into the stage act on occasions, of which the water pistol routine was one notable example. These were more innocent times.

While Eve Taylor was announcing her defection from the Will Collins Agency to MCA (taking as many of her acts with her as she could including The JB7, Adam Faith, Jackie Dennis and Des Lane), she had lined up further concert and TV appearances for the Seven during March, one of which was an appearance on *The Melody Dances* from the Majestic Ballroom, Finsbury Park, for ITV. Far more prestigious was the 'S.O.S Charity Concert' held at The Empire Pool, Wembley. This read like an 'A to Z of British Showbiz' and featured Adam Faith, Cliff Richard, Winifred Atwell, Shirley Bassey, Alma Cogan, Lonnie Donegan, Robert Earl, Dave Lee, Dennis Lotis, Vera Lynn, Joan Regan and

Dickie Valentine. The JB7 included 'Peter Gunn' and inevitably 'Hit and Miss' amongst its repertoire that night. Sandwiched in between these events was a recording session with The Five Dallas Boys.

An extension of the Granada Cinemas tour occurred not long after over April, this time more widely spread albeit without the resurgence of any water-related incidents. Aside from Adam Faith, a different full supporting cast was assembled that included The Honeys, Joan and Paul Sharratt, Johnny Worth, Larry Grayson and Don Arrol. Among the venues were East Ham, Burnt Oak, Birmingham, Norwich, Grantham, Woolwich, Tooting and Greenford.

Nevertheless, one Sunday date at Scarborough later in June, was marked by a one-off recurrence of those unrestrained aquatic antics, although this time the band went a tad too far even by the their own standards and, if anything, it was borne out of petty squabbling rather than innocent horse-play. Just a mere five minutes before going on stage, one unnamed member of the band decided to pick up a fire bucket full of stagnant water and throw the entire contents over most of his band mates. The stage uniforms were absolutely drenched to the point of saturation; gleaming white shirts were now all fifty shades of grey! "Playing an hour set in wet socks and underwear is not a pleasant thing to have to do", Vic Flick would later recall painfully.

The JB7's appearance at Sutton was given prominence in *The Stage* as follows: "With terrific driving force, The John Barry Seven also went over big. This is one group that has survived the age of rock 'n' roll; deservedly so because its musicians – comprising two really twanging electric guitarists and two rasping saxists (*sic*) – have genuine talent, are musical and put over their offerings with plenty of gusto. Even those who are anti their type of music cannot help but see that they're the tops."

∽

Adam Faith fan Michael Bush, who attended the show at Burnt Oak, has nothing but fond memories of what for him was a truly wonderful experience: "My very first 45 record was 'What Do You Want'? – a Christmas present that actually arrived about three weeks later, bought for me by my cousin Sheila. She had to order the disc from the local record shop because it had sold out, and I can still remember the 45's bright red label with silver writing. It was a joy to my ears! As a result of having both a paper and a grocery round, I was able to save enough money to buy two tickets for 'The Adam Faith Show', one for me and another for my classmate, Tim Clarke. We went along to the 'Savoy Theatre' in Burnt Oak (near Edgware), where we were first entertained by compère Don Arrol, who was a very funny man! The John Barry Seven played its set before Adam Faith came on standing right of stage. I remember during 'Singing in the Rain', Don Arrol came running onto the stage to interrupt the band by announcing that one of The Seven had just become father to a baby girl (this would have been Dougie Wright), and there was Vic Flick in the middle of his solo cut off in his prime! My other outstanding memory was the presence of four local female violinists being conducted by John Barry during 'Someone Else's Baby', which concluded the evening."

~

Les Reed would later reveal how the band managed to re-produce that pizzicato sound live on those occasions when such a string section was unavailable on any given night. This would be achieved by juxtaposing the sounds of the piano at the high end of its register with a dampened guitar note effect.

After completing the soundtrack for the Adam Faith film *Beat Girl*, Barry was soon hard at work scoring Faith's second movie, *Never Let Go*, which clearly provided the inspiration for the next single; the first example whereby Barry was able to stretch his orchestral muscle for that format. Both 'Beat for Beatniks' and 'Big Fella', recorded between 2 p.m. and 4 p.m. on 14th March, were written with the film in mind. A larger budget enabled Barry to utilise as many as nineteen musicians to provide the fuller, big band, brass-led sound he was aiming for (four trumpets, four trombones, five saxes, two basses, two drums, guitar and piano). This was by no means an obvious follow-up to 'Hit and Miss', and in all likelihood was never intended as such, since on release it was billed as being recorded by 'John Barry and His Orchestra' as opposed to simply The Seven, who had been augmented by no fewer than twelve additional musicians, among them established jazz players such as saxophonist/flautist Johnny Scott and trumpeter Dicky Hawdon. Sales figures seemed to suggest that this single only appealed to the more specialist jazz market inasmuch as it attracted just 16,949 buyers. It was simply too 'off centre' for the mainstream record-buying public. Nevertheless, it still managed to sneak into the Top Fifty for a couple of weeks by late April.

The A-side 'Beat for Beatniks' had, in effect, already previously found a home when Barry was hired to record a number of self-penned pieces of library music for Chappell – one of several labels that employed composers and musicians to record 'production' or 'stock' music for lending out to various media outlets such as TV, radio, advertising and film for a fee. This was another way a jobbing writer or player could earn a crust in such an insecure profession. Chappell's version of 'Beat For Beatniks' was entitled 'Mood Three' and was virtually identical to the Columbia single except for the addition of a guitar solo (courtesy of Vic Flick). 'Big Fella', was similarly Elmer Bernstein-inspired, and a taster of Barry's work on *Never Let Go*. Both cuts were completely alien to anything previously recorded by the Seven on 45 and were light years away from the typical guitar-led pizzicato approach for which Barry was becoming renowned. He was quite obviously using JB7 recording sessions as workshops for perfecting these early attempts at film scoring. The Columbia contract was giving him more leeway to experiment and extricate himself from the confines of a seven-piece ensemble, thereby enabling him to distance himself from his pop persona. 'Beat for Beatniks' was a clear statement to the wider music community as a whole that he was more than a 'one-trick pony' *a la* 'Stringbeat'. Thus, even during the first flushes of success, here was the first hint that a parting of the ways was inevitable.

The single was such a radical departure for Barry that it took the jazz-dominated *Melody Maker* completely by surprise. Naturally, given the paper's stylistic leanings, columnist Maurice Burman fell head over heels for the single: "I put on the record without a lot of interest, and after the first four bars I nearly fell through the floor! The record is like nothing he has done before – it is modern jazz with a fresh approach, tinged with Kenton-ism. It stamps John Barry as a first-class modern arranger and composer with a daring mind."

The *New Musical Express* was equally as effusive in its praise and as accurate as any in identifying the single's terms of reference: "'Beat for Beatniks' is the sort of title that might lead you to anticipate something unusual, but JB's recording on Columbia of his own composition is way, way out. I don't mean off the target, but out of the rut; a wild, pounding, big-band noise with strong jazz suggestions. Not quite morbid in mood but there's an element of cruelty about it, belonging as it does, to the same broad category as Bernstein's Staccato's Theme. Like the top side, the flip ('Big Fella') is also penned by Barry. This has an easier pattern to it, but is still an instrumental broadside – an onslaught that can leave you limp. This latest waxing places Barry somewhere between Johnny Dankworth and Elmer Bernstein!" Given that the style of both sides was the first coupling on which Barry's own musical tastes were being truly reflected, this must have been the type of review he had always dreamt of receiving.

The same paper was also highly appreciative of the *Beat Girl* soundtrack's artistic merits, which was released at the same time – the first LP of its kind ever released in the UK for a domestic film. "Played by John Barry's wild and rockin' orchestra," it enthused, "the net result is a terrific Columbia album, which should gain him international recognition as Britain's reply to Henry Mancini's *Peter Gunn*. With 18 tracks, it contains some of the most exciting and novel rock instrumentation ever heard." Praise indeed. By this time, The JB7 were beginning to incorporate their own contributions to the *Beat Girl* LP into their regular repertoire. Tracks such as 'Lindon Home Rock', 'The Stripper', 'Time Out', 'Beat Girl – Main Title' and 'Kid's Stuff' were as good a reflection of the band's dynamic live sound as anything they ever recorded.

In the meantime, the Granada tour trudged on regardless interrupted only by yet another *Saturday Club* spin-off held at The Royal Albert Hall (12th April), on this occasion billed as 'The Big Beat Concert'. Compèred as ever by Brian Matthew and headlined jointly by Craig Douglas and Adam Faith, this *pot pourri* of British pop also included The Lana Sisters, Duffy Power, Dickie Pride, Bert Weedon, Johnny Wiltshire and The Trebletones. Towards the end of the tour, the participants played weekly residences at the Finsbury Park Empire (London) as well as the Manchester Hippodrome. Speaking to the press, Barry, donning his PR hat, remarked with the following: "Nothing but a hurricane would keep us away from these concerts, we love them so much. Each time we take part we win more and more fans."

Launched on ITV's opening weekend by impresario Val Parnell on 29th September 1955, *Sunday Night at the London Palladium* quickly established itself as one of the most prestigious programmes on British television and helped to attract massive audiences for the fledgling commercial networks. By 1960, an appearance could guarantee half the viewing population tuning in for their weekly fix of wholesome entertainment (an incredible 28 million!). Based on a variety bill model, it successfully managed to transcend age and class barriers and as a result of its standing in the television firmament attracted most of the biggest names in showbiz. For anyone booked to appear, it became a indication of one's standing in a notoriously competitive and hierarchal business, and in some cases, it was considered the pinnacle of one's achievements. That's why you can imagine just how gutted Jimmy Stead must have felt when he fell ill on the very day The JB7 (and Adam Faith) were given the nod to appear on the show broadcast on 17th April during which they performed 'Hit and Miss'. It was more miss than hit for poor Stead. "Missing *Sunday Night at the London Palladium* has to be my most disappointing moment as a member of The JB7," he later recalled. "However, my absence was covered at short notice by someone I never actually met – a fellow sax player, Frank Gillespie, who did a great job."

If *Sunday Night at the London Palladium* was a measure of just how far one had climbed the ladder of success, it palled in comparison to an invitation to appear on *The Royal Variety Show*. Although it may now have lost the lustre of old due to the multi-platform media available to the 21st-century consumer, but in 1960 it was considered the ultimate accolade for any entertainer treading the boards – akin to reaching the summit of Mount Everest. Dating back to 1912, the first Royal Variety Show (or Command Performance) was a charity event held in the presence of King George V and Queen Mary in aid of the Variety Artistes' Benevolent Fund for elderly entertainers. From 1921 onwards, it became an annual showpiece on the instructions of the King, whereupon it attracted the cream of show business from all over the world, interrupted only by the outbreak of war and the Suez crisis,

On 16th May Adam Faith and The Seven were honoured to perform on what was to be the first ever televised transmission of the show, broadcast that year from The London Victoria Palace. The resplendently suited and booted JB7 took to the stage to back Faith, himself dressed completely in white, on 'What Do You Want?' and 'Play It Cool', after which they all changed into top hat and tails for the grand finale. The presence of Faith and The JB7, alongside Cliff Richard and The Shadows and Lonnie Donegan, was an admission by the promoters (at last) of the growing emergence and existence of a teenage audience with musical tastes of their own. Held in the presence of Queen Elizabeth II and The Duke of Edinburgh, the remainder of the bill read like a 1960 'Who's Who of the Show Business Establishment': Max Bygraves, Nat 'King' Cole, Russ Conway,

Billy Cotton and His Band, The Crazy Gang, Sammy Davis Jr., Diana Dors, Jimmy Edwards, Bud Flanagan, Benny Hill, Robert Horton, Frankie Howerd, Hattie Jacques, Liberace, Vera Lynn, Bob Monkhouse, The Tiller Girls, Norman Wisdom and Harry Worth, with Bruce Forsyth acting as compère.

Of all the star-studied turns on display that year, 1960's show is always likely to be best remembered for a truly mesmerising, show-stopping performance from Sammy Davis Jr, whose energy sapping song-and-dance act had critics in raptures. As far as the *Daily Sketch* was concerned, "In eight electrifying minutes, he (Davis) made the word 'star' seem inadequate." For certain members of The JB7, however, recollections of a more personal nature took precedence.

Dougie Wright, for instance, clearly recalls this as the one and only time the band was ever expected to wear top hat and tails. They may have been hired from as reputable an outfitter as Moss Bros, but in Wright's eyes, "I looked a right prat, because the entire look didn't really seem to suit me on account of my size." Les Reed, on the other hand, fondly remembers not only meeting his musical hero, Nat 'King' Cole, backstage, but also being photographed alongside him. Such a proud moment would have stayed with him forever had not a mix-up at the developers seen the print winging its way to Adam Faith rather than himself; sadly, an error Faith would never rectify over the course of his lifetime.

Vic Flick's own reminiscences include the stylish gold-embossed invitation that arrived from Buckingham Palace, having to use a room above a pub across the street from the theatre in which to get changed, and then having to walk all the way to the venue in full make-up and regalia, with instruments in hand, which would solicit some very odd looks from passers by. The sheer sense of excitement and anticipation marked this out for him as no ordinary show with even the usual backstage chaos adding to the sense of occasion: "Juggling acts mixed with be-plumed dancing girls; stage hands moved with skill and ease through all the props and ropes and theatrical paraphernalia, while the stage manager made sure the next act was ready – like any other show on the surface maybe, but with an aura only a Royal Command Performance could create."

Within a matter of days (on the morning of 29th May), The Seven were soon brought back down to earth recording the two tracks that would make up both sides of the next single: 'Blueberry Hill' and 'Never Let Go'. On this session, twelve musicians were used at a cost of £88: four violins, two electric guitars, tenor sax, baritone sax, piano, bass, bass guitar and drums. EMI's way of balancing Barry's eagerness for experimentation with the need to maintain The JB7's chart momentum was to release these two startlingly different tracks on the same single. Overt commercialism in the form of a straight 'stringbeat' rendition of Fats Domino's 'Blueberry Hill' (with identifiable pizzicato strings and guitar twang) was juxtaposed with Barry's more sombre, tension-riddled 'Never Let Go', another example of Barry's cinematic tendencies, which was taken from the film of the same name. Although the officially designated B-side, 'Never Let Go' managed to receive almost as much air play and, as a result, was chart-listed in its own right. The custom of the day at participating chart return shops was to record a purchase according to the title actually requested by the customer, which could sometimes lead to the reverse 'out-selling' the recognised A-side. As 'Blueberry Hill', the single peaked at 34, whilst as 'Never Let Go', at 49. Even so, what would have been considered a significant achievement at the start of the year was something of a disappointment now when placed in comparison to the popularity of 'Hit and Miss'. Admittedly, the sales figure was hardly inconsiderable, but it was still down by a quarter to 32,252 (albeit twice as many as 'Beat for Beatniks', mind you). Who knows, the decision to attribute the single once again to 'John Barry and His Orchestra' may well have had a bearing on matters with the hardcore JB7 fan base not buying into the name change; i.e. failing to perceive them as the same band they saw live every week. The fact that neither track featured in concert rather reinforced that perception, one suspects.

Few insights, if any, could be gleaned from the music press on reviewing the single. *Melody Maker* edged in favour of 'Never Let Go' on account of it "having a little more character", while *New Musical Express* simply noted the use of plucked strings and slower tempi.

The Seven then resumed a series of one-weekly variety appearances at venues in Shrewsbury, Newcastle and Liverpool (with Johnny Worth, Don Arrol, The Honeys, Larry Grayson and The Munro's). The start of the Newcastle week, on 30th May, was the final act of a manic period of performances, recordings, broadcasts – and even weddings! It's worth having a look in detail at what took place:

~

A FORTNIGHT IN THE LIVES OF 'THE JOHN BARRY SEVEN': 1960-style

Monday 16th May to Monday 30th May

Mon 16th:	*The Royal Variety Show (with Adam Faith) recorded*
Mon – Wed 16th-18th:	*Never Let Go film soundtrack recorded.*
Wed 18th:	*Easy Beat* (BBC Radio) – two episodes recorded.
Thu 19th:	Vic Flick's wedding.
Fri 20th:	*Easy Beat* (BBC Radio) – two episodes recorded.
Sat 21st:	*Saturday Club* (BBC Radio) – live appearance *Les Reed's wedding.* St Ermin's Hotel (London) – concert.
Sun 22nd:	*The Royal Variety Show (ITV) – broadcast.*
Mon 23rd:	Shrewsbury Granada – one week's engagement (with Adam Faith and co.).

A FORTNIGHT IN THE LIVES OF 'THE JOHN BARRY SEVEN': 1960-style

Monday 16th May to Monday 30th May

Wed 25th: 'When Johnny Comes Marching Home' recorded at
              Abbey Road for Parlophone (with Adam Faith).

Sun 29th: 'Blueberry Hill' and 'Never Let Go' recorded at
              Abbey Road for Columbia.

Mon 30th: Newcastle Empire – one week's engagement
              (with Adam Faith and co.).

Such was their popularity that Adam Faith and The JB7 were now lined-up to embark on what would be the highlight of the summer, headlining a twelve-week season at Blackpool Hippodrome. The show was first tested at The Globe, Stockton, before the entire cast assembled for what became a sell-out set of shows commencing on 24th June. The full line-up comprised of: Adam Faith; The John Barry Seven; Emile Ford with The Checkmates; Morton Fraser's Harmonica Gang; The Lana Sisters; The Marie De Vere Dancers; Van Dam and His Orchestra, with compère Don Arrol.

For the rhythm section of The Seven, this was a particularly stamina-sapping experience, since they were also requisitioned to accompany every musician featured on stage as well as performing in their own right. So demanding was the schedule that other worldly distractions became something of a necessity; the only problem being that breaks were few and far between and had to be synchronised with split-second timing. Accordingly, a forty-minute window sandwiched between the first half finale and Adam Faith's closing appearance in the second half was soon identified by the band as 'snooker time'. This amounted to lightning quick visits to a local snooker hall situated a good few miles away. With cars parked strategically to accommodate this mad dash to the hall, it was nothing compared to the speed of departure back to the theatre, which was always left as late as was feasibly possible – arriving back on stage just in time to play the opening instrumental number before Adam was introduced. If members of the audience ever wanted to know the reason why the band was out of breath for the first part of Adam's act, this was it!

Negotiating notoriously unreliable stage props became somewhat of an occupational hazard for the band wherever they played whether on TV or on the stage. The Blackpool Hippodrome was no exception. Backstage sophistication amounted to nothing more than a series of manually operated ropes and pulleys back in 1960. The rostrum on which they would stand to start the show just prior to Adam Faith's entry on stage was a case in point. As the curtain went up and the band began playing a crowd-stirring instrumental, all seven members faced the audience head on. Once Faith was being introduced, it then split into two to form an inverted 'V' shape through which the star singer was able to make his dramatic entrance. Now, this all sounded good in theory, but more often than not, some mishap would inevitably scupper the plan: stagehands on either side might pull either too quickly or too slowly, but never as one, for example. The wheels might find an obstacle over which they couldn't roll or the cables simply refused to budge. What this meant for the musicians was a tricky and delicate balancing act, whilst simultaneously attempting to play instruments to a competent standard, which was by no means an easy task in light of these distractions and disruptions. For Vic Flick, these were traumatic moments night after night: "I used to play standing up, balancing on one foot with my other foot on a volume/tone pedal. Some nights I had to leap from my rostrum onto the stage and then clamber back on – playing all the time. The experience was quite daunting and led to some forceful recriminations after the show, I must say. Having said that, Adam always put on a great show and the audience loved him."

The Stage made a number of pertinent sociological observations in its review of the show by alluding to the growing spending power afforded to the burgeoning baby boomers, who were forcing traditional theatrical entrepreneurs to move in an altogether completely different direction. No generation in history was enjoying the financial and personal freedom bestowed upon the 1960s teenager. Leslie Grade's 'Seeing Stars' presentation (as this show was billed in Blackpool) was a direct response to that fact, for this was a *bona fide* 'pop' package in all but name, purely and simply aimed at attracting the newly found 'wealth' acquired by a younger consumer now awash in disposable income by dint of earning money in a country virtually in full employment. Ironically, as a direct result of this approach, Variety (in its traditional form) was sewing the seeds of its own demise, because in wooing teenage culture in this manner, it was alienating its core audience, who were older in both age and outlook. Maybe a decision later in the year to attach Adam Faith to a pit band rather than The JB7 in future variety shows (as opposed to one-nighter 'pop' shows) was Eve Taylor's way of managing this dichotomy in an attempt to appease the purists and all parties concerned. Nevertheless, the 'pop' package tour was about to become Variety's son and heir and would reign supreme thereafter.

To quote *The Stage*'s glowing review. "The appeal of the 'Seeing Stars' show is beamed directly at the teenagers, for in Adam Faith and Emile Ford, its co-stars, they have two top pop recorders; the Lana Sisters are vocalists in the best modern tradition; and The John Barry Seven are among Britain's foremost modern groups of instrumentalists. The Morton Fraser Harmonica Gang is good fun for any type of audience but they also have a special teenage appeal. Adam Faith certainly excels in the tunes of today: casual, relaxed, but capable of swift transition into action, he sings with obvious sincerity and has a style that is distinctly his own while being recognisable as belonging to his generation. His appealing, at times slightly bewildered look, certainly gets over to the womenfolk. The John Barry

Seven, accomplished musicians to a man, give him wonderfully loyal and, at times, inspired support."

If teenagers *per se* were, indeed, 'never having it so good', then it was a golden era for young professional musicians with no ties, money in their pockets and a licence to travel. Not for them a regimented nine-to-five existence, six days a week; having to clock-in and clock-out with every second accounted for; nor the daily drudgery of production-line repetition or monotonous, mindless clerical filing. On the contrary, they were providing the escapism that the average working teenager was desperately seeking after a hard week's graft tied to the factory floor, building site or office. What's more, a musician could stay up late and sleep off any early morning excesses.

And what better way of celebrating one's 21st birthday than with a bunch of fellow troupers gallivanting throughout the night, which was precisely how Jimmy Stead marked his 'coming of age' (as it was termed back then) despite the consternation of a plethora of residents in Bispham (a suburb of Blackpool no more than one and a half miles from the town centre) where old friend Bill Marsden (and his group The Crescendos) had rented a house for the season and from where, as a favour, he had loaned the use thereof for the purpose of Jimmy's party. "I still have a local newspaper cutting that contains a report on neighbours complaining about the noise! Happy days, eh?", so reminisced Stead.

Even *The Stage* got wind of the fracas to the point of naming names and identifying the disreputable venue: "Jimmy Stead, baritone saxophonist of The John Barry Seven, didn't have a place large enough to accommodate his many friends, so he consulted Bill Marsden, leader of the locally based Crescendos instrumental/vocal group, of whose orchestra in Leeds he was once a member, for the loan of his rented house in Bispham. Bill was only too happy to co-operate. Party operations opened just before midnight and a lively pitch was maintained until five the next morning. It was a great success as whoopee-makers the Lana Sisters, Clinton Ford, the Checkmates, the Zio Angels, and members of the Barry Seven are prepared to testify. But you cannot suit everybody, as the anonymous letter delivered to the Crescendos at the Central Pier the following day goes to prove.

This read as follows: "'Dear Crescendos, If you must celebrate from midnight to milking time, perhaps you will be good enough to transfer the operations to the sea-end of the Central Pier. The fish may appreciate them more than we — Your Sleepless Neighbours.'" Evidently, Bispham and a rock 'n' roll lifestyle were not ideal bedfellows.

One highlight of the summer season was on being invited onto the bill of a one-off concert at the legendary Tower Ballroom, but for Vic Flick, however, the group's rather brief appearance there is now best renowned for a calamitous guitar string malfunction at a most inopportune moment. Playing to a packed house of several thousand people, The JB7 had been booked to provide an eight-minute medley of hits, which of course, necessitated several guitar solos. No sooner had the band started than Flick's second string broke as he launched into the second power chord as part of the opening salvo. Since the guitar had a built-in tremolo arm, the disruption caused by the breakage of one string affected all of the others, which meant that the guitar immediately went horribly out of tune. There was nothing else he could do but rush off stage in a frantic attempt to fit a new string, while Les Reed's piano took over the lead chores on the intro. Unfortunately, what should have been a simple operation turned out to be anything but, since for all his efforts, he could not dislodge the offending string. For what seemed like an eternity, it took the stage manager and a pair of enormous pliers to rip out it out, along with half of the main body's back plate. While all this was going on, Barry had instructed the rest of the band to indulge in some 12-bar improvisation, vamping and riffing to fill in the holes. By the time Flick returned on stage ("sweating like some wild animal," as he put it), he was just in time to play the very last chord! "And yet after all that," much to Flick's complete astonishment, "the audience crazily applauded the group's performance – which does makes one start to wonder."

To fulfil its radio commitments whilst the Blackpool season was in full swing, the band pre-recorded all their appearances on *Easy Beat*, as well as a *Saturday Club* slot on 16th July when they lined up with Adam Faith, Lance Fortune, The Zodiacs, The Bert Weedon Quartet, Bill Bailey's Hop County Boys and Mr. Acker Bilk's Paramount Jazz Band. Even ATV's *Val Parnell's Star Time* simply used footage from the Blackpool show to feature the main acts performing there: Adam Faith; Emile Ford; The John Barry Seven and The Lana Sisters. Also filmed in advance was an appearance on ATV's latest music extravaganza, *The Tin Pan Alley Show* on 25th June. On this particular edition The JB7 were joined by Jack Parnell and his Orchestra; The Kaye Sisters; Emile Ford and Lionel Bart.

Whilst performing day-in, day-out to a live audience remained the lifeblood of any working musician, this still had to be delicately balanced between recording, TV and radio commitments. Unless there was material already in the can, no artist could ignore a call for laying down new material. Given the insatiable clamour for more Adam Faith product at a time when no other singer (bar Cliff Richard) could claim to be as popular, then one can imagine the pressures exerted on Faith, Barry and The JB7 by EMI for them all being whisked back into Studio 2, Abbey Road at every conceivable opportunity. Hence, an overnight journey on a Saturday night from Blackpool to London, immediately after a 'Seeing Stars' show, was the order of the day to enable Adam Faith to record his next single ('How About That!'/'With Open Arms') and start his debut album (with 'A Girl Like You'). That Sunday, 14th August, was, therefore, no day of rest nor was the following Sabbath when the same six-hour session was repeated. As this clearly demonstrated, the recording process at that time had to be fitted in and around touring schedules. The idea of retreating to a recording studio for months on end would have been laughed out of the boardroom. Time meant money and if that

SIX-FIVE SPECIAL!

JOHN BARRY SEVEN · JIM DALE
JIMMY JACKSON · KING BROTHERS
KEN JONES · DON LANG
LAURIE LONDON · GEOFF LOVE
TONY OSBORNE · TERPY WAYNE
and THE RITA WILLIAMS SINGERS

PARLOPHONE

JACK GOOD'S 'OH BOY!'

WITH ACKNOWLEDGEMENTS TO THE HISTORIC A.B.C. TELEVISION PRODUCTION

mono

BBC's TELEVISION SHOW

DRUMBEAT

Music from the film

'BEAT GIRL'

'BEAT GIRL'

mono

JOHN BARRY
ADAM FAITH
SHIRLEY ANNE FIELD

COLUMBIA

SATURDAY CLUB

mono

PARLOPHONE

SATURDAY CLUB

(By Arrangement with the B.B.C.)

JOHNNY ANGEL
JOHN BARRY
TOMMY BRUCE
DANNY DAVIS
COLIN DAY
KEITH KELLY
JOHNNY KIDD
KING BROTHERS
GARRY MILLS
TONY OSBORNE
SYLVIA SANDS
RICKY VALANCE
BERT WEEDON

BLACKPOOL NIGHTS

mono

BLACKPOOL NIGHTS

those appearing

ALYN AINSWORTH · JOHN BARRY · EDDIE CALVERT
ALMA COGAN · TONI DALLI · REGINALD DIXON
ADAM FAITH · BRUCE FORSYTH · TEDDY JOHNSON & PEARL CARR
KEN MACKINTOSH · KEN MORRIS
RUBY MURRAY · PETERS SISTERS · JOAN SAVAGE

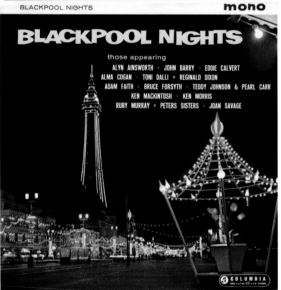

COLUMBIA

THE BIG BEAT

THE JOHN BARRY SEVEN

THE JOHN BARRY SOUND

THE JOHN BARRY SOUND

JOHN BARRY THEME SUCCESSES

mono

THE HUMAN JUNGLE

CUTTY SARK

THE JAMES BOND THEME

THE LOLLY THEME

FROM RUSSIA —WITH LOVE 007

EMB E.P. 4551

ember

THE JOHN BARRY SEVEN AND ORCHESTRA

JAMES BOND IS BACK

THE THEME MUSIC FROM THE FILM COMPOSED AND CONDUCTED BY JOHN BARRY

ZULU STAMP

EMB S 185

ember

THE JOHN BARRY SEVEN

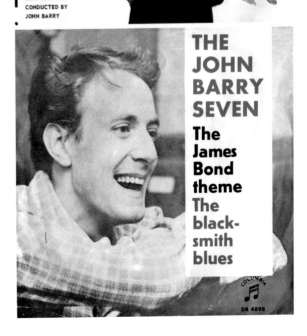

THE JOHN BARRY SEVEN

The James Bond theme
The blacksmith blues

DB 4898

The Stars Turn on
PARLOPHONE

ZIP ZIP
(Kaye Barnes)
JOHN BARRY AND THE SEVEN

78 R·P·M RECORD

BIG GUITAR
(De Rosa—Genovese)
THE JOHN BARRY SEVEN

EVERY WHICH WAY
(Torme)
THE JOHN BARRY SEVEN

Parlophone
DEMONSTRATION RECORD
NOT FOR SALE

THREE LITTLE FISHES
[Dowell]
JOHN BARRY AND THE SEVEN

FARRAGO
(White)
THE JOHN BARRY SEVEN

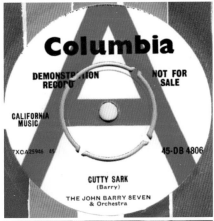

COLUMBIA

Columbia Graphophone Co.Ltd. · All rights of the Manufacturer and of the Owner of the recorded work reserved

CHAPPELL & CO.

7XCA 25124 45

RECORDING FIRST PUBLISHED 1960

MADE IN GT. BRITAIN

45-DB 4446

BEAT FOR BEATNIKS
(Barry)
JOHN BARRY
AND HIS ORCHESTRA

Unauthorised public performance, broadcasting and copying of this record prohibited

THIS RECORD MUST
BE PLAYED AT
45
R.P.M.

COLUMBIA

Columbia Graphophone Co.Ltd. · All rights of the Manufacturer and of the Owner of the recorded work reserved

FILMUSIC PUBLISHING CO. BIEM/NCB

7XCA 25185 45

RECORDING FIRST PUBLISHED 1960

MADE IN GT. BRITAIN

45-DB 4480

NEVER LET GO
(from film "Never Let Go")
(Barry)
JOHN BARRY AND
HIS ORCHESTRA

COLUMBIA

Columbia Graphophone Co.Ltd. · All rights of the Manufacturer and of the Owner of the recorded work reserved

MILLS MUSIC NCB

7XCA 25359 45

RECORDING FIRST PUBLISHED 1960

MADE IN GT. BRITAIN

45-DB 4554

BLACK STOCKINGS
(Barry)
THE JOHN BARRY SEVEN
with accompaniment directed
by John Barry

COLUMBIA **45** R.P.M.

B. FELDMAN & CO LTD.

7XCA 25999 45

RECORDING FIRST PUBLISHED 1963

45-DB 4941

THE LOLLY THEME
(from film "The Amorous Prawn")
(Barry)
JOHN BARRY SEVEN
AND ORCHESTRA

MADE IN Gt. BRITAIN

COLUMBIA **45** R.P.M.

ACTIVE MUSIC LTD.

7XCA 28054

Recording first published 1964

DB 7414

SOLD IN U.K. SUBJECT TO
RESALE PRICE CONDITIONS
SEE PRICE LISTS

TWENTY-FOUR HOURS AGO
(Suede)
JOHN BARRY SEVEN

MADE IN GT BRITAIN

meant cramming in as many unsocial hours as possible to cut a twelve-track LP, then that was how it would be.

Even more remarkable was the fact that The JB7, in between the Faith tracks, still managed to find time on the 14th to record their own new single, 'Walk Don't Run'/'I'm Movin' On', during the 6.30 p.m. – 9.30 p.m. session, having to use Studio 3 in which to do so. Both Barry and EMI were keen to have this all done and dusted in haste as a result of expectant competition from the very record on which The JB7's version was based, by The Ventures, whose own 45 had entered the US *Billboard* charts on 18th July (and would eventually sell two million copies in the US alone). There was no time to waste. Dougie Wright recalled how Barry had succeeded in obtaining an advanced demo copy of The Ventures' single before playing it to the band in the dressing room. "I loved it from the start," he clearly remembers, "and everyone thought it was great, so we immediately started to think about how best we could improve upon it. It was my idea to alter the drum introduction slightly to make it more interesting, and in the end I think our version had more urgency about it."

'Walk Don't Run', a jazz instrumental written by Alabama-born guitarist Johnny Smith, was picked up by Chet Atkins for inclusion on his 1957 LP, *Hi-Fi in Focus*, and it was this rendition, which would capture the imagination of The Ventures' lead guitarist Bob Bogle, whose use of vibrato would give the piece its distinctive hallmark twang. Barry clearly saw the potential in creating an anglicised version specifically for the UK market utilising Vic Flick's adept lead work. What's more, the field had been left clear at Columbia on account of The Shadows having turned it down in spite of them all admiring the track, according to bassist Jet Harris.

Vic Flick's overriding memory of recording 'Walk Don't Run' remains one of sheer dismay, for he was mortified to discover on listening to the vinyl for the first time that the wrong take had been used. This was all because of Barry's and/or Norman Newell's insistence on replicating Bob Bogle's tremolo arm effect. On this session, The Seven had been augmented with Eric Ford on rhythm guitar to add depth to the sound. Although each band part had been transcribed directly from The Ventures' 45, there was no original desire to ape Bogle's style until a change of heart ensued once the first take had been analysed in the control room. This meant Flick having to swap his own Clifford Essex Paragon acoustic for Ford's Gibson 375, simply because of the two axes, that was the one with the Bigsby tremolo arm attached. For Flick, adapting to the slim-bodied Gibson when used to a fat body acoustic was bad enough, but to throw in the tremolo arm under the pressure and glare of the 'red light' on-switch in the heat of the studio was enough to test the nerve of any seasoned pro. Consequently, he was absolutely distraught on later hearing his slightly over-cooked, off-key tremolo technique blaring out from the radio, for it was take two that the company had chosen to release. From Flick's standpoint, this was a rush release that was far too rushed.

An out-of-tune tremolo arm notwithstanding, what Flick failed to foresee was that 'Walk Don't Run' would prove to be The JB7's biggest selling single by amassing sales of 152,825, which easily matched the success of The Ventures' single in the UK as well as trouncing another cash-in cover by Rhet Stoller (on Decca). In terms of chart position, The Ventures peaked at No. 8 as opposed to The Seven at No. 11, but it was a mightily close call.

On reviewing the single, *Disc* foresaw the potential competition with Stoller's 45 while also alluding to the use of the pizzicato 'four' on the B-side, 'I'm Movin' On'. This was an instrumental cover of Hank Snow's 1950 country standard that had been successfully revived by Don Gibson in the USA when released in 1959 – a version that was produced by Chet Atkins. Clearly Bob Bogle was not the only one with his radar on what Atkins was doing in Nashville. *Record & Show Mirror* admired both sides in its characteristically clumsy style, enjoying the "frontal attack" of the "top-side" and the "pizzicato plunks" on the reverse. "For them that wants instrumental rock and wants it good – here it is," was its final summary.

If the first half of 1960 marked a dramatic change in fortune for The JB7, it was nothing in comparison to John Barry's own elevated standing within the executive corridors of the music business. Eve Taylor, throughout this period in the throes of re-negotiating Barry's recording contract with EMI, was now able to do so from a position of considerable strength in light of the phenomenal profits being generated by Adam Faith's 'What Do You Want' and 'Poor Me'. Moreover, The Seven's sudden sales surge was another bargaining chip to bring to the table. Not only that, but earlier in February, another Barry arrangement, Lance Fortune's 'Be Mine', had also taken the charts by storm albeit this time on a rival label, Pye. Unwittingly, Barry's chosen production style for Faith had suddenly become the yardstick by which the industry was now measuring future revenues. His recipe in the studio had become 'flavour of the month', his name a byword for success. Naturally, EMI was ultra keen therefore in tying Barry down to an exclusive recording and production contract that prevented him from working independently as he had done so under the pseudonym Johnny Prendy for the Lance Fortune record. In truth, the longer-term acquisition of Barry was more highly prized than that of The JB7, which is why his signing of a three-year deal was acclaimed as a major coup when it was announced to the media as August drew to a close. After taking several weeks mulling over the offer before taking the plunge, Barry couldn't contain his delight on claiming to have become one of the highest paid MDs in the business. The days of moonlighting under a thinly veiled assumed name were over!

Not that Barry minded one iota. For him, this was an ideal arrangement, since it gave him even greater latitude for experimentation. No longer simply one of a large roster of artists signed to the label, he was also now part of its core production team, given licence to augment The Seven whenever he saw fit from a wider pool of session players should the demands of an arrangement require it, whilst at the same time able to retain a nucleus of first-rate musicians to continue to promote his band as a live act outside the confines of the studio on stage, screen and radio. And in light of EMI's huge investment in him, there was little doubt that the name John Barry would also receive a higher profile than ever before (certainly in terms of media exposure) to the detriment of the rest of The JB7 from there on in. For example, reviews and features in future editions of EMI's own trade paper *Record Mail* would now inevitably focus on Barry, and Barry alone.

With the Blackpool season a distant memory, the rest of the year's diary was being rapidly filled with a series of live dates (either in variety, at charity concerts or 'pop' packages); numerous radio and TV assignments, and pressing recording commitments. There was no let-up. The JB7, now riding the crest of a wave, had managed to catch the musical *zeitgeist* perfectly, for 1960 ushered in what would eventually become known as the 'golden age of the instrumental'. Timing being all-important in the music business, The JB7's could not have been better. The rock 'n' roll 'old guard' (Elvis Presley, Chuck Berry, Little Richard, Jerry Lee Lewis and Buddy Holly) had been suddenly silenced, neutralised or exiled on account of draft board conscription, jail sentences, moral condemnation or early death. Something was needed to fill a gap in the market to satiate the ravenous hunger of an ever-growing number of young record buyers. Cliff Richard and Adam Faith may have captured the hearts of the 'teenybopper', but there was no denying the excitement generated by the sound of the electric guitar for any muso in search of an alternative.

In early September alone, The Shadows' 'Apache' and Duane Eddy's 'Because They're Young' were No 1 and No. 2 respectively and, as already documented, The JB7 and The Ventures both succeeded in reaching the Top Twenty with competing versions of the same composition. By the end of the year, no less than fifteen instrumentals had been placed amongst the top hundred selling singles of 1960; 'Apache' being the second best-seller on that list, eclipsed only by The Everly Brothers' 'Cathy's Clown'. In the UK, The Shadows and The JB7 were the undisputed brand leaders, as the *New Musical Express* Readers' Poll of that year would soon confirm. Published on 28th October (coincidentally on the same day the film *Beat Girl* was premiered at The London Pavilion), The Shadows topped the 'small group' section in amassing 14,673 votes compared to The Seven's 11,529 in the runners-up spot. Lonnie Donegan may have come third, but was some way off his competitors with a total of 3,333 votes. Bear in mind too that to register a preference in 1960 was not as straightforward as simply texting one's choice. The act of writing, then posting one's entry involved a far greater investment in time and effort. Less likely to have been done on a whim, the resultant straw poll was clearly a genuine reflection of the readership's current tastes.

Since changing their name from The Drifters (so as not to be confused with the more established American harmony group of the same name), The Shadows had gone from strength to strength. The universal appeal of 'Apache' had enabled them to steal a march on The JB7 (and every similar band of that ilk). Nonetheless, although Cliff and The Shadows would eventually surpass The JB7 in terms of fan base, longevity, influence, and sheer volume of hit records, throughout 1960 they were very much neck and neck in the popularity stakes (as the poll indicated). From EMI's (and, in particular, Columbia's) perspective, this was like manna-from-heaven, a rich harvest of a year; a rivalry – real or imagined – worth encouraging just so long as the yearly turnover continued on its upward trend. Barry's divergent interests would in time provide The Shadows with a clearer runway; a close-knit involvement with Cliff Richard via stage, film, television and pantomime would ultimately cement their all-round family appeal.

≈

As regards The Shadows, there was never any animosity between the two bands even though they were close rivals. As Mike Peters would confirm, they often compared notes over a convivial drink: "When 'Apache' first entered the charts, we were in Blackpool doing a Sunday special for TV, and as it happened, The Shadows were also around and so dropped in to see us. This enabled us all to have a morning celebration together over a few cans of ale they had brought with them. In fact, it was the first time we had ever drank out of a can. Hank Marvin and I often met up in London for the odd tipple or two during those days."

≈

Being the two biggest draws of the day, Cliff Richard and Adam Faith were rarely seen performing on the same bill, which is why when it did occur, the clamour for tickets was overwhelming. That's why promoters of charity events were all the more keen to see this happening, just as it did on 18th September when both singers performed at the Printers Pension Corporation Charity concert at The Royal Albert Hall, London, with The JB7 supporting Adam as well as performing their own set.

The autumn and winter months of 1960 were inevitably linked to the recording and stage demands of Adam Faith, with Eve Taylor fixing up a punishing string of dates from October right up to the middle of December. In all, no fewer than twenty-eight one-night stands had been arranged covering the length and breadth of England and Wales: from Carlisle to Devon, Cardiff to Cleethorpes. In addition, weekly residencies had been secured at the Birmingham Hippodrome (from 10th October); the Leeds Empire (24th) and the Sheffield Lyceum (31st). Monthly guest appearances on *Saturday Club* would also ensue.

But firstly, prior to all this and whilst in the throes of a week's stint at the Brighton Hippodrome, there was that little matter of Adam Faith's debut LP, *Adam*, to complete at Abbey Road. In its embryonic years, a 12-inch release was a luxury granted only to those considered able to sustain sales, or to those with proven pedigree. In Faith's case, the former applied, with pressure mounting to satisfy public demand. Such an eagerly awaited event had already been delayed by seven months on account of having to find room for recording amidst a relentlessly heavy workload, with only one track at that point already in the can. Consequently, throughout that week, the band's wagon could be spotted regularly hurtling up and down the London Road before and after the curtain call at the Hippodrome. Eleven Faith tracks were recorded on the 21st, 22nd and 23rd September with the Seven laying down 'Saturday's Child' – their one contribution to a forthcoming EMI album entitled *Saturday Club* that featured an array of artists who had regularly appeared on the programme. On this, a stripped down JB7 line-up was used, devoid of the brass section or pizzicato stings, comprising two guitars, bass, bass guitar, drums and piano; arguably the nearest they ever came to sounding like The Shadows.

One of those nights at the Leeds Empire was picked up on by *The Stage* whose reviewer, while noting a change in Faith's appearance and act, also highlighted the acclaim afforded to The Seven. Opening the second half of a bill comprising Joan and Paul Sharratt, Larry Grayson, The Honeys and Johnny Worth, The JB7 was described as "swift moving and lively" with this particular scribe blown away by the sheer scale of audience reaction, a genuine reluctance to let them leave amid "a storm of applause and whistling – a response that almost equalled that of the main idol of the evening, Faith himself."

On the eve of starting the November/December Adam Faith tour (11th November), The JB7 reconvened at Abbey Road with John Burgess for an evening shift to record the next single earmarked for the lucrative Christmas market; 'Black Stockings'/'Get Lost Jack Frost', both of which were Barry compositions. Although credited this time solely to The John Barry Seven on release (a lesson maybe learned), no fewer than twenty-three musicians were used on the session: twelve violins, four violas, two electric guitars, bass guitar, acoustic bass, drums, piano, xylophone at a total cost of £173. Once again, neither saxophones nor trumpet were deemed necessary, and as was becoming the norm, the fluid guitar work of Vic Flick dominated both sides, this time augmented by The Rita Williams Singers on the A-side and a perky xylophone part on the reverse. Released on 2nd December, 'Black Stockings' sold well enough to reach a creditable No. 27 in the charts, eventually selling 41,744 copies. With no discrepancy of identify, sales held up reasonably well. Indeed, Keith Fordyce, writing in the *New Musical Express*, was notably upbeat in his assessment and in unreservedly recommending 'Black Stocking' described Barry's 'stringbeat' blueprint as "a perfect example of the new trend and blend in pop music, and a welcome and interesting one, too," considering it "a more than worthy successor to Walk Don't Run." As for 'Get Lost Jack Frost', by juxtaposing electric lead guitar with xylophone, he stated, "John Barry contrives to weave new and unusual sounds."

Incidentally on release in the USA, 'Black Stockings' was indeed attributed rather more accurately to 'John Barry and His Orchestra' as opposed to 'The Seven', the marketing strategy there clearly different. According to Les Reed, he remembers Barry stating how he wrote 'Black Stockings' as an homage to his then-wife, Barbara: "a beautiful lady, who paid our wages every week!", he would add.

Among the more noteworthy dates in December's touring calendar was a one-off band-only appearance on 14th at that now famous Liverpool launch pad, The Cavern Club (Mathew Street), which up to as recently as 25th May, when the first all 'beat night' was staged (featuring Rory Storm and The Hurricanes), had been a strictly jazz-only venue. Although Lennon and McCartney had played there before playing skiffle as part of the Quarrymen during lunchtime sessions, The Beatles' first appearance was still two months away (9th February 1961). So while John Lennon was licking his wounds after returning four days earlier from Hamburg following the deportation of Paul McCartney and Pete Best for alleged arson and of George Harrison for being underage and lacking a work permit, The JB7 was already wowing the 'cellar full of noise' with its own brand of rock 'n' roll, supported by The Duke Duval Rockers plus Cass and The Cassanovas, who would later morph into The Big Three.

As Christmas arrived in readiness of an appearance on *Bernard Delfont's Sunday Show* on ATV (with Adam Faith) and then a prime-time spot on the Christmas Eve edition of *Saturday Club* (alongside Adam Faith, Lorrie Mann, The Brook Brothers, The Trebletones, Arthur Greenslade and The Gee Men, Mick Mulligan and His Band, and George Melly), The JB7 could look back on 1960 in utter wonderment at what had been a truly memorable year on both a professional and a personal level. No one month could epitomise this better than the one in May already alluded to when amid the whirligig surrounding a full-scale tour with Adam Faith, multiple appearances on *Easy Beat* plus *Saturday Club*, not to mention *The Royal Variety Show*, both Vic Flick and Les Reed got married (on 19th and 21st respectively) while Jimmy Stead met his wife-to-be Rita during a week in Shrewsbury. In terms of record sales (over 300,000 in total), The JB7 notched up five top Fifty singles (six if you count Adam Faith's 'Made You') and, in doing so, spent thirty-seven weeks in the charts throughout the year.

When Prime Minister Harold Macmillan described a "wind of change" blowing through Africa in speaking out against South Africa's system of apartheid on 3rd February 1960, he might just as well have been talking about the gathering storm swirling all around a music industry that was only just beginning, albeit begrudgingly, to open its doors to a younger generation with a different perspective on the world. For one veteran balladeer the writing was being indelibly daubed on the wall. Recognising the accent on youth, popular crooner and fifties hit maker, Jimmy Young, decided to bite the bullet in making a tentative career-changing move by presenting *Housewife's Choice* for a fortnight on The Light Programme during June. At 43 years old, John F. Kennedy became the youngest elected president of the USA. 'Out with the old and in with the new' appeared to be the prevailing mantra, with 1960 witnessing the last locomotive steam train being built as the diesel revolution began to take shape, whilst more cinemas and theatres closed down with the emergence of alternative interests such as ten-pin bowling and televised wrestling. The 1960s was up-and-running and starting to swing. For The JB7, staying at the top amid these changes was the challenge ahead.

THE JOHN BARRY SEVEN
plus FOUR
Hit and miss/Rockin' already
COLUMBIA 45-DB4414

EACH new issue by John Barry shows him as a truly remarkable young man. His career continues in an ever upward trend and, if not backing successful singers, he is making his own mark in the musical field. This latest, particularly "Hit and Miss", displays his musical talents to the full. The scoring is intriguing, impelling, and a wonderful contribution to the disc scene.

There's a special appeal too about his arrangement of "Rockin' Already".

JOHN BARRY
Blueberry hill/Never let go
COLUMBIA 45-DB4480

THIS is John Barry with his full orchestra, creating yet another fresh sound. Guitars take the melodic lead on the grand old melody topping the platter, the shimmering strings joining in later.

JOHN BARRY

It's another very danceable item on the other deck. Barry plays the theme from the new Adam Faith movie of the same name. A top disc for all the fans of Britain's brightest young music maker.

NOW No. 6 ! THE HIT VERSION of

WALK, DON'T RUN

BY THE

JOHN BARRY SEVEN

on Columbia 45 DB4505

136

Robin Jacques

DAY

Light Programme
1,500 m. (200 kc/s)   247 m. (1,214 kc/s)
VHF: Holme Moss 89.3 : Pontop Pike 88.5 : Douglas 88.4 : Sandale 88.1 Mc/s

6.45   1,500 m.
Greenwich Time Signal
Shipping Forecast

* * *

8.55 Your Holiday Weather
by the man from the 'Met' Office

9.0 Big Ben
'Jesus Christ is risen today'
SILVER CHORDS
with 'David'
Kelvin Thomas, Keith Griffin
The Silver Stars
Conductor, Hubert C. Williams
and the strings of the
BBC Welsh Orchestra
(Leader, Philip Whiteway)
Introduced by Dillwyn Owen
Programme arranged and
conducted by Rae Jenkins
(BBC recording)

9.30 News Summary
A SEQUENCE
of music for Easter
arranged by Denys Gueroult
(BBC recording)

Three | 2.40 to 5.0

464 m. (647 kc/s) 194 m. (1,546 kc/s)
VHF: Holme Moss 91.5
Pontop Pike 90.7 : Douglas 90.6
Sandale 90.3 Mc/s

4.0 CHESS
The One and the Many
Analytical comments on the
Simultaneous Display by
Svetozar Gligoric in January
2—Peter Clarke on
J. E. Littlewood v. Gligoric

The World Championship
Talks by Harry Golombek
6—From Alekhine to Botvinnik

* * *

Report from Moscow
The latest news of the
World Championship Match
between Tal and Botvinnik
(BBC recording)

4.30-5.0 TALKING ABOUT
MUSIC
Antony Hopkins
In this series of weekly programmes
Antony Hopkins usually discusses a
work to be broadcast during the week;
sometimes he goes further afield in his
choice of topic.
Repeated Monday at 9.25 a.m. (Home)

9.45 THE ARCHERS
(Omnibus Edition)
A story of country folk
Written by
Edward J. Mason and Geoffrey Webb
Edited by Godfrey Baseley
Daniel Archer................Harry Oakes
Doris Archer............Gwen Berryman
Jack Archer................Denis Folwell
Peggy Archer............Thelma Rogers
Philip Archer..........Norman Painting
Jill Archer................Patricia Greene
Christine Johnson......Lesley Saeward
Paul Johnson................Leslie Dunn
Walter Gabriel............Chris Gittins
Tom Forrest..................Bob Arnold
Pru Forrest..................Mary Dalley
Carol Grey..................Anne Cullen
John Tregorran............Basil Jones
Ned Larkin....................Bill Payne
Mabel Larkin..............Kay Hudson
Jimmy Grange..........Alan Rothwell
Mr. Grenville............Michael Shaw
Produced by Tony Shryane
(BBC recording)

10.30 EASY BEAT
with
The John Barry Seven
Plus Four
and Maureen Evans
Going Up!
Members of the audience comment
and give their opinion on three new
records
Folk Beat
with the Joe Gordon Folk Four
and Steve Benbow
Produced by Brian Matthew
(BBC recording)

11.0 TWENTY QUESTIONS
Anona Winn, Joy Adamson
Jack Train, Richard Dimbleby
and Gilbert Harding
Produced by C. F. Meehan
(Recording of last Tuesday's broad-
cast in the Home Service)
(' *Twenty Questions* is broadcast by
arrangement with Maurice Winnick)

11.30 PEOPLE'S SERVICE
for Easter Day
from the Church of the Holy
Ascension, Upton by Chester,
conducted by the Rev. Eric
Mercer, assisted by the vicar, the
Rev. J. Wheldon Williams
Those taking part . .
3—Sinner!
Organist, John Ross

11.55 1,500 m.: Shipping Forecast
247 metres and VHF: 'Good Listening
Some news of current programmes

12.0 Greenwich Time Signal
TWO-WAY
FAMILY FAVOURITES
Records for Service men and
women stationed abroad and their
families at home
Presented from London and Cologne
by Jean Metcalfe and Bill Crozier

1.15 THE BILLY COTTON
BAND SHOW
Laugh with the Cotton Boys
listen to
Alan Breeze and Kathie Kay
with The Bandits and
Mr. Wakey-Wakey (himself)
Script by Eddie Gurney
Produced by Glyn Jones

1.45 Bebe Daniels, Ben Lyon in
LIFE WITH THE LYONS
8—' The Stranger from Sorrento
(Last Wednesday's recorded broadcast)

2.15 Kenneth Horne in
BEYOND OUR KEN
A sort of radio show
Produced by Jacques Brown
(Last Friday's recorded broadcast)

2.45 MOVIE-GO-ROUND
A sound approach to the cinema
Introduced by Peter Haigh
and including
Around the British Studios
with Peter Noble
*Highlights from
Bottoms Up'* starring
Jimmy Edwards with Arthur Howard
A Few Words from Jack Cardiff
Director of ' Sons and Lovers '
Sounds Familiar (or otherwise)
to test your memory
of films old and new
Presented by
Desmond Carrington and Spencer Hale
*Pocket Edition
Please Don't Eat the Daisies*
starring Doris Day and David Niven
and co-starring Janis Paige
Spring Byington and Richard Haydn
Adaptation by Roy Bradford
Script by Trafford Whitelock
Programme edited and produced
by Alfred Dunning
(Recording)

3.30 Peter Yorke in
MELODY HOUR
featuring Andy Cole
Edward Rubach
and Robert Docker
and The Peter Yorke Orchestra
Introduced by Tony Raymont
Produced by Eric Arden
(BBC recording)

4.30 Trevor Martin
and Marjorie Westbury in
DR. BRADLEY REMEMBERS
The novel
by Francis Brett Young
arranged by Lionel Brown
PART 8
Emma................Marjorie Westbury
Dr. Bradley................Trevor Martin
Matthew................Brian Smith
Janet................June Tobin
Martin Lacey................Rolf Lefebvre
Wheelan................Charles Simon
George Perks................John Saunders
Produced by David H. Godfrey
(BBC recording)

Every Day. ' The French Have a Word
For It '; 7.45 a.m. (41.89 m., 7160 kc/s).
Monday to Friday. 10.0 p.m. (218 m.,
1376 kc/s). **Saturday and Sunday.** 2.0
p.m. (41.44 m., 7240 kc/s)
Sunday. 3.0 p.m. Mahler: Symphony No.
4, in G (Hilversum 402 m.)
3.45 p.m. *Les Cloches de Corneville:*
operetta by Planquette (France III, 280 m.)
6.0 p.m. RTF Philharmonic Orchestra
(France I, 1829 m., and France III, 280
m., in stereophony)
7.40 p.m. Light Classical Concert, conducted by Paul Bonneau (France III, 280 m.)
8.0 p.m. Vienna Symphony Orchestra,
with soloists (France I, 1829 m.)
8.45 p.m. Opera Concert (Hilversum 402
m.)
11.20 p.m. ' By the Blue Danube ' (France
I, 1829 m.)
Monday. 2.20 p.m. Radio Philharmonic
Orchestra, conducted by Bernard Haitink;
Theo Olof (violin): Mozart and Stravinsky
(*The Rite of Spring*) (Hilversum 298 m.)
4.25 p.m. *La Périchole:* operetta by Offen-
bach (France III, 280 m.)
8.5 p.m. RTF Philharmonic Orchestra
(France III, 280 m.)
8.15 p.m. Concertgebouw Orchestra: public concert (Hilversum 402 m.)

From the Continent

9.0 p.m. Opera Concert (Italian National
Programme 457, 334, 225 m.)
11.5 p.m. Reger (Serenade in G) and
Fortner (Movements) (Hamburg 309 m.)

Tuesday. 8.5 p.m. Chamber Music: Bach,
Beethoven, Schubert (France III, 280 m.)
8.20 p.m. Beethoven: Missa Solemnis (Hilversum 402 m.)
8.50 p.m. *Turandot:* opera by Busoni
(France I, 1829 m.)
11.25 p.m. Chavez (Toccata for Percussion) and Henze (Symphony No 3) (Hamburg 309 m.)

Wednesday. 8.30 p.m. Suisse Romande
Orchestra: Weber, Schubert Debussy,
Fortner, and Roussel (Sottens 393 m.)
10.0 p.m. Symphony Concert (Italian
Second Programme 355, 290, 269 m.)
10.25 p.m. Concerto No. 1, by Louis de
Meester (Brussels 324 m.)
10.50 p.m. ' Jazz at the Champs-Elysées '
(France I, 1829 m.)

Thursday. 8.5 p.m. Orchestre National,
conducted by D. E. Inghelbrecht (France
I, 1829 m.; France III, 280 m.)

8.5 p.m. Radio Chamber Orchestra:
Geminiani, Delden, Respighi (Hilversum
298 m.)
9.0 p.m. *Nabucco:* opera by Verdi (Italian
National Programme 457, 334, 225 m.)
9.30 p.m. Lausanne Chamber Orchestra:
Boccherini, Saint-Saëns, and Hindemith
(Sottens 393 m.)
Friday. 7.15 p.m. Radio Chamber Choir
(Hilversum 402 m.)
8.0 p.m. Two one-act operas: *Léonidas*, by
Pierre Wissmer; *Maître Patelin*, by Henry
Barraud (France III, 280 m.)
8.30 p.m. Promenade Orchestra: light
classical music (Hilversum 402 m.)
9.0 p.m. Turin Orchestra (Italian National
Programme 457, 334, 225 m.)
Saturday. 2.40 p.m. Chamber Music:
Gounod, Saint-Saëns (France III, 280 m.)
3.50 p.m. Radio Orchestra, with Jakob
Krachalnik (violin): Wieniawski (Concerto
No. 2) and Kodály (Hilversum 298 m.)
6.0 p.m. Organ Recital by Paul Ealry
(Brussels 324 m.)
8.0 p.m. ' La Vie Parisienne ' (France I,
1829 m.)
8.30 p.m. *Aida:* opera by Verdi (Italian
Second Programme 355, 290, 269 m.)
11.5 p.m. Vienna Festival Concert (France
III, 280 m.)

*Eve Taylor, who managed both
Adam Faith and The JB7.*

*Brian Matthew, who produced and presented
many BBC radio shows featuring The JB7.*

★ ★ ★ ★ **PROGRAMME** ★ ★ ★ ★

Star Cinemas in conjunction with Helena Presentations present

THE HIT PARADE SHOW

COMPÈRE
JIMMY TARBUCK
Friend of the Stars

JIMMY TARBUCK

introduces the DECCA RECORDING STAR
MIKE PRESTON
HIT RECORDER OF "MR. BLUE"

COLUMBIA RECORDING STARS
THE AVONS
high on the hit parade with . . . . .
"SEVEN LITTLE GIRLS SITTING IN THE BACK SEAT"

THE SENSATIONAL NEW SINGING STAR
EMILE FORD
AND THE CHECKMATES

— INTERVAL —

JIMMY TARBUCK

introduces BRITAIN'S No. 1 BEAT GROUP
THE JOHN BARRY SEVEN

and now

"WHAT DO YOU WANT?"
ADAM FAITH
Dynamic star of Films, TV, Radio and Parlophone Records

— FINALE —

Programme subject to alteration at the discretion of the Management.

The John Barry Orchestra

BEAT FOR BEATNIKS

and Big Fella

45-DB4446

COLUMBIA RECORDS

E.M.I. Records Ltd · 8-11 Great Castle Street · London W.1

Backstage with their award after the NME Pollwinners' concert in 1960.

Jimmy Stead, John Barry and Dennis King at a Royal Albert Hall concert presented by Roxy, Marilyn and Valentine magazines on 18th September 1960.

140

Publicity photos for the band's Blackpool summer season with Adam Faith and Emile Ford.

★★★

☆ **POLL-WINNERS' CONCERT PROGRAMME** ☆

Items to be selected from the following, but subject to alteration.

Billy Fury
Let's Play House   Collette   Break Up

The John Barry Seven
John Barry (leader-trumpet), Vic Flick (guitar), Doug Wright (drums), Mike Peters (bass), Jimmy Stead (baritone sax), Les Reed (piano), Dennis King (tenor sax).
Hit And Miss.   Peter Gunn.   When The Saints Go Marching In.
Red River Rock

The Mudlarks
Fishmonger's Song   Candy   Waterloo

Bert Weedon
Teenage Guitar   Guitar Boogie Shuffle   Big Beat Boogie

Cliff Richard
Living Doll, Voice In The Wilderness, I'm Walkin', Whole Lotta
Shakin' Goin' On, Baby I Don't Care, Love

Gene Vincent
Be-Bop-A-Lula.   Somewhere Over The Rainbow.   Wild Cat.
Say Mama

Russ Conway
Windows Of Paris, Forgotten Dreams, Side Saddle, Time After
Time, My Concerto For You, Royal Event

Craig Douglas
Only Sixteen   Pretty Blue Eyes   Sandy

Emile Ford
and The Checkmates
Emile Ford (leader), John Cuxsley (drums), Ken Street (electric guitar), George
Ford (electric bass).
What Do You Want To Make Those Eyes At Me For, Slow Boat
To China, Lucky Old Sun, You'll Never Walk Alone

Compere : PETE MURRAY ☆

The Dallas Boys
Baubles Bangles And Beads. Old Macdonald Had A Farm, I'm
Forever Blowing Bubbles, A Nightingale Sang In Berkeley Square

Eddie Cochran
C'mon Everybody, Hallelujah I Love Her So, Sweet Little Sixteen,
Somethin' Else

Alma Cogan
You Do Something To Me   I Love To Sing   We Got Love

Lonnie Donegan and his
Skiffle Group
Lonnie Donegan (leader/guitar banjo/vocals), Les Bennetts (guitar),
Peter Huggett (bass), Nick Nicholls (drums).
Battle Of New Orleans, Rock My Soul, San Miguel, Fancy Talking
Tinker, Talking Guitar Blues, John Hardy

PRESENTATION OF AWARDS

Ted Heath and his Music
Ted Heath (leader), Bobby Pratt, Bert Ezard, Duncan Campbell, Eddie Blair
(trumpets), Don Lusher, Wally Smith, Johnny Edwards, Ken Goldie (trombones),
Leslie Gilbert, Ronnie Chamberlain, Henry Mackenzie, Bob Efford, Ken Kiddier
(saxes), Derek Warne (piano), Johnny Hawksworth (bass), Ronnie Verrell (drums).
Cherokee, Tuxedo Junction, From This Moment On, Sing Sing
Sing, Skin Deep, Flying Home, Rhapsody For Drums

Marty Wilde
Mack The Knife,   In Love Again,   Donna,   Old Black Magic,
Just A Little Too Much

BOB MILLER AND THE MILLERMEN

Gene Vincent and Eddie Cochran appear by arrangement with Larry Parnes

★★★

JOHN BARRY
Walk don't run/I'm movin' on
COLUMBIA 45-DB4505

HERE'S another Columbia side bound for the top. The
number comes from the States, but it's a tremendous
treatment by the Barry Seven that makes it. Lots of guitars and
beat pound along at a medium pace for some music that is ideal
for dancing or just listening.

The seven becomes the eleven on the other side as the violins
move in. In parts, it sounds like the fine backings he's provided
for Adam. Another exciting side.

TODAY'S PROGRAM

1. JOHN BARRY SEVEN   *Columbia Recording stars*

2. JULIE RAYNE   *H.M.V. recording star—*
   the new singing star

3. MIKE MARTIN   *your comedy compere*

4. LITTLE TONY   *Decca recording artiste and*
   star of "Boy Meets Girl"

★interval

5. JOHN BARRY SEVEN

6. THE LIDDELL TRIPLETS   *Glamorous and*
   tuneful trio

7. WHAT DO YOU WANT?

ADAM FAITH
Parlophone record star
and star of T.V., films and radio

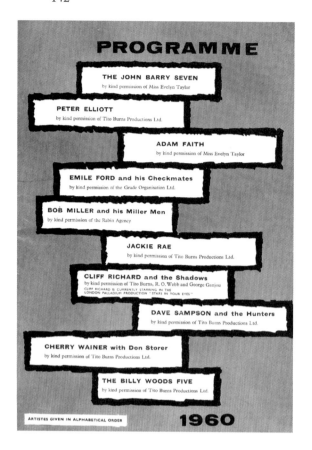

PROGRAMME

THE JOHN BARRY SEVEN
by kind permission of Miss Evelyn Taylor

PETER ELLIOTT
by kind permission of Tito Burns Productions Ltd.

ADAM FAITH
by kind permission of Miss Evelyn Taylor

EMILE FORD and his Checkmates
by kind permission of the Grade Organisation Ltd.

BOB MILLER and his Miller Men
by kind permission of the Rabin Agency

JACKIE RAE
by kind permission of Tito Burns Productions Ltd.

CLIFF RICHARD and the Shadows
by kind permission of Tito Burns, R. O. Webb and George Ganjou
CLIFF RICHARD IS CURRENTLY STARRING IN THE
LONDON PALLADIUM PRODUCTION "STARS IN YOUR EYES"

DAVE SAMPSON and the Hunters
by kind permission of Tito Burns Productions Ltd.

CHERRY WAINER with Don Storer
by kind permission of Tito Burns Productions Ltd.

THE BILLY WOODS FIVE
by kind permission of Tito Burns Productions Ltd.

ARTISTES GIVEN IN ALPHABETICAL ORDER

1960

THE BBC LIGHT PROGRAMME

presents

SATURDAY CLUB
'Jazz and Rock'

with

Mr. Acker Bilk's Paramount Jazz Band

Terry Lightfoot's New Orleans Jazzmen

The John Barry Seven

and

Adam Faith	Al Saxon	Craig Douglas
Cuddly Duddly	Betty Smith	The Five Dallas Boys
The Lana Sisters	Miki and Griff	Diz Disley
Clinton Ford	George Chisholm	Bert Weedon
Dill Jones	Eric Silk	Ike Isaacs
Sylvia Sands		Ken Jones

compère: **Brian Matthew**

production by **Jimmy Grant and Terry Henebery**

Programme

WINIFRED ATTWELL ❀ **SHIRLEY BASSEY** ❀ **JOHN BARRY SEVEN**

ALMA COGAN ❀ **LONNIE DONEGAN** ❀ **ROBERT EARL** ❀ **ADAM FAITH**

DAVE LEE ❀ **DENNIS LOTIS** ❀ **VERA LYNN** ❀ **JOAN REGAN**

CLIFF RICHARD ❀ **DICKIE VALENTINE**

PROGRAMME SELLERS

Avril Angers, Audrey Bishop, Liz Bresslaw
Jill Browne, Maudie Edwards
Elspet Gray, Diane Hart, Hattie Jacques
Rena Lotis, Monti Mackey
Pamela Manson, Carol Marsh, Stella Moray
Margaretta Scott, Gay Sharples
Liz Valentine

MUSICAL DIRECTORS

Tony Osborne, Norrie Paramor
Woolf Phillips, Cyril Stapleton
Bob Sharples

PRODUCER

Dick Hurran

There will be an interval of 15 minutes.

BUSKERS

Frederick Bartman, John Blythe
Bernard Bresslaw, Tito Burns
Max Geldray, Donald Houston, David Kossoff
John Le Mesurier, Francis Matthews
Brian Rix, Peter Sellers, Ronald Shiner
John Slater, Edward Underdown
Tony Wright

Empire Pool
WEMBLEY

5 FOCUS ON YOUTH

Produced by Jack Good

with

LONNIE DONEGAN

and the

LONNIE DONEGAN GROUP

LES BENNETTS
PETER HUGGETTS
NICK NICHOLLS

ADAM FAITH

with the

JOHN BARRY SEVEN

JOHN BARRY	DENNIS KING	JIMMY STEAD
VIC FLICK	MIKE PETERS	DUGGIE WRIGHT
	LES REED	

CLIFF RICHARD

and the
SHADOWS

JET HARRIS
HANK MARVIN
TONY MEEHAN
BRUCE WELCH

THE VERNONS GIRLS

Dance Direction: LESLIE COOPER

A page from the Royal Performance souvenir brochure.

The John Barry Seven rehearsing for The Tin Pan Alley Show.

EASYBEAT – SUNDAY 10.4.1960

Pre-recorded 23.3.1960 – TLO 13533

With: The John Barry Seven Plus Four
Maureen Evans
Dorita Y Pepe
Steve Benbow

JOHN BARRY SEVEN PLUS FOUR
Signature tune: Easy Beat

JOHN BARRY SEVEN
Black Bottom

DORITA Y PEPE
La Mucura

MAUREEN EVANS &
JOHN BARRY SEVEN
I Enjoy Being A Girl

JOHN BARRY SEVEN PLUS FOUR
Theme From A Summer Place

GOING UP? – Panel: Bob Knight / Barry Peacock /
Trevor Peacock / Syd Green

RECORDS (DUBBED):

ADAM FAITH
Someone Else's Baby

MIKE PRESTON
A Girl Like You

DAVY JONES
Amapola

DORITA Y PEPE
En De Que Te Vi

MAUREEN EVANS &
JOHN BARRY SEVEN PLUS FOUR
Do You Mind?

STEVE BENBOW
O'Rafferty's Pig

JOHN BARRY SEVEN
Manhunt

JOHN BARRY SEVEN PLUS FOUR
Signature tune: Easy Beat

Produced by Brian Matthew

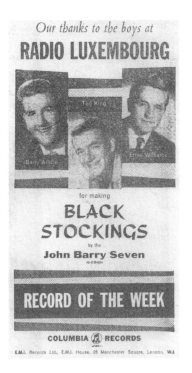

EASYBEAT – SUNDAY 17.4.1960

Pre-recorded 4.4.1960 – TLO 12832

With: The John Barry Seven Plus Four
Maureen Evans
Joe Gordon Folk Four
Steve Benbow

JOHN BARRY SEVEN PLUS FOUR
Signature tune: Easy Beat
Rockin' Already

JOE GORDON FOLK FOUR
Borrow My Nut Brown Maiden

MAUREEN EVANS &
JOHN BARRY SEVEN
Autumn Leaves

JOHN BARRY SEVEN
Two Way Stretch

GOING UP? – Panel: Ian Ralphini / Roger
Clifford / Matt Monro / Bob Knight

RECORDS – DUBBED:

GORDON JENKINS ORCHESTRA
& CHORUS
The Clock Song

JOHN BARRY AND HIS ORCHESTRA
Beat For Beatniks

DORIS DAY
Any Way The Wind Blows

JOE GORDON FOLK FOUR
By The Bright Shining Light Of The moon

MAUREEN EVANS &
JOHN BARRY SEVEN PLUS FOUR
But Not For Me

STEVE BENBOW
The Spinning Wheel

JOHN BARRY SEVEN PLUS FOUR
Like Young
Signature tune: Easy Beat

Produced by Brian Matthew

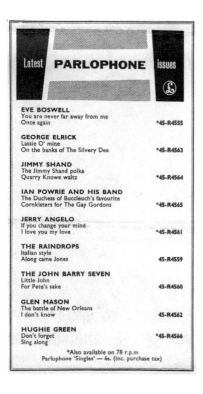

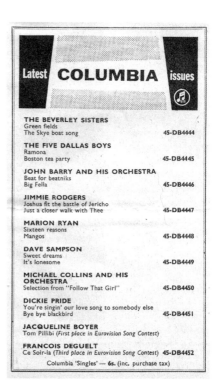

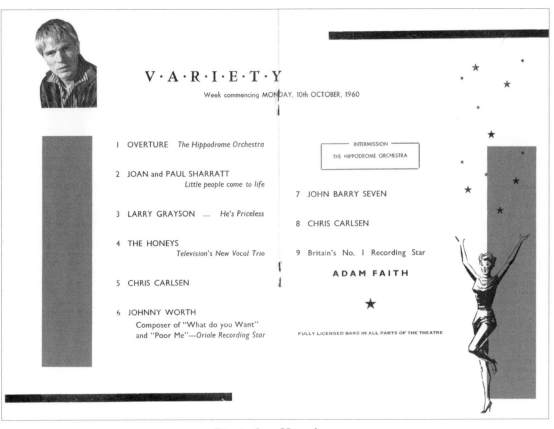

V·A·R·I·E·T·Y

Week commencing MONDAY, 10th OCTOBER, 1960

1 OVERTURE   *The Hippodrome Orchestra*

2 JOAN and PAUL SHARRATT
   Little people come to life

3 LARRY GRAYSON ... *He's Priceless*

4 THE HONEYS
   Television's New Vocal Trio

5 CHRIS CARLSEN

6 JOHNNY WORTH
   *Composer of "What do you Want"
   and "Poor Me"—Oriole Recording Star*

INTERMISSION
THE HIPPODROME ORCHESTRA

7 JOHN BARRY SEVEN

8 CHRIS CARLSEN

9 Britain's No. 1 Recording Star

ADAM FAITH

FULLY LICENSED BARS IN ALL PARTS OF THE THEATRE

Birmingham Hippodrome

HIPPODROME - BLACKPOOL Telephone 24233

Proprietors:
Associated British Cinemas Ltd.

Managing Director:
D. J. Goodlatte

Assistant Managing Director:
W. Cartlidge

Licensee and Manager: Harold Jarvis

LESLIE GRADE presents

"SEEING STARS"

A FABULOUS FAST-MOVING STARAMA OF TALENT AND FUN

"SEEING STARS"
with
THE MARIE DE VERE DANCERS
Who in turn introduce Our Compere
DON ARROL
Who with the help of the Girls presents
THOSE DYNAMIC SINGING SISTERS
THE LANA SISTERS
* * *
COMEDY FLASH with
MORTON FRASER'S HARMONICA GANG
A Riot of Fun and Music
* * *
DON ARROL
This Up and Coming Comedian
* * *
The One and Only
EMILE FORD
with
THE CHECKMATES
Hit Recorders of " What Do You Want To Make Those Eyes At Me For ? " and
" Slow Boat To China "
* * *
— INTERVAL —

"GUYS & DOLLS"
with
THE MARIE DE VERE DANCERS
* * *
DON ARROL
Sets the scene
* * *
"A WESTERN BAR"
with
THE BAR-ROOM HOSTESSES
and
THE MORTON FRASER GANG
INTRODUCING THE
JOHN BARRY SEVEN
Jimmy, Dennis, John, Douglas, Mike, Vic and Les
The Number One Recording Star of " What Do You Want " and " Poor Me "
ADAM FAITH
With The Inspired Backing of
THE JOHN BARRY SEVEN
VAN DAM AND HIS ORCHESTRA
* * * * * *
THE SHOW STAGED BY ALBERT J. KNIGHT
DANCES BY MARIE DE VERE

Company Manager .... (For The Grade Organisation Ltd.) .... Sid Maurice
Stage Director .... (For A.B.C. Cinemas Ltd.) .... Owen Pryce

RULES AND REGULATIONS in accordance with the requirements of the Blackpool Corporation.
(a) The public may leave at the end of the performance by all exits and entrances other than those used as queue-waiting rooms, and the doors of such exits and entrances shall at that time be open.
(b) All gangways, passages and staircases shall be kept entirely free from chairs or any other obstructions.
(c) Persons shall not be permitted to stand or sit in any of the intersecting gangways. If standing is permitted at the rear of the seating, sufficient space shall be left for persons to pass easily to and fro.
(d) The safety curtain shall at all times be maintained in working order, and shall be lowered at the beginning of and during the time of every performance.

Autographed programme from the Blackpool Hippodrome season.

Dennis, Jimmy and Dougie in Blackpool.

Saxophonists Jimmy Stead and Dennis King "seeing stars" in Blackpool!

THE JOHN BARRY SEVEN

Blueberry Hill Never Let Go	DB4480
Beat for Beatniks Big Fella	DB4446
Hit and Miss Rockin' Already	DB4414
Twelfth Street Rag Christella	R4582
Little John For Pete's Sake	R4560
Long John Snap 'n' Whistle	R4530
Farrago Bee's Knees	R4488
The Big Beat E.P....	GEP8737
The Beat Girl L.P. ... ... (from the Soundtrack)	33SX1225

JOHN BARRY SEVEN FAN CLUB

c/o Starcast,
14 Great Russell Mansions,
60 Great Russell Street,
London, W.C.1.

E.M.I. Records Ltd.

Dennis and Jimmy relaxing in Blackpool.

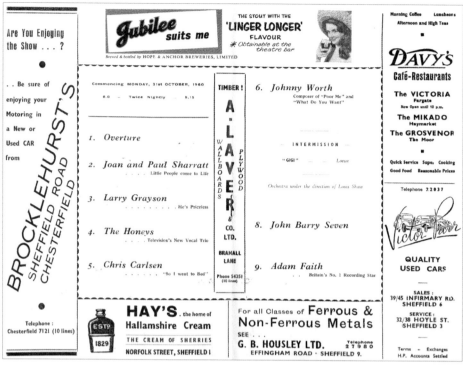

Commencing MONDAY, 31st OCTOBER, 1960

8.0   —   Twice Nightly   —   8.15

1. Overture
2. Joan and Paul Sharratt . . . . Little People come to Life
3. Larry Grayson . . . . He's Priceless
4. The Honeys . . . . Television's New Vocal Trio
5. Chris Carlsen . . . . . "So I went to Bed"

6. Johnny Worth
Composer of "Poor Me" and "What Do You Want"

INTERMISSION

"GIGI" . . . . . Loewe

Orchestra under the direction of Louis Shae

8. John Barry Seven
9. Adam Faith . . Britain's No. 1 Recording Star

Success ! Success !

The Story of the John Barry Seven begins when bandleader Vic Lewis heard the group when he played a one-night concert date in York, with the fabulous 'Platters' vocal group. He was so impressed that he enthused about them to Johnnie Ray. The result . . . when Johnnie played a concert in York on April 7th, backed by the Lewis Orchestra, the 'John Barry Seven' had a big spot in the show. Again, the reaction was sensational! And the loudest applause of all came from a dressing-gowned figure standing in the wings—Johnny Ray !

When Johnnie went back to London, next day, he was full of praise for the 'Seven'. Word reached the ears of agents Lew and Leslie Grade. . . . Then ace showman Val Parnell heard about them. A few days later, the boys were on their way to London . . . and an audition at the London Palladium for Val Parnell's commercial TV show, "Startime". They passed with flying colours ! Said Mr. Parnell: "I like the boys very much".

While in London, the 'Seven' had a private recording session . . . and cut six discs.

Yes the Boys with Britain's freshest Beat "Had Arrived ! "

Birmingham Hippodrome concert programme.

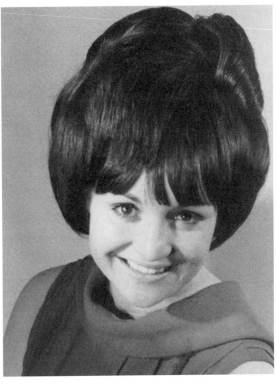

*Julie Rayne, who toured with The JB7 during 1960
and helped initiate "Water Pistol Wars"!*

*Maureen Evans, who starred in Easy Beat,
when she was accompanied by The JB7.*

john barry 7

Photo by courtesy of Record and Show Mirror

JOHN BARRY (leader-trumpet)
VIC FLICK (guitar)
DOUG WRIGHT (drums)
MIKE PETERS (bass)
JIMMY STEAD (baritone sax)
LES REED (piano)
DENNIS KING (tenor sax)

With their successful record releases, and their stage, radio, and TV appearances, John Barry and The Seven have built themselves a great following. During his army service, John had played with a military band and studied orchestration and composition. Then he had the idea of forming his rocking "Seven" in a jazz club. He got in touch with some of his army friends. After intensive rehearsals in an 18th-century barn they cultivated the "freshest beat" in Britain.

Shortly afterwards the "Seven" were discovered by top impresario Val Parnell. Harold Fielding went to Blackpool to book them on the spot. On tour, The John Barry Seven got a tremendous "hand" wherever they played. In London, they stopped long enough to cut six records, two of them original compositions by John—"We All Love to Rock" and "Rock-a-Billy Boogie." Johnny Dankworth said, "He has a great future ahead of him."

A record contract soon followed, with Parlophone, and their first disc, "Zip Zip" and "The Three Little Fishes," was released. It displayed their talents to the utmost and showed that The John Barry Seven had really arrived. John Barry has also won acclaim for directing the musical accompaniment for such recording artists as Adam Faith, The England Sisters, and Johnny Gavotte.

February 5, 1960   RADIO TIMES   23

TELEVISION PROGRAMMES

SATURDAY EVENING

FEBRUARY 13

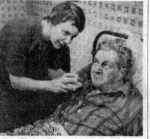

Maureen Pryor and Rupert Davies

SATURDAY PLAYHOUSE PRESENTS

'GOING LIKE A FOX'

A disgraced politician—something of a rogue, something of a hero—spends the last day of his life as he has lived it, scheming and plotting with ruthless disregard for the feelings of those around him. He dominates the whole household, an inescapable influence whose only saving graces are his uncomplaining courage and humour, but that too, is seen in a different light when his niece, a woman of solid substance, takes a sudden and romantic decision to free herself from the people who stand in her way.

The play, a contemporary tragedy, has qualities of violence and realism which relate it to the real problems of our time.

AT 8.40

6.0 JUKE BOX JURY
Presenting
before a young audience
the latest in popular records
with the opinions of
**Pete Murray, Alan Freeman
Carolyn Townshend, Esmée Clinton**
In the chair,
David Jacobs
The programme devised by
Peter Potter
Presented by Russell Turner
See page 9

6.28 YOUR SUNDAY WEATHER

6.30 JACK WARNER
as
DIXON OF DOCK GREEN
Stories of a London Policeman
by TED WILLIS
'The Slinger and the Slush'
Characters in order of appearance:
P.C. George Dixon........JACK WARNER
Sergeant Flint.............ARTHUR RIGBY
Cadet Jamie MacPherson
...........................DAVID WEBSTER
Mr. Norden..............ANTHONY WAGER
Mr. Bakewell.................JOHN LEWIS
Sgt. Grace Millard......MOIRA MANNION
Det.-Sgt. Andy Crawford.PETER BYRNE
Mary..............JEANNETTE HUTCHINSON
P.C. Lauderdale........GEOFFREY ADAMS
Tony Beeny............MALCOLM KNIGHT
Edith Beeny...............EDNA MORRIS
Marion Wiltshire...VERONICA TURLEIGH
Sailor......................BRYAN DREW
P.C. Nightingale.......DAVID PHETHRAN
Bill Jordan.............PATRICK NEWELL
Slim Vachos.............WALTER RANDALL
Designer, Malcolm Goulding
Production by DOUGLAS MOODIE

7.0 'LARAMIE'
A Western film series, starring
**JOHN SMITH, ROBERT FULLER
ROBERT CRAWFORD, Jnr.**
and
HOAGY CARMICHAEL
in
'The Legend of Lily'
Guest star,
CONSTANCE MOORE
The men of the Sherman ranch are always ready to help people in trouble, but when they go to the aid of a lady in distress who is a beautiful actress their efforts cause unexpected results.

**7.50 THE
JIMMY LOGAN SHOW**

with
**THE KING BROTHERS
THE CARLU CARTER TRIO
NINA AND FREDERIK**
The George Mitchell Singers
The Dancers:
Pamela Barrie, Elaine Carr
Sandra Hampton, Isabelle Mileno
Anna Sharkey
Elaine Skelton, Ann Talbot
Script by
TERRY NATION and JOHN JUNKIN
Original lyrics and music by
Peter Myers and Ronald Cass
Orchestra directed by
Malcolm Lockyer
Designer, Cephas Howard
Produced by BRYAN SEARS
(Nina and Frederik were specially filmed for the BBC by the Danish Television Service)

8.35 NEWS SUMMARY

**8.40 SATURDAY
PLAYHOUSE**
presents
**RUPERT DAVIES
MAUREEN PRYOR**
and
RALPH MICHAEL
in
'GOING LIKE A FOX'
A tense drama of family life
by ALUN RICHARDS
Production by David J. Thomas
Cast in order of appearance:
Jeffrey Harris.............PETER GILL
Jeanie.....................JOY LEMAN
Mrs. Harris...........MAUREEN PRYOR
Councillor Harris.......RUPERT DAVIES
Glyn Harris............RALPH MICHAEL
Captain Jenkins........BECKETT BOULD
Mr. Watkin...........LLYWELLYN REES
Film cameraman, Bill Greenhalgh
Film editor, Terry Laurie
Designer, Alan Taylor
From the BBC's Welsh studio
(BBC recording)

10.0 SPORTS SPECIAL
featuring Football
Introduced by
Kenneth Wolstenholme
Sportsview film cameras
bring you today's sport tonight
Among the films it is hoped to include:
ASSOCIATION FOOTBALL
EVERTON v.
WOLVERHAMPTON WANDERERS
RUGBY LEAGUE CHALLENGE CUP
First round:
ST. HELEN'S v. WAKEFIELD
RUGBY UNION:
England v. Ireland
Programme edited by Ronnie Noble
Presented by A. P. Wilkinson
Viewers whose sets are tuned to Kirk o' Shotts will see Sports Special from Scotland from 10.0-10.30

10.30 SMALL WORLD

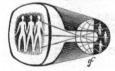

An inter-continental conversation
THE SPEAKERS:
In Washington:
Senator Mike Mansfield
A member of the United States Senate Foreign Relations Committee
In Paris:
Jean-Jacques Servan-Schreiber
Editor of a Paris newspaper
In New York:
Emmet John Hughes
Chief of Foreign Correspondents
for *Time-Life*
The host in Geneva:
Edward R. Murrow
THE TOPICS:
Defence, the future of NATO American politics and foreign policy
Produced for CBS Television
by EDWARD R. MURROW
and FRED W. FRIENDLY

10.55 NEWS SUMMARY
Weather and Close Down

The John Barry Seven was heard weekly on BBC TV's Juke Box Jury for many years, via its theme tune, 'Hit and Miss'.

5

THE MAGNIFICENT SEVEN

JANUARY – DECEMBER 1961

*With such a busy concert schedule, The Seven got used to driving
into towns with no idea where we were playing until
we saw the advertising posters.*

– Vic Flick (lead guitar/leader in waiting)

*Once, when driving between gigs on a deserted Irish road, we came
across a donkey. Our driver, Nuggy, stopped the bus and out we
got hoping to befriend it. Fortunately, this was a people-friendly
animal, but with every failed attempt at mounting it meeting
with more and more hilarity, the task became harder and harder.
However, I did manage to succeed in the end and Mike took a photo
for posterity. We had so many laughs on those Irish tours.*

– Jimmy Stead (baritone sax)

As Big Ben chimed for the twelfth time to usher in 1961, the farthing coin
was no longer legal tender, National Service conscription was formally ended,
and The John Barry Seven were now *bona fide* pop stars. In the role of Adam
Faith's court musicians, they were experiencing mass adulation by association
on a grand scale, playing to screaming audiences night after night in packed-out
venues throughout the country. 'Black Stockings' was still lodged firmly in the
Top Fifty where it would remain for nine weeks. Barry, Faith and Eve Taylor
hosted a lavish party at Barry's new Coleherne Court apartment to celebrate
these achievements. The juggernaut – or more accurately the band's wagon – was
rolling on relentlessly with the coming year looking all the more likely to be as
rosy as the last. However, a decision made by its leader involving a change in
personnel during September would have lasting repercussions that would change

the internal dynamic of the band irrevocably, and one which would ultimately alter their status in pop's hierarchy.

During the early part of the year, though, the band were playing the 'pop game' impeccably, the result of which even saw them appearing in the myriad of magazines that had flooded the market between 1956 and 1960 aimed at the young female consumer. Titles such as *Mirabelle, Romeo, Valentine, Jackie, Boyfriend, Princess, Judy, Marty, Honey* and *Date* sold in spectacular quantities during this period. In fact, *Valentine*, the brand leader, sold in excess of 400,000 copies per week! One such example was the 11th February edition of *Roxy* (published by Amalgamated Press from 1958 to 1963), which under the headline "Meet The Fellas!" featured Barry (as ever the sole interviewee) introducing the rest of the band to its readership. Here we learned that Dennis King loved photography; Mike Peters, curries; Les Reed, cars; Jimmy Stead, food; Dougie Wright, practical jokes, and Vic Flick, (not surprisingly) guitars. Barry also revealed that the band's current stage uniform consisted of colour-coded jerseys; anyone who saw The JB7 live in 1961, therefore, would have witnessed Vic in red, Dougie in green, Mike in mauve, Les in dark blue, Dennis in light blue and Jimmy in navy blue. Such minutiae formed the staple diet of any star-struck teenage magazine at that time.

Recording, stage and radio commitments continued unabated throughout the early months of the year. Towards the end of January, The Seven played a Sunday concert at The Coventry Theatre with Faith and a new hopeful by the name of Gerry Dorsey, who since November had become a regular name on the bill and whose presence was inextricably linked to the time and investment both Barry and EMI were about to lavish on the singer's fledgling recording career. The significance attached to friendships struck up with the rest of the band, and in particularly Les Reed, would not have seemed in any way special to the twenty-four-year-old touring the provinces as the apprentice in this particular entourage. Sitting in that Midlands dressing room, Dorsey could never ever have envisaged that by the end of 1967 – in his new guise as Engelbert Humperdinck – he would have recorded the two biggest singles of that year... and that the architect of the second of these, 'The Last Waltz', would turn out to be that piano playing, card school mate of his in The JB7. For Dorsey/Humperdinck, touring with the band was to be an invaluable learning experience and a reminder of just how far he had travelled on his own personal journey towards the top. "We had some fun times," he would later recall, "moving from here to there in shabby buses that always smelled of our aftershaves and hair creams."

It wasn't until February before the year got fully into gear. In between a string of one-night dates (Loughborough, Nantwich and Birmingham included), the band were back on the radio recording an edition of *Saturday Club* that was broadcast on the 4th with Barry's latest protégé Johnny De Little; The Rabin Band; The Quintetto Italian, and Riddell, Frazer and Hayes. Within three days of this appearance, the touring was once again interrupted by an evening at Abbey Road busily cutting both sides of the next single. The A-side was a version of Elmer Bernstein's memorable main theme to *The Magnificent Seven*, which was a gift of a 'made-to-measure' signature tune for a band comprising of seven members. Given the huge popularity of the film, this ought to have been a heaven-sent chart opportunity, but an uncharacteristically lacklustre and undercooked performance produced only moderate sales of 48,025. True, competition from American Al Caiola – an altogether bigger-sounding record – may have divided sales, but it was noticeable that the rival's version grabbed the higher chart placing – 34 against 48. Writer and musician David Toop once described the single as anorexic in comparison to Bernstein's original fleshed-out arrangement; a tad harsh, maybe, but there's no denying that The JB7 sounded at best undernourished when sat alongside the full-bodied opulence of the film score. Barry's decision to go with a stripped down line-up for the session seemed at odds with what was required to replicate the dynamic sound experienced in the film. Maybe a strict £79 budget dictated a line-up pared down to three electric guitars, electric bass, drums, piano and double bass.

No wonder The JB7's interpretation sounded so lightweight when judged against Bernstein's orchestral richness. Clearly, a full John Barry Orchestra arrangement would have been a more appropriate proposition. The B-side, 'Skid Row', turned out to be much more representative of the Seven's trademark style – close-miked pizzicato strings vying with Vic Flick's melodious fretwork. The record became The JB7's sixth successive Top Fifty hit.

As if to illustrate the production-line precision of the music business in 1961, this single was recorded and on record shop shelves within a mere seventeen days; just about as soon as 'Black Stockings' was finding its way into the 'ex-jukebox' bargain racks. Such short-term-ism, characterised by a rapid output policy, was the business model of the day.

In his *New Musical Express* review of 24th February (the date of the single's release), even Keith Fordyce appeared underwhelmed by the main cut by actually nailing his colours to the 'Skid Row' mast: "'The Magnificent Seven' comes from the film of the same name, and as a title it just had to be recorded by The JB7. It turns out to be a standard rock instrumental with guitars doing most of the work. The coupling – a Barry original – is, to my ears, far more interesting than the topside; a more imaginative piece with the whole mood more intriguing." *Disc* followed suit a week later. In rating 'Skid Row' as the more commercial proposition, it was described as, "a well played twangy beat item with both eyes firmly fixed on the current state of the market." Whatever the outcome of the single, the group could find some solace via the current LP chart, which saw the *Beat Girl* soundtrack listed throughout February whereupon it would peak at No. 11 and rack up sales of 14,938. This was a formidable achievement to have cracked what was at the time the more upmarket, adult end of the vinyl market.

Sandwiched in between a number of concerts in the North of England (Southport, Spennymoor and Nelson), both small and big screens beckoned when The JB7 were hired for cameo appearances in an up-and-coming MGM feature film, *A Matter of WHO*, as well as for a more substantial role in a new one-off BBC TV drama entitled *Girl on a Roof*.

Rehearsals for the latter took place in London and Manchester before being filmed from the BBC's Manchester studios, which necessitated three nights away from home. The BBC reimbursed train fares (at a cost of £3 17s – £3.85) and also paid each band member £7 10s (£7.50) for three nights' subsistence, which was hardly a King's ransom even by 1961's standards!

Broadcast on 16th February, *Girl on a Roof* was originally conceived as a vehicle for Adam Faith, who was earmarked for playing the part of Red Mayne, a pop singer about to become the object of a young fan's obsession (played by Waveney Lee). When Faith pulled out of the production (due to extending his pantomime commitments at the Wimbledon Theatre), the role was assigned to Ray Brooks, who had to dye his hair blond accordingly. Johnny De Little, whose first Barry-produced single – 'Not Guilty' – had only just been released in January, was also given a small part as a singer named Snowy. The JB7's function was to provide the backing for both fictional characters in addition to performing an array of instrumentals from their own current repertoire ('Bee's Knees', 'Black Stockings', 'Kid's Stuff', 'Mad Mab', 'Not Guilty', 'Saturday's Child', 'Skid Row' and 'Walk Don't Run'). They backed Brooks and De Little on two songs, each based on Barry's arrangements: the former on 'Flea Brain', the latter on 'I Did What You Told Me' and both on separate versions of 'I Want You Baby'. The play was written by ex BBC TV producer Stuart Douglass, who also supplied the lyrics for 'I Want You Baby'. The producer was Chloe Gibson. For Brooks, being backed by a band as renowned as The JB7 made the whole venture entirely worthwhile and was the ultimate thrill as he would later enthuse: "Singing live with The John Barry Seven behind me was big news for me; that powerhouse sound behind Adam Faith had a massive reputation,"

For *A Matter of WHO*, a drama starring Terry-Thomas that was later noted for introducing his nephew Richard Briers to cinema audiences, The JB7 were given the task on camera of playing an instrumental version of Edwin Astley's main title theme, which sounded like an absolute breeze in theory. However, the reality was very different. According to Jimmy Stead, the Seven's three minutes of fame on this film took what seemed like an eternity to perfect, and all because of the ineptitude of its leading man. "Our scene was at a party in a large apartment," he recalled, "where Terry-Thomas makes his entrance to inform the dancing audience that some of them might have a serious medical problem or words to that effect. Now we were the band playing for that audience, but it took him thirty-two 'takes' to get that short scene eventually and successfully 'in the can' which, as you could imagine, took almost a day in the studio! Mike Peters reminded me that we were paid by the hour for the gig, which was just as well, because we were well pissed off with Mr. Thomas by the end of the day, I can tell you!"

The JB7 laid down their studio version of 'A Matter of Who' at Abbey Road on 17th April alongside an unissued cut written by Brian Fahey, entitled 'Dark Rider', immediately after returning from a two-week tour of Ireland. On these tracks, all seven members were employed plus, inevitably, the almost obligatory violin quartet on a session costing. in total, £97. No carefully constructed simultaneous multi-platform launch strategy existed in 1961, so when The JB7's recording was released as the B-side to 'Starfire' on 1st September, it was a good month ahead of the film's 3rd October premiere – a film which lost MGM a reported $142,000!

The most prestigious event during March occurred on the 5th when The JB7 made their second (and, as it turned out, final) appearance on the bill of the *New Musical Express* Poll Winners' Concert, which was held once again at the 10,000-capacity Empire Pool, Wembley. This particular event was noted for being the first to be filmed since its inception, highlights from which were televised later that same month (on the 25th) to a reported audience of 15 million as part of ABC's networked Saturday night entertainment show, *Big Night Out* on which performances by Cliff Richard, Adam Faith, Connie Francis, Lonnie Donegan, The King Brothers, Emile Ford and the Checkmates, The Shadows, The John Barry Seven, Lyn Cornell, Ted Heath and His Music, plus Bob Miller and the Millermen were broadcast. Also present on stage, but not transmitted that Saturday, were The Mudlarks, Mark Wynter, Jerry Lordan, Bert Weedon, Russ Conway, Alma Cogan, Billy Fury and The King Brothers. Connie Francis was given the honours of handing Barry the 'small group section' runners-up trophy on behalf of the band during the actual awards presentation.

According to the concert's official programme, The JB7 were lined up to play 'Hit and Miss', 'Walk Don't Run', 'Cerveza', 'Blueberry Hill' and 'The Magnificent Seven', and just as they did the previous year, the band backed Adam Faith, who was now appearing as a poll winner in his own right. Faith's lengthy set included 'Wonderful Time', 'Singin' In The Rain', 'What Do You Want?', 'Worried Man', 'Lonesome Traveller', 'Who Am I?' and 'When Johnny Comes Marching Home'. Both the *New Musical Express* and *The Stage* were at pains to praise The JB7's combined role as main act and backing band. In the staid and archaic parlance of the day, *New Musical Express*'s Keith Goodwin was positively gushing just as he was the previous year: "The big beaty sound created by The John Barry Seven is the sort of thing that makes teenagers want to clap their hands and stamp their feet, which is just what they did when the multi-talented Barry led his men through hits like 'Hit and Miss' and 'Walk Don't Run'. For big beat music at its best, Barry is undoubtedly the tops!" Similarly, *The Stage* liked what it saw: "Compère David Jacobs set The JB7 going with 'Hit and Miss' of 'Juke Box Jury' fame – this polished group of musicians played excellently, before backing the next act, Adam Faith."

One of the constant niggles espoused by just about every incarnation of the band was the baffling geographical randomness of the touring schedule that necessitated what seemed like countless miles of needless travelling. This was never better summarised than by Vic Flick when reflecting on his days with The JB7: "As good a business woman as she was, Eve Taylor had no sense of geography whatsoever, or so it seemed to the members of The Seven." By way of combating the inevitable fatigue that resulted, many a late night *en route* to the next venue involved stopping off wherever possible at a nearby service station, but with an undeveloped motorway network (still in the throes of construction), these were few and far between in 1961. This is why 'The Blue Boar Cafeteria' situated at Watford Gap services between junction 16 and 17 on the M1 became the most fondly remembered watering hole of that era. It was there, just about every touring musician gravitated towards, and if any astute fan wanted to collect autographs *en masse* then that was the place to hang out. Flick recalled many a conversation struck up with fellow muses over a fry up and a mug of coffee at 'The Blue Boar': "It became quite a meeting place for groups as well as the few remaining big bands like Bob Miller and The Millermen, The Squadronaires, Nat Temple and a few others."

Flick also alluded to the liberal use of amphetamines amongst touring musicians throughout this period purely as a practical way of staying awake and alert for as long as possible. Alongside caffeine, the drug Benzedrine (or 'bennies' as they were colloquially christened) enabled the tired and exhausted to remain *compos mentis* into the early hours of the morning thereby minimising the need for sleep. Also known as 'pep pills', 'speed' and, 'jets', such stimulants or 'uppers' – "unsophisticated drugs" was how Flick described them – were seen as a necessary part of a musician's armoury at a time when they were being worked rigorously hard.

As if to illustrate the point perfectly, yet another exhaustive tour was arranged for March (by promoter Arthur Howes), which no doubt would have tested the skills of any designated navigator-come-map-reader during these pre-'Sat Nav' times. As part of a bill that also included Adam Faith, Gerry Dorsey, The Honeys and Johnny LeRoy, The JB7 once again traversed the length and breadth of the country taking in locations as far apart as Bristol, Hull, Maidstone, Cambridge and Banbury. On 21st March, East Ham, London, was the venue; the same day on which The Beatles debuted at The Cavern – paths that were seemingly destined never to cross.

~

Although all evidence points towards The JB7 and The Beatles never once sharing a stage on the same bill, interviewed in 1996 Barry did allude to a conversation he once had with Paul McCartney years later backstage at Carnegie Hall, New York during which McCartney actually admitted to having seen The JB7 live at The Cavern as a paying member of the public. Apparently, what impressed him most of all back then was the amplification they used, which was well advanced for its time. Indeed, Mike

Peters echoed this by recalling an interesting exchange of ideas occurring on that very subject between various members of the two bands inside The Cavern on the day of the concert.

~

For any travelling band governed by tight deadlines, in many instances with digs to find and invariably with equipment to set up, the onset of mechanical failure was arguably the most dreaded hazard of them all. Arguably even worse, a breakdown could be especially galling when desperate to return home to one's loved ones after many weeks on the road. Vic Flick recalls one particular hair-raising journey southwards post concert alongside Barry at the wheel of his Triumph, when in the face of all sorts of ear-splitting clanking noises and with smoke pouring out effusively from the back of the vehicle, he stubbornly refused to admit defeat and kept driving on despite all evidence to the contrary. As the bangs got louder and the fumes thicker, the language inside the car grew demonstrably bluer and bluer! "For God's sake slow down and stop, we all cried," recounted Flick. Unfortunately, Barry's logic was not that of a trained mechanic but of a homesick traveller. "I don't want to break down any further from home than I have to. The faster I go, the nearer I'll get," he explained rather unconvincingly. Needless to say, the car ground to an inevitable spluttering, stuttering, smoke-filled, steaming halt without any intervention from the driver. Thankfully, no one came to any harm, but to this day, Flick has no idea how anyone on board managed to find a way back home that night.

Throughout our research over the years, the events that readily resonated with members of the band when reminiscing tended to be those involving the mishaps, the accidents, the inconveniences and the bloopers. That these should stand out first and foremost is hardly surprising bearing in mind the hundreds of routine concerts undertaken and the thousands of miles travelled. A dance date at Wimbledon Palais on 30th March is a prime example – an evening which proved memorable for Dougie Wright though not for the right reasons!

One of the highlights of the set-list was an arrangement of 'When the Saints Go Marching In' that was aimed at putting Wright's virtuosity in the spotlight. Consequently, the stage was set up to ensure that the drum kit was visible by being perched on a high rostrum at the back. Now as a means of preparing himself a few bars prior to his solo, Wright would habitually play with one hand while adjusting his drums, cymbals and stool with the other; a ritual that normally worked perfectly well. However, on this occasion something was definitely amiss. As the rest of the band raised their hands to usher in the solo (before shuffling off-stage for a welcome fag break), Wright had inadvertently lost his drum stool after overstepping the rostrum when making his adjustment. The back leg had slipped off and with it, the entire stool. So there he was, holding on for dear life to anything remotely bolted down while at the same time attempting the most intricate of rolls. "It wasn't one of his better solos but it certainly was one of his more spectacular," Flick amusingly recalled. "It's amazing how long the human form can suspend itself in space and how many movements it can make before gravity takes over. Poor Doug disappeared in a tangle of tom toms, snares, cymbals, stands and music behind the stage."

Primitive living conditions in transit also lodged themselves firmly into the collective memory banks and, in particular, the basic amenities afforded the touring buses of the time. Forget the luxurious grandeur enjoyed by the rock gods of the 1970s such as Led Zeppelin, whose rented 'Boeing 720-B', known as the 'Starship', was furnished with shag pile carpeting, brass-trimmed lounge bars, waterbeds and an extensive video library. The best The JB7 could ever hope for was a vehicle with seats (and even these were never guaranteed with equipment to transport)! As for a toilet, well that was like asking for the earth, as Vic Flick vividly recalled, looking back at the way in which many of the hired Timpson coaches suddenly developed mechanic defects as a direct result of the inevitable calls of nature that ensued whilst on the move. The corrosive effect of urine on metal severely affected the rear brake assembly when, as Flick put it, "It became common to lift the inspection hatch over the back axle and relieve oneself onto the road as the bus sped along." Once the firm's mechanics got wind of such practises, however, locked covers were installed over the hatches with only the driver having access to the key with which to undo them, and gone were the "relief stations" (as Flick called them); holding on till bursting point became the order of the day.

Like the coaches, The Seven often found the venues also lacking in basic amenities and state-of-the-art equipment with house amplification always a major concern. Jimmy Stead stressed that throughout his tenure with The JB7, the p.a. system was always provided by the theatre alongside at least one microphone, a piano plus main power for the amplifiers. Consequently, the sound quality on the night was dictated by the standard of hardware provided, which could vary from one gig to the next. Mike Peters was particularly in awe of Les Reed's transposition skills, for many a time he became saddled with a beaten up, out-of-tune keyboard, that required him having to compensate, virtually 'on the hoof', by altering the key for every piece on the night's set-list – unlearning, in effect, what he had erstwhile rehearsed. Vic Flick will never forget being faced with one temperamental sound system at a local cinema in Pontefract that had been hastily converted into a concert venue for the evening. Throughout the first half of the show the sound had been so bad that often the crackling noises and buzzes would be interspersed with no sound whatsoever. "By the time The JB7 were about to start the second half," he explained, "Barry, standing in front of the microphone, turned to me and said "This mic will never work. You could say 'Bollocks!' into it ...", and at that precise moment, the sound system roared into life heralded by JB's epithet ringing around the auditorium. No wonder we were met with an icy reception thereafter!"

On 12th April, while Russian Soviet cosmonaut, Yuri Gagarin, was heading into history by becoming the first human being to orbit the earth, The JB7 were broadening their horizons on a much more modest scale in the midst of the first of two trips to Ireland that took in venues throughout both North and South including The Top Hat Ballroom (Portstewart, Northern Ireland) and Londonderry City Hall (ROI). Travelling in a hired VW split screen van (rather than a Vostok 1 spaceship), this tour lasted two weeks and was a thoroughly enjoyable experience for all concerned. Jimmy Stead clearly remembered the remoteness and primitive nature of some of the destinations, in particular the Roseland Ballroom in Moate (Co. Westmeath, ROI). Somewhere 'out in the sticks' away from the local community and situated in isolation on a field that allowed for ample parking, Stead was soon to discover that its 'revolving stage' had to be operated by sheer brute force with help from the locals. There was simply no power supply available, so in the absence of any electricity, the promoters had to rely on manpower to push it around. This would have been much easier to accomplish had it not been for the fact that the concrete track over which the stage moved was so uneven, the music and cymbal stands stood to fall over at a moment's notice. The band also soon realised that concerts in Ireland followed the conventions set by most dances with a start time of 10 p.m. and a finish as late as 2 a.m. As such, The JB7 made sure that they were never the last men standing. What stood out in Dougie Wright's mind was the wording of a poster announcing the arrival of The JB7 in one of the smaller outposts on the itinerary. "I can only imagine that the printer must have been instructed by telephone, because the posters read – 'Appearing tonight – The Jamboree Seven...!'"

On returning from 'The Emerald Isle', The Jamboree Seven were quickly back up-and-running on the 'touring/TV/radio/recording' treadmill once again, with the touring, as ever, taking precedence being the lucrative money-spinner that it was. In his later autobiography *Acts of Faith*, Adam Faith revealed how he was earning as much as £1,000/week on tour (minus manager's fees) throughout this period, which is why a further lengthy circuit of dates ensued all over England and Scotland during May, June and October. To tie in with the May concerts, Faith had a new single to promote, 'Easy Going Me'/'Wonderin'', which was recorded with the Seven prior to the Ireland jaunt. An appearance on the annual 'Our Friends The Stars' charity show at the Victoria Palace (23rd April) with Russ Conway, The Allisons and other top artistes served the same purpose, as did another spot on *Saturday Club* the following week (the 29th) where Faith and The JB7 were joined by The Brook Brothers, Dinah Kaye, Mike Shaun, Ricky Baron, Tommy Sanderson and The Sandmen, and Arthur Greenslade and The Gee Men.

When BBC TV decided to make a token concession to teenage musical tastes with the introduction of *Six-Five Special* in 1957, The JB7 had featured prominently, just as they would continue to do so on the most significant and groundbreaking alternatives that immediately followed in its wake, *Oh Boy!* and

Drumbeat. In fact, well before they were ever welcomed on radio, the band was part of an 'A-list' of coveted performers deemed appropriate for the small screen. Hence, come 1961 it was hardly surprising to find them once again invited to appear on one of the earliest editions of television's latest mainstream pop vehicle, ABC's new Saturday evening series, *Thank Your Lucky Stars*, which had only just been launched in April. As it transpired, this would be the last trailblazing pop programme on which The JB7 would be an automatic pick, but on 6th May 1961, no one was to know that.

Although not initially networked nationally, *Thank Your Lucky Stars* was conceived by producer Phillip Jones as a direct competitor to *Juke Box Jury*, the success of which had left the commercial channels floundering somewhat. Each edition was filmed at Birmingham's Alpha Studios (in Aston) on Sunday night in front of a live audience before being transmitted on the following Saturday, and was a vehicle for introducing new releases in a more visual way compared to its well-established rival, more akin to a variety rather than a panel show. Despite appearing 'in the flesh', as it were, artists invariably mimed to their records, which did not meet the wholesale approval of The Musician's Union, A *Spin-a-Disc* section was soon introduced that deliberately cloned the *Juke Box Jury* format, whereupon teenagers in the audience were asked to judge the merits of three new releases, and then mark them accordingly by awarding points out of five. This made a star of one such participant, sixteen-year-old office clerk Janice Nicholls, whose Black Country dialect turned her comment "Oi'll give it foive" into a national catchphrase.

Two hundred and forty-eight episodes of *Thank Your Lucky Stars* were eventually transmitted spanning the years 1961 to 1966, and hosted by a plethora of presenters among them Keith Fordyce (the first), Brian Matthew (the most) and Jim Dale (the last). It is probably best remembered now for ushering in the next generation of pop stars by positively embracing the Mersey Sound and for giving The Beatles their first fully networked prime-time opportunity. The JB7's debut appearance saw them mime to 'The Magnificent Seven' on a Pete Murray-presented show that also featured Adam Faith, Matt Monro, Gerry Dorsey, Susan Grey and Ken Jones. As it was pre-recorded, the band was elsewhere playing Stockton on the latest Adam Faith tour during that very evening. The JB7 would eventually appear on *TYLS* on three further occasions, but, sadly, none of their filmed appearances have survived – a disturbing trend that has resulted in nearly all of their performances on both UK TV channels being either lost or destroyed.

During 3rd May, the first of two lengthy recording sessions took place at Abbey Road Studios, ostensibly to lay down tracks that would later form part of John Barry's first non-soundtrack LP, *Stringbeat* (which is discussed more fully later). Recorded that day were 'Sweet Talk', 'It Doesn't Matter Anymore', 'Spanish Harlem', 'Zapata', 'Rollin' Along' (aka 'There's Life in the Old Boy Yet'),

'Iron Horse', plus the two cuts that would form both sides of the next single, 'The Menace' and 'Rodeo'.

In spite of being lauded at the time by *New Record Mirror* as "some of the best work Mr Barry has done and presented in a way that spells success", 'The Menace'/'Rodeo' 45 was an unexpected commercial failure set against the previous year's sales figures. Released on 2nd June and credited to John Barry and His Orchestra (again, possibly an error of judgement), in total only 15,821 copies were sold, which was a considerable disappointment; this, despite the most encouraging of reviews and arguably the Seven's most assured outing to date, which stylistically, acted as a perfect trailer for the *Stringbeat* LP. In fact, 'The Menace' was the first single since 'Twelfth Street Rag' to fail to register on the charts (and the first on Columbia) at a time when the popularity of the instrumental was at its zenith. Both sides conveyed a filmic quality that was the clearest indication yet of the way in which Barry's career would develop, but neither failed to stir the public's imagination sufficiently enough to propel it into the hit parade.

By the time *Stringbeat* was being recorded (during these two intensive sessions – morning, afternoon and evening – the second being on 14th July), Barry had gathered together a reliable cache of seasoned instrumentalists from which to draw upon according to the individual requirements for each specific track; in fact, a combination of twenty-four musicians were used throughout these sessions at a total cost of £931. At the core of this pool of talent, of course, were the Seven, on whom he was also able to rely for original material, with both Les Reed and Vic Flick chipping in with a track apiece for the forthcoming LP. Flick submitted a composition entitled 'Zapata', a track characterised by a then innovative 'fade-intro' which gradually builds up the tension to reveal a taught, almost western-like, theme, while Reed's contribution, 'Donna's Theme', was inspired by the birth of his daughter and was the first recorded composition in what was to become an illustrious song-writing career.

In Les Reed, Barry had at his disposal someone whose grasp of music theory was arguably more advanced than his own at that point of his career; a contemporary able to add clarity to his own innovative ideas. According to Reed, "Because John studied the Schillinger method of scoring using counter melodies to build up chord structure, there were at times simply too many melodies going on all at once, which wasn't a very satisfactory system in my eyes. I told him as much, and he did take note of what I was saying." Not only that, but Reed was also able to correct Barry's less-than-precise piano technique with his wider vocabulary of chords. "Being a trumpet man," he added, "Barry wasn't quite *au fait* with the finer elements of chord-work being used by Wes Farrell and Barney Kessel at that time and he was terrified of flattened 5ths, added 9ths, root notes and the like. Not his fault, but a bit frustrating for me at the time having to listen to him trying to discover the correct chords on his piano! Having said that, he was a fine composer, bless him."

In Vic Flick, Barry was able to rely on a consummate professional with the perfect temperament for session work. Flick once described his work on *Stringbeat* as a major turning point in his own career, given that the entire sound of the LP hinged on the fluidity of his lead guitar work, together with his ability to ad-lib sixteen bars when a fill-in solo was required. Consequently, two lengthy, energy-sapping days in the spotlight at Abbey Road recording the album in the direct gaze of just about all of the most influential contractors and fixers from within the business (themselves doubling up as session players) would turn out to be, in hindsight, the most rigorous of auditions ever imaginable. To this day, Flick is convinced that it was the result of how well he handled both nerve-jangling occasions, which cemented his post-Seven life as an in-demand session player.

Another musician whom Barry was to rely on during the recording of *Stringbeat* (primarily on the second session and, indeed, on later ones throughout the year) was jazz pianist Ted Taylor whose ability to create ethereal high register sounds out of a crude, sensitive electronic keyboard device called the 'Clavioline' was to inform tracks such as 'Moody River', 'Man from Madrid', 'Rum-Dee-Dum-Dee-Dah', 'Like Waltz' and 'Starfire' (earmarked as the next single) with an other-worldly quality that was later to serve The Tornados' 'Telstar' (1962) and The Beatles' 'Baby, You're A Rich Man' (1967) far more famously. The Seimer Clavioline, devised in 1947 by Versailles inventor Constant Martin, was actually the first electronic instrument of its kind to reach a mass market. Because of its high sensitivity, it required the mere deftness of touches to illicit the sound required, which was why Taylor was drafted in, being one of the few musicians able to perfect this novel and unusual instrument at the time. "My big pal Ted Taylor taught me how to master this little piece of new technology, but I would let him play the complicated parts on record," Les Reed would later enthuse. "As a result, he became the revered eighth member of The JB7," he noted.

The May and June dates that embraced the North of England and Scotland with the familiar company of Adam Faith, The Honeys, Johnny Leroy and Gerry Dorsey was bolstered by the introduction of a fresh compère, Irish-born comedian Dave Allen, whose skills as a card shark left an indelible mark on everyone who shared a hand with him during the tour. Long before he came to fame as the chain-smoking, whiskey (in reality, ginger ale) swilling, bar stool raconteur, Allen hosted various pop packages including Faith's and Helen Shapiro's. Now of all the activities spent whiling away those tedious long journeys from venue to venue, the card school reigned supreme, and as an avid and wily gambler, Allen organised regular games of poker, blackjack and blind brag, more often than not to the consternation of the rest of the troupe.

As Les Reed confirmed, "Hours on the road were spent playing poker with Dave Allen; only we didn't know he was marking the cards back then. Needless to say, we were always broke by the end of the week." For Gerry Dorsey (Humperdinck), he could only rue how much he lost pursuing such an expensive pastime. "The only entertainment on offer as the miles sped by came in the form of card games and gambling, and by indulging in this, it got me into heavy debt and cost me my entire wages on that tour!" Vic Flick explained that because seats had been taken out of the back of the coach to make room for equipment, luggage and instruments, there was always plenty of space for competitors to gather round a large bass drum case, which doubled as a card table. As very little actual cash was available, all transactions were recorded on a complicated system of I.O.U.s dreamed up by Allen. This is where the trouble started. "Going for the big pot, and subsequently losing, left some without any money at all for the rest of the tour," Flick added, concurring with Dorsey. "Amounts in the region of £75 were lost and owed, which was a fortune in those days. Rumour has it that some I.O.U.s remain unpaid to this day, and by people that could well afford to pay them off," he concluded.

On being given responsibility for yet another new weekly Light Programme during 1961 (entitled *Music with a Beat*), Brian Matthew decided once again to engage the services of The Seven during which, in addition to their own spot, they would back singer Kay McKinley. From a musical standpoint, the *modus operandi* leaned more towards an easy listening style, which provided Barry with an opportunity to include some jazz material – the type of numbers that they would often stretch out on during dance gigs. Therefore, 'St Louis Blues', 'Lonesome Road' and 'Tuxedo Junction' found their way into The JB7's repertoire alongside their accompaniment of McKinley's 'How Wonderful to Know', 'Half of My Heart' and 'Little Boy Sad'.

The Seven's performances had to be pre-recorded (on 25th May) as the band were still touring relentlessly. The programme broadcast on 1st June included 'Long John', 'The Menace', 'The Magnificent Seven', 'Tuxedo Junction' and a new Barry original, 'Trouble Shooter' – the only known JB7 recording of a number written specifically for Bob Miller and The Millermen (the A-side of their Parlophone debut). Returning two weeks later, The Seven played 'Cerveza', 'St. Louis Blues', 'The Menace' (released a fortnight earlier), 'A Matter of Who' and 'Lonesome Road'. One final appearance would ensue in September.

Geographically challenged once again, among June and July's locations were Preston, Brixton, Redruth, Oxford, as well as a dance at Mellow Lane Comprehensive School (Hayes). From Peters' perspective, the dances were welcome respite from the concert set-list, since they were more musically satisfying in allowing for a wider repertoire, a greater freedom of expression and an opportunity to improvise "More from our pleasure than the audiences, I liked the dances as we got more time to play some nice instrumental music as opposed to playing behind the main star for most of the show," he reflected.

The summer months provided the band with the opportunity of recording Adam Faith's next single ('Don't You Know It?'/'My Last Wish') on 19th and 26th June, and by the end of September, the back had been broken on the completion of his second, and eponymous LP. In addition, the aforementioned second *Stringbeat* session had also been fitted in, which spawned the following: 'A Handful of Songs', 'Baubles, Bangles and Beads', 'Man from Madrid', 'Like

Waltz', 'The Challenge', 'Starfire', 'Donna's Theme', 'Moody River', 'Rum-Dee-Dum-Dee-Dah' and 'Smokey Joe' with only the latter failing to make the cut. In and amongst this flurry of studio activity, a weekly season of dates over a nine week period had been arranged for the band at three separate seaside venues – Morecambe (Wednesdays), Weston-super-Mare (Fridays) and Folkestone (Saturdays) – resulting in gallons more petrol being consumed often in their own vehicles. As Mike Peters put it, "Doing three nights through the summer was no picnic. The motorways that were open then weren't long enough to impact on those locations. Still, at least we were working."

Media promotion work also continued in the form of a TV appearance on ABC's *Sunday Break* (30th July), this time with singer Danny Williams, followed a week later by a *Saturday Club* stint on a show that also included Adam Faith, Helen Shapiro, Tommy Sanderson and The Sandmen, Bob Wallis's Storyville Jazzman, plus their former colleague, the now solo Keith Kelly. Barry and Faith appeared on the cover of that week's edition of *New Record Mirror* pictured at the BBC recording of the programme.

Danny Williams, incidentally, was now being represented by a new agency calling itself Topline, which had been set up in June as the brainchild of its co-directors: Barry, wife Barbara and musician/arranger Geoff Love, managed on a day-to-day basis by Tony Lewis. This was another example of Barry diversifying his music business interests even further. Also on the books were various artists whom he would produce in his capacity as MD at EMI: Johnny De Little, Anita Harris and Mark Tracy.

Barry would record Harris's Parlophone debut on the afternoon of 22nd August, the same session on which he would also produce an altogether different act calling itself 'Michael Angelo and his Orchestra' that sounded not unlike The JB7. In truth, this was The JB7 in all but name, wrapped up in a pseudonym, augmented by a small string section together with 'eighth member', Ted Taylor, on clavioline.

One suspects that this development may well have been an attempt by Barry of emulating his friend, label mate and new business partner, Geoff Love, who in 1959 launched a series of highly successful South American influenced recordings on Columbia under the nomenclature, 'Manuel and his Music Of The Mountains'. By 1961, this strategy had resulted in two hit singles ('Theme from Honeymoon' and 'Never on Sunday') plus a top twenty LP, *Music of the Mountains*. Barry's *nom de plume* was aimed more at targeting an Italian audience whose appreciation of Barry's pizzicato stylising on Adam Faith's records had proved immensely popular there; so much so that a reputed £200,000 offer from an Italian businessman, which would have secured an exclusive four-year contract for Barry and The Seven, had been placed on the table and firmly rejected. Understandably, for Michael Angelo's debut, Barry selected Italian composer Nino Rota's theme from the latest Visconti film, *Rocco and his Brothers,* as the A-side, which was coupled with a Barry original, 'Spinneree', named after a quaint café he frequented in

Cumberland calling itself 'The Spinnery'. 'Rocco's Theme' delightfully captured the kind of surreal circus and carnival atmosphere so evocative of Rota's Fellini scores, but didn't sell in great quantities. However, with sales of 3,242, it more than covered costs thereby justifying the go-ahead for a follow-up in the New Year ('Tears'/'The Roman Spring of Mrs Stone'). Any attempt that may been made at concealing the identity of the mysterious Michael Angelo, however, was short-lived when Bruce Welch of The Shadows let the cat out of the bag in his weekly column for *Disc* not long after the single's release on 15th September.

The JB7's own official new 45 'Starfire', released just a fortnight earlier, fared a lot better from a sales perspective in totalling 26,754 (almost twice as many as 'The Menace' managed to shift), and yet it still didn't make any impression on the charts. Even commissioning Jerry Lordan (composer of 'Apache') to pen the A-side was unable to launch it into the pop stratosphere. Likewise, Keith Fordyce's endorsement in the *New Musical Express* failed to ensure lift-off. "Partly repetitive, although interesting all through," was his conclusion in recommending 'Starfire's' "crisp beat, fascinating tune and a wide and varied use of instruments," However, he did feel that the B-side, the earlier recorded theme to *A Matter of WHO*, sounded naked in comparison to Roy Castle's vocal version despite "lots of twangy guitar sounds." Emulating 1960's hit-making accomplishments was proving to be anything but easy.

The release of the single neatly coincided with yet another prestigious appearance at The Empire Pool, Wembley; this time as part of *New Musical Express's* 'Big Stars of 1961' extravaganza held on Sunday 10th September. This sell-out event boasted a terrific line-up: Cliff Richard, Adam Faith, Billy Fury, Jess Conrad, The Brook Brothers, The Allisons, The Shadows, The Temperance Seven, Eden Kane, John Leyton, The Bob Wallis Jazzmen, and Bob Miller and The Millermen with Pete Murray officiating. Curiously (and ominously), The JB7 did not back Adam Faith on this occasion. That honour befell The Red Price Combo; a clear indication that Faith was hatching a plan of his own concerning his future music career, that would ultimately not include The Seven. Without the added responsibility of accompanying Faith, the 10,000-packed arena was able to witness The Seven focus solely on unveiling 'Starfire' along with 'Tuxedo Junction', 'Hit and Miss', 'The Magnificent Seven' and 'When the Saints Go Marching In'.

A third episode of *Music with a Beat*, broadcast on 14th September, gave The Seven another opportunity to promote 'Starfire', along with 'The Magnificent Seven', 'A Matter of Who', 'Route No. 1' and 'Lonesome Road'. Since these performances were, as usual, pre-recorded, on that same day the band were holed up again at Abbey Road, this time devoting attention to six further tracks destined for the *Adam Faith* album.

On 17th September, The Seven played the Pop Prom for Printers concert held at the Royal Albert Hall, which was an annual fundraising event in aid of the 'Printers' Pension Corporation' promoted by the teen magazines *Valentine*, *Marilyn* and *Roxy*. Now on the surface, this was just a routine gig of no great significance, but for The JB7, it was soon to become a major landmark, because immediately afterwards, John Barry took the rather unusual (and arguably unprecedented) step of quitting his own band. No longer would he be performing with them on stage from there on in, apart from the odd one-off event to which he was already contractually obligated. He had decided that this concert would mark the end of his on-stage playing career with the band, and having made up his mind, the classic line-up was no more. He clearly left on a high, however, since according to one report, "The JB7 received rousing applause as they stormed through 'The Magnificent Seven', 'Walk Don't Run' and 'Hit and Miss' with the latter earning mass hand-clapping."

Barry's withdrawal from performing had been a gradual one, since he had not appeared on a JB7 recording since 'Farrago' in October 1958, but now that he was being pulled in all sorts of different directions, he felt no longer able to commit himself to the rigours of touring full-time. For a start, he already had lifelong designs on a career as a film composer after having experienced a further taste of it during May (28th) when he supplied the music to *Falling in Love* for ATV, a documentary study of young love (now sadly erased or destroyed). Even more pressing was his commitment to fulfilling his responsibilities as a Musical Director for EMI, nurturing and producing talent whilst continuing to make his own records, as contracted, under The JB7 banner. Although the 'Tin Pan Alley' edifice may have been crumbling, Denmark Street remained the hub of the music industry in 1961, and so he needed his ear to the ground there, more so now that his new joint enterprise, Topline, was also up-and-running. Perhaps most importantly, his bosses at EMI had offered him the prospect of undertaking a 'fact finding' mission throughout the USA during the coming October as a means of learning about the more advanced recording techniques available at the best studios there. This was an opportunity he could ill-afford to refuse and would necessitate three weeks out of the country. Therefore, an interim replacement would have been required in any case.

Two huge decisions affecting the future of The JB7, therefore, now had to be made: the appointment of a new on-stage leader plus the introduction of a new permanent trumpet player. It was Vic Flick to whom Barry turned to for taking on the added responsibility of leading the band, which he accepted, albeit with some reluctance, out of a sense of loyalty to both Barry and the rest of his band mates (a loyalty "misplaced" was how he would later describe it). Knowing full well how potentially stressful being top dog was likely to be through his own experiences at Butlin's, Flick feared some initial resentment from amongst the band, itself, as well as the flak he was bound to receive from promoters expecting to see Barry – and he was vindicated on both counts. This was hassle he could have well done without and, in hindsight, he has since regretted making that move. Nevertheless, he succeeded in steadying the ship, seamlessly smoothed over the transition, and then skilfully oversaw the day-to-day management of a band that was gradually losing pace with its contemporaries.

A constant problem remained thereafter in always having to reconcile the loss of the band's eponymous figurehead and mouthpiece, who by choice, as the designated 'face of The JB7' had over the course of time become its only member with any media profile; a predicament that Barry, himself, had deliberately cultivated, but which was counter-productive without him at the helm.

Northumberland-born Bobby Carr was the musician entrusted as Barry's *heir apparent* by dint of reputation rather than audition by virtue of being already known to Vic Flick and Les Reed as a first-rate blower. As Reed confirmed, "Bobby was such a beautiful man and divine trumpet player. Vic and I 'discovered' him in 1958 playing 2nd trumpet to Alan Moorhouse in The Eric Winstone Band. He was always the obvious choice to replace John Barry."

Carr, born at 9 Pioneer Terrace, Bedlington on 6th March 1930, learned to play trumpet as a boy in the local Salvation Army band out of which a love for the instrument rapidly grew. He would eventually become widely regarded as the North East's number one trumpet player, and when he returned there in later life, became one of the leading lights in its thriving jazz scene, often mentoring young hopefuls. Ruth Caleb, a former girlfriend, believes that Bobby was asked by Barry to join not only because of Flick and Reed's personal endorsements, but also because he was aware of his reputation via appearances with The Eric Delaney Band and as part of the general London scene. Once he had started rehearsing with The Seven, Carr was very quickly nonplussed at just how rudimentary his parts were. "I've never had to play rhythm trumpet before!," he once commented, since Barry – at best merely competent – tended to write his contributions accordingly. As Flick later recalled, "After three months Bobby often complained how he couldn't envisage getting another job in a band as his lip had gone. Playing nothing much above 'C' in the treble clef all night didn't stretch his capabilities much at all. Still, as he said, once the money keeps coming in and you get used to it, it becomes difficult to give it all up."

With the summer season at an end, Barry decided to give the band a fortnight off, which allowed the rhythm section to accompany Adam Faith on his debut in cabaret at the Room at the Top (Ilford) on 18th September. This may have been a major departure for Faith and somewhat of a gamble for him, but from Mike Peters' perspective, it acted as a welcome breather, as he vividly remembers: "Such an easy gig, backing Adam as part of a quartet at the same venue for a fortnight... and with Jimmy and Dennis surplus to requirements, they were off on their holidays, so it enabled me to stay at their flat for the duration." During this brief cessation of band duties, Peters, Reed and Flick were also able to accept some promotional work on behalf of 'Vox' amplifiers at a local music shop where they took part in a photo session alongside the brand's products.

In addition, the respite enabled Peters to engage in a spot of networking of his own. As a result, he managed to secure a number of sessions recording for Woolworth's Embassy Records at its studio in New Bond Street, Mayfair. Produced and manufactured by Oriole Records for F.W. Woolworth & Co Ltd from 1954 to 1965, Embassy supplied cover versions of current hits exclusively to the chain, retailing at a cut-price bargain 4s 6d, with both sides of each 45 boasting a well-known hit. Because some of these releases reportedly outsold the original (Maureen Evan's version of 'Stupid Cupid' being one of those, as previously stated), it led to the budget labels being excluded from the official chart count. Run on a tight seven-day turnover from studio to shop, musicians of the calibre of Peters were highly prized and as such, this became a useful way of supplementing one's income. "It earned me a bit of spending money," he fondly recalled. "Happy days!"

No sooner had Faith completed his successful transition onto the cabaret circuit than he was back in the studio with the Seven recording the next two singles ('The Time Has Come' and 'Lonesome' respectively) as well as completing the remaining tracks earmarked for the second LP, *Adam Faith*. Despite a level of fame above and beyond his wildest dreams, Faith had become increasingly disenchanted with the way in which his career was being steered throughout the year. Various trigger points had darkened his mood, which he expounded in *Acts of Faith*. Firstly, he was unhappy about being browbeaten into recording 'Lonely Pup' (a song he dismissed as nothing more than a "kiddie's ditty"). Secondly, he was piqued at having to wear a suit on stage (looking like a "prissy twit" as he termed it) when he was much more comfortable in torn jeans and scuffed-up leather jacket. Thirdly, he was growing ever resentful of Eve Taylor's dictatorial and confrontational management style, and fourthly, he was feeling increasingly neglected by what he perceived as Barry's less-than-attentive commitment towards his recording career, claiming that the second LP took far too long to finish on account of his mentor's constant unavailability. In fact, this sense of neglect would eventually engulf the collective morale of The JB7 in the fullness of time.

Consequently, Faith was determined to initiate some changes of his own making, namely the formation of his own backing band, The Roulettes; a clear attempt at emulating what Cliff Richard had already got going with The Shadows (the inclusion of a saxophonist being the only difference). Faith saw 'The Roulettes' in the same mould – as his band and his band alone – which was the first indication of the trusted Barry-Faith-Seven triumvirate approaching a natural conclusion. Faith was hell-bent on asserting his independence amidst a changing musical climate and in having a younger set of musicians behind him – exclusively – this was how he envisaged keeping up with the times. So, for the entire October tour (1st – 15th), The Seven experienced the unusual sight of having to watch another group back Faith once they had finished their own set. As it transpired, this particular incarnation of The Roulettes didn't prove up to the task and was shortly abandoned. However, a determined Faith was to persevere again the following year with greater success whereupon he would ditch the sax player and adopt an archetypal 'lead/rhythm/bass/drums' beat group format. Even so, The JB7 found themselves back *in situ* during the following February for the interim period while Faith was putting his Mark II version together.

The October tour – comprising Adam Faith, Des Lane, Johnny LeRoy, David Macbeth and Dave Allen – gave Bobby Carr the perfect opportunity for bedding in and for familiarising himself with The Seven's repertoire without the added distraction of having to back Faith. Les Reed was absolutely delighted to have a musician of Carr's calibre on board, in whose ability he was keen to exploit. The most talked-about jazz LP throughout the summer months had been the Dave Brubeck Quartet's *Time Out* LP from which an edited version of 'Take Five' had just been released as a single. Reed immediately set to work on his own arrangement for incorporating into the act, and it immediately went down a storm. In Reed's eyes, "My take on 'Take Five' came to life with Bobby Carr in the line-up. Mind you, Mike Peters loved the bass line so much, he played it constantly, even when we were playing 'God Save the Queen' at the end of our gigs!" Peters' own recollections were similarly glowing. "Among all of the arrangements we used, one great one was Les's treatment of 'Take Five' (then in the charts). We used to love to watch any would-be dancer trying to figure out what dance to do in 5/4 time."

A review in *The Stage* of the Harrow concert on the 3rd was equally as positive describing The JB7 as playing "big, beaty ding-a-dong music in their well-known inimitable style," as part of "a popular and well-presented show," However, according to Bobby Carr's then girlfriend, Ruth Caleb (who was studying in Bristol at the time), by the end of the tour, Carr's enthusiasm was rapidly beginning to pall. Referring to The Colston Hall (Bristol) date on the 13th (the thirteenth of the fifteen scheduled), Caleb stated that Carr told her he wasn't enjoying the experience one iota and, she felt that, in all likelihood, he was only carrying on because the money was so good. "Hated wearing the 'monkey suits' and not having time to play his jazz," she recalled, adding that, "Bobby felt frustrated, Playing crap music for tons of screaming Adam Faith fans who only really wanted to see Adam Faith was not for him. At that time I recall him saying that he wanted out." Even so, the rest of the band remained excited by his presence and undoubted ability.

By the start of October, The Shadows had become, unassailably, the UK's most popular group in creating history by topping three charts simultaneously. From those compiled on 7th, 'Kon-Tiki' was the No. 1 single; *The Shadows*, the No. 1 LP, and *Shadows To The Fore!*, the No. 1 EP. Just as impressive was the fact that they were never out of the singles chart throughout 1961. In comparison, The JB7's chart career had stalled markedly. Whilst remaining a top live draw, the result of the *New Musical Express*'s 1961 Annual Readers' Poll (published in December) was a sobering reminder to 'team JB7' that the exposure generated by a hit single via radio, TV and the press was all-important for remaining in the public eye and for being perceived as fashionable. Although The Seven once again came a creditable second in the 'small group' section, the margin of votes cast against those of the winners, 'The Shadows', indicated the shifting fortunes. Whereas The JB7 attracted 2,874 readers, The Shadows hauled in a whopping

37,419. Just as significant was in not being invited to appear on the bill of the New Year's Poll-Winners' concert – possibly the first indication that The JB7's star was on the wane.

Even more portentous were the stirrings of a new generation of pop stars emerging. Two days after the October tour ended, London School of Economics undergraduate Mike Jagger was bumping into an old primary school friend of his by the name of Keith Richards on Platform 2 of Dartford Station, himself heading for Sidcup Art College, both allegedly carrying Chuck Berry LPs under their arms. Future Monkee Davy Jones was developing his stagecraft by portraying Ena Sharples' grandson in *Coronation Street*, while a pre-Herman's Hermits Peter Noone would be following suit in December as Stanley Fairclough, son of Len. During that same month (on the 9th), The Beatles, now under the guidance of a new manager, Brian Epstein, were venturing southwards for the very first time (the day after The JB7 were, ironically, up North gigging in Nelson, Lancashire) whereupon they would play for four hours at The Palais Ballroom (Aldershot) in front of a mere eighteen people; this after *The Aldershot News* had failed to place a paid advert for the show in that week's edition.

Making the best possible record was, therefore, imperative were The JB7 to stand any chance of rebooting its chart prospects, which is probably why Barry decided to remake the next-planned single, 'Watch Your Step', after having returned from his aforementioned 'working holiday' in the USA. The first version had been recorded prior to the October tour, on 28th September, but after having visited the country's best studios in both LA (Capitol) and New York (RCA and Atlantic), dropped in on Neal Hefti and watched Lee Hazlewood mixing, felt he could do much better. Barry was most impressed with the multi-track approach adopted by Ahmet Ertegun at Atlantic Records when he sat in on the recording of The Drifters next single (most likely 'Sweets for My Sweet'), and where he also met Leiber & Stoller, Phil Spector and Mort Shuman. The technique of taping individual instruments and artists on separate tracks, thereby making it possible for engineers to balance and produce a finished article after the performers had departed was a revelatory idea, as was the way in which each instrument was carefully and individually close-miked prior to recording. It was this latter approach that Barry was keen to adopt for 'Watch Your Step' Mark II, and which he was eager to explain in the music press at the point of release.

'Watch Your Step' was an instrumental adaptation of a song written by Washington-based soul-blues singer and guitarist Bobby Parker, whose vocal version reached No. 51 in the *Billboard* Top 100 during June. Although not an obvious choice for a JB7 single, its pulsating, hypnotic guitar riff was an ideal vehicle for Vic Flick's fretboard dexterity over which Ted Taylor and Dennis King could extemporise around the main melody. The B-side, 'Twist It', the title for which was inspired by Barry's own experience of witnessing the new dance craze first hand at New York's Peppermint Lounge, was in truth his own take on 'Watch Your Step'. Musically speaking, they were like fraternal twins – strikingly similar, but different. Just like John Lennon would do three years later by re-working Parker's riff to form the basis of his intro to 'I Feel Fine', Barry felt inspired to write his own naggingly repetitive guitar figure in the same mould. He was clearly quite taken by the song's potential since a new vocal interpretation was soon to provide Adam Faith with the opening track for his second LP.

At a total cost of £67, the remodelled 'Watch Your Step'/'Twist It' session on 1st November proved even cheaper to record than the one that spawned 'The Magnificent Seven'/'Skid Row' 45 earlier in the year. Eight musicians were used: two electric guitarists, plus bass, tenor sax, Hammond organ, piano and drums. From Dougie Wright's perspective, it remains a source of constant irritation and complete bafflement as to why he was completely overlooked on this particular date in favour of seasoned session drummer Andy White. In hindsight, he is convinced that Barry had an inexplicable preference (obsession, even) for using session players at the expense of regular members. Irrespective as to whether this was true or not, the snub still clearly rankles to this day. The irony, of course, was that Dougie Wright would become one of the most sought-after session musicians in the country after leaving The JB7.

Despite a favourable review in *New Record Mirror*, describing the A-side as "a good romp" whilst stressing the important roles played by both lead guitar and electric organ, 'Watch Your Step' was not to be the single to resuscitate the band's chart life when released on 24th November. Even an appearance on *Thank Your Lucky Stars* the following day (alongside Joe (Mr. Piano) Henderson; Ricky Stevens; Paul Raven; The McGuire Sisters and host Brian Matthew) failed to attract the all-important Christmas market in sufficient quantities. 'Watch Your Step' was to sell a disappointing 18,073 copies, which was a far cry from the dizzy heights achieved by 'Walk Don't Run' a mere fifteen months earlier.

It's just as well that the *Thank Your Lucky Stars* slot was pre-recorded, because on the following day the band set off on yet another arduous excursion – this time a ten-date whistle-stop tour of Scotland covering all the major urban centres (including Glasgow, Inverness and Aberdeen) as well as arguably the most northerly venue possible (at a village hall in Wick with a population of just over 7,000). With their appearance already filmed and 'good-to-go', the prospect of an inconvenient, energy-draining about-turn all the way back to Birmingham on the Saturday was therefore thankfully averted. Not that the band minded TV work as a general rule. On the contrary, since the going rate was "the princely sum of £10," to quote Dougie Wright, a mere three minutes-worth of miming in front of the cameras was even more lucrative than the then £7 10s (£7.50) standard fee paid for a three-hour recording session at Abbey Road!

As would happen, the Scotland tour was not without incident. Vic Flick vividly remembers driving along many a long, winding, open and deserted road travelling through the Highlands. On one occasion, he noticed that the car immediately tailing him, which contained the tour's promoter (already struggling with a fractured leg) was suddenly no longer in his eye line and nowhere to be seen.

Despite protestations from some of The Seven to press on, Flick decided to turn back and look for the errant vehicle. What they found was said car overturned on its side, stuck slap bang in the middle of a marsh with the poor promoter now cradling a broken arm as well as a broken leg! The problem then was to seek help in order to contact a doctor; easier said than done when stranded in a remote and desolate corner of Scotland. After traipsing a good while, they managed, eventually, to come across a dark and foreboding house miles from anywhere that was occupied by a suspicious, elderly lady who allowed only one of the search party into her home to make the necessary 999 call. For the rest of them, they were all left shivering outside on what was one the most inhospitable of wintry nights. Once treated, the promoter retired hurt from the rest of the tour, never to be seen again, and consequently, procuring money owed to them afterwards became just as arduous as the tour itself.

Incidentally, whilst The JB7 were in Scotland, Barry was busily recording 'March of the Mandarins', 'The Aggressor' and 'Onward Christian Spacemen' at Abbey Road on 22nd November (at a cost of £275), which was the clearest indication yet that he was already beginning to make the studio his priority and that he had no qualms about drawing upon session players when The Seven were otherwise engaged. He was already starting to differentiate between the concert JB7 and the studio JB7. On this occasion, no fewer than thirty-two musicians were called upon to realise these orchestral arrangements: twelve violins, four violas, four celli, four horns, trumpet, tuba, oboe, bassoon, bass and three percussionists. Evidently, it wasn't specified at the time as to what purpose these particular tracks were likely to serve.

～

Considering the amount of time and effort The Seven put it at Abbey Road, EMI was not renowned for its generosity in respect of providing gratis copies for those directly involved. Quite the opposite, in fact, as Les Reed confirmed, for he had to buy his own records, the result of which once led to one awkward transaction with a sales assistant who evidently was not much of a fan of the band. "Yes, it was rare for most companies in those days to dish out freebies. I remember proudly walking into Maxwells Music store in Woking to enquire at the counter about the latest JB7 release. "Not that horrible group that's on the TV every Saturday night? You must be joking!!" snapped the assistant serving me. Well, I dare not tell him I was a member and so hastily scurried off after buying the record. Poor old EMI – you would think they could have afforded to give away seven records wouldn't you"?

～

The Scotland tour was an opportunity for The JB7 to promote the release of the *Stringbeat* LP, which finally hit the record racks on 3rd November in both mono and stereo format. Of the eighteen cuts recorded during the two sessions in May and July, fifteen were selected for the final track listing. *Stringbeat* was a deliberate and elaborate attempt at showcasing Barry's mastery of what had become his 'trademark' (and highly marketable) sound – heavily reverbed pizzicato twang – in short, *Stringbeat*. If this was a pre-planned conceptual blueprint, the outcome was indeed an impressively cohesive selection, combining older with specially commissioned material (five of which were Barry's own). *Stringbeat* worked by dint of its daring, and in places, unconventional instrumental juxtapositions, together with its impressive overall sound. As David Toop succinctly put it, "This was light music, but not necessarily lightweight."

Only one of the tracks was issued as a single, the aforementioned 'Starfire', which was actually re-recorded during a separate evening session at Abbey Road on 31st July (at a cost of £154). On that occasion, the following instrumentation was used: four violins; four violas; four cellos; four horns; two electric guitars; bass; bass guitar; piano; organ (clavioline); drums and percussion. *TWW*, the ITV station then serving South Wales and the West Country, would soon adopt 'Starfire' as the theme to its Kent Walton-hosted pop programme, *Discs a Go-Go*.

Stringbeat was particularly impressive in its aural clarity, allowing each instrument in whatever combination a defined place within the final mix. As such, a sense of tonal purity, spaciousness and depth was achieved. Housed in a distinctive Modernist sleeve design – like an abstract montage of vividly coloured snooker balls in motion – 'Stringbeat' was sleek, slick, oozed class, and looked every bit the sixties artefact it was. On release, the LP was attributed to John Barry alone, not The JB7, and would accrue a healthy 6,545 in sales (1,205 of which were purchased in the 'new fangled' niche stereo alternative). It attracted positive notices all round as epitomised by Allen Evans' review in the *New Musical Express*, who promptly gave it a four star rating. In describing *Stringbeat* as "exceptional", he was particularly taken with its "imaginative tempos and volumes," concluding with the following: "All tracks have thoughtful treatments, producing exhilarating mixtures of sound. Top marks for something fresh and ahead of its time." Praise indeed.

One only has to listen to *Stringbeat* to appreciate just how much care and attention Barry lavished on the production. Credit must also be due to the painstaking backroom work of engineer Malcolm Addey, who was responsible for overseeing *Stringbeat*, and, indeed, all of The JB7's Columbia recordings, ably assisted by Norman 'Hurricane' Smith, who were both integral parts of the control room team alongside producers Norman Newell or John Burgess. Les Reed went so far as describing Smith as a "sensational man and engineer, who always 'pulled out the stops' to create our sound of the day," adding that "The JB7 and Adam Faith sessions were wonderful times and a joy to be involved in." Addey, who was employed by EMI from 1958 to 1965, and therefore at the epicentre of the musical revolution taking place within the confines of Abbey Road at the time, pointed out to the authors on re-visiting both *Stringbeat* and

Beat Girl (following their CD re-releases in 1990) that both LPs were as good, sonically, as anything with which he has ever been associated before or since. So highly regarded were they that he often used these albums as yardsticks by which he measured the quality of those recordings produced by trainee engineers whom he was teaching.

Towards the latter part of the year, live engagements seemed to peter out somewhat. The authors could find no definitive explanation for this, although whether this had anything to do with John Barry's absence from performing is certainly open to conjecture. One envisages that explaining away a John Barry Seven line-up without the presence of its leader (and principal spokesperson) could not have been the easiest of sells to make to any would-be promoter. To a layperson, this could easily have been interpreted as a downgrade even. Who knows, this might well have been the issue that caused Mike Peters to inexplicably cross out a slew of dates as "cancelled" in his own personal diary entries for early November (all earmarked for backing Adam Faith) prior to the Scotland tour.

Of the year's remaining dates, one in particular (on 2nd December) would have etched itself firmly onto the memories of both Mike Peters and Jimmy Stead, since it saw them return to their West Yorkshire roots playing at Ossett Town Hall. Other dates in December included a fourth appearance that year at the Nelson Imperial Ballroom, this time without Adam Faith (on the 8th), and another at the Margate Winter Gardens. Tellingly, it was the Red Price Combo and not The JB7, who backed Faith at the Malvern Winter Gardens on 28th December.

By the end of 1961, The JB7 were undergoing an unprecedented period of transition after having suddenly changed leadership, but regardless of that, remained a well-established and well-respected part of the live circuit guaranteed to add value to any bill, and yet their combined record sales had taken a disappointing and unexpected nose-dive when measured against the previous year's successes. This was all the more perplexing in light of the fact that the instrumental, *per se*, was enjoying a greater percentage of the market than ever before.

If 1960 was considered a golden year for such records, then 1961 could easily be classed as a vintage one, since the charts were awash with instrumentals, strongly led by The Shadows (with five hits) and a trad jazz boom reaching its peak (as epitomised by Kenny Ball and His Jazzmen's 'Midnight in Moscow'). Duane Eddy, Floyd Cramer and The String-A-Longs continued to fly the flag for America (with 'Pepe', 'On the Rebound' and 'Wheels' respectively), while The Dave Brubeck Quartet confounded the purists by taking jazz into the Top Ten via 'Take Five' (as previously noted). Even more curiously, the retro throwback 1920s sound of The Temperance Seven (which was predominantly instrumental) would provide the industry with two of the biggest selling singles of the year, one of which was the chart-topping, 'You're Driving Me Crazy'.

So why was it that The JB7's singles fell through the cracks? While this is not easy to discern, a number of possible causes could be cited as plausible. Above all, reduced media exposure throughout the year is likely to have had the most significant bearing. During 1960, The JB7 figured in over thirty radio programmes broadcast by the BBC Light Programme alone (thanks largely to being regulars on *Easy Beat*) in comparison to a mere six during 1961, and of those, only the three *Saturday Club* appearances would have commanded a large audience.

Moreover, the power of a two-station dominated television network could not be underestimated either. When actor John Leyton played pop singer Johnny St. Cere in one July episode of ATV's Monday night soap opera, *Harper West One*, performing 'Johnny Remember Me', such was the reaction that following its rush-release on 45, it became the fourth highest selling single of the year. Likewise, after being first broadcast in September, Mr Acker Bilk's haunting theme to a Sunday-afternoon serial, *Stranger on the Shore*, about a young French *au pair* living in Brighton, would secure him the second biggest hit of 1962, eclipsed only by Frank Ifield's 'I Remember You'! In contrast, The JB7 were seen only five times on national television throughout 1961 and of the two *Thank Your Lucky Stars* appearances, the first was not networked. Nor were they able to exploit the kudos and the ratings afforded to such high profile appearances on *The Royal Variety Show* and *Sunday Night at the London Palladium*, which they were able to do the previous year. As if to help remedy that situation, at least two television appearances were guaranteed for broadcasting during 1962, for on 9th and 10th November, the band had already recorded its contributions to two episodes of a forthcoming brand new music show entitled *All That Jazz*.

Some confusion over the changing identity of the band might also have been a contributory factor. With 'The Menace' promoted extensively in the music press as performed by 'John Barry and His Orchestra', this would have created a gap of almost seven months between the releases of two consecutive singles attributed to 'The John Barry Seven' ('The Magnificent Seven' and 'Starfire'). In the fast, fickle, faddish firmament of the fashion-conscious pop scene, this was a considerably long time. What's more, when a teen-oriented mainstream pop weekly such as *Disc* started to devote an entire page (out of sixteen) purely to the trad jazz scene and then also to recruit both Hank Marvin and Bruce Welch to write weekly columns, it was evident just how The JB7 had lost ground over the year in terms of high profile publicity, the odd feature spotlighting solely on Barry notwithstanding.

The year 1961, therefore, left The JB7 in a state of uncertainty without John Barry at the helm. Much was now expected of Vic Flick to carry the ship forward into the New Year, and with Adam Faith having already made his intentions crystal clear by his first attempt at jumping that ship, not to mention the dip in record sales with only five weeks spent in the lower reaches of the charts, it was imperative to maintain some much-needed stability.

The turbulence felt by The JB7 on a personal level, significant as it was to them, was but a blip placed in the context of the world stage as the 'Cold War' began to escalate alarmingly following the erection of the notorious 'Berlin

Wall' on 17th August, thereby splitting Germany territorially, politically and ideologically in two. Never before had the polarised East/West divide been so visibly apparent. On the other hand, Britain was attempting to build bridges (rather than walls) after having made an application to join its allies in Europe as part of 'The Common Market' for the first time. On the domestic front, the launch of the Jaguar E-Type sports car and the After Eight Mint would, by the middle of the decade, prove particularly pertinent to John Barry's lifestyle and career, but those days were still some way off. 1962 was likely to have been met with a more cautious optimism.

From left to right: Les Reed, Dennis King, Jimmy Stead, John Barry and Dougie Wright, touring Ireland in April 1961.

179

The JB7 at EMI's Manchester Square headquarters in 1961.

*The JB7 pictured on the set of All That Jazz, with Bobby Carr (4th from right)
replacing John Barry on trumpet.*

John Barry, Vic Flick, Les Reed and a photographer's monkey in Morecambe.

Les Reed performing on Morecambe Central Pier.

The JB7 performing on Morecambe Central Pier.

The JB7 performing on Morecambe Central Pier.

THE JOHN BARRY THREE

Bandleader. John Barry became a proud "dad" last week, when his wife Barbara gave birth to a baby girl, Suzanne. They are pictured in Queen Charlotte's Hospital, London.

Jimmy and Les off-duty in Morecambe.

Jimmy Stead and Dennis King in Morecambe.

 THE JOHN BARRY SEVEN
COLUMBIA RECORDS

Photo: Dezo Hoffman

Columbia promotional card for the band with new leader Vic Flick in October 1961.

Publicity photo taken by Dezo Hoffman, with new leader Vic Flick, in October 1961.

GIRL ON A ROOF – THURSDAY 16th FEBRUARY 1961

19.55.05 (55 mins)

From Manchester

CAST:

The Group	John Barry Seven	Police Inspector	Campbell Singer
Red Mayne	Ray Brooks	1st Constable	Dickie Owen
Mr. Green	Robin Wentworth	2nd Constable	Edward Brocks
Ernie Practise	James Belchamber	Mr. Smith	Ivor Dean
Harry Charles	Stanley Meadows	Mrs. Smith	Dandy Nichols
Jim	Howard Lamb	Police Sergeant	Bryan Hulme
Shirley Smith	Waverley Lee	Reporter	Barry Jackson
Mr. Horrocks	Bryan Kendrick	Snowy	Johnny De Little

Walk Ons:

Rex Boyd / John Foster / Czeslaw Grocholski / Gerald Cowan
Nan Hargreaves Jones / Ann Rushbrooke / Neil Phelps /
Richard Coe / Anthony Foyle / John Scott Martin /
William Lyon Brown

Author – Stewart Douglass
Telesnape – John Cure
Orchestration – John Barry

AMPEX RECORDINGS

RAY BROOKS & JOHN BARRY SEVEN (For Opening Captions) (2.15)
RAY BROOKS & JOHN BARRY SEVEN (0.19)
All music recorded on tape

MUSIC SPECIALLY TAPED

JOHN BARRY SEVEN
with RAY BROOKS
Flea Brain

JOHN BARRY SEVEN
Skid Row
Mad Mab

JOHN BARRY SEVEN
WITH JOHNNY DE LITTLE
I Did What You Told Me

JOHN BARRY SEVEN
Saturday's Child
Not Guilty
Walk Don't Run

Kid's Stuff
Black Stockings

JOHN BARRY SEVEN
with JOHNNIE DE LITTLE
I Want You Baby

JOHN BARRY SEVEN
Bee's Knees
I Want You Baby

JOHN BARRY SEVEN
with RAY BROOKS
I Want You Baby

Produced by Chloe Gibson

BBC TV's Girl on a Roof, with Ray Brooks and The JB7.

From left: Johnny De Little, who appeared with The JB7 in "Girl on a Roof",
with Frankie Vaughan, Steve Cassidy (Norman Fowler) and Jack Prendergast.

186

A KIWI SHINE GIVES 4 WAY* PROTECTION

*from water *from dirt *from cracking *from scuffs

Use Kiwi—and you give leather not only the famous Kiwi shine—you give protection in four specific ways. The reason—Kiwi's unique formula, which consists of the finest waxes, dyes and solvents blended together by a special 'temperature control' process. Result—Kiwi sinks deep into the leather, *feeding* it and giving it greater resistance. Kiwi's shining unique 4 way protection makes all your family's shoes last longer. Take Kiwi home today.

Look what KIWI does!

* Kiwi, with its special waxes—the secret of its unique formula—sinks deep into the leather, makes shoes water resistant (*yes, even stops damp getting in at the seams!*)
* Kiwi makes shoes more resistant to dirt, prevents it penetrating
* Kiwi prevents drying and cracking because it *feeds* as it shines, giving the leather the natural nourishment it needs—makes shoes last longer
* Kiwi's special rich waxes protect the leather, reduce damage caused by knocks and scuffs

KIWI—THE POLISH THAT DOES SO MUCH MORE THAN SHINE

44

SATURDAY Nov 25

5.45   NEWS
The latest from the newsroom of ITN

5.50   THANK YOUR LUCKY STARS
introduced by
BRIAN MATTHEW
This week's stars
THE JOHN BARRY SEVEN
JOE "Mr. Piano" HENDERSON
perform their latest records and present their tips for tomorrow's hit parade
RICKY STEVENS   PAUL RAVEN
and Guest Appearance of America's song stars
THE McGUIRE SISTERS
A panel of teenagers and disc jockey
DENNY PIERCY
comment on the latest American releases in
Spin-a-Disc
Designed by Robert Fuest
Directed by PHILIP JONES
ABC Weekend Network Production

6.30   MOVIETIME
presents
EDWARD G. ROBINSON
HUMPHREY BOGART
in
BULLETS OR BALLOTS
Johnny Blake ...... Edward G. Robinson
Lee Morgan .... Joan Blondell
Capt. Dan McLaren .... Joseph King
Kruger .... Barton McLane
"Bugs" Fenner .... Humphrey Bogart
Directed by William Keighley
A detective is put back on the beat when he attempts to clean up New York rackets. Hated by police and crooks alike, he strives to do his duty as he sees it.

7.40   OUR HOUSE
starring
HATTIE   BERNARD
JACQUES   BRESSLAW
in
BATTLE OF THE BOROUGH
Teleplay by
BRAD ASHTON and BOB BLOCK
Series originated by
NORMAN HUDIS
Featuring
Frederick Peisley   Leigh Madison
Harry Korris   Eugenie Cavanagh
with
Cameron Hall Ernest Bale Eric Nicholson
Music conducted by Norman Percival
Produced by ERNEST MAXIN
Our House object to an increase in the Local Rates, and find themselves fighting a Battle of the Borough
ABC Weekend Network Production

The JB7 appeared on Thank Your Lucky Stars, performing 'Watch Your Step'.

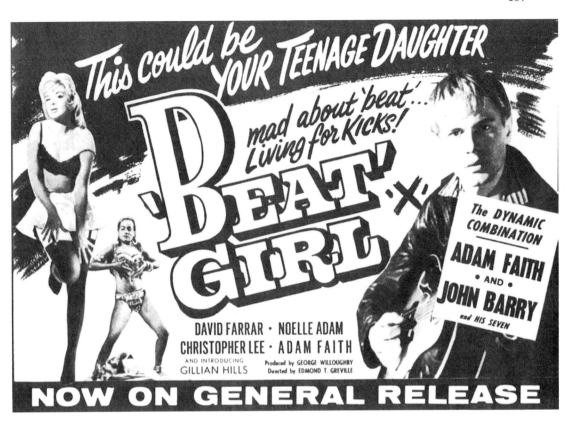

188

PROGRAMME

THE ALLISONS   JOHN BARRY SEVEN   MR. ACKER BILK AND HIS BAND

EVE BOSWELL   TOMMY BRUCE   ALMA COGAN   RUSS CONWAY

ADAM FAITH   KING BROTHERS   GARY MILLER   MATT MONRO

THE MUDLARKS   JOAN REGAN   RICKY VALANCE   BERT WEEDON

PROGRAMME SELLERS:

Avril Angers, Jill Browne,
Maudie Edwards, Elspet Gray,
Diane Hart, Brenda Hogan,
Charmian Innes, Hattie Jacques,
Jacqueline Mackenzie, Pamela Manson,
Carol Marsh, Stella Moray,
Muriel Pavlow, Mabel Pickles,
Sylvia Syms, Thelma Ruby.

THE PROGRAMME WILL BE INTRODUCED BY

DAVID JACOBS

MUSICAL DIRECTORS:

Ron Goodwin, Norrie Paramor,
Woolf Phillips, Bob Sharples,
Cyril Stapleton.

PRODUCER:

Johnnie Stewart

There will be an interval of 10 minutes

BUSKERS:

Frederick Bartman, Ian Carmichael,
Derrick De Marney, Maurice Denham,
John Horsley, Donald Houston,
Sam Kydd, John Le Mesurier,
Francis Matthews, Michael Medwin,
Alan Melville, Wilfred Pickles,
Brian Rix, Graham Stark,
Charles Tingwell, Tony Wright.

ALSO ASSISTING THE BUSKERS—GEORGE CHISHOLM AND THE JAZZERS

George Chisholm, Trombone - Tommy McQuater, Trumpet - Billy Amstell, Saxophone - Alfie Reece, Tuba - Jack Peach, Drums - Jack Emblow, Accordion

SOS Concert at Victoria Palace, London in April 1961.

New Musical Express' Pollwinners' Concert programme, March 1961.

Adam Faith and The JB7 at the New
Musical Express's Poll–winner's Concert
at Wembley, March 1961.

The JB7 at the New Musical Express's Poll-Winners' Concert at Wembley, March 1961.

Adam Faith and The JB7 at the New Musical Express's Poll-Winners' Concert at Wembley, March 1961.

Brian Matthew, Adam Faith and John Barry,
prior to an appearance on Saturday Club.

Les, Vic and Mike at a Vox promotion event in September 1961.

Les at a Vox promotion event in September 1961.

Mike at a Vox promotion event in September 1961.

New Musical Express' 'Big Stars of 1961', September 1961.

Programme pages featuring The JB7 from a tour with Adam Faith, Wolverhampton, October 1961.

6

I'M MOVIN' ON

JANUARY – DECEMBER 1962

*I told John Barry that unless we start singing, we will go down the
pan, but he would have none of it. "Just do exactly as I say,"
was his response.*

– Vic Flick (lead guitar/leader)

*Makes me proud to think of all the tracks we laid down in those hal-
cyon days of The JB7. John and the lads were just sensational people
to work with. I was honoured to work with each and every one
of them for three glorious years, but it was the right
time to leave when I did.*

– Les Reed (piano/keyboards)

The first day of 1962 was greeted by London's heaviest snowfall since records
began in 1940 and by the coldest New Year's Day for 75 years. This was the day
on which an aspiring four-piece beat group from Liverpool trudged into Decca's
West Hampstead recording studios for an eagerly anticipated audition all the
worse for wear after having experienced the most hazardous of overnight journeys
imaginable; a trek that took ten hours in total. That The Beatles actually failed
to convince engineer/producer Mike Smith of their worth may not have been
the stuff of headlines back then, but what their rejection did demonstrate was
the current mood of the music industry at the time.

The commercial climate in 1962 had no appetite whatsoever for groups playing
any variant of rock 'n' roll with the charts then awash in solo singers and trad
jazz bands. One only had to glance through a list of the type of artist whom
John Barry was producing at EMI to realise this: Gerry Dorsey, Peter Gordeno,
Anita Harris, Johnny Worth, Johnny De Little, Mark Tracy, Tony Rocco, Dennis
Lotis, Darren Young and so forth. When Decca's head of A&R, Dick Rowe, was

quoted as saying, "Groups are out; four-piece groups with guitars particularly are finished," he was merely espousing the widespread view held by just about every record company executive in the country. There was little evidence to suppose otherwise given that erstwhile British rockers such as Cliff Richard, Billy Fury and Marty Wilde were now consistently (and successfully) churning out ballads in various styles with every subsequent release, as was the 'King' himself, Elvis Presley. Adam Faith was no longer the 'worried man' either. Out of the ashes of rock 'n' roll, the modern-day crooner had emerged. The Shadows, it seems, were seen as the one-off exception proving the rule.

Not only that, but prominent media insiders such as Brian Matthew had already performed the last rites on rock 'n' roll by predicting how trad jazz would soon become the dominant musical force for the foreseeable future. In his book *Trad Mad*, published that January, Matthew needed little convincing. "The top men of 'Trad' are entertainers, and they are going to set their seal on this decade," he exclaimed enthusiastically, adding further how they "emerged from their jazz cellars and clubs, and invaded the pop world like conquering heroes." The weight of proof appeared to be overwhelming what with *The Best of Barber and Bilk Volumes 1 and 2* having ridden high in the LP chart for the best part of a year, and what's more, the BBC had already championed the cause in commissioning a Saturday night TV programme, *Trad Fad*, exclusively for the genre as early as the previous July. And as if to put a seal on the common consensus, Richard Lester's first foray as a film director, *It's Trad, Dad!*, would feature a roll call of trad's main movers and shakers (Kenny Ball, Acker Bilk, Chris Barber, Bob Wallis, Terry Lightfoot *etc*) when released in March.

Where then did this leave The John Barry Seven in 1962? To an extent, somewhere between a rock ('n' roll) and a hard place. The portents may not have been particularly promising for a band that had just lost its focal point and principal PR man, but what The JB7 had in its favour and in abundance were experience, musicianship, know how, a fine reputation, a chart pedigree and strong management. In truth, they were now a well-established mainstream act. As it transpired, the year turned out to be something of a rollercoaster, which saw the departure of two long-serving and influential members, only for their replacements themselves having to be replaced after only a few months. Significantly, the nationwide package tours with Adam Faith came to an abrupt end once Faith and Barry decided to go their separate ways, but by the end of the year, the band's profile had been bolstered enormously by a return to the charts on the back of two hit singles, the second of which, the iconic 'The James Bond Theme', was in the throes of becoming their biggest seller since 'Walk Don't Run'. For new leader, Vic Flick, his crucial contribution in the creation of this, arguably the most famous film theme of all time, would loom large in his legend to this very day.

From the band's perspective, the year actually began with appearances at a dance gig at Leyton and a concert at Nantwich on 8th and 13th January respectively.

Shoe-horned in between was the first visit of the year to Abbey Road (on the 11th), the purpose of which was to record four tracks for a re-modelled edition of *Stringbeat* that was being prepared and exclusively tailored for the USA market. The inclusion of such familiar standards as 'Blueberry Hill' (a new version), 'Cherry Pink & Apple Blossom White', 'I'll Be With You in Apple Blossom Time' and 'Volare' in trademark style was seen as more likely to attract the American consumer. However, for reasons undisclosed, the plan was ultimately dropped; neither version of the LP would ever surface across the Atlantic. Moreover, not one of the four tracks managed to secure a UK release either and, despite finding a home on a US compilation at a later date, they would languish in the vaults of EMI until released as part of a CD retrospective in 1995. Producer John Burgess originally hoped to have released these tracks as part of a stand-alone EP entitled *More of the John Barry Sound*, but that project was also eventually cancelled without any explanation given. Perhaps the decision to release four cuts from the *Beat Girl* LP in EP form during March had a bearing on the matter.

As noted in the last chapter, The JB7 had already recorded two editions of ATV's latest music vehicle, *All That Jazz*, way back in November – this, the brainchild of Rita Gillespie, who had cut her TV directing teeth on *Oh Boy!*. The first of these shows was broadcast on 19th January in a line-up that also included Chris Barber's Jazz-band, Ottilie Patterson, The Dallas Boys, Gary Lane, and Jack Parnell and His Orchestra. Despite its obvious musical leanings, all twenty-six episodes of *All That Jazz* reflected the prevailing preference for jazz bands and singers; therefore, each edition would invariably see artists of the calibre of Chris Barber, Johnny Dankworth and Tubby Hayes rubbing shoulders alongside the pop styling of, say, Billy Fury, Frank Ifield or The Dallas Boys, The second show featuring The JB7 (transmitted on 2nd February) simply replicated the same acts save Sheila Southern in preference to Gary Lane.

In the meantime, Les Reed had been left with a major decision on his hands after being head-hunted by the then 'A&R' manager at Pye Records, Ray Horricks, to fulfil the role of musical director at Piccadilly Records, which after having been launched as an adjunct to its parent label in April 1961, had not exactly set the music world alight. Horricks was in the midst of taking over the overall management of Piccadilly, and, as such, was looking for someone able to harness new talent by way of combining the roles of producer, arranger, orchestra and combo leader plus accompanist... and clearly, Reed fitted the job spec perfectly. Reed recalled being approached by Horricks after he had played piano for Rosemary Squires on a radio broadcast. "By 1962, I knew everything about the pop business," he later explained, "and it was natural from then on to get into it in a bigger way." In his own mind, Reed had reached a point in his career when he wanted to be closer to the hub of the music business community in and around Denmark Street and Archer Street on a day-to-day basis. With longer-term pretensions towards song writing and record production, this was too good an opportunity to miss and so, as a result, he duly accepted Horrick's offer.

Les Reed was, therefore, about to become a major competitor to John Barry in the record making stakes (both employed as 'MDs' at their respective labels) and right from the off, he made a good impression, for it didn't take him long before he struck gold in masterminding the label's first big hit: Joe Brown and the Bruvvers' 'A Picture of You', which peaked at No. 2 after first charting during May to become the twelfth biggest selling single of the year. Brown was to notch up five further sizeable hits under Reed's guidance spread over an eighteen-month period that included two more 'top tenners', 'It Only Took a Minute' (1962) and 'That's What Love Will Do (1963), with Reed even playing the celeste on the former's B-side, 'All Things Bright and Beautiful'.

As Les Reed would later confirm, being a member of a predominantly rock 'n' roll based outfit like The JB7 proved, undoubtedly, to be a valuable training ground for a jazz-orientated musician initially wary of entering the pop scene. By the time he left the band, he would readily admit to having been won over by its endless possibilities and, as a result, wanted to become a bigger part of the hit-making process. Here's how he would sum up his JB7 years on looking back over his career: "When I first joined The Seven, I had to adapt my mind considerably after having come from a strictly jazz background. Just having to provide only basic chords was extremely hard for me to adjust to, but the money was good and the experience allowed me to meet many 'pop' people along the way; people who became a very important part of my future. My life with The JB7 was wonderful inasmuch as it provided me with a unique insight into the machinations of the 'popular music' arena." It is fair to say that following his sudden departure, Les Reed never ever needed to look back, given that even greater success was awaiting him just around the corner.

Following such an unexpectedly hasty exit, a massive void needed to be filled with some urgency. Fortunately, Reed was able to recommend a ready made replacement in the form of Brian Hazelby; a fine pianist grounded in the classics whose musical preferences for Bach and Chopin very quickly came to the fore whenever he arrived at a new venue, much preferring to practise assiduously rather than unload any gear. Such was his proclivity for flamboyant keyboard flourishes that the nickname 'Rachmaninov' soon began to stick amongst his new band mates – to such an extent that Vic Flick had great difficulty in remembering his real name, as we shall shortly discover.

After being demobbed in 1958, Hazelby started to play professionally at the Pump Rooms in Leamington Spa during which time he also met his future bride, Pauline. After three years on the local treadmill, he made the bold decision of focusing his energies on the music scene in London instead. With a wife and baby daughter, Ella, now to support, seeking fame and fortune in the showbiz capital seemed a sounder strategy since it was more likely to offer better prospects. For Hazelby, there simply had to be more to life than playing for "the genteel folk of Royal Leamington," as he succinctly put it. Many an hour was spent knocking on doors and filling phone boxes with "those heavy pennies" in order to contact various agents, but the legwork eventually paid off with a variety of engagements ranging from house parties, working men's clubs to more exclusive West End ones. Both ends of the spectrum were catered for and along the way he was able to cultivate a number of contacts and friendships within the music business, Les Reed and family among them. This was to reap dividends when, in January 1962, he received a telegram from John Barry inviting him to join The John Barry Seven following Reed's decision to leave the band. In fact, Reed recalled how he and his wife, June, passed the baton on cordially by inviting the Hazelbys for a meal at their Wimbledon flat.

To this day, Hazelby can clearly remember his debut as a member of The JB7 and for good reason: "My first gig was at Whitehaven (in Cumbria). I went by train, met the chaps there only to discover that I had to work without any 'dots' (i.e. music). As a consequence, I needed to rely on Mike Peters to shout out the chords for me!" If that alone wasn't memorable enough, it was the journey home that would indelibly stick in his mind. Once the show was over, Vic Flick drove him part way home – "at great speed and through the roughest of terrains" – until he ended up waiting several hours at Shrewsbury Station for the connecting train back home to Leamington. Unfortunately, poor Brian fell asleep at precisely the wrong time, eventually waking up a good few miles past Leamington Spa with the loco now bound for Paddington Station. "I eventually got home," he added, "but only after experiencing what must have been the longest gig on record!"

Hazelby's virtuosity, combined with his extensive knowledge of the Great Composers' repertoires, was instrumental in digging The Seven out of one notable hole during a concert at The Floral Hall in Scarborough when the band was wrongly scheduled to perform a full two hour set and not the half-hour one as originally agreed. In order to avoid an embarrassing failure, a lack of material and a reliance on repetition, 'Rachmaninov' was only too delighted to provide the paying public with an exhibition of the full range of his undoubted talent. Therefore, after the band had played a couple of numbers, up strode Hazelby behind the keyboard to give the solo performance of his life.

According to Vic Flick, there were no more than around a hundred or so folk in the audience that night and, as such, proceedings opened to a mere rippling of applause. "And when we roared into our two opening numbers," he explained, "these, too, received an anaemic reaction. Then when I announced 'Ladies and Gentlemen, for your pianistic delight, I give you Brian – ', well, my mind went completely blank. I had been calling him Rachmaninov for so long I had forgotten his last name!" Fortunately, at that point, Hazelby took it upon himself to grab the microphone, by announcing the full extent of his planned recital, and much to a startled audience, not to mention Flick's great relief, that was precisely what he proceeded to do: "Returning to the piano, Brian started on what he must have thought of as his solo concert début either at the Wigmore or Carnegie Hall. It went on and on and on and on. Not only did it succeed in thinning out the audience by about 50%, but it also gave us the break we needed!"

Hazelby was soon in his stride, cutting his teeth at venues such as Darlington, Bloxwich Baths, plus 'Grand Dances' at Bradford Kings Hall and in Maesteg, when, come February, The JB7 were once again re-united with Adam Faith for an extensive 20-date tour of England's cinemas (mainly Granada ones) starting at the Adelphi (Slough) on 3rd and ending at the ABC (Exeter) on 25th – an itinerary interrupted only by a JB7-only dance engagement in Harrogate (on the 11th). Also on the bill were Des Lane, Brad Newman, Johnny LeRoy and compère, Dave Reid.

This was Hazelby's first experience of witnessing at such close quarters the mass hysteria generated by a teen-idol. Faith once described the effect as "a gale of sound crashing up and over me, like some physical force – two thousand supercharged girls screaming at full pitch." No wonder Hazelby, on revisiting the heat, the noise and mania from way back in 1962, was still able to summon up such minute detail well over fifty years later: "Brad having a pull-away jacket, which fans tore off; Adam crashing his Jag, and Des opening with 'Caravan' on his penny whistle," were among some of his more vivid snapshots from that tour. What wasn't obvious at the time, though, was that this would be the last one on which The JB7 would back Faith, but with Faith still resolved on reforming The Roulettes, albeit this time with an altogether more accomplished set of musicians, The Seven's days were numbered and so, after filling in on this tour effectively as a stop-gap, they were now on the brink of being ousted. Only bassist, John Rogers and guitarist Pete Thorpe were to remain from The Roulettes' rather ramshackle first line-up.

Surprisingly, the band's pre-tour radio appearance on *Saturday Club* broadcast on 3rd February (pre-recorded on the 2nd) – alongside Adam Faith, The Polka Dots, Ray Pilgrim, Joy and Dave, The Eric Delaney Band, and Arthur Greenslade and The Gee Men – was to be their last appearance on this show until 1965! Why this was exactly is not entirely clear. However, an internal memo discovered in the BBC archives revealed a reticence to pay the band the same rate now that Barry was no longer on board. Furthermore, an adjudged 'below par' performance (courtesy of Jimmy Grant) with regards to this appearance on the show may have also influenced matters, but even so, it does seem odd that a band, who, up to that point, had been one of the show's regular contributors, was not invited to appear again for some considerable time even when they re-entered the Top Twenty later in November. Barry may well have taken the BBC's patronage a tad too much for granted when he decided to jettison the live work.

～

The JB7 had a chequered relationship with Jimmy Grant, the principal producer of Saturday Club *and other BBC music programmes. It was Grant who oversaw The JB7's radio audition in September 1957, at a time when they were already appearing on BBC TV's* Six-Five Special, *and it was he who turned them down.*

They finally made their Saturday Club *debut almost two years later, after they had become highly popular through their weekly* Drumbeat *TV appearances.*

Having made this breakthrough, Grant proceeded to book them fairly often, both with and without Adam Faith. In fact, he was apparently so impressed after just two or three appearances that he floated the idea of them becoming the house band.

Melody Maker's 16th January 1960 issue reported: "The John Barry Seven will take over as the house band for the BBC's Saturday Club as the show moves to include pop and rock oriented material into its format".

Ultimately this didn't happen; in fact, unlike Easy Beat, Saturday Club *never had a house band of its own, instead ensuring that a band capable of providing suitable accompaniment was always on the bill to support the various guest vocalists. Outfits headed by the likes of Ken Jones, Arthur Greenslade, Bob Miller, David Ede, Bert Weedon, Ronnie Price, Tommy Sanderson and Ted Taylor were semi-regulars for long periods, but The JB7 relied mostly upon regular guest appearances.*

However, this all came abruptly to an end with the aforementioned appearance on 3rd February 1962. The band's line-up at this stage, remember, saw Bobby Carr replacing John Barry on trumpet and Brian Hazelby on piano following Les Reed's departure.

The Seven also accompanied Adam Faith on this programme, just prior to them all starting a lengthy tour of the UK. Faith had also become a regular guest on the programme though in fact his last appearance had been several months previously, once again with The JB7.

The long gap of almost eight months can be attributed to the limited availability of both artistes, since they were touring regularly, but The JB7 could not have realised that this 1962 appearance would have been the last for almost three years! Indeed, as far as this line-up was concerned, it was the band's last ever appearance on the BBC.

Neither act had new releases to promote on the 3rd February; their latest singles being 'Lonesome'/'Watch Your Step' (Faith) and 'Watch Your Step'/'Twist It' (JB7). However, on the session, The JB7 did perform 'Watch Your Step' in a set that also included Cliff Richard's 'The Young Ones', 'Image' and 'It Doesn't Matter Anymore', while accompanying Faith on 'You and Me and the Gang', 'The Time Has Come', 'As Long As You Keep Loving Me', 'Lonesome' and 'If I Had a Hammer'.

Weeks and then months passed without any invitation for a return visit to the show, but when The JB7's management attempted to get them back on BBC Radio, producer Grant responded in July 1963 by way of the aforementioned internal memo criticising their last performance (i.e. 3rd February '62 one) as "rather poor" and also claiming that now John Barry no longer played in the band, their fee made them an expensive hire.

One can only guess as to what Grant didn't like about The JB7's performance, assuming that was the genuine reason for them being sidelined. However, it's also possible that something else might have been going on behind the scenes, involving Eve Taylor. The latter was infamous for some outlandish demands on behalf of her clients, threatening withdrawal of their services at times, and perhaps her bluff may have been called on a future occasion.

Certainly it was notable that quite apart from The JB7's long stint on the sidelines,

Adam Faith had to wait another eight months before his next appearance, backed on that occasion by his new band, The Roulettes, and this at a time when he was as popular as ever.

We may never know if Grant and Taylor did fall out over money, but it's perhaps interesting to note that when The (new) John Barry Seven finally returned to Saturday Club *in 1965, their producer was Brian Willey, and Taylor no longer managed the Seven.*

≈

No amount of gigging could ever equate with the pull of a hit single for raising a band's national profile. After an eleven-month absence from the charts, it was imperative for The JB7 to reconnect with the record buying public. Airplay and media interest, in general, would naturally follow as a result of a Top Forty placing. Both sides of the new single – 'Cutty Sark'/'Lost Patrol' – were recorded in the middle of the Adam Faith tour (on 20th, and 12th February respectively). Now although in all probability the touring JB7 would have recorded 'Lost Patrol', as there was no concert scheduled for the 12th, it is highly unlikely that 'Cutty Sark' (the designated A-side) would have involved any of the touring party since they were all playing with Faith at the newly re-named ABC Cinema in Carlisle (formerly the 'Lonsdale') on the day of recording.

Here was a clear sign that Barry had no qualms whatsoever in differentiating between a studio and touring variant of the band. On release, the single was attributed to 'The John Barry Seven and Orchestra', but in truth the personnel was made up entirely of session musicians. Once again, this upset Dougie Wright in particular, who took exception to having been replaced on drums by Art Morgan for the recording of 'Cutty Sark' – understandably so given his mastery of the instrument, but in weighing up the practical considerations, the decision was likely to have been borne out of simple pragmatism rather than a slight on Wright's capabilities. The logistics of having to travel over 300 miles from Tunbridge Wells to Carlisle via Abbey Road inside a day was likely to have held sway. Nevertheless, the seeds of discontent amongst the 'foot soldiers' were being planted.

'Cutty Sark' was a clever pastiche of The Dave Brubeck Quartet's 'Take Five', which, of course, The Seven had already recently introduced into their stage act. Clearly inspired by the 'West Coast' 'Cool School', right down to the tone of Paul Desmond's alto sax and Joe Morello's drumming style, here was Barry's 'West Riding' equivalent – an equally distinctive and highly original jazz instrumental only this time characterised by a strikingly rhythmic staccato brass arrangement. In contrast, the B-side, 'Lost Patrol' (written by New York composer and harpist, Robert Maxwell, and based on Tchaikovsky's 'Capriccio Italien'), evoked the type of martial music that would have been 'meat and drink' to the Band of the Green Howards during Barry's period of National Service, and hence an ideal opportunity for putting into practice what he learned from them.

Both sides proved just how mature and adaptable Barry's writing had become when 'Cutty Sark' was chosen as the signature tune for ITV's current affairs programme *Dateline London*, and also when 'Lost Patrol' served a similar purpose for the BBC TV regional news slot, *Look North*. In fact, the latter even went global when picked up by ABC-TV (Australia) as the theme to its hard-hitting topical news show, *Four Corners*, the result of which saw it surge into various Antipodean regional Top Tens throughout the during July/August 1963, re-titled as 'The Four Corners Theme'. (There was no national chart in Australia until October 1966.) Released in the UK on 23rd March 1962, 'Cutty Sark' would finally restore The JB7 to the UK Top Forty, whereupon it would peak at No. 35 and sell a respectable 25,768 copies.

Reviews of the single in *Disc* and *New Record Mirror* were both on the positive side. Whereas the former was quick to make the comparison with 'Take Five' (whilst acknowledging 'Cutty Sark's' "cool melody" and "fastidious" alto saxophone playing) and to recognise the military influences on 'Lost Patrol', the latter was keen to praise Barry's versatility, and comment on how far he had travelled since departing from his rock 'n' roll origins. "Friendly, but not too pretentious, John can tackle literally every kind of music," was its conclusion. Barry was at a point in his pop career where he could do little wrong and was regularly being touted as one of the industry's 'bright young things'. This was epitomised perfectly when, during a *Melody Maker* interview with Bobby Vee in a February edition, the singer readily admitted to using Barry's arrangements for Adam Faith as the template for his own records.

The JB7 were able to promote the new single a mere two days after its release with an appearance on the seventh *Daily Express*-sponsored annual star-studded 'S.O.S, Record Star Show' held at 'The Empire Pool', Wembley, on the 25th. For the price of just 10s 6d (52.5p), the packed audience was able to witness live many of the biggest names on the British scene at the time: on this occasion, The Shadows alone (Cliff Richard being ill on the day), Adam Faith, Helen Shapiro, Kenny Ball and His Jazzmen (with Beryl Bryden), Lonnie Donegan, Tommy Bruce, Rosemary Squires, The Brook Brothers, Doug Sheldon, Des Lane and Ron Goodwin, with David Jacobs acting as compère.

Ironically, rather than 'Cutty Sark', it was The Seven's "clever" version of 'Take Five' that was singled out by Norman Bowles of *The Stage* as being "particularly well received". No doubt the band were also able to promote the two tracks that had also just been issued as part of the *Beat Girl* EP, 'The Stripper' and 'Main Title – Beat Girl' – both proven staple parts of the live repertoire. From The JB7's perspective, the event turned out to be a particularly significant one, for when Adam Faith finished the first half of the show to a tremendous reception (in a set which included a rollicking version of Chubby Checker's 'Let's Twist Again'), this would be the last occasion on which the band would accompany Faith in a live setting. No longer would the two acts share the same stage again. Now whether or not this was known by either party at the time is a moot point.

The release of the *Beat Girl* EP may well have been a canny ploy by Columbia of cashing in on Parlophone's most popular act given that the other two cuts making up the four were two of Faith's three songs from the soundtrack LP, 'I Did What You Told Me' and 'Made You'. Fierce sibling rivalry may have persuaded Columbia to release the EP amongst a glut of other titles bearing Adam Faith's name that were being issued by Parlophone during the early months of 1962. No fewer than five new EP titles hit the record shops between January and April without actually counting the *Beat Girl* one!

Tellingly, the entire *Beat Girl* EP package completely expunged any reference at all to the contributions made by The JB7. It appeared to be specifically designed to promote Barry (and to a lesser extent, Faith), thereby demonstrating once again how the Columbia contract in essence was a vehicle for furthering Barry's career and no one else's.

What is worth pointing out is just how lucrative the EP market had become by the time of *Beat Girl*'s release; in fact, it was entering its golden age. In acknowledging the trend, the *Record Retailer* first introduced an 'official' EP top ten chart on 10th March 1960 (soon expanded to twenty two weeks later). The EP format in the main collected together an artist's two most recent hit singles (A- and B-sides) housed in an attractive colour picture sleeve and was released once the sales of those 45s had peaked. It was a way of selling the same product twice, in effect, and at 11s 3d (56p) was cheaper than buying both singles separately (each costing 6s 6d (32.5p) in 1962). It also acted as a bridge between the 45 and LP markets, appealing to the younger record buyer whose budget could not stretch to a pop album (priced at £1 14s 6d, £1.72.5).

Although Cliff Richard and The Shadows (both collectively and individually) registered the most hits on the EP chart – and by some distance if you add the two together (42) – Adam Faith's chart-topping 'Adam's Hit Parade' was to become the seventh most successful EP of all time in terms of longevity (77 weeks in total, of which 76 were consecutive). The JB7's only listing was 'The John Barry Sound', which peaked at No. 4 during 1961. Featuring both sides of the hit singles 'Hit and Miss' and 'Walk Don't Run', it sold a healthy 13,630 in the UK. The *Beat Girl* EP, though less successful, still racked up decent sales of 4,442 despite failing to make the chart.

The dissolution of The JB7/Adam Faith performing partnership was but a prelude to a much higher profile 'divorce' when in early autumn Barry and Faith formally announced that they, too, would be parting company by mutual consent. No longer would Barry be acting as Faith's Musical Director. In the music press, this was treated as big headline news – the lead story by some distance – and a huge shock, which was hardly surprising given the nature of their hitherto gold-plated relationship. Barry had overseen no fewer than twelve hits (among them two No. 1s and another seven Top-Tenners) within a narrow time frame of less than three years. What's more, the latest, 'As You Like it', had been one of Faith's biggest and best received for almost a year. Although handled very diplomatically in public by all concerned, as previously stated, Faith had long since harboured various frustrations behind the scenes. It would not be long before the entire producer/writer/band backroom team of Barry, Worth and The JB7 would be replaced by Johnny Keating, Chris Andrews and The Roulettes respectively.

Having so many other irons in the fire by this stage of his career meant that Barry was able to afford to severe links with Faith without enduring any hardship. Amongst these was hands-on, creative involvement in no fewer than five up-and-coming feature films (*The Amorous Prawn*, *Mix Me A Person*, *The Cool Mikado*, *Dr. No* and *The L-Shaped Room*), which was where his ambition always lay from the outset anyway.

In knowing full well of Faith's intention to resurrect The Roulettes as soon as he was able, it was probably no coincidence when Barry also decided to end his (and The JB7's) association with Eve Taylor at precisely the same juncture. Any chance of The JB7 ever appearing again with Faith on package tours booked by Taylor was in all likelihood remote once the new band was *in situ*. Moreover, Barry was now busily trying to steer the careers of many other lesser-established artists in his MD role at EMI, some in whom he had a further vested interest given their affiliation to his co-owned agency, Topline Artists. It, therefore, made better sense for him to throw in his lot with Tony Lewis who was now looking after the day-to-day running of the agency and was already acting as his own agent anyway. Assuming the management of The JB7 simply became yet another act for Lewis to take responsibility, albeit an important one.

So as from the end of February (the 'SOS' concert notwithstanding), The JB7 bandwagon kept on rolling throughout the length and breadth of the UK albeit without Adam Faith as part of the equation. During the end of March, the band began an eleven-day tour starting at New Brighton (Merseyside) on the 29th and ending at Southsea (Portsmouth) on 13th April.

Sandwiched in between, during one Sunday off (the 8th), they managed to fit in another appearance on *Thank Your Lucky Stars* due for broadcast on the 14th. That week's edition of *TV Times* gave it a big splash in light of the fact that this was the first in a brand new series and, as such, it portrayed a montage of featured artistes on its front cover, one of whom was John Barry himself (and not one member of The Seven, note). Given such prominence, it was no wonder that he opted to partake, and was seen participating on screen conducting the band running through 'Cutty Sark' – with some irony, miming to a recording on which they did not play, in effect. Exposure on such a high profile, peak-viewing, nationally networked, youth-targeted programme achieved its prime objective, for within a fortnight, 'Cutty Sark' was entering the UK Top Fifty at No. 36. Among the other artists appearing on this Brian Matthew-presented series opener were Gene Vincent, The Brook Brothers, Chas McDevitt and Shirley Douglas, Susan Maughan, Johnny Worth, and Danny Rivers alongside guest DJ, Jimmy Henney.

These occasional cameo appearances by Barry were to become a source of much irritation to members of the band over the course of the year, because of his penchant for hogging the limelight when it suited him and also for picking the higher profile events as well as choosing the obvious crowd pleasers whenever he was on stage. True, sometimes a promoter might insist on his presence at a venue due simply to the wording of a contract, but in his autobiography, *Guitarman*, Vic Flick recalls having to consciously bite his tongue when after performing at the opening ceremonies of the Streatham Silver Blades Ice Rink during December (28th/29th), some of the skaters remarked at how much better The JB7 were whenever Barry was present; this, after he had insisted on cherry-picking the best numbers ("curtain raisers" as Flick would call them) for the entirety of his much trumpeted twenty-minute 'special guest appearance'. "That doesn't leave us much for the rest of the night," Flick complained at the time, to which Barry retorted, "That's OK, I won't be here." There lay one of the problems of having to accommodate an absentee leader with an eye for a photo opportunity.

From 22nd April to 6th May, The Seven returned to Ireland, once again facing a schedule that took them to the most remote of locations. For Vic Flick, it remained a complete wonder to him as to how often, after driving miles and miles through the most deserted and desolate countryside, the entourage would suddenly be confronted, as if out of the ether, by an enormous ballroom that looked as if it had been thrown together with nothing like the grandeur of, say, The Rialto, York! And yet these bleak, impersonal, isolated constructions suddenly came to life once dusk descended on the surrounding vista when fields rapidly became crammed with cars and trucks after having transported the multitude, now all tucked inside, elbow to elbow and alcohol fuelled, eagerly awaiting the night's festivities.

On this particular tour, the band flew into Dublin from Heathrow courtesy of Aer Lingus and from the outset they were kept constantly entertained (just as they were during the previous tour) by the 'larger than life' personality of their roadie/driver, Nuggy McGrath, whose antics often left the entire touring party in hysterics, among them one memorable botched attempt at water skiing in Killarney. Sat behind the wheel of the VW split-screen van provided for the tour, Nuggy's Irish charm often came in handy for courting favour with the traffic police on point duty in and around Dublin.

According to Flick, much credit for the tour's smooth organisation could be attributed to the promoter, Louis Rodgers (father of singer Clodagh), whose unflappable demeanour emitted a soothing, calming presence wherever they went, be it North or South. This proved particularly useful when having to skilfully negotiate with local promoters weaned on the Irish dance band scene's tradition of staging 'all-nighters'. Initially, this clash of cultures often left Flick having to stand up for the band in no uncertain terms, reminding organisers and house band leaders alike that as a headline act, The JB7 would only be performing the two one-hour slots previously agreed and nothing more. Thankfully, he was able eventually to delegate these often-heated exchanges to the implacable Rodgers thereby enabling the beleaguered guitarist to concentrate on what he did best – music.

Despite these backstage altercations, the band found the Irish way of life most agreeable, each and every one of them thoroughly enjoying the experience. In what spare time was permitted, they attempted a round of golf, sampled the local hostelries and even embarked on a little horse riding. The breathtaking scenery provided Mike Peters with the perfect backdrop for indulging his favourite pastime, photography.

No sooner had the band returned from Ireland than they were back clocking up the mileage throughout England and Wales. Reviews were decidedly mixed. One particular date in Cardiff failed to meet the approval of *Disc*, seemingly the first of its kind hinting at a sea change in the air. "The much publicized JB7 concert/dance at Cardiff turned out a let down. Although their more serious music came over well, particularly a trumpet version of 'Moanin', there was little soul, style or drive to keep the mainly teenage audience moving." In redressing the balance, however, an appearance at Lowestoft in July was much better received, at least according to *The Stage*: "The new John Barry Seven, with trumpeter Bobby Carr taking Barry's place in the group, entertained a large audience of holidaymakers at the Sparrow's Nest, Lowestoft, recently. John Barry now handles behind-the-scenes production work for The Seven. Working everything from modern jazz to classics into their programme, The Seven revealed great talent for playing their varied instruments, and kept the audience 'in the groove' for two hours."

≈

Brian Hazelby revealed that the aforementioned 'Moanin' was a favourite of Bobby Carr's. "Bobby and I would try to get to the gig early, him driving his beloved little Sprite car, in order to have a blow. Always started with that great jazz tune, Art Blakey and The Jazz Messengers' 'Moanin'."

≈

With so many performances to look back upon (and, in 1962 alone, The JB7 took to the stage on more than 150 occasions), it was always those appearances that were either of a more personal nature or simply slightly out of the ordinary, which stood out above all others for just about every member of the band. Take Jimmy Stead for example. Of all the gigs throughout the years to which he was party, one that involved his father has etched as firmly as any in his mind ever since. During the summer season, The JB7 were booked for a residency at Folkestone and since his father was staying with him in Luton at the time, he decided to take him along, which was the first time he had ever done so as a member of The JB7. "Although it was a long day, what with driving there, setting up, playing the gig and then driving back to Luton, he enjoyed the experience,"

Stead fondly remembered. Brian Hazelby recalled the same set of dates albeit for entirely different reasons: "Every Wednesday, Mike Peters and Bobby Carr would visit my home in Leamington Spa whereupon I would drive them to Folkestone for the gig."

It may not have resonated with quite the same significance amongst members of The JB7, but for John Barry, June 1962 was to become, as he often alluded, the most significant month of his entire career. Not only did he start work on the now iconic 'The James Bond Theme', but he was also given the opportunity by director Bryan Forbes of contributing to *The L-Shaped Room* (thereby initiating two richly fruitful long-term collaborations that were to cement his reputation as a film composer *par excellence)*.

Recording 'The James Bond Theme' for *Dr. No* sign-posted Barry's future direction as impressively as any track could ever have done, resulting in a massive hit single and, more importantly, future commissions for the franchise. After having being originally recorded at CTS Studios for the original soundtrack on 21st June by an augmented JB7, it was remade between 10 a.m. and 1 p.m. on 23rd July at Abbey Road as part of the deal that led to Barry agreeing to work on the film in the first place. It was this latter version, released on Columbia later in September that catapulted The JB7 (and Orchestra) back into the Top Twenty.

Precisely who else played on either or both of these sessions, apart from Vic Flick, has long remained a mystery, more's the pity, particularly when the number of musicians who have *claimed* to have done so runs at approximately twice the size of the actual orchestra used! Sadly, the authors were unable to solve this particular conundrum; names could not be named, as no documentation came to light with the salient information, but with access to EMI's archives, it was possible to find out precisely what instrumentation was used on the session for the Columbia Records hit single. This reads as follows: four trumpets, four trombones, bass trombone, two French horns, five saxes (four doubling flutes), two electric guitars, piano, bass, two percussion, and drums – in total, twenty-three musicians.

This backs up the comment made by John Barry when he later insisted that no strings were ever used on the theme, which will no doubt come as a disappointment to any string player who may have laid claim to have played on it! Recorded on the same session, incidentally, was an embryonic attempt at tackling what would become The JB7's follow-up single – 'The Lolly Theme' – which would explain the necessity for four of the sax players lending themselves to the flute parts integral to the arrangement thereof. The entire three-hour session cost £166.

Engineer Malcolm Addey, who as a fledgling at Abbey Road in 1958 was chiefly responsible for masterminding the authentic rock 'n' roll sound achieved by Cliff Richard and The Drifter's breakthrough hit 'Move It', was at pains to point out to the authors that by 1962, Barry felt no compunction whatsoever in recruiting as many musicians as he felt necessary to produce the sound he was striving for, much to the consternation of his then boss at Columbia, Norman

Newell, whose eyes were fixed firmly on the balance sheet. Barry and Addey were indeed kindred spirits in their quest for securing the perfect recorded sound, both having discovered the virtue of precise close microphone placement via differing routes; Barry by dint of his field trip to the US and Addey by virtue of painstaking day-to-day 'hands on' studio experimentation. Addey would later joke that The JB7 should have been renamed The JB47 by the time 'The James Bond Theme' was recorded, although as we have now since discovered, The JB23 would have been more accurate!

Without wishing to trawl through well traversed waters already covered in our earlier tome (*John Barry: The Man with the Midas Touch*), suffice to say that having been given a mere two days to deliver the goods (i.e. a memorable musical motif for agent 007), Barry was able to transform what in essence was a barely developed fragment of a slow Raga-like melody (as written by Monty Norman) into something utterly unrecognisable, compelling and unique: into what became the archetypal spy theme now known the world over. He was soon to be rewarded with the musical keys to the James Bond kingdom as a direct consequence, even though at the time he had no reason to believe that that would definitely happen. What it certainly did achieve back then, however, was to enhance his reputation as one of the music industry's 'hottest properties', and although it did not bring the same lasting success to individual members of The JB7, it did no harm whatsoever in cementing Vic Flick's credentials as a session guitarist of note, even if his only financial reward was the bog-standard three-hour session fee and nothing more – £7 10s (£7.50), according to Flick.

The release of 'The James Bond Theme' during September came at a time when the UK record industry had finally started to successfully tap into the hitherto underdeveloped and potentially lucrative market generated by the TV and film tie-in. With only two television networks legally permissible, the potential rewards were enormous. By releasing a main theme attached to a weekly drama that commanded a massive multi-million audience, for example, there was every chance of it succeeding simply by association. Likewise, a box-office hit was highly likely to attract the same reaction. The precedent had already been set by the release of Mr. Acker Bilk's theme to the BBC drama *Stranger on the Shore* in November 1961. Not only did it remain in the UK charts for an astonishing 55 weeks (incredibly almost the whole of 1962), but it also became the first UK single ever to top the American Hot 100, as widely reported throughout the music press during May. Other labels were quick to follow Columbia's lead. As a result, themes from three of 1962's most popular television programmes benefited from this strategy with Joe Loss's 'The Maigret Theme' (on HMV); Johnny Keating's 'Theme from 'Z Cars' (on Les Reed's Piccadilly) and Johnny Spence's 'Theme from Dr. Kildare' (on Parlophone) all notching up sizeable sales by reaching the Top Twenty.

At the beginning of August, The Seven travelled to Shepperton Studios to film a cameo appearance in Michael Winner's *The Cool Mikado*, which as its title suggests, was an updated, yet truncated, take on Gilbert and Sullivan's *The Mikado*. Joining Stubby Kaye, a regular American visitor to the UK, were a plethora of British stars including Frankie Howard, Tommy Cooper, Dennis Price, Mike and Bernie Winters, and Lionel Blair. The presence of Blair proved a slight irritation and distraction to both The JB7 and its legion of fans, since he and his dancers tended to hog the limelight (and the cameras) throughout what was to be the band's only number, 'Tit Willow Twist'. Although credited to Barry as sole composer, this was no more than a guitar instrumental of the Gilbert and Sullivan song.

As was the case on *A Matter of WHO*, The JB7 quickly discovered that capturing two or three minutes' worth of celluloid onto the big screen took rather longer than a few minutes to set up and film. For Brian Hazelby, this was a tedious and exasperating experience: "I remember having to spend days waiting around, and yet when the moment arrived for us to do our spot, we mimed the entire scene. That's showbiz!"

Not long after this frustrating escapade, Hazelby decided it was time for him to move on. The point had been reached where the thrill had long since gone, his health was taking its toll and he was not playing the style of music he so longed to play. As he put it, "It seemed great at first but, for me, it became a nightmare. I was taking tranquillizers to keep going and to stay awake. I so wanted to do my own thing on piano. Also, by this time, I felt The Seven were beginning to wane." With 'The James Bond Theme' already in the can, Hazelby was not to stick around to witness The Seven's Top Twenty renaissance during November.

Kenny Salmon was quickly drafted in to take Hazelby's place. Born in Hainault, Essex in 1933, he did not descend from a musical family, but after having been evacuated to the home of an aunt and uncle during the war, was offered the chance of taking piano lessons. This proved to be an astute move, for by the time he had left school he was already playing with amateur dance bands in and around the Portsmouth area, where the family had since moved, as well as starting to write his own arrangements. National Service, as was often the case, interrupted this young man's career path, for despite having being conscripted as a bandsman in the 4/7 Royal Dragoon Guards Band, it turned out to be an unedifying experience. Vowing to put his musical ambitions back on track thereafter, he then joined the resident orchestra at the Mecca dance hall in Edinburgh, which later transferred to Mecca's equivalent in Sheffield. By 1956, he had returned to the London area where he would spend the rest of his life. There, he first played with Frank Weir's band, until around 1960, he took up with The Eric Delaney Band, which toured Germany several times. As a composer, he co-wrote 'Rolling the Tymps' with Delaney, during which time he started playing the Lowrey organ in addition to the piano. From then on, he was somewhat of a musician for hire: playing with Bob Miller and The Millermen on BBC Radio sessions for the Light Programme (on programmes such as *Go Man Go*, *Easy Beat* and *Parade of the Pops*); often deputising when needed in the Oscar Rabin Band at the Wimbledon Palais, plus playing in an array of other ensembles before joining The John Barry Seven.

No sooner had Salmon settled himself into the routine of band life with The JB7 than Dougie Wright decided to go the other way entirely by promptly quitting the band forthwith. To his fellow band mates, such a bold move as this was unlikely to have come as a huge surprise. After a series of rows with Barry over various aspects of musical policy, in addition to the gradual reduction of regular tour dates – soon to be exacerbated following the management's decision to disassociate The Seven altogether from the Adam Faith bandwagon – enough was clearly enough in the eyes of the disillusioned drummer. He was leaving to try his luck elsewhere in the music business, and with a growing reputation as a consummate session player, was about to utilise his network of contacts to seek work in and around the London studio scene. In many ways, his departure marked the end of an era for The JB7 and a sign of what was to come; in other words, this would no longer be the stable, coterie of musicians of old, with personnel changes becoming the norm rather than the exception.

Dougie Wright's final gig with The Seven was an appearance at Whitehall, East Grinstead on 24th August. To this day, he remains extremely bitter about how Barry treated and used the band for his own purposes and, in particular, critical of the way in which he neglected them once he stopped touring to pursue his other music interests. To quote Wright directly, "From my point of view, Barry was in it entirely for himself. We were, primarily, a vehicle to give him a leg up, and once he had achieved his aims, he left and allowed us to dwindle away." He was also piqued at receiving scant recognition for their musical input, adding, "Nor were we given proper credit. Barry used to write out our parts and we would often improve them by chipping in ideas of our own, and on some tracks we made considerable contributions to the overall outcome." The issue of financial remuneration (or lack of it) was another major irritation: "There was never any question of royalties with Barry either, since we were simply salaried musicians and therefore not entitled to anything other than our session fees as far as he was concerned. I found him ruthlessly ambitious, and he had an obsession about using session men at the expense of regular group members." As previously recounted, Wright was 'dropped' from playing on 'Watch Your Step' and 'Cutty Sark' in favour of Andy White and Art Morgan respectively, which may well have acted as the final straw for Wright (even if Barry may have argued that this was done purely for practical reasons and nothing more). Nevertheless, Wright felt insulted by the snub. "It was a ridiculous practise," he insisted, "Because all of the post-'59 band were capable of handling anything that was thrown at them, and in any case I went on to do more session work than Art Morgan ever did." Indeed, Wright soon became, alongside Clem Cattini, Andy White and Bobby Graham (about whom we shall learn more later), the 'go-to percussionists' whenever a session drummer was required throughout the sixties and beyond.

Another cause of bitterness revolved around Barry's apparent refusal to adapt to the changing musical climate that was emerging at the time. Members of the touring JB7, as a natural consequence of relentlessly performing the length and breadth of the UK, would have been perfectly placed for witnessing the sudden proliferation of the beat group, whose song-dominated repertoire necessitated a lead vocalist. In fact, there were reported to have been no fewer than five hundred or so such combos playing in the Merseyside area alone throughout this period! The JB7 would have had to have been blind not to have become aware of the prevailing trend, as Wright later confirmed: "Times were changing, other styles were coming in, and so I said to Vic Flick, 'We've got to become a vocal band or else we'll get left behind,' and yet my advice was not heeded even though we were regularly having dates cancelled. I saw the light and the writing on the wall. I said to myself, 'Do something and do it now.' I left the band after a blow-up with Barry on the telephone. The work had been going gradually downhill, and to cap matters he became insulting, and so I told him that I was finished."

This festering discontent was confirmed by Jimmy Stead, who recalls Dennis King's repeated requests for the introduction of one or two vocal numbers in their set being continually met by deaf ears. And that wasn't the only grumble! Stead was similarly irritated by Barry's apparent indifference whenever day-to-day problems arose on tour. "Take one minor point as an example: when the trousers of my stage-wear had become threadbare, I wrote to Barbara Barry requesting a replacement, but received absolutely no response." In an almost perfect echo of Wright's gripes, Stead added. "It was obvious that John Barry had his eyes on 'the main chance', but what could any of us do about it? Don't forget that we had a contract of employment with Barry and were paid by him for each engagement as employees, carefully managed by his then wife, Barbara. We paid for the running of the band van out of our own earnings, as well as tea, coffee, digs, transport café meals, *etc.* Oh, happy days!" Nonetheless, even though Stead knew full well that Barry formed the band as a means to his own end, not once has he ever regretted the opportunity of being part of the band. "I for one would definitely state just how lucky I was to receive Barry's phone call inviting me to join The Seven. We had really, really great times with so many good memories," he would later reflect. Evidently, from his perspective, the good times outweighed the bad.

Dougie Wright's replacement on drums was a former flatmate of Vic Flick and Les Reed, Dickie Harwood. In fact, Reed and Harwood were well acquainted long before Reed himself joined The JB7: "Dickie and I played for The Harry Singleton Orchestra at the Lido Restaurant, Swallow Street, London W1 from 1957 to 1959, which was prior to me moving on to join The JB7. We shared a flat together in Notting Hill Gate until 1961. He was a fine drummer and when Vic moved into the flat with us, soon got to know a great deal about The JB7, and he also played as part of a trio with Vic and I on a few jazz gigs outside of The Seven concerts."

Regrettably, Harwood's stint behind the drums was a short-lived affair, and following his departure, session drummer Andy White was recruited to fill in, although regular studio session work invariably restricted his availability. However, as both Brian Hazelby and Dougie Wright pointed out, this problem was likely to have been ameliorated unintentionally by the sudden shrinkage in bookings, for the band was by now nowhere near as busy as they had been when working regularly as Adam Faith's trusted backing band. What was once an incessant schedule involving five and sometimes six gigs per week had been pared down drastically to regular weekend ones augmented by the odd mid-week engagement or two. The entire itinerary from September right up to the end of the year conformed to this pattern. Hence, only ten dates were confirmed for October, followed by fourteen each throughout the months of November and December. Compared to The JB7's previous heavy workloads, these were slim pickings indeed.

To make matters worse – as Dougie Wright and Dennis King sagely pointed out to the management – direct competition from a new generation of four- or five-piece vocal groups had become a stark reality. Promoters, with eyes firmly fixed on the profit and loss account, were now thinking twice about hiring a seven-piece band when a cheaper option was available. Recording sessions during the autumn months had also petered out to a large extent restricted only to the recording of the B-side to 'The James Bond Theme' (an instrumental beat-group-like cover of Ella Mae Morse's 1952 million-seller on Capitol, 'The Blacksmith Blues') during August (the 29th).

Fortunately, the September release of 'The James Bond Theme', did bring some much-needed attention and chart success for The JB7, even if the record was actually accredited to 'The John Barry Seven and Orchestra' in recognition of the big band ensemble assembled for the recording. However, the respective EMI and Topline Agency publicity machines appeared to have missed a huge trick or two in failing to exploit the popularity of the single. Astonishingly for what was to become such a massive hit, no TV nor radio promotion ensued whatsoever, which amounted to a golden opportunity lost – the showbiz equivalent of an own goal, surely; neither did its success appear to have made much difference to the volume of bookings thereafter. One would have at least anticipated an appearance on *Thank Your Lucky Stars* at some stage of the 45's eleven-week chart run, but it was not to be. The JB7's absence on the UK's then-premier pop programme remains a mystery when one considers just who was booked to appear on the show during this period: The Eric Delaney Band, The Flee-Rekkers, Peter Jay and The Jaywalkers, The Spotniks, The Temperance Seven, *etc*. One can't help thinking that this was one more example of team JB7 taking an eye off the ball just at a point when maximum mainstream exposure would have done wonders for updating the band's image and upgrading its place in pop's hierarchy.

Reviews of 'The James Bond Theme' were both sparse and mixed, but despite that, the record succeeded in reaching No. 13 in the charts, and by April 1963, had amassed sales of 89,381. Given its now worldwide status, *New Musical Express*'s curt one-line "a sort of 'Harry Lime' of the 60s" review was cursory to say the least, albeit an apposite one, with 'The Blacksmith Blues' judged as "a fairly routine guitar instrumental." *New Record Mirror* was more thoughtful, but even they failed to recognise its chart potential: "Very large orchestra; very main-streamy effort. Some very good big band sounds on this quite dramatic effort. We liked it. Can't see its commercial prospects except as a film theme. Shows yet another facet of John's versatility but maybe he'd like a hit once in a while, too, like he used to, with Blacksmith Blues. Quite good but less interesting." It was left to *Melody Maker* to make the most succinct and accurate prediction: "The John Barry Seven and Orchestra make a first class job of the theme from Dr. No, which could score heavily."

Entering the charts on 1st November, 'The James Bond Theme' was to become The JB7's last hit single for EMI. The official Top Fifty, as published by *Record Retailer*, on 13th December provided the industry with a prescient glimpse into the future. This was the week in which the debut single from one of EMI's newest signings, The Beatles, outsold their more established stable mates. As The JB7 slipped out of the Top Twenty to No. 22, The Beatles entered it for the first time at No. 19. Proof enough, by virtue of changing chart positions, that the old order was on the cusp of being evicted. Earlier in April a 20-year-old blues enthusiast by the name of Brian Jones met two like-minded students, Michael Jagger and Keith Richards, at The Ealing Club, and by July, all three were making their stage debut at The Marquee Club as members of a five-piece group calling itself The Rolling Stones – yet another glimmer of a major paradigm shift approaching. Within a few short months, the charts would be awash in home-grown vocal groups, and yet nobody associated with the management of The JB7 appeared to take notice – or if they did, appeared not to be particularly bothered.

Of course, the success of the single was due entirely to the popularity of *Dr. No*, which was premiered on 5th October at The London Pavilion, Piccadilly. While a carefully selected few were enjoying the glitz and glamour of a red-carpeted West End night out, The JB7 were over two hundred miles away earning a crust in Morecambe! Not that Barry was on the guest-list either, although he did manage to slip into the same cinema on the following Sunday afternoon. His initial reaction, there, vacillated from shock and horror to incredulity. Hearing his potent amalgam of rock 'n' roll and bebop splattered willy-nilly all over the final cut was not what he had expected or bargained for. Not that he should have minded too much. The fact that it was so liberally featured on screen amounted to a vote of confidence in his abilities from the producers and, what's more, once put on general release, much like the film, the single took off big time (entering the Top Fifty a month later on 1st November). What particularly irked Barry was in accepting a one-off payment of £250 rather than a share of the royalties; a complaint that received short shrift when the subject was later brought up in conversation with Vic Flick. "Well, I played on it – and only got seven quid!", was his curt response.

As has already been recounted, The Seven were now mostly relying on weekend work for live work. One such regular Saturday haunt was Nantwich Civic Hall, a venue that attracted some of The JB7's most fervent fans. Jimmy Stead, on recalling one such occasion when events didn't go quite as smoothly as usual, was effusive in his praise of those "wonderful" regulars there, all of whom stayed loyal to the last. He vividly remembered turning up one night fully expecting to be the headline act only to find Bob Miller and The Millermen arriving there with the same idea. "The booking agent must have got his wires horribly crossed by double booking us in error. As a result, we tossed a coin to decide the running order and everything went swimmingly. Having only the one dressing room did prove somewhat of a problem but there's no doubt the audience got their money's worth and had a great night!"

Among the dance dates played in late October was one at Ossett, a town dear to the heart of Mike Peters. "I arranged the gig in Ossett with the help of my mother, who at the time was working in the Cock and Bottle pub, which was also the local hostelry of a mutual friend. Now he happened to be organising the yearly dance at the Ossett Town Hall aimed at raising money in aid of the local football team. When he told me how much they usually made, I suggested he could make more by booking The Seven, and so I got in touch with Barry, via Vic, to arrange a Saturday date to play there. As it turned out, the club made more profit that night than they had ever made before; such a good gig." Jimmy Stead concurred wholeheartedly: "It was a one-off but quite memorable as many friends turned up – some even from my school days."

Two days after the Ossett experience, a nineteen-piece John Barry Orchestra was holed up at The Remembrance Hall (Chelsea) rehearsing for the pilot of a planned new music-related TV show for BBC Television that was intended as an adjunct to *Juke Box Jury* on which chart acts were featured in a live setting – a very early precursor to *Top of the Pops*. However, despite being telerecorded at the BBC TV Centre some three days later (with Bobby Vee as star guest), the idea never got the go-ahead.

With only three to four dates per week booked for the foreseeable future, it was now imperative, by dint of economic necessity, to try to fill up the time vacuum productively. In Vic Flick's case, living in and around the London area certainly enabled him to draw upon his address book of contacts that he had managed to accumulate over the years either through his stage or studio work – and like Mike Peters before him, he was soon about to enter the world of the lucrative hit single covers market; only this time he was about to join the team of musicians who supplied the backing for Cannon Records' regular stream of EPs rather than for Embassy. What led him there was his longstanding friendship with musician Alan Moorhouse, who had been appointed Cannon's Musical Director. (Both Flick and Moorhouse had been members of the Eric Winstone Band in the late fifties.)

Cannon Records, formed by Australian music entrepreneur Allan Crawford in April 1961, was to release twenty-five six-track EPs right up to September

1964. Some titles issued on the Cannon imprint were also duplicated on parallel releases found on sister labels, Crossbow and Rocket, although this was not always the case. Whereas Embassy Records sold exclusively through the Woolworth's chain of shops, Crawford targeted the nation's petrol stations, newsagents and supermarkets (where they existed) for his sales outlet. Recording sessions took place at either Lansdowne Road Studios (Notting Hill) or IBC Studios (Portland Place). Much like Embassy, Crawford was able to attract a high calibre of musician to deliver what was required – i.e. authentic replica versions of the biggest hits of the day – since each flat fee per session was fixed at a competitive rate.

Many of the players were, in fact, moonlighting and, as such, preferred to adopt pseudonyms in order to protect their identities. Hence Ross McManus, away from his day job as vocalist for the Joe Loss Orchestra, became Hal Prince or Frank Bacon, whereas John Shakespeare and Kenneth Hawker (aka John Carter and Ken Lewis) became members of The Sparrows. In Mark Lewisohn's weighty Beatles biography, *All These Years*, Shakespeare attributes Flick as the acoustic guitar player in The Sparrows, whose take on 'Love Me Do' would hold the honour of becoming the first ever cover version of a Lennon-McCartney song. Somewhat contrary to protocol, Vic Flick was actually given a genuine credit on no fewer than five of Cannon's releases even though he did attend many more sessions than that. On the sleeves of the later releases the banner "Stars from 'Easy Beat' and 'Saturday Club'" was also emblazoned in bold on the back to add kudos to the release in a further bid to attract the buyer.

On those where he was singled out, as part of a billing that read "The Alan Moor Four featuring Vic Flick (guitar)", no fewer than four of the titles ('Foot Tapper', 'Shindig', 'Geronimo' and 'Theme for Young Lovers') were copies of the then most recent Shadows' hit. The irony would not have been lost on Flick, whose involvement on these tracks acted as a perfect metaphor for the way in which The JB7's career had stalled. In 1960, they were vying neck and neck with The Shadows as the most popular instrumental group, yet, by 1962, Flick was being paid handsomely simply to replicate Hank Marvin's licks. *New Musical Express*'s annual Reader's Poll confirmed as much, which saw The JB7 relegated to third spot behind The Shadows and The Tornados (then enjoying their moment in the spotlight with 'Telstar'). It was the disparity in the number of votes cast that was most telling: The Shadows amassing a staggering 45,951 in comparison to The JB7's more modest 2,292! Clearly, Vic Flick was spreading his wings wisely in accepting these intermittent offers of session work. With his eyes fixed on the long term even at this early stage, he was keeping his options open. Ever loyal to John Barry and the band at that point, it would not be long before his enthusiasm and patience would begin to wane, particularly with his ex-leader.

While the world watched nervously as Jack Kennedy, America's dynamic young President, became embroiled in a seemingly implacable thirteen-day stand-off with the leader of the Soviet bloc, President Khrushchev, over the installation of nuclear-armed Soviet missiles in Cuba, The JB7 pressed on with the more mundane business of fulfilling a series of dance dates in Preston, West Bromwich, Stafford, Solihull and Stetchford. Another personnel change was soon in the offing – the introduction of yet another new drummer, Ray Cooper, as replacement for the in-demand Andy White, whose commitments elsewhere limited his presence considerably.

Cooper, a more than capable alternative, had been playing regularly with The Billy Ternent Orchestra. As a child, his first dalliance with music began by way of violin lessons, but it was switching to drums that lit the blue touch-paper for him. By the age of fourteen, he was already being paid as a direct result of playing various engagements in and around the Birmingham area, so by the time he was called up into the army and posted to the North Staffordshire Regiment Band at the age of eighteen, he was almost like a seasoned pro. Touring India and parts of Burma for three and a half years harnessed his talent further and cemented his musical ambitions. Thus, on leaving the forces, he continued in the same vein playing with orchestras in and around London.

During the morning of 9th November, an expanded JB7 was back at Abbey Road, this time refining 'The Lolly Theme' in addition to recording 'March of the Mandarins' and 'The Party's Over'. For the sake of numerical accuracy, this was actually The JB18 (albeit billed as 'The John Barry Seven and Orchestra' on vinyl) comprising of another 'mix 'n' match' ensemble: four flutes (two doubling as piccolos); two bassoons; two trombones; two French horns, tuba, electric guitar, harp, bass, drums, two percussionists, organ, at a total cost of £104.

'The James Bond Theme' had made such a strong impact on the charts that it had not yet peaked by the time 'The Lolly Theme', the main theme to the film comedy, *The Amorous Prawn,* was released on 30th November. Here once again was ample evidence of Barry exploiting Abbey Road's advanced studio techniques whilst experimenting with unusual combinations of instruments amidst an ever expanding musical palette – and it was hoped that as the last single had taken off on the back of a box office hit, then the latest one would do the same. The *New Musical Express*'s summary was positive, describing the A-side as "a blend of humorous novelty; Scottish and military – entertaining and ear-catching", while the B-side ('March of the Mandarins') was considered "a bold, striking, impressive and unusual number that must be heard." *Disc*'s Don Nicholls was cautiously optimistic for its chances: "'The Lolly Theme', a natty novelty that skips along merrily with cash register effects underlining the title, could easily catch on if the picture does well, while 'March of the Mandarins' is a much more dramatic piece evoking a stalking darkness that I find very effective. Excellent use of strings heightens the atmosphere." Rush-released to coincide with the film's 26th November premiere, 'The Lolly Theme' failed to emulate the success of its predecessor (likewise the film in comparison to *Dr. No*), but nevertheless, still managed to rack up sales of 9,287 by the end of April the following year.

The last recording session of the year designated for The JB7 took place at Abbey Road on 3rd December and was devoted to laying down the main title to ABC Television's forthcoming ITV series *The Human Jungle* then at post-production stage. A full twenty-five-piece orchestra was used on this occasion, twenty being the string section alone. Costing £138 in full, the exact break down of the instrumentation used reads as follows: twelve violins, four violas, four cellos, organ, alto sax, electric guitar, bass, drums. Note that this recording was commissioned by the television company and should not be confused with another session in the New Year that would result in The JB7's follow-up to 'The Lolly Theme'.

Further gigs at Coventry, Birmingham, Portsmouth, Plymouth, and Barnstable during November and December allowed Ray Cooper to bed into his new role, and it didn't take him long to make a big impression on *de facto* leader, Vic Flick, by virtue of his diligence and devotion to duty. Reliable almost beyond the call of duty, two particular instances epitomised these qualities perfectly.

The first of these occurred on Sunday 25th November when The JB7 was asked to headline the Annual Ball of the Grand Order of Water Rats taking place at the Grosvenor Hotel. Unsuspectingly, Cooper had found himself double booked for the evening at that very same event due to having already agreed the previous year to perform with his erstwhile employer, Billy Ternent, whose orchestra had been contracted to back the supporting artists in the cabaret there as well as supplying all the music for the general dances. To resolve this dilemma required delicate, diplomatic negotiation skills, since Ternent was not at all likely to take to the idea of lending 'his' drummer to an 'upstart' rock group too kindly. Fortunately, Cooper had all these attributes in spades and was able to solve the issue amicably following several lengthy discussions. Flick was full of admiration for Cooper's way with words: "As long as there was some sort of interval between the two bands' appearances, so people had time to forget the drummer's face, Billy acquiesced to the idea of a double date. Ray had to change from his tuxedo into his JB7 uniform – a shiny, grey mohair type suit – from behind the bandstand. Suitably garbed, he performed admirably for both combos and made twice as much as any other musician that night!" A major row was therefore averted.

The second was due entirely to dense smog that suddenly descended upon London during the early evening of 4th December. Despite the introduction of the 1956 Clean Air Act, the capital remained susceptible to these debilitating 'pea soupers' that severely reduced visibility. On this occasion, on the eve of a pub date at Eltham for the South London Fairground Association, the combination of fog and fuel-infused air pollutants became so blinding that, as Flick recalls, "I couldn't see my hand with my arm extended in front of me." All but Cooper had arrived at the venue early, and with no sign of him as curtain-up time approached, Flick was beginning to fear the worst. Cooper lived no more than three miles from the pub in Bexleyheath, but even so, "with the severity of the fog, this might have well have been three hundred," as Flick later remarked. Fortunately, Cooper showed his guile and initiative. With time of the essence, Flick suddenly became aware of a dim light waving in the gloom: "Slowly, through the swirling fog, there emerged a figure shrouded in scarves and warm clothing, a cap placed low on his head and, tied to a pole, swung a Storm Lantern. The pole was secured to a wheelbarrow piled high with his drums. Ray staggered to a stop, sweat dripping from his brow, and collapsed on a seat by the entrance. 'I couldn't drive and I couldn't let you down, so here I am!'" Much to Flick's relief, the show was able to go on without so much of a hiccup.

With Christmas approaching, the band returned to Scotland for a few dates that took in East Kilbride, Eyemouth and Dundee's Ritz Ballroom. The gigs themselves may not have been particularly memorable in Mike Peters' eyes, but the local facilities certainly made a lasting impression on him, in particular the ballroom at Eyemouth (situated near the docks), the hospitality provided by the landlord at the local pub where they stayed, not to mention his first taste of the whiskey-based liqueur, Glayva.

So as 1962 was drawing to a close and with the UK about to be gripped by weather conditions even more severe than the previous winter's, The JB7 was still managing to hold its own albeit in the face of fiercer competition from an increasingly crowded market. The ever-bulging youth population was helping to absorb the growing influx of fresh aspirants to a degree, but what was becoming abundantly clear was that they were craving role models of their own to follow. The JB7 was beginning to be perceived as belonging to the old guard and would soon be seen as looking staid and safe when placed alongside the new generation of beat groups sprouting up in their droves. Such a dramatic shift in the musical climate – meteorologically mirrored by the coldest winter since 1740 – presented enormous challenges ahead for both band and management in order for them to survive as a successful touring and recording outfit. For The JB7, 1963 would prove to be as disruptive and as uncomfortable as the big freeze that heralded the New Year.

Donkey-trekking in Ireland, with Les, Jimmy and Nuggy.

Vic recording for posterity the attempts of Jimmy and Nuggy to board a local donkey.

From left to right: Mike Peters, Louis Rodgers (tour promoter), Bobby Carr, Vic Flick, Jimmy Stead.

The JB7 touring Ireland in May 1962.

222

Unused Columbia publicity photos with Vic Flick as new leader in early 1962.

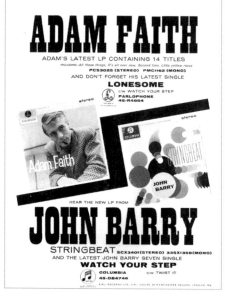

Programme and ticket from the last appearance with Adam – March 1962.

223

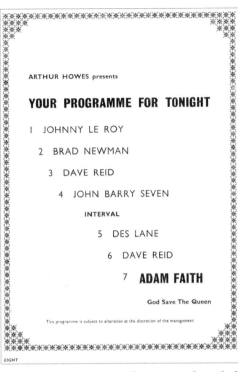

ARTHUR HOWES presents

YOUR PROGRAMME FOR TONIGHT

1 JOHNNY LE ROY

2 BRAD NEWMAN

3 DAVE REID

4 JOHN BARRY SEVEN

INTERVAL

5 DES LANE

6 DAVE REID

7 ADAM FAITH

God Save The Queen

This programme is subject to alteration at the discretion of the management

EIGHT

NINE

Adam made his film debut in " Beat Girl "

Programme from the last tour with Adam – February 1962.

The band in late 1962: Back row from left: Mike Peters, Vic Flick, Kenny Salmon;
front row from left: Jimmy Stead, Dickie Harwood, Bobby Carr, Dennis King.

John Barry with Jack Parnell and Chris Barber on the set of All That Jazz.

225

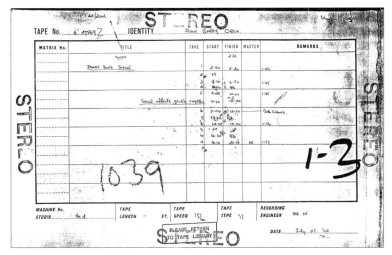

*EMI log for the recording of The James Bond Theme
on 23rd July 1962, at Abbey Road.*

*Sean Connery with JB7 producer John Burgess, second from right; back row,
as members of the Showbiz football team.*

From the left, Mike Peters, Vic Flick and Brian Hazelby on the set of The Cool Mikado.
JB7 fan Terry Martin is seen to the left of Mike Peters.

Congratulations!
from
JOHN BARRY
New Columbia Release
The John Barry Seven and Orchestra
"THE JAMES BOND THEME" from "DR. NO"

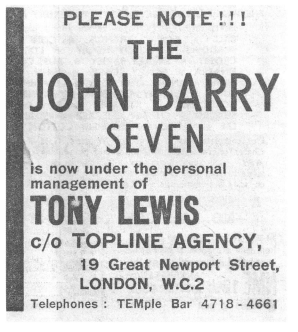

PLEASE NOTE!!!
THE
JOHN BARRY
SEVEN
is now under the personal
management of
TONY LEWIS
c/o TOPLINE AGENCY,
19 Great Newport Street,
LONDON, W.C.2
Telephones : TEMple Bar 4718 - 4661

7

SEVEN (NEW) FACES

JANUARY – DECEMBER 1963

*Had I known that Barry had blown a solo contract for me
with EMI, I would have left a long time before –
and with no notice!*

– Vic Flick (lead guitar/leader)

*It became obvious we were on the downward slide when we played a
'Young Farmer's Dance' in the wilds of East Anglia, and were sharing top billing with a then relatively new group – Gerry and The
Pacemakers, whose latest recording was at No. 1; so you can imagine
which of the groups were the more popular with the young farmers!*

– Jimmy Stead (baritone sax)

One cannot overestimate the chaos that was caused by the severe winter of 1963
and the debilitating impact it made on the entire infrastructure of the country.
Lasting right up until the end of March, blizzards produced snowdrifts of up
to 20ft (6m) deep, resulting in mass school closures, wrecked phone lines and
in power cuts affecting thousands of homes. Lakes, rivers and roads froze to a
point where, in some areas, daily milk rounds had to be delivered on skis, with
temperatures plummeting so low that even the sea froze, and in Braemar's case
(in Aberdeenshire) dropping to a staggering -22.2 degrees centigrade on 18th
January. Nevertheless, despite snow lying knee deep for up to three months and
thereby causing all sorts of disruption to the road and rail links, somehow The
JB7 managed to fulfil all of its engagements, comprising a plethora of dances
throughout the most affected months of January and February at venues as scattered
as Maidstone, Cheltenham, Birmingham Plaza, Manchester, Wimbledon Palais
and York Assembly Rooms.

The turbulence caused by this, the harshest winter in living memory, turned out to be nothing in comparison with the upheaval that would blight the band as the year progressed. A complete overhaul of its entire personnel in October could not have been anticipated by the line-up that was then in the throes of overcoming those tricky, hazardous ice-impacted journeys amid sub-zero temperatures. For Vic Flick (lead guitar), Mike Peters (bass), Bobby Carr (trumpet), Ray Cooper (drums), Jimmy Stead (baritone sax) Dennis King (tenor sax) and Kenny Salmon (keyboards), it was simply a case of 'business as usual'.

The year 1963 has often been cited as the year when the sixties finally began to swing, which was given credence by the way in which various cultural and political events converged to convey a society in transition alongside a collective sense of anything being possible. In his 1967 poem, 'Annus Mirabilis', Philip Larkin mischievously wrote, "Sexual intercourse began in 1963/ (which was rather late for me)/ Between the end of the Chatterley ban/ And the Beatles' first LP" – and this, in many eyes, summed up the mood of the time. A shift in the moral climate was being implicitly inferred from within the still very much London-centric entertainment and advertising industries, helped it must be said in no small measure by a political scandal – reported with an almost salacious zeal – that would soon put paid to an age of deference in favour of one built on scepticism. The notorious Profumo Affair – in which the War Minister (John Profumo) lied in Parliament over his affair with a model and showgirl (Christine Keeler) whose links to a Soviet embassy official (Yevgeny Ivanov) compromised his position – revealed the full scale of the hypocrisies surrounding the Establishment, and this would arm an emerging band of young satirists (the likes of Peter Cook, Alan Bennett and Jonathan Miller) with further licence and ammunition to lampoon the then-Conservative administration mercilessly. Such irreverence, viewed by some as impertinence, had never before been so blatant. Harold Macmillan's tenure at No. 10 Downing Street would not last much longer. Just as significant, a British-made contraceptive pill was being made available for the first time, so that the idea of a sexually liberated modern, independent young woman, as personified by Julie Christie's character Liz in the film *Billy Liar* (released that August), was there on the screen for all to behold as a defined future role-model.

And then, of course, there emerged The Beatles as *the* dominant force in popular culture bar none. January presaged what was to come when the second single 'Please Please Me' entered the charts on the 18th, and would become the band's first chart topper in just about every chart (including those printed in the *New Musical Express* and the *Melody Maker*) except the one used jointly by *Record Retailer* and the BBC. During the course of the year, The Beatles would never be out of the Top Forty and would notch up a further three No. 1 singles in addition to two multi-million-selling LPs. "Four piece groups with guitars," it would appear, were not quite the dodos that Dick Rowe had envisaged. For saxophonists like Dennis King and Jimmy Stead, this would be bad news indeed. Through their boundless energy, enthusiasm, talent, charisma and youthful good looks, The Fab Four would capture and enrapture the hearts of the nation like no other pop group before or since, and by dint of their provincial background and creative self-sufficiency would shake up a complacent recording industry with the force of a hurricane, tsunami and raging bushfire rolled into one.

Unfortunately the emergence of The Beatles (together with the Merseybeat sound that followed) coincided with a fairly dramatic decline in the fortunes of The John Barry Seven, whose pure instrumental style could not be fortified by chart hits such as those enjoyed by The Shadows, whose close bond with Cliff Richard kept them regularly in the public eye, be it on stage, or on small or large screens. However, it would be all too easy to attribute The JB7's diminishing media presence and popularity solely to the arrival of the beat group explosion. Although a mitigating factor for sure, this would be a superficial analysis. As will be revealed, managerial indifference; disillusionment amongst the ranks; a failure to adapt to the prevailing trends; fewer bookings and little TV or radio exposure all played their parts.

On the morning of 18th February, The JB7 attended what would become their final recording session at Abbey Road under Barry's direction in a bid to capitalise on the scheduling of ITV's latest drama, *The Human Jungle*, due for transmission on 30th March. Two tracks were cut on this particular session: a re-working of the same Bernard Ebbinghouse theme first recorded in December, plus a routine guitar and clavioline-dominated Barry original (minus the trademark pizzicato effect) entitled 'Twangin' Cheek' (which was originally logged in the archives, curiously, as 'Double07'). Altogether, twenty-seven musicians were used at a total coat of £150: twelve violins, four violas, four cellos, alto sax, clavichord/ piano, two electric guitars, electric and acoustic bass and drums. There's no doubt that Barry pulled out the stops with regards to the A-side, which saw Vic Flick's best Duane Eddy-like stalking twang lock horns with an eerie string/ clavioline blend and brooding sax as intimidating and as menacing as Barry ever concocted. As a musical backdrop for a weekly psychological thriller set in the underbelly of an urban metropolis, the arrangement was just about perfect. It was as if Barry was subconsciously serving notice of his exit from mainstream pop music by recording such an esoteric masterpiece even if his actions at the time suggested no such thing, for he had already entered discussions with Jeffrey Kruger (owner of Ember Records) by then over a possible role there as some kind of musical *supremo*, frustrated by what he saw as a lack of producer recognition from EMI.

On 30th March – during that very evening *The Human Jungle* premiered and the day after the single was released – The JB7 promoted the new 45 on *Thank Your Lucky Stars*, via a pre-recording made the previous Sunday at Teddington Studios in South West London. Billed as The John Barry Orchestra on this occasion, The Seven were joined on the programme by Billy Fury, Mike Preston, Bobby Rydell, Marcie Blaine, and Lionel Blair and His Dancers.

Reviews in the music press were decidedly mixed. The *New Musical Express* described 'The Human Jungle' as "powerfully impressive yet hardly uplifting". Any uplift, it added, was by way of the B-side, Barry's own 'Onward Christian Spacemen', which was described as "interesting and unusually entertaining, but not commercial in the pop sense." *New Record Mirror*'s staccato-like review arched more towards the positive: "Slow guitar opens this one then strings join in. Moves along very heavily – has bags of atmosphere – well performed – with lots of appeal and a haunting tune. The flip again has sax on it – moves along at a fair pace. Well performed but not as commercial as side one." *Disc*, however, was not particularly smitten by the downbeat ambience of the top side: "Television series theme music, 'The Human Jungle' is dark mood music for the John Barry Seven who get lush string backing as they plant it. Atmosphere is gloomy and there's plenty of it. 'Onward, Christian Spacemen' is a clever instrumental with original ideas in conception and scoring. Seems a pity to give it a title that might lead folk imagining it to be a novelty re-write of 'Onward Christian Soldiers'. It isn't."

What was becoming evident, much to the irritation of Norman Newell, was that Barry was now spending ever increasing, valuable studio time and resources over elaborately textured B-sides – a potential source of conflict that may well have accelerated his departure from EMI – for, as Newell later admitted, he often found difficulty booking into a studio as a result of Barry always being there. Vic Flick also made the same point, in suggesting that Barry probably pushed his luck a tad too far by using Abbey Road to construct demos for films he was chasing at EMI's expense. As was now becoming routine, each new JB7 single featured a full orchestra, and with each new arrangement becoming more ambitious than the last, this necessitated a broader orchestral canvass and a greater financial outlay. Indeed, the session used to record 'Onward Christian Spacemen' (on 22nd November 1962) used thirty-two musicians at a cost of £275, which was a far cry from the £79 charged against the recording of 'The Magnificent Seven' less than a couple of years earlier (on 7th February 1961), and whereas the cheaper charted, the bigger-budgeted recording failed to make so much as a dent.

It was clear to everyone that Barry's position as MD at EMI was becoming less tenable. From his perspective, the role was now far too constricting for maintaining his interest for much longer. He had more 'irons in the fire' to stoke than simply recording production-line three-minute pop records every day. His horizons stretched way beyond those confines since he was on the brink of breaking into the film world, and with Abbey Road at his disposal, no wonder he used his position there to further his own cause. From Norman Newell's vantage point, Barry's roster of artists was not producing any hits in any case now that Adam Faith had broken ranks. The severing of ties was always likely to have been amicable, as a result, and rationalised by both parties that way as mutually beneficial.

By this time, Barry was not the only one considering his position. Vic Flick, too, was seriously weighing up his future prospects. As March approached, he made the monumental decision of serving notice to Barry of his intention to leave the band permanently in September. He felt that this would give Barry ample time to line up his replacement, and it was not difficult to understand Flick's reasoning given a developing conflict of interests between what was becoming regular session work and his JB7 live duties. The attraction of being completely divested of the domestic disruption caused by having to adhere to a haphazard touring schedule and, instead, becoming part of the capital's very own unofficial 'Wrecking Crew' was tremendously appealing. Moreover, he would finally rid himself of the added responsibility of being the band's on-the-road manager with all the day-to-day headaches that this entailed. Turning down just one prestigious session in favour of, say, one night at the Grimsby Mecca Gaiety Ballroom, might easily have caused catastrophic consequences for the long term were a studio life the path he was genuinely aiming to take, for there was always likely to be another 'axeman' waiting in the wings willing to wield the axe, so to speak (in more ways than one).

Take February as an example. The JB7 were pencilled in to fulfil a mere eight dates throughout the month compared to the twenty or so other varied extra-curricular engagements Flick had already pencilled into his diary for the same period. It didn't really need a mathematician to do the sums. On the week commencing 14th February, for instance, after returning from a JB7 gig at the Prestatyn Royal Lido on the 14th, Flick found himself holed up on the 15th fulfilling two sessions at Abbey Road and CTS Studios during the one morning alone followed by one at Decca during the afternoon. Similarly, after playing the Kingston Coronation Hall with The Seven on the 16th, there he was back in session mode the very next day at Decca throughout the afternoon before fulfilling a regular evening residency in Purley. By Friday (the 18th), he was once again at EMI in the morning, then playing for BBC Radio as a contributor to *Music While You Work* during the entire afternoon. Some weeks were busier than others, admittedly, but it was clear to Vic Flick that very soon, something had to give, with difficult choices needing to be made. It was becoming ever more apparent just how important it was for him to be on call at short notice in order to keep his name in the frame and, to be able to do this, he could no longer be part of a touring entourage. Consequently, his days as a member of The JB7 were now officially numbered.

As Flick would later explain, "Driving all night long to get to London in time to do three recording sessions the next day, then back on the road for a couple of nights and then having to repeat the process became impossible, and so I decided to quit the roadwork and concentrate on recording sessions, broadcasts and television!"

Throughout March, and with no let up to the bad weather in sight, The Seven appeared at Tunbridge Wells Assembly Rooms, Bath, Nuneaton, the Portsmouth Savoy (with the Benny Freedman Orchestra) and The Empress Ballroom, Burnley. More regular work came during the summer season at such venues as Morecambe

Central Pier, Folkestone, Paignton, Torquay and Blackpool. During June, rumours began to circulate throughout the music press hinting that Barry's long and fruitful association with the renowned Norman Newell – and therefore with EMI – was about to end. There was no smoke without fire, it seems, since it later emerged that Barry was already recording Annie Ross for his future new employer, rival label Ember, despite still being officially under contract to EMI.

∽

The engagement at Bath on 18th March happened to coincide with the filming on location of director Val Guest's latest production, 80,000 Suspects, *starring Richard Johnson and Claire Bloom. Also appearing, in a somewhat less distinguished role, was one Terry Martin, who was there in his capacity as an 'extra' – one of a tiny but dedicated band of individuals who were paid a small fee for making up the numbers on set where crowd scenes, 'walk-on' parts (and the like) were required. Unheralded, but indispensable, these individuals rarely became known to the general public, since their names seldom appeared in the film credits.*

Now, what relevance does this have to the story being told, you may ask? Well, Martin had another string to his bow. He was regarded by just about everyone connected with the band as The John Barry Seven's number one fan. He followed them all over the UK, and even managed to appear alongside them in his capacity as film 'extra' in The Cool Mikado, *much to his delight. On this particular occasion in Bath, he was portraying a Guildhall Sergeant, but it is unlikely that this prevented him from taking his usual place in the concert audience on the night of the 18th.*

Les Reed was one ex-member with fond memories of Martin's staunch loyalty and undoubted devotion: "Yes, Terry Martin was the biggest JB7 fan of all time. He was in virtually every town and gig in which we performed and because he was also a film 'extra', he was able to appear in a couple of films we made. He has sadly passed away, but he was a very nice man and so dedicated to the cause of The JB7."

∽

One of Barry's final assignments at EMI resulted in a fortuitous meeting of musical minds that would prove significant for both parties later on in the year. Masquerading as a group calling itself The Boys was Marty Wilde's then-backing band, The Wildcats, who were given the go-ahead to record a one-off single for Parlophone with Barry producing. This came about on the back of Barry having overseen Marty Wilde's Columbia single, 'Lonely Avenue', in February. The A-side in question, 'Polaris', was an instrumental penned by Wilde that bore a striking resemblance to the track that inspired it – the Tornado's multi-million seller 'Telstar' – complete with a Joe Meek-like arrangement and tongue-in-cheek title to match (Polaris being the brightest star in the constellation of Ursa Minor). Sitting behind the drum kit on the session was Bobby Graham, who by this stage of his career had already gained a considerable reputation as one of the best drummers in the business. Watching a master technician at such close quarters gave Barry ample food for thought, and no doubt he made a mental note of Graham's capabilities for future reference.

What Barry and Graham were soon to learn was that they not only worked well together, but also shared much in common. Both started working life as trainee film projectionists (Barry at The Rialto and Graham at The Regal Cinema, Edmonton) were equally fastidious in perfecting their musical bent, and even more significantly were huge admirers of The Stan Kenton Orchestra, so much so that many an hour was spent listening to and dissecting this band's recording legacy in each other's company. With Graham reputedly possessing one of the finest collections of Kenton records in the country, the pair easily bonded; such mutual respect and musical empathy developed into a firm friendship, and when Graham discovered that Barry once studied musical arranging under the tutelage of a member of The Stan Kenton Orchestra, he was enraptured.

Meanwhile, miles away elsewhere in the UK, The JB7's stuttering road show rolled on, and given the need to keep working as often as possible in the face of a disappointing falling-off in bookings, no engagement was off limits. One week in June epitomised this policy perfectly. Within the space of five days of one another, The JB7 moved from the rarefied circles of a prestigious event held at Balliol College Oxford to playing what in essence was a vegetable-packing station at a remote village near Cambridge.

For Balliol College – founded in 1263 and one of Oxford University's constituent colleges – the year 1963 was clearly a landmark one in its history. As a way of commemorating the 700th anniversary, then-Chairman Timothy Ades hired The JB7 as part of an impressive line-up of acts providing the evening's entertainment for the 24th June Ball. Also on the bill that night were The Temperance Seven, Tommy Kinsman and His Orchestra, The Russ Henderson Steel Band and Bill Savill and His Orchestra. A double ticket cost seven guineas (£7.35), which was a record amount at the time for a Balliol Ball, with seven bands appearing in total. Additionally, a cabaret boasting Lance Percival, Cleo Laine, and a display of Scottish traditional dancing was also laid on for the paying guests. So there they were, The JB7 performing on an Oxbridge campus for the revelling 'champagne and caviar' set at the very place where Prime Minister Harold Macmillan graduated.

Compared to such a grandiose spectacle located in the opulent setting of one of the nation's pre-eminent universities, the next gig was situated in a venue that couldn't have been more different. Affectionately known as 'The Barn', it was located in the village of Chatteris, and being nothing more than a rather large, glorified shed, could best be described as primitive – more 'spit and sawdust' than 'glitz and glamour'. Owned and hired out by one of the local farmers to such organisations as the local Conservative Club for concerts and dances, it proved to be a popular attraction. Marianne Faithful was another act said to have appeared there, according to villagers. Sadly, the barn was later demolished, though on a positive note, this was in favour of a new doctor's surgery. And so while The Seven were playing in the less-than-salubrious surroundings of 'The Barn', their founder was busily ensconced in a London recording studio, producing Annie Ross for his new label, Ember Records.

Another memorable date occurred at Great Stukeley, near Huntingdon, on 27th July, for this was the weekend of The Great Stukeley National Gala, which was a mid-summer's cavalcade of non-stop entertainment: of donkey races (organised by then champion jockey, Josh Gifford), helicopter rides, aerial displays, trick motorcyclists, gymnastics, keep-fit displays, country dancing, Scottish pipers, local farmers demonstrating their wares, football and 'push ball' matches – and, of course, top pop acts with chart pedigree performing live. Having recently moved into the village with his wife, 85-year-old Eric Tring (who is still a resident there) could, to this day, vividly recall the occasion well and with great fondness. Even now, the couple refer to the gala as "a weekend to remember."

Sited on a carefully chosen field by the local Round Table committee due to its proximity to the A1, A603 and a British Rail station, the gala was a two-day festival aimed at raising sufficient funds to purchase a special coach for disabled patients from the nearby Papworth Village Settlement. Blessed by good weather throughout the weekend, it ran from 10 a.m. to midnight on both the Saturday and Sunday and would draw a crowd of over 10,000; by doing so, a sum in excess of £2,000 was raised, which in 2018 terms would work out at around £40,000. The dance itself was a complete sell-out and alongside The John Barry Seven, the Trings were able to see The Alan Price Rhythm and Blues Combo and The Temperance Seven as well as other lesser-known groups, who entertained the crowd in between those headliners. What impressed Eric Tring in particular was the generosity shown by the main acts towards the charity for although they were each scheduled to play specific one-hour spots, they willingly extended their sets.

One excited reveller, packed into the marquee ostensibly to watch The JB7, was life-long fan, Peter Wallis, who vividly remembers the band following The Temperance Seven's set and, in particular, Jimmy Stead pouring perfume on the microphone to negate the stench of their cigar smoke. Bobby Carr was unfortunately waylaid getting there, which necessitated having to start without him. Vic Flick managed to turn this hiccup into hilarity by announcing 'The Magnificent Seven' as 'The Magnificent Six'! In similar jocular fashion, 'In the Mood' was introduced as 'Twisting in the Nude'.

A good time was clearly experienced by all those attending, with the music adding immeasurably to the carnival atmosphere. The numbers of organisations that attended and contributed included the Royal Air Force and the United States Air Force (from its bases in Molesworth, Alconbury and Lakenheath), the latter supplying hot-dogs, burgers, donuts, *etc.* plus one of its larger aircrafts to fly over the site, so that, for the sum of half a crown (12.5p), punters could try and guess its altitude and speed to win a crate of whiskey! Marquees were manned courtesy of various brewers, whilst an array of refreshment tents served up teas, coffees, sausage rolls, Cornish pasties, soft drinks and ice-cream, with the weekend star raffle prize (priced at £2 per ticket) being a weekend in Paris for two!

As the summer schedule continued to proceed in a somewhat 'stop-start' fashion (with eight dates in July and a further ten in August), another crack appeared in the band's armour when Mike Peters, one of its staunchest mainstays, decided to leave. Acutely aware of Flick's intentions of quitting, Peters had originally agreed to stay on until Flick's final appearance, but alas this was not to be. His premature departure left Flick with the tricky dilemma of having to find a suitable replacement at such short notice. That he managed to secure the services of Russ Stapleford to fill in on bass on a temporary basis was credit to his growing list of contacts and powers of persuasion, but it is fair to say that by this time, he was finding it increasingly difficult to balance session work with leading and organising the band. His focus was changing in any case. Having long since given Barry notice of his own decision to leave, which by then was now fast approaching, overseeing the affairs of The JB7 was understandably becoming less and less of a priority for him by the day.

While this was all unfolding, the news finally broke over Barry's departure from EMI to Ember Records, after Barry himself had spilled the beans to the *New Musical Express* on 26th June. This caused major ructions from within the industry at the time, since Ember was considered but a tiny minnow when measured against EMI's whale-like might. However, Barry was presented with such an attractive package that it was very difficult for him to turn down. As he later revealed, what he wanted above all else was due acknowledgement for his role as a producer, which was something EMI had refused to give him, so when Ember's owner, Jeffrey Kruger, guaranteed him a producer credit with a salary of £400 a week (the equivalent of around £8,000 a week in 2018's terms), this was the proverbial 'offer he couldn't refuse'. It certainly put the standard session fee of £7 10s (£7.50) into perspective!

Whether or not being totally immersed in this new role as 'associate producer and creative A&R man' at Ember caused him to become complacent with regards The Seven is debatable, but there is little doubt that Barry's attitude towards Vic Flick's period of notice did appear surprisingly casual to say the least, bordering on the blasé, much to the guitarist's constant frustration. Maybe he hadn't taken Flick seriously enough, since no genuine attempt had been made to replace him throughout the six-months notice period, or so it seemed to the perplexed guitarist. The 'wake up call' occurred on 8th September after a JB7 concert at the Torquay Princess Theatre (on a bill with singer Danny Williams). It was then when Flick, encouraged by his long-suffering wife, Judy, was forced to make it crystal clear to Barry that he had now served his notice and, forthwith, had finished being a member and leader of The Seven, the result of which meant that he would not be fulfilling the following week's engagements. In short, Vic Flick had now finally left the building, from which there was no turning back.

Having nobody willing or indeed able to step seamlessly into Vic Flick's shoes (after having seemingly completely ignored Flick's overtures for months now), Barry felt he had no alternative other than to cancel future bookings and disband the group forthwith. So just imagine the shock Jimmy Stead must have felt when he was handed his dismissal letter, terminating his contract of employment with the band from immediate effect, as he disembarked from the RMS Empress of Britain at Liverpool Docks on its arrival from Canada after a fourteen day working holiday on board the cruise ship. "It was the end of my being a professional musician," he would later reflect ruefully on receiving that "dismal letter from Barbara Barry."

With bookings dwindling, members of The Seven had been forced to consider other opportunities from within the business to make ends meet, as perfectly illustrated by Jimmy Stead's decision to take up the cruise ship offer. Similarly, Kenny Salmon looked elsewhere, albeit closer to home. His reputation as an extremely competent and reliable keyboardist stood him in good stead, for he was never short of offers. However, he had designs on forming his own band or small group very much in the mould of The JB7. Tired of being a peripheral figure in the background, he wanted to play the same style of music but leading from the front, which is precisely what he had started to do during the weeks immediately prior to the axe falling on his JB7 career. Throughout July and August – at a time when The JB7 couldn't even get so much as a toehold onto the stage of the BBC's Playhouse Theatre – there was Kenny Salmon, no less, leading both The Kenny Salmon Quintet and the Kenny Salmon Seven on programmes as popular as *Music While You Work* and *Steppin' Out*. With some irony, he even included Vic Flick in his band, the leader now being led. How a member of his 'team' had managed to land these BBC gigs that had since become so elusive to The JB7 must have bewildered Flick no end, which must have stiffened his resolve to make the break when he did, one suspects.

To make better sense of this sudden spiralling of events, one needs to take a more considered look at the principal reasons behind The JB7's fall from prominence that led to Barry having to take such drastic action.

Why then did bookings begin to drop so dramatically towards the middle of 1962 and throughout 1963? Leaving The Beatles' spectacular game-changing emergence to one side, which coincided almost simultaneously with the period under discussion and which most certainly had some bearing, other factors – mostly of their own making – played their part just as significantly.

In truth, the problem might well have begun as far back as October 1961 when John Barry decided to finish playing with the band. From that moment on, The JB7 was no longer his priority, and rarely was it a 'hands-on' relationship any more. Granted, he still made occasional special appearances after that, mainly to honour contracts or to be seen at the more prestigious events (as previously explained), but by this time, he was far more concerned with cultivating his writing, arranging and recording careers than he was with promoting The JB7. The band was no longer high on his pecking order of commitments.

Dispensing with Eve Taylor's services was also highly significant. She managed both Barry and The JB7 with ruthless efficiency right up until 1962 when Tony Lewis, then overseeing the day-to-day running of Barry's Topline Artists agency, was assigned the band to add to his portfolio of clients. Now whether by accident or design, this backroom change coincided with a noticeable diminution in the flow of bookings, which was further exacerbated once Barry and Adam Faith went their separate ways, musically speaking, in the summer of that year. Up to that point, so inextricably linked were Barry and Faith that it almost went without saying that The JB7 would be part of any nationwide package tour on which Faith would be headlining. Not only would The JB7 be backing him, they would always be offered a slot in their own right. Without the comfort of such a guilt-edged guarantee, they now had to rely on their name alone for securing a place on these lucrative tours, and what's more, a JB7 line-up without John Barry was always likely to be a harder sell.

As a consequence, such opportunities just did not happen. The cost of hiring a seven-piece band was likely to have been a stumbling block to certain promoters for starters, and arguably Tony Lewis did not share the same flair for management as Eve Taylor nor, indeed, her negotiating nous. The facts spoke for themselves, since the last major tour undertaken by the 'classic' JB7 ended on 25th February 1962 when Adam Faith headed that bill. For the remainder of the year and right through 1963, The JB7's erstwhile place on such package tour bills was now being taken by the likes of such 'younger models' as Peter Jay and The Jaywalkers, Sounds Incorporated, The Flee-rekkers and The Tornados. In an industry that was not built on the foundations of longevity at that time, The JB7 were now being viewed as part of the older guard; as first-generation British rock 'n' rollers. Times had moved on and as Paul Simon once succinctly put it in his song 'The Boy in the Bubble', "every generation throws a hero up the pop charts". This 'new generation' were now muscling in on the much coveted radio and TV work that The JB7 once had 'in the bag' not that long ago. Regular appearances on *Saturday Club* and *Easy Beat* were now a thing of the past, and although they did secure a couple of TV spots on ITV's *All that Jazz* and *Thank Your Lucky Stars*, only one TV appearance was forthcoming throughout the whole of 1963.

The absence from the small screen was particularly odd and more difficult to explain away, given that the band had been regular performers on the only pop programmes of any note from 1957 to 1959. The fickleness of fashion might on the surface be the likeliest explanation, since the 1961 drama, *Girl on a Roof* turned out to be The JB7's last ever appearance on BBC Television, but this fails to account for the reason why BBC TV would ignore them completely throughout their chart breakthrough year, 1960, when arguably at their peak.

Securing air time on radio fared no better: a single appearance on *Saturday*

Club during 1962, then absolutely nothing at all throughout 1963, by which time the band was now back in the hands of the Starcast agency, whose representative, Barry Saunders, endeavoured, albeit fruitlessly, to rekindle a working relationship with the BBC. Evidently, Jimmy Grant's damning internal memo (as revealed in the previous chapter) appeared to have put the kibosh on all his efforts. When such an influential figure as Grant, producer of *Saturday Club*, considers the band's last session sub-standard in comparison to previous ones, not to mention more expensive in the absence of its leader, is it any wonder that the rest of BBC Radio's Light Entertainment Department sat up and took notice? The damage had been inflicted irrevocably, or so it appeared.

~

On 9th August '63, Rediffusion TV launched the groundbreaking and iconic pop show, Ready Steady Go!, *which was to become as much an emblem of the swinging sixties as the mini skirt and the Mini Cooper. Hosted initially by Keith Fordyce, then soon accompanied by Cathy McGowan,* RSG! *quickly became* the *show to watch on a Friday evening. Sadly The JB7 was never asked to appear. Admittedly, it was not the kind of show on which an instrumental group was regularly featured; not even The Shadows were invited on. However, more significantly and with some irony, it did employ an extremely capable and versatile house band, among which were two familiar names: ex-JB7 members Dougie Wright and Vic Flick, for whom this would prove particularly lucrative – and who else in his role as musical director hired them for the show? Well, none other than ex-JB7 member, Les Reed.*

~

Clearly, in 1963, The JB7 was as capable as ever of fulfilling any number of radio and television appearances, in terms of ability, but seen through the prism of a growing number of fresh-faced turns and latest trends, they were now being deemed unfashionable. Most disconcerting was the blinkered approach adopted by their management, who were seemingly oblivious to that fact almost to the point of negligence. Although Barry has to take some share of the responsibility for this, he wasn't the only one culpable. Bearing in mind he was incredibly busy at the time, both professionally and personally, he could at least lay claim to having a legitimate excuse. Not only had he just taken up the reins at Ember and was producing Annie Ross and Chad & Jeremy, he was also writing scores for a TV special, *Elizabeth Taylor in London*, as well as his Bond debut, *From Russia with Love*. On top of this, he had left his wife and was expecting a child with his current girlfriend. Managers/agents Lewis and Saunders, on the other hand, were much closer to the coalface and should have been aware of the prevailing market, but if they were, it didn't show.

One by one, every member of the 'classic' line-up had gradually dropped out.

No doubt Vic Flick must have looked over his shoulder in envy at the way in which Les Reed and Dougie Wright were now forging successful careers from within the music industry since parting company, and this may well have given him the courage to do likewise, for there were sure to be occasions when he was forced to turn down a JB7 gig in order to maintain his hard-won place on the session circuit. Whilst understandable, he knew full well that this was hardly fair on the rest of the band for whom regular gigs meant regular wages. As much as he tried hard to bow out as smoothly as possible by giving plenty of notice, followed by numerous reminders, the moment of reckoning proved to be anything but. For Flick, the difficulty lay entirely at Barry's door: "Just a week before I left, he refused to accept that I was leaving. Even on my last appearance in Torquay, he got mad at me because I refused to do the following week's schedule, and yet I couldn't do a thing about it." Flick was already committed to being elsewhere, and no way was he ever going to jeopardise his good name by letting down those fixers with whom he had worked hard on cultivating an amicable working relationship. Had he done so, that would have been tantamount to professional suicide.

Ignored also was the air of despondency and disquiet then creeping in amongst the band regarding the content of the set-list. The feeling was that it had now become outdated, jaded, and unadventurous (predictable even), when judged against the fresh-faced beat groups that had started to make an impression on the charts. Almost to a man, the band were sick to death of playing 'When the Saints Go Marching In' night after night and most vociferous about the urgent need to introduce a vocal element into the act. Even The Shadows had done this (in fact, each of their first two LPs contained vocal tracks). Being on the shop floor, as it were, they were all too aware of what was now exciting the paying public, but Barry was adamant – to the point of stubbornness – over The JB7 remaining an instrumental outfit, despite repeated overtures to the contrary. This was one bone of contention bound to raise the hackles and reduce morale accordingly, and it succeeded in doing so. When reasonable requests for replacement stage gear were also being brushed aside, this only succeeded in rankling the rank and file even further.

Now no employer ever feels comfortable with a disgruntled workforce at the best of times, however justified the complaints may be. Barry, in all likelihood, would have been no exception, which may very well have compounded his decision to make wholesale changes in the form of a seemingly ruthless mass cull. By doing so, that would have put the criticisms to bed in one fell swoop, as well as clearing the way for freshening things up. After all, his bass player had already left, and his guitarist and leader had refused to reconsider his position, while drummers were coming and going on an ad hoc basis. There was clearly less to lose by going the whole hog and dispensing with the entire band when three regulars had already fled the nest. The timing of Vic Flick's departure certainly forced Barry's hand despite having been forewarned for six months. Without a leader and guitarist, Barry had no other option but to abandon operations; his display of petulance towards Flick's actions borne out of irritation, one suspects – a misjudgement on his part in taking Flick's loyalty for granted. Barry, had assumed on counting on his goodwill, as he so often had done in the past, in order to bail him out of a tricky predicament, only to be faced with the one and only occasion on which Flick would have none of it.

≈

Years down the line, Vic Flick was to seriously question his unwavering loyalty towards The JB7 after learning from EMI producer John Burgess that a proposed solo career was squashed on the spurious grounds, proffered by Barry, that Flick was under an exclusive contract to him. Not wanting to offend the company's rising star, no one within EMI attempted to verify this with Flick. "Who knows, Duane Eddy and Hank might never have got a look in!," he would later wryly rue.

≈

A telling advertisement in the 'musicians wanted' section of an August edition of *Melody Maker* offering "A great opportunity for young pro Lead Guitar, Bass and Drummer. Must be able to read. Vocals asset" lends credence to the theory that Barry's 'Night of the Long Knives' was far more calculated in its execution than might have first appeared, with only the actual timing of it failing to go to plan. Obviously, the existing members of the band would have had no idea of what was being hatched by the management covertly during this time (in fact, not all of them even knew about Flick's own intentions to leave). Even so, as Jimmy Stead later revealed, although startled by the precise point of exit, he did have a strong inkling that it might soon be coming. For one avid reader of *Melody Maker*, however – a certain ambitious young sixteen-year-old guitarist by the name of Ray Russell – the bold decision to reply to that said advert was to be a life-changing one.

Another soon-to-be-recruited member, trumpeter Alan Bown, recalled being 'spotted' and approached by a member of Barry's agency in early August, whilst playing at The Richmond Jazz Festival, which was weeks before the 'final' gig played by the ousted JB7 on 7th September. Being specifically headhunted as opposed to being auditioned via the advertisement, Bown recalled that at the time of being interviewed both Vic Flick and Kenny Salmon were still in the band. When he eventually signed on, drummer Bobby Graham and tenor sax player Bob Downes were already in place, and he was given the impression that he was actually replacing Barry himself on trumpet rather than Bobby Carr. What appeared to clinch Bown's appointment was not necessarily his actual playing style but his uncanny physical resemblance to Barry. Such was the likeness that he was often able to pass himself off as the eponymous leader even to the point of signing many an autograph to eager punters as if he actually was the main man, himself.

Given that his own career was now in the ascendancy and moving into overdrive, Barry's decision to reboot the band with an entirely new line-up less than four weeks after handing out redundancy notices remains a difficult one to fathom. For a man who was already busy enough at the helm of Ember, let alone in the throes of writing his first major film and TV scores, one might have forgiven him for jettisoning the idea of The JB7 as a live vehicle for good. He could easily have conceded that the band had served its purpose and reached its natural conclusion, but evidently not. On the contrary, wearing his business hat very much like his father JX might have done, he still saw The JB7 as a viable commercial proposition, with a proven brand name able to exploit the lucrative college/university circuit. This was precisely how Barry sold his vision of the future to Bobby Graham – now a regular fixture on most sessions for Ember – when he first offered him the post of drummer-come-leader (and musical arranger/director) following Flick's departure. What with 'fresher's week' fast approaching during the first week in October, there was no time to lose.

The official line, as portrayed to the music press at the time, may well have been one of disbandment, but it was clear from the evidence presented that Barry had already planned a major clear-out well in advance of Vic Flick leaving. Only, from Barry's perspective, this 'sudden' exit happened to have occurred at a most inconvenient moment, for he hadn't yet found suitable permanent replacements on lead and bass guitar; that is, until the late arrivals of Ray Russell and Ray Stiles. Nevertheless, such a wholesale transition of this magnitude would have needed to have been a painstaking, well-organised and orchestrated operation for such a disparate group of musicians – newly recruited and under-rehearsed – to then appear as a tightly knit unit at barely a moment's notice.

And so it came to pass that the newly installed Graham (with Barry's full backing) led an entirely new John Barry Seven on a series of dates around the UK, while its former members remained oblivious to the behind-the-scenes machinations that had led to what was a truly stunning 'reincarnation'! As far as they were all aware, The JB7 no longer existed – the one notable exception being Kenny Salmon, for he was asked by Barry to fill in from time to time right up until Tony Ashton was able to bed in.

Official word proclaiming the rebirth came via an article emanating in an early October edition of the *New Musical Express*. Breaking the news of Bobby Graham's appointment as leader, the article also claimed that three of the members would also perform as a vocal trio; a nugget of information, which turned out to be entirely bogus. The full line-up of the new JB7 read: **Bobby Graham (leader/drums), Ray Russell (lead guitar), Alan Bown (trumpet), Terry Childs (baritone sax), Tony Ashton (keyboards/vocals), Ray Stiles (bass guitar) and Bob Downes (tenor and alto sax).**

The first gig was not, as one might have expected, at a place of learning, but at the Locarno Ballroom, Coventry, on 4th October. Bobby Graham was delighted to have received a good luck telegram from none other than Barry's father, Jack Prendergast, on the night in question.

For Graham, the concert venues that had been lined up for the new-look Seven may have been entirely different to the type he was used to playing, but he would find the student audiences highly appreciative, responsive and accommodating. Recalling his new role as band leader, he remembers just how difficult it was to get to see Barry on a one-to-one basis right from the outset. Even at this early stage in his new role, all appointments had to be negotiated through Barry's redoubtable secretary, Zena Ackers. Mind you, when the two did manage to catch up, time would be agreeably spent listening to Stan Kenton records for hours on end, impressed as Barry was by Graham's vast collection of vinyl.

Born Robert Francis Neate on 11th March 1940, Bobby Graham was brought up in Edmonton, North London by father, Robert, a GPO telephone engineer and mother, Elsie, a housewife. Although the family was not musical, they did own a wind-up gramophone together with a limited collection of 78s, and it was Bobby who soon became its principal user. His father decided to build Robert a drum kit when he was just seven years old for fear of his son breaking the crockery from his habit of constantly tapping his dinner plate with a knife and fork. Although rudimentary, it enabled the precocious youngster to practise hard, and practise hard he did until he was deemed good enough to own his first 'real' set bought from Ted Warren's Drum Shop in Bow, East London.

Consisting of a second-hand snare drum, a bass drum with mounted tom-toms and a single small ride cymbal, his bedroom practice sessions became ever more intense. He played along to the rhythm sections emanating from his parents' 78s, and when the family bought a newer record player, he was able to slow the tracks to 33 1/3rpm to allow him to isolate the drum part more easily thereby enabling him to hear the nuances and stylistic subtleties better. When the guitarist son of the family's landlord found his local band bereft of a drummer with a wedding booking to fulfil, he persuaded Bobby's parents to allow their son to deputise. He was just twelve-years-old at the time, but practice had, indeed, made his playing perfect for he was able to cope with everything thrown at him, despite never having previously rehearsed with the band. This was clearly a sign of things to come.

After leaving school at the age of fifteen without any formal qualifications or the self-belief to seek a musical career, he found work at The Regal Cinema in Edmonton, as previously stated. Fortunately, this was the perfect location for studying the best orchestras and bands of the day on account of the fact that many of them – The Stan Kenton Orchestra included – played Sunday evening concerts there. Young Bobby watched from the wings assiduously, learning all the time from the professionals passing through. A chance discussion with one of the usherettes led to him being invited to join her son's skiffle group, The Hangmen, who were very popular in the local village halls playing all the hits of the day. As a result, Bobby became more familiar with different styles of music and started to fraternise with other musicians, among them trumpet-player, Mike Brown. At the time, Brown was playing in a jazz band, which played each Sunday at a smoke-filled, dimly lit basement in Hampstead calling itself The Witches Cauldron. Once invited to sit in. Bobby rapidly established himself as the resident drummer, and on a whim, Robert Neate thus became Bobby Graham.

Although jazz was his first love, – much like Barry and most other previous members of The JB7 – the newly-christened Graham gradually began to expand his repertoire by buying more and more rock 'n' roll records, although remaining careful of concealing the fact to any of his jazz friends who might call round. A friend then invited him to join what would become 'The Outlaws' (a group of musicians who would ultimately act as Joe Meek's studio band) thereby launching his career in the pop world. By 1963, Graham's pedigree was already impressive. Before moving into regular session work, he had been a member of Joe Brown's Bruvvers before becoming one of Marty Wilde's Wildcats, whose one certain recording session at Abbey Road would lead him to the path of John Barry.

The other fresh faces in the new Seven were a mix of youth and experience, though even the experienced ones still had youth very much on their side.

Like the majority of schoolchildren at the time, Alan Bown – born in the front room of his parents' house in Slough, on 21st July 1942 – failed his eleven plus exam, thereby leading him to William Penn Secondary Modern, a single -sex school with a reputation for being tough and combative. Bown knew he needed to be able to look after himself there, and so developed a keen interest in boxing, whereupon he became schoolboy champion in the flyweight division for three years. Prior to commencing his secondary education, he had already just started to play cornet with The Slough Town Military Band that rehearsed once a week at The Slough Town Boys Club, situated no more than five minutes walk from his home. Because he was only ten years old at the time, he was considered under-age, but was allowed to sit in on account of his boundless enthusiasm. It was through band leader Sid Brown's encouragement that Bown began to take up trumpet, cutting his teeth on a Besson silver model.

After leaving school at fifteen, Bown continued to fit in his musical pursuits around full-time work based on Slough Trading Estate: firstly at the Hazel Offset Printing Company and then at The Standard Box Company. Through acquainting himself with the Joe Harriott Quintet, by regularly attending their residency at The Dolphin Hotel, he met trumpeter Henry 'Hank' Shaw, from whom he would take formal lessons every Saturday (whilst still working). Shaw would eventually become mentor-in-chief to the young Bown to the point of even fixing up his first permanent paid residency when he joined Shaw as a 2nd or 3rd trumpet player in The Danny Mitchell Orchestra (based in Redcar, Yorkshire).

On returning to London in January 1961, he was soon back in the routine of playing at The Boys Club and it was there where he was encouraged to audition for The RAF School of Music. And so, not long after passing, there he was, as an eighteen year old, a full-time bandsman in The Central Band at the RAF base in Uxbridge. He soon became friends with saxophonist and flautist, Bob Downes, who being slightly older than his contemporaries was one of the last of those conscripted into National Service. Among other members of this particular regimental band was bass player Herbie Flowers, who was to become another member of London's session musician elite many years later, and best remembered for creating the bass line on Lou Reed's 'Walk on the Wild Side' as well as writing Clive Dunn's 'Grandad'.

Bown's experience in the RAF was not a particularly happy one; the six-week training programme at Henlow Camp, which mostly involved marching up and down the parade ground in all weathers, being a notable low point. The experience of living in cold and damp quarters might have conceivably contributed to the emergence of fluid on the lungs, for it wasn't long before he was medically discharged on grounds of ill health. The upside of it all was in meeting fellow musicians of a like mind and for focusing his energies on a career in music once his lungs had fully recovered. As an ex-regular, he started gigging on and off with The South London Jazz Orchestra, before joining The Embers, who had secured a three-night residency at The Café des Artistes (in Chelsea). Following a brief sojourn in Germany, members of the band then went their separate ways.

On being reunited with The South London Jazz Orchestra for the 1963 Richmond Hill Jazz Festival, Bown found himself unexpectedly approached afterwards by Len Black, who was then part of John Barry's Topline agency, the purpose of which was to set up a meeting between Bown and Barry at his office in Great Newport Street with the proposition of an offer of work on the table. It was on this occasion that Bown could remember first meeting Barry's secretary, the aforementioned Miss Ackers, who struck him as being very kind by making him feel so welcome. Barry explained how he needed a trumpet player for The John Barry Seven and, on Black's recommendation, offered him the position there and then. For a twenty-year-old musician with limited experience, this was a marvellous opportunity.

What also delighted Bown was in being able to team up with Bob Downes once again, whose sense of the absurd and quirky humour was always likely to create much hilarity on the road. He didn't disappoint. One particular ruse of his whilst playing out in the provinces was in demonstrating to the audience a fictitious new dance craze he called 'The Windmill', which he claimed was now the current sensation doing the rounds in London. At that point he would proceed in demonstrating this routine by flailing his arms in time with the music and encourage the audience to copy him. "Made up on the spot, this resembled the 'U' and 'N' in semaphore or someone drowning or waving for help," Downes later explained. "It was such a ridiculous spectacle that I had to look away or risk blowing out of tune," Bown fondly recalled. Another memorable moment of slapstick that brought the house down was the sight of Bown riding Downes piggyback style whenever The Seven played a self-penned tune of Downes' entitled 'Monkey on my Back'.

Bown also remembered being often mistaken for John Barry, which he admitted exploiting to the full. He claimed that both he and Bob Downes would take it in turns to assume Barry's identity since audiences were none the wiser, but according to Ray Russell, Barry openly encouraged Bown to do so on account of his doppelganger looks "so that punters wouldn't realise John Barry wasn't playing in the band." By doing so, it certainly allowed the real John Barry to appear as if he was in two places at the same time, even if, as Bown later pointed out, "there's a few forged John Barry autographs out there!"

For Bob Downes, born in Plymouth during 1937, picking up the tenor sax for the first time at the age of nineteen came right out of the blue following a period of adversity after having been flung off his bicycle by a reckless car driver, resulting in multiple injuries that included a broken jaw as well as a number of broken teeth. Determined to help him through a difficult period of depression caused by the collision, his mother decided to present him with the said sax to keep him occupied. It proved to be a masterstroke and a major turning point in his life, because up till then, he had no prior knowledge of music whatsoever. Almost immediately, he found himself able to compose and improvise instinctively and he even started to construct his own method of notation given that he had no idea of how to read music. "Even today," he will readily admit, "I have no knowledge of music theory, as I believed it would only hinder my freedom. I reckon I was right." Possessing a natural aptitude (or "animal instinct" as he defined it) for being able to extemporise around a chord sequence shaped his playing style.

Downes' formative working life was spent completing five years as an apprentice electrical fitter based in the Devonport Dock Yard, Plymouth, before being called up for National Service, which was an experience he later described as "a complete waste of time." Mind you, this was where he first crossed paths with Alan Bown. After responding to an advert in Melody Maker not long after being demobbed, passing his audition with The JB7 was to be the break he needed to enter the music business professionally.

Baritone saxophonist Terry Childs, who had known Bobby Graham as a seventeen year old, contacted his old pal not long after having returned to the UK in 1963 following three years working abroad in France and Spain. The timing couldn't have worked out better. When Graham told him he was about to lead The JB7 and, as a result, was in the throes of helping Barry put together the new line-up, Childs was asked whether or not he would be interested in becoming part of the set up. It didn't take him long to make up his mind.

Childs was around thirteen years of age when he first started to play a musical instrument whilst at school. Taught by a music teacher whose main instruments were piano and horn, he didn't realise at the time just how much these early lessons had placed him at a disadvantage, for the mouthpiece of the clarinet he had been given to practise on was virtually unplayable on account of it being previously doctored. Only when he began to take saxophone lessons from his cousin did he find out that this was the case. As a result, he soon discovered how playing a woodwind instrument was nowhere near as difficult as he had first experienced. When he later resumed playing clarinet, the amount of time he had wasted on those ill-delivered early lessons soon became fully apparent. Nevertheless, Childs made up for lost time astutely, for before turning pro at the age of eighteen, he studied under the watchful eye of legendary saxophonist Don Rendell, who was a founder member of The Johnny Dankworth Seven and then stalwart of Ted Heath and His Music.

Although born in Blackburn in 1946, Tony Ashton grew up in Blackpool in what was a musical family. He took piano lessons from an early age and by 1959, whilst a student at St. George's School, played keyboards and rhythm guitar in a local group, The College Boys. By the time he left school at the age of fifteen, he was already an accomplished pianist with a leaning towards jazz. This resulted in the formation of his own combo, The Tony Ashton Trio, alongside John Laidlaw (drums) and Pete Shelton (bass), and a residency at The Picador Club in Blackpool throughout 1961 and 1962.

Bobby Graham remembered Ashton with great fondness, describing him as the joker in the pack. Never one to shy away from a practical joke, Graham could never forget one night when he was completely up-staged by the prankster whilst in the midst of his show-stopping 'grand finale' drum solo that formed part of the band's James Bond medley, during which time he was, as a rule, the sole centre of attention. Not a bit of it this time. Instead of the usual rousing applause, all he could hear was raucous laughter. Even when he redoubled his efforts, side-splitting guffaws from all over the auditorium continued unabated and refused to subside, much to his utter confusion. Little wonder: when he glanced behind him, there was Tony Ashton cycling around the stage with a broom balanced on his nose! Bob Downes (whom Ray Stiles recalls was another one prone to riding a bike on stage) was also quick to acknowledge Ashton's wicked sense of fun, which he admitted more than made up for his annoying tendency of being tucked up in bed when he should have been with the rest of the band *en route* some place in their unreliable Ford Transit. On many occasions, they had to pick him up from his home on a way to a gig, "but as soon as he got into the van, all was quickly forgotten as he had such a dynamic personality," Downes recalled.

Considered very much the baby of the band when he joined The JB7 on account of his tender years (sixteen), Ray Russell knew from a very young age that his career was destined to be in music, such was his passion for the guitar, after having being captivated by the West-Coast jazz style adopted by a near neighbour. He began playing on a four-string ukulele before acquiring a Spanish acoustic, his first six-string guitar. From his early days, Russell was keen on rock 'n' roll and jazz, and at only twelve years old he sat in at the legendary 2i's club in Old Compton Street, Soho. At school, he formed a band with his friend George Bean – George Bean and The Runners – as a means of showcasing his lead guitar licks on a new Burns Vista-Sonic, and when still only twelve, he made his very first TV appearance on the Carroll Levis junior talent show. Accompanying himself solo on guitar, he sang Paul Anka's 'I Love You Baby', although his one abiding memory is in having to be nudged awake after falling asleep during the summing up!

On leaving school at the earliest possible opportunity and determined to gain a foothold in the music business in some shape or form, he found work at Hinrichsen Edition Ltd, a company based in Baches Street, near Old Street, London N1, specialising in supplying orchestral parts for classical music. When an order was urgent, as often they were, he and his colleague, fellow teenager Paul Buckmaster, would deliver them personally using Paul's Vespa scooter. Neither of them could have guessed that a few years later they'd be working together again – on a James Bond film soundtrack no less! Throughout this period, Russell remained on constant lookout for any suitable opportunities a budding guitarist itching to make his mark as a professional musician could respond to and, sure enough, when scouring through the 'musicians wanted' section of *Melody Maker* in August, as he did on a regular weekly basis, he answered one such advertisement that led directly to him auditioning for the lead guitarist role in The John Barry Seven. So determined was he to succeed (after having previously failed a similar experience with Eric Delaney's band two years earlier) he resorted to the kind of subterfuge that deserved every success given its sheer nerve, for he bluffed his way into the band by pretending to sight-read. He did this by buying every JB7 record he could afford with a view to fastidiously learning the lead guitar part on every track until he was note perfect. "It was fortunate for me that my Dansette Half-Valve played records perfectly, because a semi-tone either way would have been disastrous had I replicated that at the audition," he later conceded.

Fully prepared, Russell arrived early for the audition in order to check out the opposition only to find there wasn't any on account of no other guitarist turning up. This seemed like a good omen until it was discovered that the designated venue – a North London cinema in Archway – was completely locked up, but so as not to waste the morning, and thanks entirely to the tenacity of Bob Downes, who managed to crawl into the pay kiosk in the foyer to plug Russell's amp to a socket, the audition was able to go ahead from the entrance of the cinema. With all the music parts spread out before him – not that he actually needed them – passers-by were then treated to a guitar master class from the young pretender. Naturally, the band was immensely impressed by his apparent reading ability; so much so, in fact, that they asked him to join there and then, which meant that the penultimate piece of the new JB7 jigsaw was now in place. By the following Friday, Ray Russell was a fully-fledged member alongside his new 'band of brothers' playing that Coventry Locarno debut.

Russell recalls that any nerves from which he might have suffered during his first appearances before an audience of hundreds were more than offset by the sheer excitement of the moment. This was, after all, his dream come true, for there he was, a professional musician at just sixteen years old being paid a weekly retainer and earning the type of money that most working men could only envy back then – £25/week – with additional bonuses whenever the workload increased. Despite his age, his parents fully supported his decision to join the band, and, over the next year, he was to receive a musical education, which would forever stand him in good stead.

~

This education began four months after joining the band once his failings were finally found out, which was the point at which it was decided to add new material to the repertoire. He really had no other option but to come clean there and then, and so with some trepidation, plucked up the courage to admit to being unable to read music to his fellow band mates. Much to his great relief, they took his confession very well to such an extent that two of the then newest recruits, Ron Edgeworth (keyboards) and Dave Richmond (bass), were both on hand to take him under their wings by teaching him the rudiments of music theory often when travelling between gigs. Incidentally, Russell wasn't the only one unable to 'join the dots' so it transpired, since it soon became apparent that Tony Ashton was also in the same predicament after failing to reproduce the written piano solo presented to him when 'Route 66' was introduced into the set. And of course, as already documented, Bob Downes could only follow a set of notation of his own making. "I never practise, I play," he would proudly proclaim, adding years later, "I don't play the flute, the flute plays me."

~

Becoming a touring musician certainly opened Russell's eyes to a completely different lifestyle: constantly being on the road travelling around in a Bedford Dormobile and having to stay in all sorts of boarding houses immediately springing to the fore. The conditions of some were often horrendous. One, situated next to a transport café at Scotch Corner on the A1, was an establishment Russell would never forget. "So very basic, it mainly consisted of one large room into which had been placed up to one hundred camp beds. Much frequented by lorry drivers, you can imagine the smell even when only 60% full; the air quality was often foul, more than likely due to the diets of the drivers! It was also advisable to sleep on your money, assuming you had any." Far more pleasing was the occasional visit to Barry's flat in Cadogan Square (Knightsbridge, London), which was always accompanied by a cup of tea and convivial conversation.

Ray Stiles had already received a thoroughly rounded musical grounding long before he took a phone call from Ray Russell suggesting he auditioned for a John Barry Seven then still desperately in need of a bass player to complete the new set-up. At the time, he was working at Selmer Musical Instruments Ltd in its grand showroom situated on 114-116 Charing Cross Road (London) after having already completed an apprenticeship with Boosey & Hawkes on leaving full-time education, where he learned all about the repairing and manufacturing of brass and woodwind instruments. As part of this training, placements at subsidiaries, Ajax Drums and Rudall Carte, enhanced his knowledge even further. At Selmer, which was considered the West End's premiere music establishment for professionals and amateurs alike, Stiles would often rub shoulders with established names alongside would-be pop stars on a daily basis. For every Tommy Steele, Cliff Richard and Mike Hurst (of The Springfields fame) whom he would regularly serve, there were no end of aspiring youngsters keen to seek out his sage advice; of the latter, one such customer was no other than Ray Russell himself.

Being part of the close-knit artistic community centred throughout the Denmark Street area enabled Stiles to augment his wage at Selmer's by becoming a regular session player at Regent Sounds Studio. For a handsome £12 10s per hour, he could simply nip out during his lunch hour and play. After all, he was a consummate musician in his own right, a classically trained guitarist and pianist, who first took to the stage when he was but a wee lad in short trousers, playing an accordion almost as tall as him, as part of his father Len's band, The Accordionaires – a popular London-based attraction that could boast future actress/comedienne Joan Turner as its singer. Even at a tender age, he was a seasoned performer, and would often give guitar recitals.

Following Russell's tip-off, Stiles passed his JB7 audition with flying colours whereupon he became the final cog in this pristine new machine and was soon fitted up in his crimson-coloured suit, with his Gibson bass at the ready, launching into 'The Magnificent Seven' – the established opening salvo – on that 'official' re-launch at the Coventry Locarno. He would later describe his time on the road with The JB7 as "the happiest days of my musical career" and can remember seeking permission from Bobby Graham to allow him and Alan Bown to travel together separately from gig to gig in order to avoid the cramped conditions associated with being hemmed in like sardines amongst all the stage gear that travelling in a transit van or Dormobile entailed (with a great deal of it spilling over onto the roof). Clearly, sharing a car with Alan Bown in the driver's seat was a far more comfortable option. Stiles described the camaraderie amongst the band as being "like a family", and although they very rarely fraternised with Barry, described Bobby Graham's leadership as "firm, fair and professional." It was only a tempting offer from Mike Hurst (to join his new group, Mike Hurst and The Methods) that would eventually entice him away from the band.

One early outing that struck a chord with Ray Russell was when playing at a rather unusual venue in Raikes Lane, Chesterfield, which was no more than a Nissen hut, named The Deep Litter Club, named on account of it serving as an actual pigpen prior to its change of usage. Owned and managed by a Mr Briscoe (who was well known to everyone as 'The Colonel'), the club was situated in the grounds of his estate and yet despite its remote location and insalubrious origin, it still managed to attract several other well-known acts such as Mr Acker Bilk and Joe Brown. The Colonel was renowned as the most gregarious of hosts, who always made an effort of entertaining that night's entertainers by putting on a generous spread with copious quantities of alcohol for the act in question at his home prior to the gig. "Although I don't think he actually attended any gigs, we would call in on the Colonel for drinks and eats. There seemed to be unlimited booze on hand, after which we would rehearse at the club," Russell clearly remembered.

In complete contrast, and just about as far flung from a pigpen as you could possibly imagine, was the venue chosen to host Ember Records' grand official re-launch party on 14th August. There, inside the luxurious ballroom of The Mayfair Hotel, Bobby Graham could be seen rubbing shoulders alongside a whole host of music industry luminaries: artists, writers, publicists, disc jockeys and journalists alike. The occasion provided Barry, under the full glare of publicity, with the perfect platform for formally announcing the signing of The John Barry Seven to the label from EMI. Of course, this was something of a misnomer for two main reasons.

Firstly, he had by this stage completely differentiated the studio personnel from the live act (Bobby Graham's contributions on both fronts notwithstanding). All of the Ember recordings were to employ the cream of the session cognoscenti from in and around the London studio scene, among them Big Jim Sullivan, Alan Haven and Ronnie Price, any one of them likely to be available at a moment's notice. No expense was to be spared whilst Barry reigned at Ember and his decision to hire the best musicians around reflected this policy. No longer being an employee of EMI, he would base his future recording operation either at CTS Studios (Bayswater) or at Olympic Sound Studios (Carlton Street, London's West End).

Secondly, it was Barry (and not The Seven) who was actually contracted to Columbia, thereby enabling him to often adjust the moniker of the band whenever he felt it appropriate (be it 'plus four', 'and orchestra' *etc.*) to reflect what instrumental combination was being employed on any given release, and also releasing 'Stringbeat' under his own name, and his name only. The pretence of retaining The JB7 name on record was a sensible one, done for the sake of maintaining continuity, for promoting the live shows as well as for taking full advantage of a hard-earned fan base. Moreover, members of the 'classic' JB7 line-up were still regularly contributing to studio recordings anyway. The name was now a well-established one, so there was little point in upsetting what had become a winning formula once 'Hit and Miss' took off.

Therefore, the studio John Barry Seven continued to issue singles throughout the latter end of 1963 even if the live wing were elsewhere whilst they were being recorded. The first of these, 'Kinky'/ 'Fancy Dance' (released in August) featured the alto sax of Johnny Scott on both sides. 'Kinky' was in fact a Scott composition, while 'Fancy Dance' was a Barry original that was later adopted as the theme to BBC TV's soap opera, *The Newcomers*. Both sides were turntable, if not chart, hits, and well received by the music press. *New Musical Express* described 'Kinky' as combining "a catchy rhythm with an air of mystery," while *Disc* expected the waltz-time melody "featuring his own well-known Seven" to "corkscrew its way into your brain and stay there quite a time." As for 'Fancy Dance', *New Musical Express* considered it "absorbing, worthwhile, but not for the pop market," while *Disc* applauded its "warm sax sound."

Two further 45s were released by Ember before the year was out, the first of which – '007'/'From Russia with Love' – was to become the last chart hit credited to The JB7 even if, as stated, it had little to do with the band that was treading the boards. Credited to 'The John Barry Seven and Orchestra', both sides showcased two prime cues from Barry's first fully-fledged Bond score. Although '007' – Barry's own alternative action theme – was originally the designated A-side (featuring, incidentally, the unmistakable guitar work of Vic Flick in session mode), it soon became overshadowed by the airplay extended to the B-side, an orchestral treatment of Lionel Bart's title song. The reviewer in *Disc* suggested that these sides should be flipped after praising 'From Russia with Love's' "brittle polish and high sense of mood lacking in Matt Monro's vocal version." Sage advice indeed, since that is precisely what occurred, resulting in the single climbing to No. 39 in the charts during a three week run from 21st November. The New JB7 was to incorporate these tracks as part of the live set in the fullness of time.

The second of the 45s – 'Elizabeth'/'The London Theme' – was being recorded at around the same time 'From Russia with Love' charted, to coincide with the screening of the CBS TV documentary, *Elizabeth Taylor in London*, scheduled for transmitting by the BBC for Christmas Eve. Both cuts were piano-led orchestral arrangements based on Barry's two main themes from the programme and credited to 'The John Barry Seven and Orchestra'. Quite why The Seven received a name-check even perplexed the *New Musical Express*'s reviewer at the time although he did acknowledge the single as "fine orchestral music, albeit more of the background type, with 'London Theme' the more tuneful of the two." This was, indeed, a valid point, since no single could possibly have been as far removed from the sound being generated from the live JB7 at University campuses all over the country as this one. Nevertheless, from Barry's perspective, he retained a vested interest in keeping The JB7's name alive on vinyl. By maintaining the illusion of the band as a studio entity as well as a stage act, the concert and recording wings of the publicity machine were able to fuel each other.

On 23rd November 1963, BBC TV launched a brand new Saturday evening science fiction drama entitled *Doctor Who*, the popularity of which continues unabated to this day. When the first lead actor, William Hartnell, was forced to relinquish the role on grounds of ill-health during October 1966, the writers came up with an ingenious way of introducing his replacement by devising the process of regeneration that would transform the physical appearance and personality of the Doctor. In many ways, John Barry's decision to revamp The JB7 in its entirety during October pre-empted this concept by three years, for here was a regeneration of sorts in all but name; intentional or otherwise, it succeeded in repositioning the band in a market place that was undergoing a seismic transformation.

This was no better illustrated than by what was revealed in *New Musical Express*'s 1963 annual music poll published that December, which was always a useful barometer of the current pop climate. Conspicuous by their absence for the very first time since 1958 were The JB7. There could not have been a clearer indication as to where the band stood in the new hierarchy than by the names occupying the 'British Small Group' section, on which a place for The Seven had been just about guaranteed for the past five years. The new brooms sweeping aside the old stalwarts included The Beatles (inevitably), The Searchers, Gerry and The Pacemakers, The Rolling Stones, Peter Jay and The Jaywalkers, The Dakotas, The Dave Clark Five, Brian Poole and The Tremeloes, Freddie and The Dreamers and The Rockin' Berries. Of the established acts, only The Shadows (who topped the section) and Kenny Ball (who also trounced the opposition in the 'Trad Jazz Band' section) stood firm.

More significantly, instrumental music *per se*, although by no means dead in the water, was not the force it had been in previous years. Of the hundred best -selling 45s of 1963, only thirteen could be described as instrumental, and of those, seven of them were in some way connected to The Shadows (if one counts the solo offerings of Jet Harris and Tony Meehan). The *New Musical Express* Top Thirty chart published on 13th December illustrated this point perfectly, since only two 45s were *bona fide* instrumentals ('Geronimo' by The Shadows and 'Maria Elena' by Los Indios Tabajaras) while the remaining listing was dominated by The Beatles (occupying six entries including the top two singles – 'I Want to Hold Your Hand' and 'She Loves You' respectively) alongside seven fellow beat groups following their lead (such as The Hollies, The Rolling Stones and The Dave Clark Five). There seemed every need for the new JB7 to adapt to the prevailing trend, but this was not to transpire until later the following year when certain changes in musical direction were to be initiated from directly within the band. Until then, as the new personnel tentatively got to grips with the repertoire, they stayed strictly instrumental, with a set-list replicating what had already prevailed; hence 'Hit and Miss', 'Walk Don't Run', 'The James Bond Theme', 'Cutty Sark', and 'The Magnificent Seven' remained integral to each concert.

With the Western world still reeling from the shockwaves caused by the assassination of President J. F. Kennedy on 22nd November, the conditions were ripe for a British invasion – led by The Beatles – to rejuvenate a nation badly in need of a collective lift. John Barry happened to be appearing on stage at The Savoy (London) with Nina and Frederick on that tragic day of the shooting, a concert that was to prelude a more substantial return to the stage a month later when he led a full orchestra backing Shirley Bassey in Cardiff on 21st December. What would soon transpire during the coming year was the sight of two John

Barry-related ensembles taking to the stage simultaneously across the UK; in effect, leading parallel existences.

So as 1964 loomed rapidly on the horizon, The JB7 could no longer be considered among the vanguard of the British music scene. Instead, it was now creating a new niche for itself through carving out a considerable reputation as a solid, dependable and entertaining live attraction (as the next chapter will reveal). In doing so, the band would become renowned for breaking in some of the finest young talent around by way of providing them with valuable touring experience. After having seemingly miraculously risen from the ashes during October, there was clearly still life in the old boy yet.

The Joe Loss Orchestra including drummer Ray Cooper, third from left, back row.

Programme

1 Harold Collins & the Princess Theatre Orchestra

2 *Our entertaining compere Chris Carlsen introduces to you* The Jetblacks

3 Himself!   Chris *in* " Comedy Cameos "

4 Brook Brothers   *Torquay favourites*

intermission

5 The Kestrels   *presented by Chris Carlsen*

6 " A word from Chris " *followed by the popular*

7 John Barry Seven

8 **DANNY** *"Moon River"* **WILLIAMS**

In accordance with the requirements of the local authority: 1. The Public may leave at the end of the performance by all exit and entrance doors and such doors must at that time be open. 2. All gangways, passages and staircases must be kept entirely free from chairs or obstruction. 3. The safety curtain must be lowered and raised once, immediately before the commencement of each performance, so as to ensure its being in proper working order. 4. No smoking shall take place on the stage except as part of the performance or entertainment.

Danny Williams' concert at Torquay Princess Theatre, featuring the last appearance of the Vic Flick-led line-up of the band – September 1963.

Norman Newell, who, with John Burgess, produced The JB7 for many years.

*John Barry and Bobby Graham at the
re–launch of Ember Records at The
Mayfair Hotel, in August 1963.*

*John Barry, Annie Ross, David Jacobs and Jeffrey Kruger at the re–launch of
Ember Records at The Mayfair Hotel, in August 1963.*

The re-formed band in October 1963, with, from left, back row: Ray Stiles, Ray Russell, Terry Childs; second row: Bob Downes, Tony Ashton, Alan Bown; in front: Bobby Graham.

The new line-up of the band at The Deep Litter Club, near Chesterfield, with its owner Mr. "Colonel" Briscoe. From left: Ray Stiles, Tony Ashton, Ray Russell, Bobby Graham, Terry Childs, Bob Downes and Alan Bown – November 1963.

GREETINGS TELEGRAM   GPO

76   APB 2/43. YORK T 19 ALLPURPOSE =

BOBBY GRAHAM JOHN BARRY SEVEN

          LOCARNO BALLROOM COVENTRY =

WISHING YOU ALL THE VERY BEST OF SUCCESS

          JACK PRENDERGAST +

Good luck telegram from Jack Prendergast to Bobby Graham on the occasion of the first gig for the new line-up.

258

The Human Jungle debuts with
the theme music played by
The John Barry Seven and Orchestra.

8

THE PARTY'S OVER

JANUARY 1964 – MAY 1965

*Many is the time Alan Bown was asked for his autograph; he never
disappointed the fans, always dutifully signing 'John Barry'.*

– Bobby Graham (Leader/Drums)

*The John Barry Seven were the first band I ever went on the road
with – all seedy hotels, brown ale and very hard work.*

– Gered Mankowitz (pop/rock photographer)

By the beginning of 1964, the youthquake generated by the baby boomer bulge
flexing its collective economic muscle was now in the midst of registering on the
Richter scale with no one quite as in synch with the zeitgeist as Bob Dylan or The
Beatles. On 13th January, Dylan released his third studio LP, *The Times They Are
a-Changin'*, which was as good an expression for the shifting social mores as any,
and when a Pan Am Yankee Clipper (Flight 101) carrying The Beatles touched
down on New York's Kennedy Airport on 7th February, 'Beatlemania' (and the
UK musical revolution it represented) was about to go global. For the new-look
John Barry Seven, they were going to have to learn to adapt to this climate change
pretty quickly, and adapt to it they did. Although no longer regarded as one of
pop's 'A-listers' any more, The Seven succeeded in consolidating a reputation for
guaranteeing a good-time, 'value-for-money' live experience.

What continued to hamper any major re-emergence alongside the elite was the
band's lack of media exposure and coherent recording strategy, and when BBC
Television launched its new flagship pop programme, *Top of the Pops*, on New
Year's Day, it more or less confined The JB7 to the live circuit, and the live circuit
alone. The entire ethos of *TOTP* throughout its forty-two year longevity was
always to promote what was happening and emerging on the current singles chart.
Therefore, any band not regularly releasing 45s, as was the case with this version
of The JB7 at the time, would automatically have been excluded for consideration

as a result of not meeting the programme's strict criteria. Unfortunately, *TOTP* arrived a couple of years too late for The JB7. Nevertheless, the profile of the band was given a considerable boost come November, when it was chosen to back Brenda Lee's UK and European tours. Several changes in personnel would have taken place well before then, however, including a change in leadership.

In complete contrast to the fortunes of The JB7, insofar as continuing to tick along nicely on an even keel without ever looking likely to regain its place amongst pop's hierarchy, Barry's own career would soon be taking off and gathering pace with almost Beatle-like momentum. Yes, 1964 was a watershed year for Barry, the year that would propel his name onto the world stage. It began with a tour of England's major city cinema venues that saw him lead his own orchestra in a concert setting for the first time. Not only was he hired to back the headline act, Shirley Bassey, but his orchestra was also allocated its own supporting spot. Among the musicians employed was none other than Vic Flick on guitar, now established in his role as a session player, and yet happily reconciled to playing the *occasional* 'live' gig now and then. Three of the films Barry scored during the year – *Zulu*, *Séance on a Wet Afternoon* and *Goldfinger* – were to rapidly secure his reputation as a go-to composer able to handle any assignment.

And so while The JB7's own touring schedule occupied venues less glamorous than the concert halls allotted to Barry and Bassey (e.g. a Saturday dance at The Winter Gardens Pavilion, Weston-super-Mare, say, as opposed to a performance at the Odeon, Leicester Square), they still more than paid their way. Nevertheless, what became evident throughout the course of the year was how Barry consciously distanced himself professionally from the touring JB7 even when opportunities may have arisen whereby a coming together might have given the band the type of exposure it was being denied.

Throughout January, in addition to his concert appearances, Barry was busily scoring the film *Zulu* after having been recommended for the job by Lionel Bart, impressed as he was with Barry's contribution to *From Russia With Love*. Co-star and co-producer Stanley Baker – a personal friend – suggested to Barry that he recorded guitar-led 'pop' versions of two of *Zulu*'s main themes. Calling them 'Zulu Stamp' and 'Monkey Feathers', this is precisely what he set out to accomplish on 3rd January at Olympic Sound Studios under the experienced guidance of engineer Keith Grant. Released later that month, here was another example of an Ember 45 attributed to a John Barry Seven, that, with the exception of Bobby Graham's drumming, had nothing to do with the set of musicians regularly representing the name up and down the country on stage.

January marked the first changes in personnel for the remodelled JB7, when Dave Richmond was drafted in to replace Ray Stiles on bass guitar, while Ron Edgeworth took over keyboard duties from Tony Ashton. As it transpired, Richmond and Edgeworth were already well acquainted prior to joining The JB7, since the two of them were members of 'The Val Merrill Band' that played at two different American air bases in Germany over a three-month period during the winter of 1961.

Both Ray Stiles and Tony Ashton decided to leave for pastures new after being headhunted by Mike Hurst, who was looking to form his own group in the wake of The Springfields having recently split up. Stiles knew all three 'Springfields' well through his job at Selmer's, and so an attractive offer from a friend held sway over any allegiance to The Seven. Therefore, he and Ashton, alongside Albert Lee (once original choice as lead guitarist Ray Smith left some weeks later), formed part of the five-piece Mike Hurst and The Methods, whose explorations into the country-rock idiom was some way ahead of its time.

Throughout his formative years, new recruit Ron Edgeworth concentrated his energies on mastering boogie, blues and twenties jazz in and around the London area, but it was his versatility and imaginative playing style that would eventually take him beyond such a specialist sphere. His ability to embrace a wide variety of musical styles ranging from pop to classics made him stand out so much that his services soon became desirable in all types of guises: as a soloist, as part of his own duo and trio (embracing both traditional and modern jazz), as an accompanist to various nightclub acts and society bands, even as a musical director in his own right – in fact, he played for anyone who would employ him, be it pub or palace!

Just to exemplify such adaptability, he subsequently went on to work in Europe and North Africa (doubling up on trombone in a military band), on the US bases in Germany with a forties-style swing band, and in England with the famous broadcasting big bands of the day – led by Ronnie Aldrich, Cyril Stapleton, Johnny Howard and Bob Miller. Introduction to the showbiz side of the music world came about when comedian and compère Don Arrol invited him to become his regular personal accompanist, whereupon he became an integral part of Arrol's stage act in theatres and nightclubs throughout the UK, as well as on radio and TV.

Whereas John Barry's enthusiasm for the trumpet and modern jazz was influenced by his elder brother's liking of Harry James, Dave Richmond's first musical influence was through a record his brother owned called 'Big Noise From Winnetka', which featured Bob Haggard on double bass and Ray Bauduc on drums. By the age of fourteen, he had started to learn the ukulele, using the 'First Step Tutor Book', and once the family moved to live in Torquay, he preferred to take lessons in Hawaiian guitar before switching to steel-stringed acoustic guitar. At fifteen, he half-heartedly enrolled on a commercial course at the South Devon Technical College, based in Torquay, but as soon as his mother realised that daily lessons in English, shorthand, typing, bookkeeping and commerce bored her son rigid, she set about to rectify such stagnancy. On having heard that the RAF was "seeking young men aged between 17 and 24 to train as musicians," she cannily wrote off and applied for an audition on his behalf.

"It wasn't until she told me a few weeks later that I had to attend an audition at the RAF School of Music Uxbridge, that I knew anything about it!," Richmond would later recall. His acoustic guitar audition in front of head of music, Wing Commander Wallace, may not have been perfect by any means, but nonetheless it proved good enough for the young applicant to have been offered a place on the understanding he would learn the clarinet rather than his preferred saxophone. After leaving the service, by which time he had become an accomplished double bass player, Richmond was to join The Mann-Hugg Blues Brothers in this capacity, only switching from double to electric bass guitar once the band had adopted the catchier moniker, Manfred Mann. However, not long after recording the band's first hit, '5-4-3-2-1' (which was soon to be adopted as the theme tune to *Ready Steady Go!*), he decided to leave in favour of The John Barry Seven, at the suggestion of Bob Downes. He particularly remembered promoting the then new single, 'Zulu Stamp', during his earlier gigs, a number on which Ray Russell distinctly recalled using a 12-string electric Burns Double Six.

≈

By 1964, several ex-members of The JB7 were already beginning to make significant inroads from within the recording industry either as musicians, writers or producers. Vic Flick, for one, was making the most of his freelance recording sessions by playing guitar on some of the biggest hits of the year including those by Petula Clark ('Downtown') Herman's Hermits ('I'm into Something Good'), Dusty Springfield ('I Just Don't Know What to Do with Myself') and Peter and Gordon ('A World Without Love'). Meanwhile, Les Reed was forging a reputation as a songwriter and musical director of note. After having set up a publishing company (Donna Music) with offices based in Denmark Street, he began to collaborate with a number of lyricists. Almost from the off, the hits began to roll off the conveyor belt: firstly in the USA, with 'Everybody Knows (I Love You)' by Steve Lawrence (words courtesy of Jimmy Duncan) and then in the UK, when 'Tell Me When' by The Applejacks (lyrics by Geoff Stephens) reached No. 7 in the UK charts during April. Within a year he would enjoy even greater writing success in partnership with Gordon Mills, when Tom Jones soared to No. 1 in the UK charts with 'It's Not Unusual'.

≈

On 7th March, the sound of wedding bells could be heard loud and clear in and around St. Paul's Church, Stoke Road, Slough, where band mates Terry Childs, Ray Russell, Dave Richmond and Ron Edgeworth could be found among those invited to witness Alan Bown tying the knot with his twenty-year-old fiancée, Jean Blackman. He had first met Jean a few years previously following a dance at the local Essoldo Cinema when he was still in the RAF, but so typical of a musician's life, there was hardly any time to enjoy the reception afterwards on account of a good many of the guests having to make a speedy exit in order to fulfil a gig later that same day.

While The JB7 continued to play venues such as The Floral Hall (Scarborough), Barry (alongside his Concert Orchestra) decided to resume his association with Shirley Bassey by embarking on a further eight dates at major concert halls throughout the spring starting at the Capitol (Cardiff) on 10th April and ending at The Guildhall (Portsmouth) on 3rd May. Not that it was all plain sailing, mind you, since the one show planned for the Colston Hall (Bristol) was actually cancelled due to poor ticket sales, which must have bruised one or two egos along the way. Nevertheless, those that went ahead were all generally well received, boosted as they were by the addition of Matt Monro on the bill.

What would have been most noticeable to anyone witnessing both of these Barry-endorsed 'ensembles' at the time was a certain symmetry with regards the set-list. Although in no doubt some distance away geographically, instrumentally and numerically, both shared the same core repertoire. For example, 'Comin' Home Baby', 'I Who Have Nothing', 'Cutty Sark', 'From Russia with Love', 'Moanin' and 'The James Bond Theme' were integral to both. Those of a sceptical nature might construe that Barry was keen to continue using already acquired and well-thumbed band parts, ostensibly as an economy measure, which was an accusation levelled at him by the previous line-up – so maybe there was no smoke without fire.

On 20th April, BBC Television launched the UK's third TV channel, BBC Two. One of its first commissions was *Impromptu*, an eight-part series, which was an early forerunner of *Whose Line is it Anyway?*. Hosted by Jeremy Hawk (as the so-called Boss Man), it also featured Lance Percival, Anne Cunningham, Betty Impey, and Victor Spinetti, whose improvisations formed the basis of the show. Also on hand to provide some dance moves of her own was Una Stubbs, with Barry engaged in leading a small group for providing the live impromptu music accompanying the mimes, plus the main theme.

Now clearly, here was an excellent opportunity for bringing The JB7 onto the small screen after a lengthy absence and back into the public's consciousness, but alas, it was not to be. Admittedly, the audience would have been small (since BBC Two could only be viewed via a 625-line set and not the then standard 405-line one), but it might well have generated a domino effect. Instead, Barry chose to enlist a group of session musicians, among them organist Alan Haven. Doubtless all fine players, but doing a job The JB7 was more than capable of fulfilling. Evidently, Barry had consigned playing alongside The JB7 to his past and therefore felt no genuine desire to go back there, but even so, one can't help concluding that a more carefully considered, 'joined-up' thinking approach might well have helped the band's cause.

The trials and tribulations associated with constantly travelling around the UK in confined quarters was to prove just as problematic, hazardous, irritating and laborious as it had been for all of the other previous line-ups, as Ray Russell was soon to learn. Of the various drivers employed during the year, he found Terry (nicknamed 'Tug') the most frustrating. At the time, 'Tug' and his brother took it in turns to drive the band from gig to gig in either of the two blue Dormobiles they hired out, one of which was notorious for breaking down. Russell recalled 'Tug', in particular, as a perpetual moaner, with one occasion standing out above all others. "I can remember he once dropped me off at a station, miles from where I lived, leaving me there completely stranded with my amp, guitar and suitcase, simply because he didn't feel like driving any more. Bearing in mind we had travelled overnight from somewhere up north, it was now 6 a.m. in the morning and I was still only eighteen, he nevertheless insisted it was far too 'out of his way' to proceed in my direction. My Mum had kittens when she saw me, and tore him off a strip when she later called him up to complain. It took a week before we could begin to laugh about it."

Neither had the quality of the guesthouses or bed and breakfast accommodations improved much either, as Alan Bown would attest. Most of the time standards could best be described as basic when it came to comfort and cleanliness, but some were downright shoddy. One such establishment that immediately sprung to mind was located in the Mumbles area near Swansea. Run by a Polish woman, her rooms were notoriously already taken by non-paying guests of the insect variety. Staying there at the same time as Bown was Tony Crane of The Merseybeats. Determined to make a point with typical gallows Scouse wit, he pinned a note to the door of his room (stating 'This room is already occupied.') attached to the remains of one of those unwelcome freeloaders, a cockroach. Henceforth, Bown would re-name the guesthouse, Mrs Bedobugska's.

Like Vic Flick and Dougie Wright before him, Bobby Graham would soon come to the conclusion that however much he enjoyed a life 'on the road', it could never compete financially with that of a session musician, nor was it as secure. As his predecessors also discovered, he, too, found that the balancing act was a difficult one to maintain and so, in the end, he plumped for the latter. Having already sampled the 'studio life' on a regular basis over the previous twelve months, the lure of £7 10s (plus porterage) per three-hour session had become overwhelming. He knew from first-hand experience precisely which side his bread was buttered, for it was quite feasible to fit in three (or even four) sessions a day, thereby making at least £27 on one day alone, which was a sizeable sum indeed by 1964's standards, when for many of his contemporaries this was considerably more than the average weekly wage (around £17/week for manual workers).

What must also have emboldened Graham's decision to leave The Seven when he actually did was in knowing just how vital his recent contribution in session had been on two of the biggest hits of the year thus far. Replacing The Beatles' 'I Want to Hold Your Hand' at the top of the charts on 16th January was The Dave Clark Five's 'Glad All Over', which was quickly followed in the Top Ten by 'Bits and Pieces'. In fact, at the beginning of March, these two singles were placed at No. 14 and No. 4 in the Top Thirty respectively during the same week. Graham's pounding 'flam beat' with both hands and feet gave The DC5 its distinctive sound, the result of which meant that he would be asked to play on all of their subsequent records right up until 1967. He would soon further his growing reputation by playing on hit records by The Bachelors, The Kinks, Dusty Springfield, Petula Clark, Kathy Kirby, Dave Berry, Them and PJ Proby, all within the same twelve-month window. Thus, Bobby Graham became one of those vital, yet unheralded, cogs in the UK's hit factory production line, a band of musicians he would collectively refer to as 'The Musical Stuntmen'.

It has to be said that, as a leader, Bobby Graham tended to divide opinion amongst his band mates. Consequently, his departure was not exactly universally mourned. Whereas his drumming credentials could not be faulted, he was evidently not the easiest of individuals to deal with on a personal level, and as such arguably not the most suitable person to lead a band *per se*. Although Ray Stiles was quick to acknowledge Graham's "firm, yet fair" professionalism and organisational skills, Ray Russell found him "difficult", while Bob Downes described him as "grumpy" and also disrespectful to his wife in front of the band. In fact Downes found that the only way he could tolerate Graham in a social setting was by taking a couple of 'purple hearts' on such occasions; for example, when the band visited Barry at his Cadogan Square apartment – something the band, he insisted, would have never ever contemplated doing normally on or prior to taking the stage.

In Graham's defence, as he later readily admitted to the authors, his period in charge of The JB7 coincided with the emergence of what would become a serious drink problem. This was the point at which he started to consume far more alcohol than was good for him, an aspect of his life he would later regret. Such excesses would eventually impact upon his long-term memory to the point where he could not always recall the exact minutiae of his past, but he was at pains to apologise to his ex-colleagues for any untoward behaviour that may have offended them all those years ago.

The decision to part company, although an amicable one, was clearly a blow to Barry, who considered Graham not only a good friend but also the ideal person to lead the band in his own image. He obviously needed to appoint a successor pretty quickly, and so decided to appoint Alan Bown, whose influence over time would prove decisive. Throughout the course of his stewardship, Bown was to gradually introduce subtle changes that would update the band's sound, i.e. by altering its musical DNA ever closer towards what was more currently fashionable; in other words, the R&B oriented material much preferred by contemporaries.

Alas, this was yet to come, for the advent of spring hardly heralded any 'green shoots of recovery' as far as The JB7 were concerned. On the contrary, work had become noticeably thinner on the ground. So sporadic were engagements that individual band members were being forced into exploring any potential commercial opportunity presenting itself, which led to four of them – at least for a short while – becoming part of an outfit called Shade Joey and The Night Owls. It was a case of 'needs must' at the time. Shade Joey, real name Brendan

Claypole, had no previous experience in the music business to speak of, and yet on 29th May, long before one solitary note had been recorded, he had succeeded in securing virtually the entire front page of the *New Musical Express* in order to announce his arrival; his publicists clearly working overtime!

The advertisement offered no clues whatsoever as to what the act was all about, but perhaps that was a deliberate ploy to create an aura of mystery. In keeping with the name of the lead singer, the four JB7 members were each wearing shades, which would have also helped in concealing their identities, since the publicity in question only revealed their first names: Dave (Richmond), Ray (Russell), Bob (Downes) and Ron (Edgeworth). When the band finally did make a record, it was produced by Joe Meek at his Holloway Road studio, but oddly enough, wasn't actually released by Parlophone until the end of September by which time any interest generated from the original launch had long since dissipated and would have been considered old hat by then. Not surprisingly, the single – 'Bluebirds Over the Mountain'/'That's When I Need You Baby' – sank without much of a trace, which has ensured it becoming a collector's item in light of the Joe Meek connection.

Bob Downes vividly recalls the whole enterprise as being rather shambolic: the four of them posing ridiculously in dark glasses for the photo-shoot; being told not to flush the toilets at Joe Meek's Islington studio in case the noise of the cistern re-filling was being picked up by the microphones, and Downes himself writing the B-side on the spot simply because no material had been planned other than the A-side. "Real naff, and didn't get us any work!", was his damning verdict. As for performing live, that too was not without comic incident. "We actually did a couple of gigs, one I believe in Stevenage, where we all tripped onto the stage half blind on account of wearing those sunglasses. After two numbers we had to remove them as we found it affected our musical communication. Dave Richmond, our bassist, always wore tinted glasses, but at least they had proper lenses in them."

Downes was to leave The JB7 shortly afterwards, not just because work was becoming ever more spasmodic, but also as a result of that old cliché, 'musical differences'. "At one point we were being lined up to become a backing band for a singer (presumably Marty Wilde), which didn't appeal to me in the slightest, for it would have meant us no longer playing any JB7 repertoire, which always gave me scope as a soloist. Not only that, but the four of us (Dave Richmond, Ron Edgeworth, Ray Russell and I) were also given the opportunity of forming a band in order to back a young black female singer. However, when we assembled for a rehearsal, we soon discovered that she just could not sing in tune. We even auditioned with her for a well-known band leader who was interested in becoming financially involved, but he obviously thought the same as us (re: the girl's vocal attributes) since we never saw him again. Thankfully that project ended abruptly." Sadly, the authors were unable to 'out' the offending singer despite tireless research, although Ray Russell was convinced she started to pursue a modelling career not long after.

The irregularity of the work eventually led to the early departures of Ray Russell, Dave Richmond and Ron Edgeworth as well, with Richmond concentrating more on session work. During his relatively brief stay, he never actually once came across Barry, and yet, ironically, a few years later, there he was playing on a James Bond film score recording, with Barry at the conductor's podium! "Strangely enough, I didn't meet John Barry (not even when I auditioned for the band) until about four years after I left it!" was how he put it. As for Ron Edgeworth, he joined a band led by Alexis Korner, while Ray Russell became part of the group Blueroots (alongside another ex-JB7 member, bassist Ray Stiles) before joining the illustrious inner circle of in-demand session guitarists.

Thus, when Alan Bown took over the reins as leader, a number of places were in need of filling, starting with the unenviable task of having to replace a drummer as capable as Bobby Graham. Understandably, he started to recruit personnel whom he knew and who shared his musical tastes. Drummer Ernie Cox, for instance, was an old friend of his from his schooldays when both were members of The Slough Centre Boys Club. As events unravelled, this particular appointment would prove to be the band's undoing, though no one was to know that at the time. One by one, as each position was taken up, a settled line-up eventually began to emerge, which read as follows: **Alan Bown (leader/trumpet); Mike O'Neill (keyboards/vocals); Ron Arghyrou (lead guitar); Stan Haldane (bass guitar); Dave Green (tenor sax/flute); Terry Childs (baritone/alto sax) and Ernie Cox (drums)**.

Both Dave Green and Ernie Cox had been members of The Flintstones, a very experienced instrumental group often found on the same pop package tours played by The Seven. Their pedigree was such that they backed Little Richard on his autumn 1963 UK tour; appeared on the Gene Vincent/Duane Eddy tour throughout November of that same year and prior to joining The Seven, had undergone a tour with Jerry Lee Lewis, Gene Vincent and The Animals during March (1964).

As was often the case in the past, word of mouth recommendation played an important part in speeding up the recruitment process. For example, Terry Childs recommended both Stan Haldane (b. 1945) and Ron Menicos Arghyrou (b. 1940), having first encountered Haldane playing bass in a band named The Counts, whilst deputising at The Café des Artistes in Fulham, and having worked with Arghyrou as part of a five-piece band engaged on American bases in France during 1962. "Two years later, Terry introduced me to Alan Bown, and as soon as I joined, I was rehearsing with the band in a hall in Hanwell," Arghyrou vividly recalled. Both made their JB7 debuts at the aforementioned gig at The Floral Hall in Scarborough.

Haldane retains nothing but fond memories when reminiscing about the-then new guitarist. "Ron Arghyrou was an out-and-out jazzer, playing an old Gibson guitar which had a lovely smooth sound. [Future vocalist] Jeff Bannister always remarks about how much Ron taught him about chords and their usage. No idea what happened to him, but I suspect he went off to play jazz somewhere. Such a brilliant guitarist."

Born in Lowton, Lancashire during 1938, Mike O'Neill was the oldest of four brothers, who having started work in a local steelworks, soon decided to teach himself the piano as a means of extricating himself from a life in heavy industry. Come 1958 he decided to hitch all the way to London, where he threw himself into the music business. Coincidentally, as if to mirror John Barry, he too initially found digs in Old Compton Street, London, except that he lived at no. 39 rather than at no. 38!

After a couple of brief stints with Clay Nicholls and Vince Taylor, he joined Colin Hicks (brother of Tommy Steele) and The Cabin Boys in the autumn of 1959 on piano. They worked in Italy for a few months, as a consequence of which they appeared in the film, *Europa di Notte* (Europe by Night), which depicted the nightlife in Europe's capitals (Rome, Paris, London, Madrid, Vienna and Brussels, *etc.*) and featured various artists performing in nightclubs.

Perhaps inspired by the Italian scene, and in all likelihood because of O'Neill's landlady in Milan dubbing him 'Neroni' (due to his hairstyle at that time resembling a Roman emperor's) The Cabin Boys decided to transform themselves into Nero and The Gladiators; and while Colin Hicks opted to pursue a solo career in Italy, the rest of the band returned to England. By 1960 they were part of the tragically ill-fated Gene Vincent/Eddie Cochran UK package tour that saw Cochran lose his life. Shortly afterwards, they began to complement their evocative name with a visual image to match, by going the whole hog with a host of props newly acquired by O'Neill allegedly from the abandoned set of the film, *Ben Hur*, i.e. matching helmets, breastplates, boots, swords, and shields, with O'Neill himself fronting the band rigged out appropriately in toga and laurel-leaf crown – New Romantics years before their time!

Nero and The Gladiators enjoyed two medium-sized hits with pop versions of 'Entry of the Gladiators' (based on Julius Fučík's famous circus tune) and 'In the Hall of the Mountain King' (loosely based on the original by Edvard Grieg). Unfortunately the BBC didn't take kindly to the latter by promptly banning it from the airwaves on account of its spoken intro being deemed "disrespectful to classical music". There were to be no more hits, but the band kept going for another two or three years with various changes of personnel, though O'Neill remained a constant. They were hired to back French singer Dick Rivers for a tour in his country, but finally disbanded in early 1964 with O'Neill returning to England and joining The JB7 around Easter time.

Playing predominantly one-nighters and now represented by the Harold Davison Organisation, Alan Bown's JB7 continued to tour the UK, as ever travelling in a Bedford van and hemmed in by equipment, but now chauffeured by a new driver/road manager, Len. On stage the band wore fashionable matching collarless shiny maroon mohair suits, with leader Bown decked out in a similarly styled light grey variant in order to stand out as leader; a deliberate throwback to the early days when Barry at the helm adopted the same policy (and one to which Vic Flick did not adhere). Like many performers of that era, applying pancake make-up to the face was necessary as a means of negating the anaemic effect on the complexion caused by the stage spotlights. Unfortunately, this method of tanning then resulted in a horrible discoloration around the point at which the shirt collar made contact with the neck, and even more disarming was the reaction caused by the band whenever they entered various hostelries for a pre-concert beverage wearing the war paint. As Bown later explained, "Seven guys draped in shiny suits and in full make-up, entering a pub in a place like King's Lynn on a Wednesday night, was bound to turn heads!"

During June, almost a year to the day after the previous incarnation had been well-received at the Balliol College Oxford's 700th Anniversary Ball, the new line-up was booked to play a similar event, this time to mark Merton College Oxford's own 700th anniversary, only on this occasion they were joined by Sid Phillips and His Band, The Fourbeats, Johnny Whatmough and His Orchestra, The Tropicannas, The Applejacks, The Joe Loss' Ambassadors Orchestra and The Crickets. And like the Balliol Ball, tickets cost 7 guineas a head. Unfortunately, summer was proving to be a difficult season for The JB7. Being closely aligned to the university/college circuit meant that the traditional, long semesters associated with the world of academia completely cut off the band's main supply line. Any hope of relying on a season at a holiday resort or two, as was the case in the past, simply failed to materialise. Yes, work was to remain thin on the ground for a while yet, even if one seaside booking did manage to buck that trend: a 23rd August concert at the Bournemouth Winter Gardens supporting The Bachelors and The Seekers.

Publicity photos indicate the band was being re-branded as 'The New John Barry Seven' at this juncture, though bearing in mind the ever-growing number of hit-making groups with whom they were now in competition on the circuit, this strategy didn't appear to have had much of an effect.

Undeterred, the band continued to refine its sound in rehearsal and, slowly but surely, Bown began to impose his own musical preferences into an evolving repertoire. Even though the hard core, non-negotiable 'must haves' remained *in situ*, 'Let the Good Times Roll' was soon to become this line-up's obligatory set opener, thereby acting as The Seven's signature tune for the remainder of the band's existence in the same way that 'Bee's Knees' and 'The Magnificent Seven' did previously. Originally recorded by Louis Jordan in 1946, The JB7 were more likely to have taken inspiration from the Ray Charles version that appeared on his 1959 LP, *The Genius Of* in line with many an R&B-influenced combo of the time (Georgie Fame and The Blues Flames being another). Alongside The JB7's Columbia hits ('Hit and Miss', 'Walk Don't Run', 'Cutty Sark', 'The James Bond Theme' *et al*), other notable instrumentals were also included (among them Cannonball Adderley's 'Sack of Woe', Henry Mancini's 'Peter Gunn', Bill Doggart's 'Honk Tonk', Jimmy Forrest's 'Night Train'. Max Harris's 'Gurney Slade', Sandy Nelson's 'Let There Be Drums', Hank Levine's 'Image' and Herbie Hancock's 'Watermelon Man') and, even more significant, with Mike O'Neill now on board, a smattering of songs started to seep into the set.

As a rule of thumb, at least four vocal numbers per show were now being included in this revamped selection, most of them emanating from the Chicago soul productions masterminded by Curtis Mayfield, Carl Davis and Johnny Pate. Not for The JB7 the Detroit sound of Motown nor the Memphis sound of Stax (as many other bands of their ilk were favouring); instead Bown was more drawn towards plundering the recent catalogue of The Impressions and other Mayfield-led collaborations. Hence, The JB7 became the first UK live act to cover Major Lance's 'Um Um Um Um Um Um' (written by Mayfield). Much to Bown's chagrin, Wayne Fontana and The Mindbenders took notice, liked what they heard, and then duly took their own recorded version of the song into the Top Five during October by more or less aping The JB7's arrangement. To emulate The Impressions's three-part harmonies, Dave Green and Stan Haldane added their own vocal colourings as they tackled the singles 'It's Alright' and 'I Need You', as well as an LP track, 'Little Boy Blue' (taken from the 1964 LP, *The Never Ending Impressions*).

Clearly, Barry's strict 'no vocal' rule had either been relaxed or simply ignored. Given that he would occasionally arrive unannounced at the odd gig or two as if he was some kind of unofficial 'mystery shopper', it suggests that the changes made must have met his tacit approval at the very least, even if the choice of songs were a far cry from the type of material he was then writing, arranging and producing. The JB7 had moved a mighty long way from its initial rock 'n' roll blueprint, and whereas it may not have always moved in synch with the times, it invariably caught up with them eventually.

By this time, Barry was less focused on his protégés in any case, for he was far more engrossed in furthering his own career. Not only was he concentrating his energies on a burgeoning film music career (*Séance on a Wet Afternoon*, *A Jolly Bad Fellow*, *Man in the Middle*, *Goldfinger* and *Muloorina* would swiftly follow each other during the course of the year) but he was also working on two stage musicals (one of which, *Passion Flower Hotel*, would reach fruition in 1965).

Nevertheless, Alan Bown, ever keen to stamp his own mark as leader, was equally determined to make a defining statement of his own by canvassing the idea of releasing a brand new JB7 45 featuring the current personnel. The fact that he managed to persuade Barry to agree to this was no mean feat, in light of the fact that Barry had still been using The JB7 'brand name' at least for his own cache of Ember singles. Recorded at CTS Studios (Bayswater), two radically different tracks were deliberately chosen to represent the stylistic changes indicative of Bown's tenure: a vocal A-side, 'Twenty-Four Hours Ago' (the first of its kind since Barry's own early efforts seven years previously), backed by a languorous twelve-bar instrumental entitled 'Seven Faces'. Here was a major sonic update inasmuch as both sides featured the kind of Hammond organ solo that was just about *de rigueur* for the period in question. The arrangement and feel of the 45 was right up there with the type of 'R&B'-influenced material being recorded by The Graham Bond Organisation, Zoot Money's Big Roll Band, Georgie Fame and The Blue Flames, early John Mayall's Bluesbreakers, and Chris Bennett and The Rebel Rousers. Pop was transforming into rock back then, and Bown wanted his JB7 to join the party.

B-side, 'Seven Faces' – which was soon to become a firm favourite live – was actually co-written by Bown alongside another of his old 'Slough Centre Boys Club' buddies, saxophonist/trombonist Keith Mansfield, who in time would be best remembered for composing many a theme tune, particularly sporting ones, among them themes for BBC's *Grandstand* and its yearly *Wimbledon* coverage. "As well as The Seven, Keith also played trombone on the track," Bown would later reveal.

Edgy, raw, and of its time, 'Twenty-Four Hours Ago' may well have sold in impressive quantities had it been marketed with any degree of vigour and shrewdness, but by the time it was eventually released on 20th November, a good two months after vocalist Mike O'Neill departed, its moment in the sun had long since passed. Not even the emergence of illegal, off-shore pirate radio stations, then seriously challenging the BBC's hitherto monopoly on needle time, could make the slightest difference. Both sides seemed ripe for airplay on Radio Caroline (which first transmitted on 27th March) and Radio London (on air from 23rd December), but sadly, they missed the boat both literally and metaphorically.

The lengthy hiatus between the recording and release dates was in all probability the result of Barry having to scout around for a suitable record deal. During April, he had announced the formation of a new company, J.B. Independent Record Productions, to enable him to produce and finance recordings of his own choosing before leasing them out to prospective buyers. United Artists was the first company to show any interest in this new arrangement when it released the single, 'Me' by A Band of Angels. The fact that 'Twenty-Four Hours Ago' was eventually picked up by Columbia was, therefore, purely coincidental, although one suspects that any previous affiliation may well have helped the sales pitch. As if to emphasise symbolically that Columbia were now dealing with an altogether different act, The JB7, on the label at any rate, dropped the definite article at a time when being 'The' something or other was practically the norm.

Reviews in the November editions of *Disc* and *Record Mirror*, were favourable, if hardly ecstatic. Both duly noted the introduction of a vocal track as well as the 'R&B' influence. The more verbose *Record Mirror* suggested that the "big, brassy noises from The Seven on an 'R&B' kick – with steady backbeat and loud efficient vocal – could create an impact," but alas, it simply fell by the wayside, as Bown later acknowledged. "Our single was given little promotion by EMI and thereby failed to attract much attention. Although Jeff [Bannister] adapted the song to suit his style once Mike [O'Neill] left, it rapidly became past tense as we moved on and introduced new songs."

It was during September when fortunes finally started to pick up for the band albeit from the unlikeliest of sources. Bearing in mind that The Seven had not appeared on BBC Radio for over two years, an invitation from the producer of the Light Programme's long-running daily teatime series, *Roundabout*, was a most welcome and unexpected boost. As previously recounted, every attempt to rekindle a relationship with the BBC on behalf of the Vic Flick-led line-up had been dismissed out of hand by producer Jimmy Grant throughout 1963. Further contact in 1964, this time to promote the Alan Bown edition, even resulted in the humiliation of being told to request an audition first. Such temerity must have hurt. The BBC Written Archives files reveal that no such reply was ever received in response to this rather derogatory and disrespectful instruction (which was hardly surprising given its dismissive tone), but nevertheless, John Simmonds (the producer of *Roundabout*) did eventually make contact. He wanted The Seven to record "about twenty minutes of music" for broadcasting on a future date.

≈

Evidently, Simmonds was somewhat of a Barry aficionado, for he sanctioned various Barry-related tracks for much-prized 'Needletime' on his show later that month, among them 'From Russia with Love' and 'The James Bond Theme', both credited to The John Barry Seven and Orchestra. Given that until 1967 (and the abolition of the Home and Light Programmes with the advent of Radios One to Four) the Phonographic Performances Ltd only allowed the BBC five hours per day of commercial gramophone records playing on air, such airtime was like gold dust.

≈

Hence, on the 10th September, The JB7 were seemingly back in favour at 'the Beeb' duly recording four tracks for *Roundabout*: 'The James Bond Theme', a cover of The Phil Upchurch Combo's 1961 US hit 'You Can't Sit Down', plus both sides of the freshly recorded but as yet to be released new single. The Bond theme apart, this was an accurate representation of the direction in which Bown was taking 'his' charges. Incidentally, the BBC's own listing credited 'Twenty-Four Hours Ago' as having been written by one 'Mickey Clark', but when the single was finally released in November, the rather enigmatic 'Suede' was given that accolade on the label. Bown told the authors that this was, in fact, a collective writing pseudonym representing the entire band in much the same way as The Hollies were using the assumed name 'L. Ransford' back then for their own song-writing collaborations. In doing so, not only did this ensure that all potential royalties would have been distributed equally, but it also avoided having to print seven

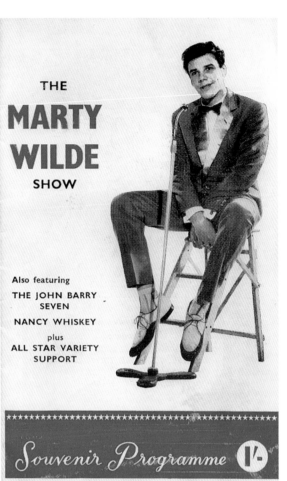

THE
MARTY WILDE
SHOW

Also featuring
THE JOHN BARRY SEVEN
NANCY WHISKEY
plus
ALL STAR VARIETY SUPPORT

Souvenir Programme 1/-

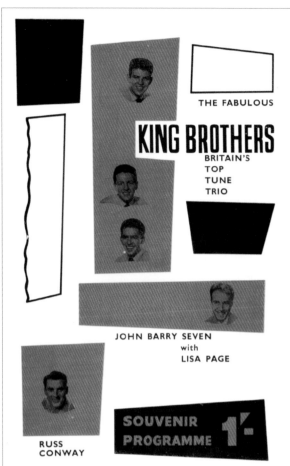

THE FABULOUS
KING BROTHERS
BRITAIN'S
TOP
TUNE
TRIO

JOHN BARRY SEVEN
with
LISA PAGE

RUSS CONWAY

SOUVENIR PROGRAMME 1/-

J. X. PRENDERGAST presents

A TWENTIETH CENTURY SHOW OF YOUTH

Souvenir Programme

HAROLD FIELDING
presents

THE
"SIX-FIVE"
STAGE SHOW

presented by the DAILY EXPRESS
in association with the Stars Organisation for Spastics

Record
star
show

Empire Pool Wembley
Sunday 27 MARCH 1960

Presented by the DAILY EXPRESS in association with
the Stars Organisation for Spastics

RECORD
STAR
SHOW

EMPIRE POOL
WEMBLEY
SUNDAY
26th MARCH 1961

Souvenir Programme Two Shillings

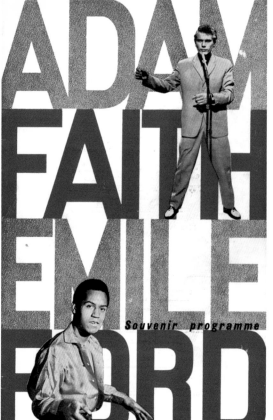

ADAM
FAITH
EMILE
FORD

Souvenir programme

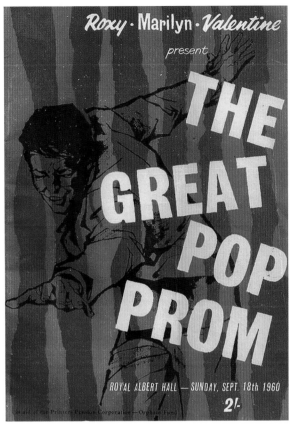

THE FIRST BIG CHA-CHA-CHA HIT !!!

★

"FARRAGO"

RECORDED BY

THE JOHN BARRY 7

ON PARLOPHONE R 4488

✳ ✳ ✳ ✳ ✳ ✳

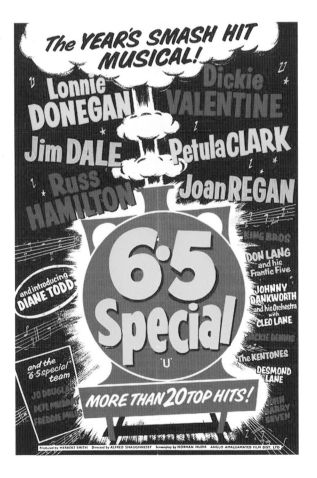

THE
CRESCENT CINEMA
PONTEFRACT

SUNDAY, MAY 5th.

Direct from their great success with the
Johnnie Ray show

The Boy's with Rhythm With'em !

THE
JOHN BARRY
SEVEN

FEATURING

DEREK MYERS	MIKE COX	KEN GOLDER
FRED KIRK	KEN RICHARDS	KEITH KELLY

— THE STARS OF TO-MORROW —

BRITAIN'S FRESHEST **BEAT!!!!**

DON'T MISS THIS EXCITING NEW GROUP

Rusholmes Printers Ltd., High Ousegate, York.

METROPOLITAN
EDGWARE ROAD   Manager: JOHN LIVINGSTON   Telephone: AMB 2478
6-30 ★ MONDAY, SEPT. 23rd, 1957 ★ 8-45

FROM B.B.C.
SIX-FIVE SPECIAL
ARTHUR FOX PRESENTS ★

FREIGHT TRAIN! — FREIGHT TRAIN!
NANCY WHISKEY
ORIOLE RECORDING STAR

BARRY ANTHONY
THE EXPLOSIVE SPARK

BRITAIN'S FRESHEST THE
JOHN BARRY 7
THE BOYS WITH THE RHYTHM WITH 'EM

HAL GARNER
BRIGHT AND BREEZY

THE TEENAGERS
SENSATIONAL YOUNG RHYTHM SINGERS

★ JUNE FRASER TRIO
THREE SMART GIRLS

ANNE HART
THE GIRL IN A MILLION
he Piano: FRANK PORTER

3 KING PINS
ROCKIN' AND ROLLING ALONG

THE "HEP" BILL

RICHARD WHEWELL (BOLTON) LTD.

RIALTO - YORK
Week commencing MONDAY, OCTOBER 21st
MONDAY at 7.15   TUES. to SAT. at 6.20 & 8.35

HAROLD FIELDING PRESENTS
ON THE STAGE

THE SENSATIONAL TEENAGE MUSIC SHOW !
THE BIG

AND GUEST STAR
MICHAEL HOLLIDAY

PRICES - 5/6 - 4/6 - 3/6

ODEON
BIRMINGHAM

ON THE STAGE
FOR 1 DAY ONLY

THURS. 19th DEC. ★ 6.15   TWO SHOWS 8.30

PRICES 4/6, 6/6, 8/6, 10/6   BOX OFFICE NOW OPEN - BOOK NOW

LEW & LESLIE GRADE Ltd. presents
FROM AMERICA - THE YOUNG SINGING SENSATION
PAUL ANKA

HIT RECORDER OF "DIANA" ETC.

GITSOM SISTERS
GLAMOUR IN HARMONY

DICKIE DAWSON
CANADA'S GOOD HUMOUR MAN

JOHN BARRY SEVEN
THE BOYS WITH THE RHYTHM WITH 'EM

BOB CORT SKIFFLE

THE ATOMIC BLONDE
BILLIE ANTHONY
At the Piano: MICHAEL AUSTIN

Poster 1 (top left)

HIPPODROME
THEATRE — BIRMINGHAM
Proprietors: MOSS' EMPIRES, LTD. Telephone: MIDLAND 2576/7
Chairman: PRINCE LITTLER Managing Director: VAL PARNELL Manager & Licensee: JOHN AVERY

6.15 — MONDAY, JUNE 16th — **8.30**
TWICE NIGHTLY

HE'S NEW! HE'S GREAT! DECCA'S 15 YEAR OLD SENSATION!

JACKIE DENNIS

RADIO & TV's ACE TRUMPETER	THE AMERICAN FUNSTER	BRITAIN'S GREAT NEW RHYTHM GROUP	BBC's FAMOUS CLOSE HARMONY TEAM
KENNY BAKER	**DON HOOTON**	**JOHN BARRY SEVEN**	**THE KORDITES**

JOE BAKER AND **JACK DOUGLAS**
THE POPULAR COMEDY PAIR

FRED LOVELLE VENTRILOQUIAL STAR

NICK DANCE STYLISTS **LUNDON & PAM**

Poster 2 (top right)

HIPPODROME
Phone: 21091 **BRISTOL** Manager: J. H. CHRISTIE Chairman: PRINCE LITTLER C.B.E.

6.25 MONDAY, MARCH 28TH **8.40**

BRITAIN'S NUMBER ONE RECORDING STAR

ADAM FAITH

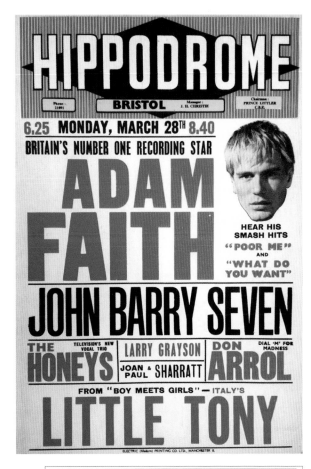

HEAR HIS SMASH HITS "POOR ME" AND "WHAT DO YOU WANT"

JOHN BARRY SEVEN

THE HONEYS	TELEVISION'S NEW VOCAL TRIO	**LARRY GRAYSON**	DIAL 'M' FOR MADNESS
		JOAN & PAUL SHARRATT	**DON ARROL**

FROM "BOY MEETS GIRLS" — ITALY'S

LITTLE TONY

ELECTRIC (Modern) PRINTING CO. LTD., MANCHESTER 8.

Poster 3 (bottom left)

MOSS' Empire
THEATRE — GLASGOW

Proprietors: MOSS' EMPIRES, Ltd. Chairman: PRINCE LITTLER Managing Director: VAL PARNELL TELEPHONE: DOUGLAS 6434/5/6 Manager: FRANK MATHIE

6.25 MONDAY, AUG. 4TH **8.40**

SCOTLAND'S OWN 15 Year Old TEENAGE STAR
HE'S NEW! HE'S HEP! HE'S FAB!

JACKIE DENNIS

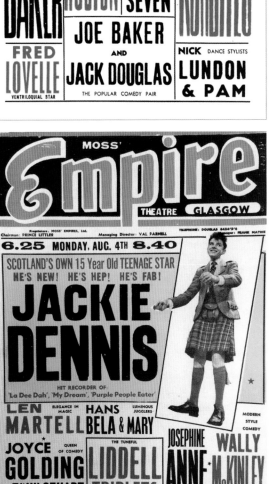

HIT RECORDER OF
'La Dee Dah', 'My Dream', 'Purple People Eater'

LEN MARTELL

ELEGANCE IN MAGIC **HANS BELA & MARY**

LUMINOUS JUGGLERS

MODERN STYLE COMEDY

JOYCE GOLDING & TONY STUART

QUEEN OF COMEDY

THE TUNEFUL **LIDDELL TRIPLETS**

JOSEPHINE ANNE CRAZY GANG'S GIRL FRIEND **WALLY McKINLEY**

THE JOHN BARRY SEVEN

PARLOPHONE RECORDING GROUP

Poster 4 (bottom right)

COLSTON HALL - BRISTOL
Entertainments Manager: T. J. PYPER

5.30 | SUNDAY, 12th MARCH | **7.45**

CHARLES H. LOCKIER presents

ADAM FAITH
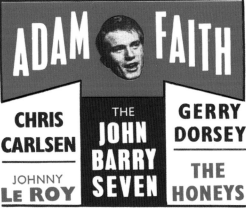

CHRIS CARLSEN	THE **JOHN BARRY SEVEN**	**GERRY DORSEY**
JOHNNY LE ROY		**THE HONEYS**

TICKETS: 10/6 8/6 7/6 6/6 5/6 Book Now
at LOCKIER'S, 29/31 QUEEN'S RD., BRISTOL, 8, Tel. 2-3885 and COLSTON HALL, Tel 2-1768
Postal applications please enclose remittance and stamped addressed envelope

POSTAL BOOKING FORM   ADAM FAITH & Co.
To LOCKIER'S 29/31 QUEEN'S RD., BRISTOL, 8, Tel. 2-3885 or COLSTON HALL, Tel. 2-1768
Please forward .... Seats at 10/6 8/6 7/6 6/6 5/6
for the 5.30/7.45 performance on Sunday, 12th March
I enclose stamped addressed envelope and P.O/Cheque value ....
Name ....
Address ....
Use this form if inconvenient to call. The best available seats will be allotted to you.
Hastings Printing Co., Portland Place, Hastings. Tel.: 2450

GRANADA EAST HAM

STAGE • ONE DAY ONLY • TUES MAR 21 • 7 o'c & 9.10

ADAM FAITH

RETURN— BY PUBLIC DEMAND

CHRIS CARLSEN	JOHN BARRY	GERRY DORSEY
JOHNNY LE ROY	SEVEN	THE HONEYS

BOOK NOW - 3/6 5/6 7/6   phone GRA 3000

WILLSONS (PRINTERS) LTD., LEICESTER.

GRANADA TOOTING

STAGE • ONE DAY ONLY • SUN APL 10 • 5.30 & 8 o'c

"POOR ME" - "WHAT DO YOU WANT?" The year's biggest record sensation

ADAM FAITH

GUEST STAR from "Oh Boy!"

LITTLE TONY

JOHN BARRY SEVEN
BRITAIN'S No. 1 INSTRUMENTAL GROUP

JULIE RAYNE HMV Record Star

JOHNNY LEROY New Young Singer

DON ARROLL Our Compere

The GLAMOROUS HONEYS

BOOK NOW 3/6 5/6 7/6 Phone: BAL 6602

TOWN HALL, LOUGHBOROUGH

SATURDAY, JAN. 2

Alfred H. Danvers presents another

BIG BEAT DANCE

with THE NEW

JOHN BARRY SEVEN

supported by **THE STROLLERS**

Dancing 8 till 11-45   Buffet

ADMISSION 6/-

Pay at the Door

ASTORIA Finsbury Park

N.4.   Telephone: ABC 2224   Manager: Mr. HIGHAM

On the Stage	Saturday, November 14th	ONE NIGHT ONLY
	6-30 Two Performances 9-0	

THE GEORGE COOPER ORGANISATION LTD present

THE WORLD'S No. 1 VOCALIST — AMERICA'S

BRENDA LEE
MISS DYNAMITE

'QUESTIONS I CAN'T ANSWER'

HEINZ AND THE WILD BOYS

MARTY WILDE

THE TORNADOS

JOHN BARRY ★ SEVEN ★

BOB BAIN COMPERE

PRICES: 10/6 - 8/6 - 6/6 - 4/6

To: THE BOX OFFICE.   POSTAL BOOKING FORM

Please forward .... (No. of Seats) at .... (Price)

for the .... (Time) Performance on .... (Date)

for which I enclose stamped addressed envelope with remittance value £   :   :

NAME: ....

ADDRESS: ....

Richard B. Whewell, Bolton.

Over fifty years on since forming The JB7, John Barry pictured at home in Oyster Bay (New York) surrounded by the trappings of his success. (Courtesy of RTÉ lyric fm's Movies and Musicals show.)

names in the writing credit underneath the title on the label, which would have been rather cumbersome. Blurting out the name 'Mickey Clark' when asked the identity of the writer was likely to have been much easier than having to explain the rationale behind the sobriquet 'Suede'. Bown later revealed that 'Twenty-Four Hours Ago' was knocked into shape during rehearsals. The *Roundabout* session formed part of the programme's 12th September content and would have been the ideal vehicle for promoting the single had it been released in time, but no, several weeks would elapse before that would happen, thereby any impetus that might have been gained was simply lost.

By the end of the month, Mike O'Neill had given Bown notice of his intention to leave after having accepted an offer of joining The Division Two, which was a new band specifically set up to accompany The Ivy League on an extensive UK tour, keen as they were to cash in on two recent top ten hits, 'Funny How Love Can Be' and 'Tossing and Turning'. Unbeknown to the rest of The Seven, the ever-enterprising O'Neill had by then already formed another band in cahoots with The Seven's road manager, Tony Colton. With JB7 bookings so thin on the ground, he saw The Crawdaddies as another way of supplementing his income and he even had the nerve to use The Seven's van and gear to do so while they lay idle. Ultimately, it was the lack of regular work that convinced him to move on. £18 per gig was good money undoubtedly, but there simply weren't enough of them at the time to warrant staying.

O'Neill's replacement, Jeff Bannister, was recommended by music agent Sidney Rose at a time when he was playing keyboards and singing in Rey Anton and The Peppermint Men. Fortunately for Bown, Bannister was becoming increasingly bored at having to play what he considered to be unchallenging and unimaginative fare night after night. As far as he was concerned, a succession of 'R&B' 12-bars could never hold anyone's interest for too long, and so he was more than ready for a change.

However, his debut with the band was a somewhat rushed affair on account of O'Neill leaving sooner than anyone expected, which meant that the band was one musician down with two weekend gigs to fulfil. Clearly, The JB7 could not go on stage as The JB6. Luckily for Bown, Bannister was all too happy to fill in at short notice; the problem being there was no time for him to rehearse or even get acquainted with the material. He was therefore going in blindly and having to wing it! His already precarious predicament was made worse during the journey to the first of these bookings – at The Samson and Hercules Ballroom, Norwich, on Saturday 3rd October – when, on being shown the music for the set numbers, he soon discovered the band would also be backing Marty Wilde! In the circumstances, he coped admirably, not only at Norwich but also at the other weekend gig at Sussex University. This led to him being offered the job on a permanent basis, after passing what amounted to be a totally unexpected and lengthy 'audition'.

Bown was delighted with just how well Bannister fitted in right from the outset. Although he had already made his mind up to offer him the position vacated by O'Neill (i.e. keyboards and vocals), he was pleased that the rest of the band agreed. "The general consensus was that he could deliver, that he looked the part and, what's more, the suit fitted perfectly!" Bannister, who was delighted to have been chosen, was clearly an inspired choice. As a result, his integration into the band was a seamless one, for he was able to handle the vocals with ease; moreover, his timbre blended well with the harmonies provided by Green and Haldane.

October brought further dates supporting and accompanying Marty Wilde. On the bill of one of these was a band called The Tea Set; despite failing to make much of an impression on The Seven, they would eventually become better known as The Pink Floyd. Several appearances were also made on Bown's home turf, Slough (the Adelphi Cinema), where he decided to introduce some theatrics into the act; a little ill-advised as it turned out, but intended as an innocent tribute to 007. The idea was that at the climax to 'The James Bond Theme', he would pull out a starting pistol to the side of the stage in full secret agent pose, and then fire two or three shots into the air for dramatic effect. The experiment was quickly abandoned when on one occasion, the blanks failed to go off ("Just a few pathetic clicks could be heard!"), which given the potential risks involved, was probably just as well.

While Harold Wilson's Labour Party was scraping home in the UK's General Election with the smallest majority since 1847 (a mere four seats) on the 15th October, despite enjoying a healthy lead in the early opinion polls, The JB7 were engaged in an equally tough struggle trying to convince proprietor Murdoch Wallace of their worth on the eve of embarking upon a two-week residency at the J.M. Ballroom, Dundee. A tough-talking, brusque, uncompromising, esteemed hub of the community, Wallace had made the erroneous assumption that The Seven were a dance band of a light music hue rather than one rooted in jazz and rock 'n' roll. On being informed of his *faux pas*, he made it quite clear that he had no qualms in cancelling their contract if he did not like what he heard. Fortunately the band went down a storm on the first night and from that moment onwards, relations rapidly thawed.

As has been thoroughly recounted throughout this tome, The JB7 built its reputation on being adept at backing any artist asked of it, regardless of style and content; think Frankie Vaughan, Paul Anka, Marty Wilde and Adam Faith, all of whom were at the peak of their popularity when the call came. By 1964, younger names tended to get the nod when asked to fulfil this function, Sounds Incorporated and The Bobby Patrick Big Six among them, but history repeated itself during November when The JB7 were selected to provide the backing for Brenda Lee's extensive tours in Europe and the UK, and like the aforementioned, the nineteen-year-old from Georgia was then riding the crest of a wave and weathering the so-called 'British invasion' better than just about any other female American singer of that era. The 1963 *New Musical Express* Readers'

Poll exemplified this perfectly, in which she topped the 'World Female Singer' category by an overwhelming margin: amassing 10,503 votes and streets ahead of her nearest rival, second place Shirley Bassey's more modest 2,361. If 1963 turned out to be Lee's most successful year in terms of UK record sales, 1964 ran it mightily close, a year in which she would spend 36 weeks in the charts on the back of four Top Thirty hits, and as if to prove the point, she topped the same *New Musical Express* poll once again when published in December.

Rehearsals with Lee took place inside the foyer of the Granada Cinema, Walthamstow, in preparation for the European leg of the tour, which was due to commence with two shows at the Paris Olympia on 3rd November. Gigs across the channel also included performances at The Star Club in Hamburg (the same venue where The Beatles had earlier honed their act), together with various American Air force bases across Germany. Had it not been for the presence of Lee's querulous and argumentative manager, Dub Allbritten, this would have been the most harmonious of experiences, since the band found the singer to be delightful company from day one. Unfortunately, Allbritten's menacing mood swings tended to negate that to a degree. As Bown put it, "Dub had an intimidating persona, so the atmosphere wasn't exactly one of bonhomie with him around."

On arriving at The Paris Olympia, Alan Bown's JB7 was faced with precisely the same embarrassing mix-up experienced by their predecessors in Ireland. There in bold letters on the front of the theatre was this giant poster hoarding advertising 'Brenda Lee avec Le Jamboree Seven'! Here was a clear case of *déjà vu* (even if none of the current band members would have known it) and, evidently, an easy mistake to make. As a result, the response to the band's opening numbers was lukewarm to say the least until, that is, they started to play 'The James Bond Theme', at which point the audience immediately recognised them for who they really were. "The audience suddenly changed into raving dervishes," Jeff Bannister recalled, "leaping out of their seats the moment they realised we were The John Barry Seven and not The Jamboree Seven."

Unbeknown to the band, however, such acclaim was not music to the ears of Dub Allbritten, clearly concerned and in fear of his artiste being upstaged. Accordingly, he immediately instructed The Seven to reduce the length of their set from forty-five to a mere twenty minutes much to their considerable annoyance, but being in no position to argue, all they could do was acquiesce. Ominously, this was a sign of things to come.

On another occasion, Bannister recalls facing a tricky dilemma on stage when Lee inadvertently removed her cloak by draping it all over his keyboard as she made her entry, thereby concealing both the keys and the music in one fell swoop. *Quelle horreur!* "I was horrified... but rather than disrespectfully throwing the garment on to the floor in front of an adoring full house, I completed the opening number by holding up the cloak with one hand and playing the keys with the other! Once the song ended, I folded up the cloak and quickly gave it to someone in the wings."

Another, more serious, problem arose when the band, in attempting to leave their Paris hotel the following morning, were accosted discreetly by the hotel manager to inform them that the bill, which should have been paid in advance by Brenda Lee's management, had not been settled. A hurried phone call to an unperturbed Allbritten made no impression whatsoever, leaving them with no alternative other than to settle the bill themselves, no doubt departing; not only out of pocket, but also seething with rage.

≈

Regrettably, very few of the band's performances on UK TV and radio have managed to remain in the archives, most of them having been unceremoniously wiped. Consequently, every single one of their BBC TV appearances on Six-Five Special *and* Drumbeat *are believed to be missing; likewise virtually all of their radio output relating to* Saturday Club *and* Easy Beat. *The situation with commercial television isn't any better with every appearance on* Thank Your Lucky Stars *reputedly destroyed and only one or two episodes from Jack Good's* Oh Boy! *series having survived the cull.*

In view of this sad state of affairs, it is perhaps ironic that The JB7's only appearance on French radio, an edited recording of the Paris Olympia concert with Brenda Lee, has actually survived the years! The authors have been privileged and fortunate enough to have heard this truncated performance, so are able to confirm the quality thereof, during the band's own spot and in providing exemplary backing for Brenda Lee. The tape enables the listener to bear witness to The JB7's faithful adaptation of 'Um, Um, Um, Um, Um, Um', after which they accompany Lee on a varied selection of her concert programme including 'Dynamite', 'Sweet Nothin's', 'All Alone Am I', 'Let's Jump the Broomstick', 'Tutti Fruiti', 'As Usual' (her biggest hit that year), 'Is It True' (the then current hit), 'What'd I Say' and 'When the Saints Go Marching In', all received with rapturous applause from the packed auditorium.

≈

On the next stop of their European adventure – The Star Club, Hamburg – The JB7 was billed as the main attraction since Brenda Lee was not contracted to appear at this venue. Now unlike most clubs, the stage there was bedecked with a curtain behind which each awaiting act was strategically placed into position, poised in readiness for the cue to begin playing. However, on the night when the Seven received their nod to start, launching as they regularly did into the intro to 'Let the Good Times Roll', the curtain opened, swirled haphazardly across the stage, and as it did so, unintentionally swiped Bannister's boom-stand and microphone up into the air!, thereby putting new meaning to the phrase 'getting off to a flyer!'

At the American airbase gig in Bielefeld, Germany, the band finally decided to confront Allbritten over the hotel bill fiasco prior to going on stage. It was time to demand the full amount owed there and then, but when Bown threatened to down tools for the night in the event of not being recompensed immediately, all hell was let loose with Allbritten become ever more abusive to the extent of threatening the entire band physically with a heavy, blunt paperweight. Although he eventually paid in full so that the gig would go ahead, this was the beginning of the end of the band's association with 'Little Miss Dynamite', for not long afterwards, Bown made it abundantly clear to Dick Katz at the Harold Davison Agency that The Seven were no longer prepared to work with Brenda Lee whilst she remained under the management of Dub Allbritten. As a direct consequence, The Bobby Patrick Big Six was quickly drafted in to fill the void for the UK part of the tour – a band that, ironically, had once opened for the Seven way back in April 1962 at the California Ballroom (Dunstable). The JB7 was to remain on board as part of the package performing in its own right and also accompanying Marty Wilde with whose material they were already more than familiar.

∼

*One unfortunate fall-out from the decision to no longer back Brenda Lee was in The Seven losing out on several BBC appearances. Contracts had been offered and accepted for them to appear with her on both radio (*Saturday Club *(twice) and* Top Gear) *and television (*Top Beat, *a new BBC Two series hosted by Alan Freeman direct from The Royal Albert Hall). Instead, The Bobby Patrick Big Six took their place in the same way they had been contracted to do so on the tour. Whereas the terms offered were not particularly generous, appearances on any nationally networked programme would have worked wonders in adding fresh impetus to a band that had sadly slipped under the public's radar. Being deprived of such a platform at the last minute was indeed an unwelcome setback.*

∼

Starting on 14th November and ending on 12th December, the UK tour was an extensive one that covered the length and breadth of England (plus two dates in Ireland). The supporting cast varied according to the location; thus, in addition to Marty Wilde and The Bobby Patrick Big Six, it might also have included any one of Manfred Mann, Johnny Kidd and The Pirates, Wayne Fontana and The Mindbenders, Heinz, Bern Elliott and The Klan, and The Flee-Rekkers. The JB7 usually opened the second half of each show with a fifteen-minute set, staying in position thereafter until Marty Wilde was introduced to join them on stage. Working with Wilde was always an enjoyable experience, which was mutually reciprocated. In fact, Wilde had at one point even entertained the idea of The JB7 becoming his regular backing band, only for John Barry to veto it out of hand, believing that the Seven's uniqueness and individuality would have been severely compromised by being regularly committed to one artist.

The 24th November edition of *The Braintree, Witham and Dunmow Herald* gave The JB7 a glowing reference in its review of the Chelmsford Odeon show held on the 16th, describing their act as "smooth and polished, as they breezed through several numbers, among them, 'Let the Good Times Roll' and, of course, 'The James Bond Theme'."

Stan Haldane evoked vivid memories of an incident involving Heinz that didn't go quite to plan. He had devised this routine during his act of running down one of the aisles, out of the front entrance, around the block to the back door, whereupon he would suddenly reappear as if from nowhere from the back of the stage just as his guitarist finished his solo. Now this was all very well as long all of the doors weren't locked, but Haldane recalled the one night that ultimately put a stop to this little ruse once and for all: "On this occasion, the fire exit had not been left open for him, which meant him having to return from whence he came through the front door and back down the aisle. We were all back stage enjoying the moment, but not so Heinz. He never did it again on that tour."

Less endearing, but equally memorable, was a horrendous night spent crossing the Irish Sea by ferry to fulfil gigs arranged in Belfast and Dublin (on 25th and 26th respectively). As a tempestuous snowstorm developed, Jeff Bannister fell out of his bunk bed numerous times while cabin mate, Stan Haldane, was soon feeling decidedly queasy. The proposed remedy was something he would never forget: "On looking a bit pale, a little Irish steward suggested I tried a whiskey and dry ginger; having never previously drunk alcohol ever before, I was soon convinced I had found a new life by the time we arrived in Ireland!"

It was during this tour that Bown was faced with the uncomfortable task of having to censure a member of the band about his over-indulgent drinking habit. This was made all the more difficult, because the person concerned was drummer Ernie Cox, whom, of course, was a very old friend of his and someone he had known since school days and during their time together at Slough Boys Club. However, something had to be done, since nothing was more noticeable than a drummer whose timing was out, so he decided to go to Cox's family home where he appealed to his parents to explain to their son the effect drink was having on him.

As previously noted, Barry was still in the habit of keeping a close eye on the band's performances on the odd occasions by watching from the sidelines, even to the point of arriving without prior notice sometimes. He remained utterly fastidious about how they should best present themselves onstage, about which Bown was once reprimanded in no uncertain terms during one particular gig when they were backing Marty Wilde. On the night in question, Wilde had persuaded them all to indulge in a few light-hearted dance-step routines, reminiscent of The Shadows. Even though the early Seven had done much the same thing at the insistence of its leader, Barry was absolutely furious – so much so that during the interval he instructed each and every one of them (Wilde included), with expletives to match that it must never happen again. What did please him, however, was in the band maintaining a clean-cut, short-haired image, albeit at a time when just about every other group was adopting the unkempt, hirsute look. Mind you, Alan Bown was always more aligned, musically and culturally, to the more sharp-suited, sartorially dressed Mod movement anyway.

Unfortunately for Cox, another sloppy performance ensued in the full glare of an unimpressed Barry during one of his impromptu visits, with Cox clearly the worse for alcohol. This led to Zena Ackers summoning Bown to an emergency meeting with Barry the very next day, at which Barry made it patently clear to Bown that substandard playing such as he witnessed would not be tolerated under *any* circumstances. This left Bown with little choice but to give Cox a final warning.

However, matters came to a head no more than a fortnight later whilst still in the midst of the Brenda Lee tour, ironically on a night off playing a prestigious solo gig at Burton's in Uxbridge. The worst possible scenario ensued: the demon drink reared its ugly head yet again, thereby leaving Bown with the unenviable task of having to fire one of his oldest friends, which must have been a painful experience. This is how he would later recount the incident: "Our first set had gone okay. Ernie played well but during the break he had a few drinks and the second set was a disaster. He was all over the place and I had to shout at him, on stage, to pull himself together, but he seemed to be in another world. In the dressing room, after the gig, I had to tell him I could no longer have him in the band." Cox did not take kindly to the news, accusing various colleagues of betraying him, but clearly he was unaware that his performances had become a liability to the band.

Placed now in a major quandary, Bown was faced with the unwelcome dilemma of having to find a suitable drummer in a hurry; fortunately, as often was the case, a fellow band member came up trumps with the perfect solution. Ron Arghyrou had known Dave Elvin for almost as long as he could remember; in fact, ever since they sat in the same class at Maynard Road School, Walthamstow. Growing up as friends, they had played a lot of jazz together, which convinced Arghyrou that his old mate would be a more than capable replacement. On recalling his recruitment, Elvin had this to say, "When The JB7 were backing Brenda Lee on her British tour at the Granada Walthamstow, Ron asked me if I would be prepared to join The JB7, and so invited me to meet them there that evening. As it transpired, not only did I know Ron, but I was also acquainted with Terry Childs from my past. I can remember having one rehearsal in a room above a pub or club on Tottenham Court Road after which I was up and running and 'on the road'."

If the Brenda Lee tour achieved anything at all, it did succeed in helping to raise the band's media profile at provincial level. For example, when the tour reached Bristol's Colston Hall on 4th December, column inches were taken up with substantial reviews in both the *Bristol Evening Post* and its sister paper, the

Western Daily Press. Whereas the former was full of praise for everyone taking part, the latter delivered a far harsher appraisal of the support acts.

The reviewer from the *Post* was astonished at Lee's stamina on stage given the unconventional way in which she and her entourage had got to the theatre. On arriving at Temple Meads Station, they could not find a single taxi available to transport them to the venue. "The queues for cabs were a mile long, and we thought we might be late," Lee later explained. "So we walked the full mile there." Such exercise did nothing to diminish the power of her performance according to the review: "Brenda Lee burst on to the Colston Hall stage to whip the audience into a frenzy of cheers and enthusiasm. Famous Lee numbers followed one after the other with a zest that earned her no fewer than seven curtain calls and three encores, and yet after a blistering half hour, Brenda still looked as fresh as a Spring morning – no screams ensued, just genuine appreciation for a great entertainer." Praise was also lavished on The JB7 (with 'The James Bond Theme', in particular, singled out) as well as Johnny Kidd and The Pirates.

On the other hand, whilst enjoying Lee's performance, the *Western Daily Press* was scathing about practically everything that preceded her. This reviewer was particularly upset over the high volume levels ruining the night on what was deemed "an over-amplified bill." The JB7 was spared the rough stuff, but Johnny Kidd and The Pirates were described as "mediocre"; The Beat Merchants as "a paler version of The Rolling Stones" and the Bobby Patrick Big Six as simply "a loud sound." The damning final paragraph put them all in their place: "Most of the groups would be fine in a beat club, but they had no stage character. There are just too many third rate beat shows rocking round Britain at the moment." Ouch!

The last night of the Brenda Lee tour was at The Opera House, Blackpool on 12th December 1964. They would never see her again.

As far as the band was concerned, the tour was not the success it might have been on account of the deficiencies demonstrated by the promoter/management team behind it: The George Cooper Organisation. In Stan Haldane's view, the name 'Cooper' and word 'organisation' was something of an oxymoron. "They should never be used in the same sentence. In fact, we used to sing the following words to the tune of 'Smoke Gets in Your Eyes': 'They asked me how I knew/ My career was through/I of course replied/I am on the slide/With Cooper on my side.'"

Nevertheless, in a rapidly changing market now awash in what seemed like a constant deluge of fresh-faced new groups, The JB7 was managing to hold its own, for as the year drew to a close, the band was enjoying its most sustained period of work for some while, rounding off with a series of one-nighters. Among those was a further visit to the California Ballroom (Dunstable), this time on its so-called 'Hot Pot Night'!. There, punters could catch The Seven, supported by Dave Curtis and The Tremors, and The Firing Squad, for a mere 5/– (25p). A return to the Winter Gardens Pavilion at Weston-super-Mare also ensued alongside several appearances at Quaintways (Chester), where on one occasion they bore witness to an early appearance by an outfit called Davy Jones and The Lower Third, whose front man would later make his mark after changing his surname to Bowie.

And so 1964 ended with the musical and cultural landscape radically transformed by the ubiquitous presence of The Beatles in just about every sphere of the media and society. With the UK conquered, world domination rapidly followed once 73 million Americans tuned in to see their debut on the Ed Sullivan Show on 9th February. Achieving the unprecedented feat of occupying the top five positions in *Billboard's* Hot 100 on 4th April just about sealed the deal. The four-piece beat group format thus became the default template for any aspiring band to emulate, which left any instrumental-only combo suddenly looking distinctly out of touch with the times. Clearly, Alan Bown's decision to gradually infuse the act with songs had been vindicated. As if to prove the point, among the year's best-selling hundred singles in the UK, only two were instrumentals: 'The Rise and Fall of Flingel Blunt' by The Shadows and 'How Soon?' by The Henry Mancini Orchestra. Come February 1965, even The Shadows would be taking the hint by releasing their first vocal 45, 'Mary Anne'.

⌛

Without a steady stream of record releases, any band placed in such a predicament was likely to remain permanently on the periphery of the music business. Furthermore, without constantly updating and expanding the repertoire, it was also in danger of becoming regarded as no more than a mere 'nostalgia' act. These were the issues facing Alan Bown's John Barry Seven at the beginning of 1965. By then, even Barry had stopped releasing his latest 45s under The JB7 banner. Both 'Séance on a Wet Afternoon' and 'Goldfinger' (issued in April and October 1964 respectively) gave the name a wide berth. What's more, he was now mixing in more exalted circles. The onus, therefore, was on Alan Bown to maintain the band's relevance in a rapidly changing music scene. Encouragingly, as a live act and from a booking perspective, The JB7 was still a viable box office proposition and had not been in such rude health for quite some while. As such, 1965 was to start promisingly with the prospect of two high profile Light Programme radio appearances on the horizon in addition to a place on consecutive Billy Fury package tours (even if this did mean slipping down the bill somewhat), but all of this was to unravel horribly thanks to the ill-discipline and unprofessional conduct of one of their own. Barry's and Bown's visions of the band's future were always likely to have ended up at odds with each other in any case, since Bown's soul leanings were steering it in a musical direction alien to Barry's tastes. Nevertheless, when the axe finally did fall, it came completely out of the blue.

However, there was no hint of any such demise on 2nd January as the band geared up to start the new year healthily by headlining 'The Big Beat Dance' at Loughborough (with The Strollers as support), on the very same day they were also booked to appear on the first of two agreed *Saturday Club* appearances – a very welcome breakthrough after more than two barren years in the wilderness. The recent spot on *Roundabout* had clearly done them no harm whatsoever. Despite competition from the pirates, *Saturday Club* was still the undisputed, most widely heard pop music show on British radio; therefore, to be back in favour was quite a coup (and a relief, no doubt). On the first of these, The JB7 was lined up to appear alongside Wayne Fontana and The Mindbenders, Brian Poole and The Tremeloes, Susan Maughan, The Barron Knights with Duke D'Mond, Marty Wilde, and The Brian Fahey Band.

On this particular edition, The Seven were allotted just one slot of their own, playing 'The James Bond Theme', since their principal role was in backing Marty Wilde. The presence of Wayne Fontana and The Mindbenders on the show must have led to some speculation as to whether they would include recent hit, 'Um, Um, Um, Um, Um, Um', with which, as has been recounted, they first became acquainted after hearing The Seven's rendition. Oddly enough they chose not to do so, but in a bizarre ironic twist, The Seven ended up accompanying Marty Wilde performing his own version of the very same song! Wilde also sang 'Baby What Do You Want Me to Do', 'Mexican Boy', 'All My Sorrows' and 'Twist and Shout'.

Unfortunately, the second scheduled appearance on the 30th January edition was dashed by dint of sheer bad luck and timing. Poised to perform alongside Acker Bilk and His Paramount Jazz Band, The Hollies, Billy J. Kramer and The Dakotas, The Spencer Davis Group and Danny Williams, this particular show had to be cancelled in its entirety to make way for the blanket coverage devoted to Sir Winston Churchill's state funeral arranged that same day. When it was rescheduled for 20th February with supposedly the same line-up of acts, as billed in that week's edition of *Radio Times*, an examination of the BBC Archives' 'programmes as broadcast' file revealed that this was erroneous, for The JB7 did not actually play a part.

On 14th February, the band made one of many appearances in and around the Birmingham area, this time at The Ritz Dance & Social Club (Kings Heath) and The Plaza Ballroom (Handsworth). Both venues were run by the renowned husband and wife team Joe and Mary 'Ma' Regan, who also owned the Brum Kavern (Small Heath) and The Plaza Dance and Social Club (Old Hill). Jeff Bannister remembers just how difficult it was logistically in having to move all of the equipment from Kings Heath to Handsworth in such a short space of time, since both gigs were scheduled for the same night! Doing a 'double' was what it was called at the time and it invariably resulted in one mad scramble. According to Bannister, being introduced on stage by Joe Regan caused so much hilarity amongst The Seven, on account of his broad Brummie accent rendering them all helpless in fits of laughter, that when the curtains finally opened, the grinning, giggling horn players could barely function.

Later that month the band was back in Birmingham playing the Student Rag Ball at the Town Hall on which The Spencer Davis Group and Tom Jones shared the bill. Throughout the gig, Jones was clearly unhappy to be there, disgruntled at having to fulfil a moderately paid function at a time when his breakthrough chart hit, the aforementioned 'It's Not Unusual', had just gate-crashed the charts. Mind you, facing a hostile student audience booing and pelting him with toilet rolls couldn't have helped his mood much either.

By early March, everything seemed to be back to normal now that Dave Elvin had bedded in well, but for Alan Bown, a huge shock was awaiting him, as Ernie Cox's misdemeanours of a few months before came back to haunt him. Called to another seemingly routine meeting to review future engagements, Barry told him he had decided to phase the band out for good, on the grounds that he felt it had run its course. It seemed that Cox's performance had been the straw that broke the camel's back, as far as Barry was concerned. Even though, as Bown pointed out, he had since replaced Cox with Elvin, his protestations fell on deaf ears. Barry was having none of it despite Bown's pleas and insistence that the current line-up was the best it had ever been. Not for turning, Barry gave Bown three months' notice of disbandment.

Naturally, the news came as a huge shock and disappointment to the rest of the band, but as a means of softening the blow, Bown had decided to hatch a plan of his own to at least provide a degree of optimism for all those affected; to wit, he vowed to form a new band with a different name just as long as he could find the right management. He also felt that in the interim period, by using the suffix 'ex-John Barry Seven', this would generate interest and, hopefully, might even boost the fee. It didn't take long for Jeff Bannister, Dave Green and Stan Haldane to all agree to join Bown in a venture that would eventually see the birth of The Alan Bown Set, with Terry Childs and Ron Arghyrou deciding to go their own ways. Later that month, those Brummie owner/promoters Joe and Ma Regan were already adorning all of their venues with posters advertising: "Coming soon: The Alan Bown Set."

There is little doubt how Barry's recent experience in watching one of his trusted employees go off the rails in such alarming fashion would have affected his thinking. He was bound to have started questioning his own commitment towards keeping the band on the road bearing in mind he could spare little time of his own now for maintaining any form of adequate scrutiny. Therefore, whereas his decision to call a complete halt to operations may have appeared an over-reaction from Bown's standpoint, it was probably anything but from Barry's own perspective. After all, he was busier than at any other time during his career, a career that was now taking off on an international scale. The worldwide success of 'Goldfinger', alone, had triggered that, the result of which had just seen him sign a three-year contract with CBS under which he would produce other artists in addition to a succession of singles and albums in his own name. Furthermore, he was writing the music for *The Ipcress File*; would soon be travelling to Hollywood with Bryan Forbes to record the score for *King Rat*; and, together with lyricist Trevor Peacock, was in the throes of completing his first stage musical, *Passion Flower Hotel*. Thus, reaching the conclusion that he could no longer spare the energy to oversee the band any more, which, after all, still bore his name, was entirely understandable. So although he had been assured by Bown that the drumming issue had been resolved satisfactorily, he was no longer prepared to risk the possibility for any further problems of that nature arising, ones which might have potentially damaged his good name and reputation irrevocably.

In the meantime, however, there was still a matter of three months' worth of dates to fulfil as The John Barry Seven. Hence, on 1st March, rehearsals for the Billy Fury tour got underway in readiness for the opening night at the ABC Cinema, Romford. On this occasion the band were back to being an augmented 'plus four', only this time billed as The John Barry Seven and Orchestra, with the four additions a combination of brass and woodwind: Ray Hutchinson (trumpet), Derek Wadsworth (trombone), Don Faye (alto sax), and Roger Waghorn (tenor sax).

Somewhat surprisingly – given how little time remained – the band was fitted out with brand new suits before the tour commenced. The choice of classic Ivy League woollen cloth might have looked the business on stage, but proved far too warm and stifling to ever be remotely comfortable. On one occasion, Jeff Bannister singed his horribly while waiting in the dressing room prior to going on stage. It might have been far worse had all those present not been alerted by a striking pungent burning smell emerging. Even so, he was still forced to adopt a rather strange gait while entering the stage in order to hide the worst of the damage, which must have alarmed or bemused the audience. Apparently in the absence of any available hooks, he had hung the offending article on a convenient nail right next to one of the bare light bulbs adorning the room, thereby causing it to smoulder.

The Billy Fury package tour was split into two distinct phases, and as one would have expected, was organised by 'Mr Parnes, Shillings and Pence' himself (Larry Parnes), the man responsible for discovering, nurturing and naming the headline act. The first raft of dates was billed as 'The All-Round Family Show' and featured, alongside Fury, The Gamblers, The John Barry Seven and Orchestra, and The Kestrels, plus compère Bobby Pattinson. The tour started on 2nd March (at Romford, as stated) and finished on the 21st March (at Leicester, De Montford Hall), all in all embracing fifteen dates (among which were two in Ireland).

After a break of about a month, a further thirteen dates were added under the banner, the 'Get Ready Steady Go Go Go!!' tour, which comprised of the same names augmented by a further four acts: The Zephyrs, Brian Poole and the Tremeloes, Dave Berry and The Cruisers, and The Pretty Things, all of whom had registered in the charts at some point during the year. With no such credentials,

The JB7, therefore, found themselves at the foot of the bill while remaining the backing band for both The Kestrels and Billy Fury.

Despite this, they enjoyed these tours far more than the Brenda Lee one, benefiting as they did from a sense of community spirit sadly lacking in the latter. All the acts bonded so well that the London-based artists and musicians made it a habit to meet by the Planetarium, north of Baker Street, in order to travel together by coach to each venue. The whole shebang started rolling on 24th April in Gloucester before winding up in Bristol on 9th May.

There was somewhat of an irony in the knowledge that The Seven were present on the night of Billy Fury's first tentative low-key start to his career and now here he was top of the bill at the very end of their own.

And yet, in spite of playing out their notice, there still remained one final twist in personnel, with Dave Elvin deciding to leave on musical grounds. Having emanated from a solid jazz background, that was where he envisaged his future evolving. Alan Bown once observed that Elvin struggled on occasions to provide the volume needed to drive a seven-piece band, since drums were not miked up in 1965, referring also to the badly blistered fingers he had experienced as a result of trying to do so. However, though admitting how problematic blistering could be at times, this was not his principal reason for leaving: "Although I am a jazz drummer, I had played various types of other music as well, but I was never a so-called rock drummer playing what I call 'knocking up a chicken shed' or 'banging a wall with a hammer' type music. Admittedly I did develop some blisters – playing, I believe, at the Pavilion (Weston-super-Mare) amid truly awful acoustics – but it was never a long term problem."

What he loved above all about his time as a member of The JB7 was in having to play 'The James Bond Theme' every night. "What a great number and one where jazz experience comes to the fore; hence, my reason for leaving. I always wanted to be creative and play jazz despite it being a more precarious way of earning a living. I was never an 'eighth note man' so in effect straightforward rock wasn't the kind of music I wanted to keep playing. Having said that, though, we had many good times and The Seven were a great bunch of guys to work with." Vic Sweeney was drafted in to take Elvin's place, a decision which would later prove fortuitous for those members intent on joining Alan Bown's new band, since they were soon to discover that here already *in situ* was just the type of drummer needed for the new venture.

Posters and flyers advertising the 'Get Ready Steady Go Go Go!!' tour boasted one additional attraction, the so-called 'Exciting new electric Flicker Sign', apparently 'for the first time ever!' Now according to Jeff Bannister, as related in his book, *The Alan Bown Set – Before and Beyond*, this was no more than a terribly cumbersome and monstrous twenty-foot long electric sign, designed to look like an iron girder, that had to be carted around on the tour coach from venue to venue. Given its bulk, weight and length, this was no mean task, since it took at least six of the musicians to carry the blessed thing at any one time under the direct supervision of the coach driver, Alf. Needless to say, very few volunteers ever came forward to offer their broad shoulders to help with the lifting; certain musicians preferring instead to scarper pronto the moment the coach had arrived at its designated stop.

One other problem pertained. Once transported, the wretched sign needed to be suspended high above the stage so that once connected to a power source, fully formed letters were able to dazzle across in motion from left to right to form words of welcome; hardly innovative, even by 1965 standards, but a gimmick nonetheless. Eventually, every bump and scrape, drop and collision resulting from having to hump the sign here, there and everywhere began to take its toll. Certain letters failed to light up, so that the much-coveted 'flicker' welcome began making no sense whatsoever, much to the amusement of the cast and the utter confusion of those in the audience!

Such was the camaraderie among acts that they often combined banter with song. On one such journey, Bown remembered Roger Cook of The Kestrels demonstrating on ukulele a new song he had just written with co-Kestrel Roger Greenaway. He was hoping that it might prove suitable for The JB7 to record sometime in the future, but the common consensus from the back of the coach was not quite as encouraging. Pity really, because 'You've Got Your Troubles' took The Fortunes to No. 2 in the charts later that year during August, thereby launching a hugely successful song-writing partnership. Ironically, it was arranged by Les Reed, ever thriving since leaving The JB7.

As with any tour, a prevalence of practical jokes were par for the course for whatever purpose, whether to relieve stress, tension, not to mention boredom. Sometimes they went beyond the pale and with the unpredictable Viv Prince on the tour bus the fine line between fun and infuriating could easily be crossed. The Pretty Things' drummer was a loose cannon ready to rumble at any moment. On one occasion, as the band sat around in their dressing room – one befitted with traditional mirrors encircled by bare light bulbs – in he burst standing at the doorway pointing a gun in their direction. After telling them to duck, he then started firing directly at said light bulbs, and despite being clearly 'under the influence' still managed to hit about ten of them before making his exit.

Prince was one of the chief architects of what turned out to be an unedifying on-stage riot on the final night of the tour at The Colston Hall, Bristol. When various cast members decided to ambush Billy Fury in full flow, the bouncers immediately leaped onto the stage in an attempt to throw them off. All hell was let loose thereafter with Prince, after having already enjoyed himself backstage by soaking all and sundry with a fire-hose, then deciding to turn his attention towards demolishing the entire drum kit in full view of the startled audience. He was eventually restrained before being wrestled off the stage in scenes of total mayhem. A disgusted Bown wasn't at all impressed, sparing his sympathies for the poor paying public, who clearly hadn't come to watch such an unruly spectacle.

Roger Bennett of the *Bristol Evening Post*, who led a jazz combo of his own, was present, and of a like mind in witnessing such bedlam. This was his first-hand account: "Police were called backstage at the Colston Hall, Bristol, last night, to keep pop stars OUT of the limelight. Constables stood guard at stage entrances in an effort to restore order to a chaotic end to Billy Fury's package tour, and just for a change, it was the pop stars not the fans invading the stage. The John Barry Orchestra suddenly found themselves with three drummers, among them Viv Prince of the hairy Pretty Things, as they backed Bristol's Kestrels. Then the night's madness became infectious."

Bennett then went on to describe how Brian Poole was led across the stage on the end of a rope during The Pretty Things' act; how several other musicians followed him there holding coats over their heads in typical Dave Berry pose; and how Poole continued to sing despite having a sack placed over his head. He described The Pretty Things as "individually looking like Sir Francis Drake, The Mona Lisa, Benny Hill, Cilla Black and an Old English Sheepdog!" and disparaged their music for being too loud and for not being as good as The Rolling Stones. Dave Berry and Brian Poole were singled out as the pick of the acts; as for Fury, he was considered a disappointment.

The *Western Daily Press* critic was also left underwhelmed by Fury's insistence on singing "un-famous songs" (*sic*); was particularly fond of Dave Berry and yet unequivocally scathing of The Pretty Things: "Looking like five clones of Benny Hill dressed as Saxons, they gave a performance so disgusting that it left me longing for the healthy exhibitionism of The Rolling Stones."

The John Barry Seven had journeyed a mighty long way since being caught up in similar riotous behaviour alongside Tommy Steele in Sweden and Scotland way back in 1958, with many a road travelled, stage trodden, guitar tuned, digs roomed, rounds bought, colds caught, cafés sought, parties thrown, solos blown since then. What a shame the last hurrah had to be marred by such an inglorious fracas.

Being embroiled in such shenanigans was an unfortunate way to bow out, no doubt, and yet most of the band soon had more pressing matters on their minds for within a matter of days newly formed The Alan Bown Set was already up and running with Vic Sweeney duly becoming the fifth member to agree to join. Bown's 'ex-John Barry Seven' promotion idea did prove helpful during the early days, since they were able to fulfil a number of dates on the college and university circuit hitherto earmarked for The JB7, albeit on a reduced fee. Although the new band readily retained the cache of songs introduced by Bown, it was considered inappropriate to persist with any of the instrumentals associated with Barry.

In conversation with the authors during the early nineties, Alan Bown remained adamant that The JB7 could have easily continued as a going concern had Barry not decided to disband when he did. Bookings remained healthy right up to the end, but he was given the distinct impression that Barry was aware of how much his input would have continued to diminish the longer he remained absent from the shop floor, as it were; an outcome he was unwilling to accept. His desire to exert more influence and control was likely to have been increasingly denied in view of demands on his time elsewhere; in particular, his ever-increasing film work. Barry's absence notwithstanding, any band without the backing of a recording contract – surely a major handicap for any act in 1965 intent on maintaining a regular profile on radio and television – was likely to have ended up at the back of the queue in any case, as the final tour starkly demonstrated. It remains an intriguing possibility that had the band been more in vogue at the time, this might have made it far more difficult, perhaps nigh-on impossible for Barry to shut down operations in the way he did – idle speculation now, admittedly.

~

Incidentally, the Bristol show not only saw the break-up of The JB7, but also that of The Kestrels, significantly two out of the three acts on that tour without any current chart pedigree at the time. Not that it encumbered Roger Cook and Roger Greenaway one jot, for after a brief period calling themselves 'David and Jonathan', they would go on to teach the world to sing in spectacular fashion thereafter by dint of their song writing acumen.

~

So as John Barry pulled down the final curtain on the band that provided him with an entrée into the music business, his own career was gathering apace and accelerating with startling rapidity. Within a couple of years, his mantelpiece would be adorned with no fewer than two Oscar statuettes for recognition of his work on *Born Free*. As The John Barry Seven smoothly morphed into The Alan Bown Set, the next Bond movie, *Thunderball*, was engaging his fullest attention, and within a matter of months, so too marriage, after having recently met soon-to-be second wife, Jane Birkin; by such time one could safely assume that the band carrying his name had already been erased from his immediate thoughts, but no doubt he remained fondly appreciative of the key part it played in shaping his career.

When The John Barry Seven first set out in 1957, almost like intrepid explorers tackling unknown territory, the UK music business could best be described as a cottage industry when placed within the context of the world stage. By the time John Barry decided to call time on his band, it had become the market leader, the trendsetter and the place where everyone gravitated towards in order to keep up with what was going on. That is why Bobby Graham could be heard on the latest recordings by Brenda Lee, why Vic Flick featured on Françoise Hardy's newest offering, why Burt Bacharach was crossing the Atlantic to record at Abbey Road, why Paul Simon was playing the capital's folk clubs, and why John Barry himself would soon be courted by Hollywood to score a film on his own doorstep. Yes, London was *the* place to be. Despite various peaks and troughs, highs and lows, hits and misses, arrivals and departures, The JB7 had successfully navigated itself through these radical, trailblazing times and in doing so, stamped its own mark on what was an exciting and innovative era. Throughout its eight-year existence, thousands of concertgoers and dancers up and down the country (and beyond) were consistently entertained and enthralled by a hard-working versatile unit and, along the way, almost forty talented musicians gained employment, experience and lifelong friendships as a result. Many would go on to enjoy lengthy, successful careers in the music business; indeed, even now some of them are as creative as ever more than fifty years on.

So, ladies and gentlemen, let's hear it one more time for The John Barry Seven!

New line-up includes Dave Richmond (far left) and Ron Edgeworth (sitting) – January 1964.

The new JB7 photographed by Gered Mankowitz at his London studio in early 1964.

Dave Richmond, Ray Russell, Bob Downes and Ron Edgeworth become
The Night Owls in May 1964 – a short-lived affair!

The JB7 after some changes: from the back: Dave Green, Terry Childs, Stan Haldane, Ernie Cox, Ron Arghyrou, Mike O'Neill, Alan Bown (leader) – autographed in August 1964.

Shirley Bassey pictured during her show at The Capitol Theatre, Cardiff,
with The John Barry Orchestra – 10th April 1964.

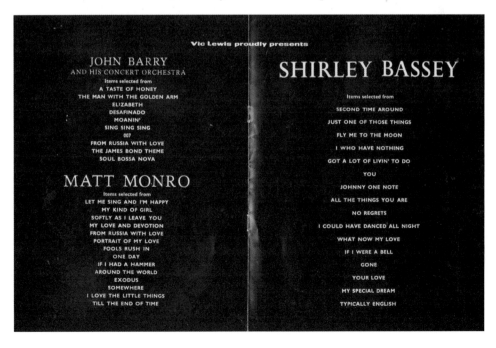

PROGRAMME OF	MUSIC AND CABARET	
Sid Phillips and his Band	Main Marquee	10.00 p.m.—Midnight & 2.00 a.m.—4.00 a.m.
The Fourbeats	The Hall	10.30 p.m.—12.30 a.m. 1.30 a.m.—3.30 a.m. & 4 a.m.—6 a.m.
The John Barry Seven	Fellows'	10.30 p.m.—Midnight
	Main Marquee	Midnight—1.00 a.m.
Johnny Watmough and his Orchestra	Grove Marquee	11.00 p.m.—Midnight
	The Hall	12.30 a.m.—1.30 a.m.
	Main Marquee	4.00 a.m.—6.00 a.m.
The Tropicannas	Grove Marquee	Midnight—1.30 a.m. 2 a.m.—3.30 a.m. & 4 a.m.—6 a.m.
The Joe Loss' Ambassadors Orchestra (Under the direction of Hugh McCamley)	Fellows'	Midnight—4.00 a.m.
The Crickets	The Hall	3.30 a.m.—4.00 a.m.
The Footlights Revue	Main Marquee	1.00 a.m.—1.30 a.m.
The Applejacks	Main Marquee	1.30 a.m.—2.00 a.m.

The 700th Anniversary Ball at Merton College Oxford, 26th June 1964.

Mike O'Neill and Stan Haldane.

The New John Barry Seven in November 1964: from left: Ernie Cox, Jeff Bannister, Dave Green, Alan Bown (leader – front), Ron Arghyrou, Stan Haldane, Terry Childs.

*New Musical Express' announcing Brenda Lee tour dates
– 6th November 1964.*

THE

George Cooper Organisation Ltd.

Presents

The John Barry Seven

Bob Bain

The Tornados

Heinz and the Wild Boys

Marty Wilde

BRENDA LEE

God Save the Queen

This programme is subject to alteration at the discretion of the management.

TOUR MANAGEMENT AND ADMINISTRATION: HARRY DAWSON & MARK FORSTER

In accordance with the requirements of the L.C.C. and the various Watch Committees of the cities and towns of this tour : 1 The public may leave at the end of the performance by all exit doors and such doors must at that time be open. 2 All gangways, passages and staircases must be kept entirely free from chairs or any other obstructions. 3 Persons shall not in any circumstances be permitted to stand or sit in any of the gangways intersecting the seating or to sit in any of the other gangways. If standing be permitted in the gangways at the sides and rear of the seating, it shall be strictly limited to the number indicated in the notices exhibited in those positions. 4 The safety curtain (where applicable) must be lowered and raised in the presence of each audience. 5 No smoking shall be allowed to take place on the stage except as part of a performance or entertainment.

★ *Get your favourites to autograph their pictures* ★

The band at a BMC promotion in conjunction with a local cinematic
screening of The Magnificent Seven – December 1964.

*Members of The JB7 and Orchestra
rehearsing with Billy Fury
– 1st March 1965.*

WINTER GARDENS - BOURNEMOUTH
Manager: SAMUEL J. BELL

Programme

Sunday, 23rd August, 1964 at 6.00 and 8.30 p.m.

1 . . . . . . The John Barry Seven
2 . . . . . . Ray Fell *introduces*
3 . . . . . . STEVE PERRY
4 . . . . . . Ray Fell *introduces*
5 . . . . . . THE SEEKERS

interval

6 . . . . . . The John Barry Seven
7 . . . . . . The Barry Sisters
8 . . . . Ray Fell
9 . . . . . **THE BACHELORS**

General Manager (for George Black Ltd.)	... ...	Harold Boyes
Manager (for George and Alfred Black)	... ...	Peter Panario
Stage Manager (for George and Alfred Black)	...	Anthony Beeston
Stage Manager (for Bournemouth Corporation)	...	Barrington Kemble

NEXT SUNDAY at 6.00 and 8.30 p.m.

George and Alfred Black present

The Fabulous

SHIRLEY BASSEY
KENNY BALL
and his JAZZMEN

12/6   10/6   9/6   7/6   NOW BOOKING

John Barry Seven

The Alan Bown Set with Cathy McGowan in 1965; five were previously members of The JB7.

Programme page from Billy Fury tour with cast and running order – April 1965.

Get Ready Steady Go-go-go!!

presented by **LARRY PARNES**

The John Barry Seven & Orchestra

Bobby Pattinson

The Kestrels

The Gamblers

THE ZEPHYRS

BRIAN POOLE & the Tremeloes

DAVE BERRY & the Cruisers
NOT APPEARING AT GLOUCESTER

THE PRETTY THINGS

BILLY FURY

This programme is subject to alteration at the discretion of the management

Tour Management and Administration — MARK FORSTER

Company and Stage Manager — SCOTT ROBERTSON

In accordance with the requirements of the local authority: 1. All gangways, passages and staircases must be kept entirely free from chairs or any other obstruction. 2. The public shall be permitted to leave by all exit and entrance doors after each performance or entertainment. 3. No smoking shall be permitted to take place on the stage except as part of a performance or entertainment. 4. The safety curtain must be lowered and raised at least once during every performance or entertainment, to ensure its being kept in proper working order.

GET READY STEADY GO-GO-GO!!! — TO SEE
THE BIGGEST ALL VALUE — ALL STAR SHOW OF 1965

★ **BILLY FURY**
'I'M LOST WITHOUT YOU'

★ THE **PRETTY THINGS**
'HONEY I NEED'

★ **DAVE BERRY**
AND THE CRUISERS   'LITTLE THINGS'

★ **BRIAN POOLE** AND **THE TREMELOES**
'AFTER AWHILE'

★ THE **GAMBLERS**

★ **THE KESTRELS**

★ THE **ZEPHYRS**
'SHE'S LOST YOU'

★ THE **JOHN BARRY 7**
AND AUGMENTED ORCHESTRA

★ **BOBBY PATTINSON**

AND SEE FOR THE FIRST TIME EVER ★ THE EXCITING NEW ELECTRIC FLICKER SIGN!

GLOUCESTER, A.B.C. Sat., April 24th, 6.15 & 8.30	EXETER, A.B.C. Wed., April 28th, 6.15 & 8.30	HULL, A.B.C. Tue., May 4th, 6.15 & 8.30
NORTHAMPTON, A.B.C. Sun., April 25th, 5.15 & 7.45	SOUTHAMPTON, A.B.C. Thur., April 29th, 6.15 & 8.30	STOCKTON, A.B.C. Wed., May 5th, 6.15 & 8.30
PLYMOUTH, A.B.C. Tue., April 27th, 6.15 & 8.30	CROYDON, A.B.C. Fri., April 30th, 6.45 & 9.00	CARLISLE, A.B.C. Thur., May 6th, 6.15 & 8.30
	DOVER, A.B.C. Sat., May 1st, 6.15 & 8.30	NORWICH, Theatre Royal Sat., May 8th, 6.20 & 8.30
DAVE BERRY & the Cruisers *not appearing* at GLOUCESTER	HARROW, A.B.C. Sun., May 2nd, 5.15 & 7.45	BRISTOL, Colston Hall Sun., May 9th, 5.20 & 7.45

POSTSCRIPT

LIFE AFTER 'THE SEVEN' – WHAT HAPPENED NEXT

Many ex-John Barry Seven members continued to work within the music business either in a full-time or semi-professional capacity, whilst a few opted for a complete change of career. Below you will find selective pen pictures of mainly those who kept the muse going over time.

John Aris — left John Barry and The Seven because his desire to get married and live in the South West of England far outweighed any allegiance he ever had to the band. To this day, he can be found in the Goa region of India for six months of the year entertaining locals and tourists by singing and accompanying himself on either ukulele or accordion.

Mike Cox — worked in several Mecca ensembles before forming his own Mecca band at Leeds Locarno and Wakefield Mecca. After this, he worked at the Wakefield Theatre Club before entering the teaching profession in 1970. Despite joining the staff of the Leeds College of Music in 1977, he continued to play professionally, in particular on productions for Granada Television and BBC Manchester.

Derek Myers — joined the Harry Gray Band at Dennistoun Palais in Glasgow, a Mecca band with a fine reputation, with whom he stayed for several years, even moving with them to Coventry, Bradford and Leeds. When Mike Cox formed his own Mecca band, Myers left Harry Gray to team up with his old band mate, and then followed him for a second time once Cox relinquished a leader's role in order to join the band of the newly opened Wakefield Theatre Club. Unfortunately, he became one of four casualties there when the band was forced to trim down to a six-piece unit after the venue had been placed into receivership following severe financial difficulties. Nevertheless, he remained in music thereafter by playing on cruiser liners operating out of Sydney, during which time he teamed up with an Australian woman who worked on the ship alongside him. They lived happily in Brisbane until his death in 2010.

Fred Kirk — had been a fitter in the RAF prior to being asked to join The JB7, and on leaving the band in the summer of 1958, moved to Wolverhampton after accepting a post in the aviation industry. He subsequently qualified as a pilot as a result of being tutored by Stan Stennett, which led directly to permanent employment flying planes for McAlpines from out of Liverpool to all over the

UK. For a time he joined Ken Golder and Ken Richards in The Ken Golder Trio, which played in and around Scarborough.

Ken Richards — returned to teaching and his smallholding post-JB7, but sadly died when only in his forties, after having suffered a heart attack while performing on stage with his friends, Ken Golder and Fred Kirk as part of The Ken Golder Trio.

Ken Golder — became drummer with The Geoff Laycock Orchestra at the Candlelight Club on the Scarborough seafront, at the time, a highly popular dance venue. He then decided to form his own band, The Ken Golder Trio, with friends Ken Richards and Fred Kirk, and in retirement, drummed for The Scarborough Concert Band for whom he would continue to play occasionally well into his seventies, that was, until becoming incapacitated by two debilitating strokes.

Keith Kelly — on leaving The JB7 in 1959, began performing at the 2i's Coffee Bar in Soho where he was spotted by George Martin, who signed him to Parlophone. '(Must You Always) Tease Me' – written by Keith whilst travelling on the London Underground – made the UK charts in May 1960, whereupon it reached No. 27 in the charts. Unfortunately, a serious road traffic accident in Nuneaton put him out of action for a good while, which prevented him from taking full advantage of his new-found success. This inevitably delayed the release of his all-important follow-up record, and even though 'Listen Little Girl' did manage to scrape into the lower regions of the Top Fifty in August 1960, the impetus was lost. Kelly would go on to appear on several editions of *Saturday Club* and, as a result, was featured twice on the LP that was released to cash in on the programme's name. His final Parlophone single, 'Cold, White and Beautiful', was adjudged by the BBC to be 'in dubious taste' because of its subject matter (suicide, with the title a reference to the corpse) and, as a consequence, was immediately banned.

Kelly would augment his singing career with various appearances as an extra in such films as Joseph Losey's *The Criminal* (1960), a film, incidentally, that Losey wanted Barry for after hearing *Beat Girl*, but was unable to secure his services since he was already in the throes of scoring *Never Let Go*. For a while, Kelly could be seen playing with The Keith Herd Rhythm Group in Hull, and not long after recording a solo single for CBS in 1965, 'Laurie (Strange Things Happen)' – at precisely the same time Barry joined the label – he spent twelve years in Sunderland, playing the local clubs, continuing to do so right up until the late seventies when many began to close. After experiencing a positive reaction playing in Jersey, he decided to try his luck over there. On a pure whim, he completely changed career direction in taking up gardening, which proved to be an astute move, for he has worked in that capacity for the same employer now for over thirty years – although he admits to not doing quite so much these days now that he is an octogenarian.

Lisa Page — (now Liza) continued singing for several years, particularly in hotels, including a long stint in Vietnam. She acted on stage, in films and on television, before eventually setting up Liza Page Productions through which she teaches elocution and creates DVDs for those customers wishing to create their own visual life stories.

Les Reed OBE — soon found himself in demand as an MD/arranger on leaving The Seven, picking up work for a number of record companies and individual managements. As outlined in Chapter Six, he was headhunted for the role of MD at Piccadilly Records, the success of which led him to join Decca. With a growing reputation came offers from radio and television seeking his services in a similar vein, which resulted in considerable runs on such shows as *On The Scene* and *Saturday Club* (for radio) and *Gadzooks*, *The Rolf Harris Show* and *Ready Steady Go!* (for television). He formed The Les Reed Combo at around the same time, through which he recorded many highly successful singles; as a result, BBC radio concerts came in thick and fast with the Combo seldom off air. Alongside his production and arranging work, he began a successful song-writing partnership with Barry Mason with whom he enjoyed several major chart hits including 'It's Not Unusual' and 'Delilah' (Tom Jones), 'The Last Waltz' and 'Les Bicyclettes de Belsize' (Engelbert Humperdinck), 'There's a Kind of Hush' (Herman's Hermits / The Carpenters) and 'Here It Comes Again' (The Fortunes). Now owner of several publishing companies, which his daughter, Donna, helps to run, he was awarded the OBE in the Queen's 1998 Birthday Honours List and has since reactivated the Chapter One label, which he first set up in 1968. At the time of writing, Les is working on his autobiography.

Dougie Wright — after leaving The Seven, joined The Ted Taylor Four, who were then resident band at The Jack of Clubs nightclub in Brewer Street, Soho, run by the son of entrepreneur Jack Iseau with a restaurant housed on the ground floor and a club lying underneath. Having already gained a reputation as one of the best and most reliable drummers on the scene, he started to receive offers of studio work, and through fixers such as Charlie Katz, David Katz, Harry Benson, Sid Sax, Alec Firman, and Bernard Monshin, soon became busy enough to leave the club scene altogether and go freelance. He also spent a couple of years as part of the *Ready Steady Go!* house band, which proved extremely rewarding, both professionally and financially. During the seventies, he joined a jazz group, The Eddie Thompson Trio, in addition to playing for Harry Stoneham, whose ensemble became *The Michael Parkinson Show*'s resident house band throughout the decade. Wright has since taught percussion at various colleges based in the Leicester area and continues to play in various bands. He also presents a regional talk show called 'My Parade of Hits', on which he focuses on those hit records from the sixties and seventies on which he contributed. These included 'The Sun Ain't Gonna Shine Anymore' (The Walker Brothers), 'Eloise' (Barry Ryan), Je T'aime (Jane Birkin and Serge Gainsbourg), 'World Without Love' (Peter and Gordon), 'Hi Ho Silver Lining' (Jeff Beck), 'Step Inside Love' (Cilla Black), 'No Milk Today' (Herman's Hermits), 'Love Grows (Where My Rosemary Goes)' (Edison Lighthouse) and 'Bye Bye Baby' (The Bay City Rollers).

Brian Hazelby — appeared on *Opportunity Knocks* during 1982 playing a Lowrey organ that was kindly loaned to him by Jerry Allen, during the same year in which he was also commissioned by Yamaha to demonstrate those keyboards duly nominated at their worldwide annual award ceremony in Hamburg. His career in music also embraced a twelve-year residency as musical director at La Reserve in Sutton Coldfield, a restaurant and cabaret venue where many a famous artist appeared. He acted as musical director for Roy Neal in the early days of the Caister festivals, and recorded numerous records, cassettes and CDs for the Grosvenor label. After such a busy life playing, he suddenly decided to pursue an academic path; these studies garnered well-earned qualifications from such renowned institutions as the London College of Music (LLCM). He also put on regular concerts of organ music to various organ societies scattered around the UK before finally retiring in 2015. His has been a lifetime steeped in music.

Andy White — was never really a permanent member of the band, but filled in occasionally when required. In fact he was still stepping in for them on the odd date or two during the 1963 September disbandment upheaval. He continued a heavy session work schedule for many years, and although he will always be known most famously for playing on a version of The Beatles' first single 'Love Me Do', he could be heard drumming on an array of other hits from the sixties, among those of Tom Jones, Herman's Hermits and Lulu; in fact, on the latter's performance of 'Shout' he was joined by Vic Flick on guitar. One of his longest-running engagements was an eleven-year stint spent as part of Marlene Dietrich's touring band during the sixties and seventies.

On divorcing his first wife, former Vernons Girl Lyn Cornell, White moved to Scotland where he played in the BBC Scottish Radio Orchestra until it was disbanded in 1983, whereupon he emigrated to New York and taught percussion: both standard drumming and drumming in pipe bands. He then married Thea White, a librarian who also supplied voices for cartoons, whilst continuing to play as a freelance drummer. He died in New Jersey in November 2015.

Mike Peters — held down numerous musical jobs as a professional and semi pro, as well as managing various music/musical instrument retail outlets in Manchester, Liverpool and Newcastle. During his time in Leeds he took a course in electrics/electronics, thereby enabling him to also work in that field for several years.

Vic Flick — undertook prodigious session work throughout the sixties and seventies on relinquishing the leadership of The JB7, before concentrating on writing and arranging for TV and films. Amongst this work has been his involvement in arranging and conducting music for a number of those from the James Ivory/Ismail Merchant stable. In 2000, he released a solo album, *Vic Flick Now* (containing his take on several Bond themes) and in 2005, he scored the film *Wilson Chance*. His autobiography, *Vic Flick Guitarman: From James Bond to The Beatles and Beyond* was published in the USA by BearManor Media during August 2008 and remains in print. He now lives in America and is often in demand throughout all platforms of the media for recounting his part in the recording of 'The James Bond Theme'.

Jimmy Stead — joined the Tony Meehan/Jet Harris band after The JB7's disbandment, but this was a short-lived affair, after which he made the monumental decision to give up being a full-time professional, thereafter resuming semi-pro work in and around Bedfordshire. He was soon asked to join such an outfit in the Luton area, but after a good run, even that disbanded. Although he continued to play a few spasmodic gigs here and there, the rising popularity of the guitar meant that hiring the services of a baritone saxophonist became ever more infrequent. In the meantime, he and his wife, Rita, had bought the lease of an established ladies hairdressing salon in Luton, Jimmy having had completed a ladies hairdressing course when he was still with The Seven. Although he didn't settle into the profession, the business continued to expand while he joined the then GPO, firstly as an engineer, then as part of their sales department. He eventually achieved a senior post at Telecom's headquarters in London and continued at various levels until early retirement at the age of fifty, after which he became a telecommunications consultant. Sandwiched in between a further three years in consultancy was a period as a director for a technology company. In retirement, he and Rita settled in Spain. They travel extensively now with bi-annual trips to Australia almost routine. With him goes his trusty sax, which enables him to jam along with many like-minded musician friends in Australia, Bali and Hawaii. After 47 years, he and Mike Cox were finally re-united at which point they wasted no time getting together for a 'tenor sax burn-off', as they call it, at a local bar in La Llosa.

Dennis King — became a busy semi-pro musician in and around London and Bedfordshire, while returning to the printing trade, eventually joining the company, Ruislip Press, where he worked until forced into retirement prematurely due to ill health. King and wife Hazel had two children, Oliver and Natalie; whereas Oliver inherited his father's musical skills and runs a rehearsal rig, Natalie works in the City. Dennis died from leukaemia on 26th December 1992.

Bobby Carr — worked extensively in the thriving nightclub scene around Newcastle and the North East at venues such as La Dolce Vita (as a member of the Bobby Stephenson Quintet) and at the Oxford Gallery. He later formed his own band, The Bobby Carr Quintet. During the seventies, he could often be seen performing at the Hofbrauhaus (a German Bierkeller in Newcastle) playing in an Oompah band wearing lederhosen! Sadly, he died while only in his forties. Saxophonist Cormac Loane, who tutors at the Birmingham Conservatoire, paid this warm tribute to him: *"Bobby Carr was my mentor as a young jazz musician, growing up in Newcastle in the 1970s. I first got to know him in 1972, playing in the Newcastle Big Band and in the Thursday night jam sessions at the Wheatsheaf in New York (near Whitley Bay), where he joined in happily with enthusiastic amateurs, including myself and the young Gordon Sumner (aka Sting) who, at the time, was learning how to play jazz on the bass guitar.*

Bobby was a truly wonderful musician and trumpet player – every phrase he played was perfectly formed and beautifully executed, whether he was playing a slow ballad, an up-tempo bebop number or an Oompah tune in the Hofbrauhaus. His commitment to the music was total, regardless of which style he was playing. Furthermore, he had a completely engaging stage presence, embodying the great jazz tradition, established by Louis Armstrong, of trumpeter/vocalist/entertainer.

Although Bobby did not teach, he was tremendously encouraging and supportive of young musicians – he gave me fantastic opportunities as an inexperienced teenage musician and treated me just as an equal, even though I was still learning the craft and he was a fully accomplished professional.

Bobby was well-known for his liking of Newcastle Brown Ale – on the way to the Hofbrauhaus in his Ford Capri, we would always stop at a Victoria Wine to buy several bottles to see him through the evening, in addition to the complementary Stein of Hofbrau lager provided by the establishment. The first bottle would disappear without trace within our first few minutes in the band-room. Bobby had a theory that, on the homeward journey, he would never be stopped by the police because they recognised his car as belonging to a musician, which provided immunity from the law!"

Bobby Carr, who died on 17th March 1979, in Peterlee, County Durham after a late night gig, left behind a son, James (b. 1969) and a daughter, Jane (b. 1964).

Kenny Salmon — on exchanging his Lowrey for a Hammond organ with a Leslie speaker, remained increasingly in demand as a session musician. From around 1964 he worked exclusively in this capacity, mainly as an organ specialist but also on other keyboard instruments as required. He played on many hit records, accompanying artists such as Tom Jones, Petula Clark, Engelbert Humperdinck and Shirley Bassey, and also featured on albums by Spencer Davis and Le London Allstars – a group of session players that included Jimmy Page and John McLaughlin on guitars. The growing popularity of the Hammond organ led to a commission to record his own LP for Decca's Ace of Clubs label: *Big Beat Organ*, released in 1966 and subsequently re-packaged as *Sounds Organised*. He also played in a variety of TV orchestras commissioned for such programmes as the Rolf Harris and Lulu shows and, for over a decade from 1965, he was a member of Johnny Pearson's *Top of the Pops* Orchestra, which provided the live backing for the songs in that week's charts. When London hosted the 1968 Eurovision Song Contest he was part of the backing orchestra, and also featured on the soundtracks of numerous films including various *Carry On* ones, *What's New Pussycat?* and *Casino Royale*.

From the early 1960s to the mid-1970s, Salmon was heard regularly performing with his own small groups on BBC radio; first on the Light Programme and later Radio 2 in programmes such as *Roundabout* and *Night Ride*. The Kenny Salmon Seven was among the guest artists who appeared on the Beatles' *From Us to You* Boxing Day special broadcast in 1963. Later sessions were more likely to have featured the pared-down Kenny Salmon Trio, with Russ Stableford on bass and John Dean on drums. Many a BBC session was also graced by Salmon's presence, particularly those specially recorded to comply with their needle-time policy. He also played on the theme and incidental music recorded for many a popular TV series including *The Persuaders*, *Department S* and *Sapphire and Steel*. Also on his CV: a 1976 tour with Cliff Richard, and a musical associate role with ATV during the late seventies for which he wrote some original music for the drama series, *All the Fun of the Fair* (1979). From the early 1970s onwards, he concentrated increasingly on writing and recording his own music, both at commercial recording studios and in his own home studio. Kenny Salmon died at Epsom, Surrey in 1994.

Ray Cooper — regularly played with London-based orchestras such as Joe Loss's, and also developed a double act called Burns & Cooper, which lasted for three years and toured all over Europe. After having relocated to the USA in 1966, he settled in Miami, Florida before moving to Las Vegas to work at major hotels accompanying the Russ Morgan, Ray McKinley and Larry Elgart Orchestras. He then formed a trio called The Dam Limeys that performed ostensibly in Las Vegas, but was also recruited for the opening of the London Bridge in Lake Havasu, Arizona. Long Beech, California, became his next destination where he put on a programme for various schools and colleges called 'The History of Vaudeville'. Thereafter, he performed for twelve years on the *Queen Mary*, long since dry-docked in Long Beach, yet now a major tourist attraction and hotel. In 1979 Cooper finally became a US citizen. He now presents a one-man show, especially for schools and colleges, entitled 'From Broadway back to Vaudeville' based on the history of Vaudeville.

Tony Ashton — joined the short-lived Mike Hurst and The Methods on leaving The JB7, before forming The Executives with whom he recorded three singles. Working with various minor Merseybeat outfits thereafter did not escape the attention of Brian Epstein, who invited him to join the instrumental group, The Remo Four, early in 1965. As well as recording in their own right, the outfit backed Johnny Sandon, Gregory Phillips and Tommy Quickly. At Ashton's instigation, the Four also developed a jazz-rock repertoire as heard on a German LP, *Smile* (1967). Back home, they assisted George Harrison on his debut solo project, the soundtrack for the Jane Birkin film *Wonderwall* (1968), which would become the first LP issued on The Beatles' newly launched Apple label. The Harrison connection paid further dividends when he was asked to play on *All Things Must Pass*, by which time the trio Ashton, Gardner and Dyke were up and running, comprising Ashton on keyboards, Remo Four's Roy Dyke on drums and Creation's Kim Gardner on bass. They managed one huge hit in 'Resurrection Shuffle', but without ever managing to consolidate on it despite releasing three albums, disbanded in 1973.

The seventies saw further collaborations with the likes of Chicken Shack, Medicine Head, Family, and Paice, Ashton and Lord – the latter via an album, *Malice in Wonderland* (1977) which was promoted with a British tour. Ashton went onto co-present the Channel 4 series, *Gastank*, with Rick Wakeman during the early eighties, but as the nineties commenced, he was already beginning to develop a secondary career as an artist. Many of his paintings were purchased by DJ/TV presenter Chris Evans for exhibition at his art gallery, Well Hung, in Notting Hill. His memoirs, *Zermattitis: A Musician's Guide to Going Downhill Fast*, were published posthumously in 2011. A well-respected figure throughout rock circles, Ashton was diagnosed with cancer as the twentieth century was coming to a close, but despite extensive treatment, he died at his home in London on 28th May 2001 at the age of 55.

Ray Stiles — left The JB7 after only a few months following an approach from old friend Mike Hurst to become a founder member of Mike Hurst and The Methods alongside Tony Ashton, Ray Smith and Nigel Menday. According to Mike Hurst, they were a great band, but unfortunately five years before their time. "Nobody was listening to country rock back in 1964," he opined. Amongst future ventures was the band Blueroots, where Stiles was re-united with Ray Russell. However, he would drop out of the touring circus for good in order to concentrate his energies on family life. Being around his second daughter as she grew up was important to him, since he had missed out on his first-born's early years as a result of constantly being on the road. As a consequence, he became an integral part of his father's business, Len Stiles Music, which with shops in Welling, Lewisham and Orpington was the premier musical instruments and sheet music outlet in the whole of South London. Music would therefore remain a huge part of Ray Stiles' life, and not just as a result of managing the shops, for he would also offer daily guitar lessons, perform guitar recitals on Sundays and regularly play the organ at local Lodges.

Bobby Graham — became a much sought-after session drummer, as previously outlined, and as such, was responsible for the percussion on many a recording despite being unable to read music, at least initially. His versatility showed no bounds. Hence, he could be heard behind full-scale orchestras employed for P.J. Proby and Dusty Springfield as well as on smaller-scale recordings by the likes of The Kinks or The Dave Clark Five. For example, it is Graham you can hear on 'You Really Got Me' and 'All Day and All of the Night', the first two Kinks hits, as well as on Tom Jones's 'Green Green Grass of Home', Dusty Springfield's 'I Only Want to Be With You', and Petula Clark's 'Downtown' amongst so many others. In 1964 he became a producer (by accident) of The Pretty Things, and recorded his own debut single, 'Skin Deep'. He also appeared in the film, *Gonks Go Beat*, alongside fellow drummers Ginger Baker, Alan Grinley, John Kearns, Bobby Richards, Ronnie Verrell, Ronnie Stephenson and Andy White; locked up in a drum prison, they were forced to play long sessions under the watchful gaze of drum master, Arthur Mullard!

Eddie Barclay, owner of the French label Barclay Records, then recruited him with a view to recording English acts for the French market, but when commercial success eluded him there, he spent four years in The Netherlands working for EMI

Holland, until forced back home when his drinking started to adversely affect his work. With the help of his parents, he sorted himself out and managed to stay clean for the rest of his life, after which he opened a record shop in Edmonton, called The Trading Post. In the 1980s he formed a company making corporate training videos, but when this tailed off, he resumed what he did best – playing drums – by forming his own band, The Jazz Experience, that played in and around North London and Hertfordshire. At around the same time, he also developed a taste for lecturing at various colleges and universities. In 2004, his memoirs were published, the aptly entitled *The Session Man*. Graham was diagnosed with terminal stomach cancer in April 2009 and died a few months later.

Ray Russell — eventually turned his back on band life by becoming a much-coveted session musician and then composer for TV. Prior to this, he played in the band Blueroots with ex-JB7 bass guitarist Ray Stiles, in tandem with his various session commitments. On one occasion at Lansdowne Studios, guitarist John McLaughlin revealed his intention of joining up with Miles Davis in the USA, and therefore wondered whether he would be interested in taking his place in Georgie Fame's Blue Flames. Naturally, Russell jumped at the chance, whereupon he would spend an enjoyable year or so working and touring with them. Further sessions then followed, some courtesy of Joe Meek and Bobby Graham, until it reached the point where he was doing as many as three per day, such was his growing reputation. He subsequently worked on various TV series such as *Dangerfield*, *A Touch of Frost* and *Bergerac*, the latter resulting in a longer-term relationship. Although originally hired as a 'musical associate', as composer George Fenton's right-hand man in effect, he would in time take Fenton's place when Fenton started to attract film commissions such as *Gandhi*. "It was literally a ten-year gig!", he recalled. Russell was to contribute to many LPs and film soundtracks over the years, including several James Bond films, some of which were composed by his old boss, John Barry (i.e. *The Man with the Golden Gun*, *Moonraker* and *Octopussy*). He also played on Barry's non-soundtrack album, *The Beyondness of Things* (released in 1999) and, to this day, continues to play occasional gigs.

Ron Edgeworth — joined the band of legendary blues guitarist Alexis Korner after leaving The Seven; Korner's influence on many an up-and-coming band in the sixties earned him the epithet, 'the founding father of British blues'. There followed many memorable one-nighters all over the country working with Alexis and his band of suburban musicians. He then joined a vocal-instrumental stage and nightclub act called The Trebletones, initially finding work in Spain with Helen Shapiro. This led them to becoming one of the first ever pop groups from the West to play behind the Iron Curtain; in this case, Poland. UK bookings for summer seasons, nightclubs and pantomime ensued, which attracted more and more bookings. Being in such demand, they were performing in just about every major theatrical venue in the UK, in shows headlined by the likes of Cliff Richard and The Shadows, Tom Jones, Engelbert Humperdinck, The Bachelors,

Frank Ifield, Dick Emery, Russ Conway, Val Doonican, and The Seekers (backing Judith Durham during her solo spot).

When Judith Durham left The Seekers, she asked Ron to become her musical director for a tour that brought him to Australia and New Zealand for the first time (a tour that also included television work) and this was followed by a trip to the United States in order to record her first solo album on which he played Hammond organ and piano alongside a Hollywood orchestra able to boast such great jazz names as Herb Ellis, Pete Jolly and Louis Belson. After marrying in 1969, the two of them continued to work together for many years, touring the world's major concert halls, theatres and nightclubs, and making numerous television appearances (among them *Sunday Night at The London Palladium* and *The Benny Hill Show*). Along the way, again with Durham in tow, he formed his own jazz band, The Hottest Band in Town, hand-picked from the cream of San Francisco's great players, which he took on the road for concerts all over the UK and Australia, providing a show-stopping opening act and exciting back-up for his wife, who headlined. Apart from his performing credentials Ron Edgeworth was also a talented composer. His theme music, which he arranged and recorded for the soundtrack of the movie *Raw Deal*, was nominated for the 1978 Sammy Awards. Tragically, he died of motor neurone disease in December 1994.

Bob Downes — is still an active jazz musician, based in Germany, and has released several albums over the years. On leaving The JB7, he played with Julian Covey and The Machine, then Dave Anthony's Moods. He also worked with singer Chris Andrews, Manfred Mann's Earth Band, and the Jimmie Nicol Band, spending two gruelling years gigging in two night clubs on the same evening, six nights a week. He left that in 1968 after securing his first commission for modern dance from the Ballet Rambert. That same year he formed his own trio under the sobriquet 'Open Music' and, over the course of time, would become the first musician in the UK to start a record label of his own (Openian) in order to promote his own music. His first LP, though, was actually released by Philips in 1969, the result of which saw him being voted best jazz flautist in an East European poll. Further collaborations followed with ex-JB7 Ray Russell's Rock Workshop and singers Elkie Brooks, Alex Harvey and Julie Driscoll. In the 1970s he was a member of Barry Guy's London Jazz Composers Orchestra and also played with The Mike Westbrook Band and The Keith Tippett Band.

Downes has since composed for modern dance on behalf of The Royal Ballet, The London Contemporary Dance Theatre, Ballet Rambert, Dance Theatre of Harlem, The Royal Canadian Ballet, Australian Dance Company, Miami World Ballet, Komische Oper Berlin, Staatstheater Stuttgart, and Hong Kong Ballet. He has also performed with the Swiss mime group Mummenschanz at various poetry festivals in Amsterdam, Paris and Rome, with William S. Burroughs, Gregory Corso and Lawrence Ferlinghetti. On the Bob Downes Open Music Trio's 1972 LP, *Diversions*, he demonstrated his versatility by playing concert, alto and Chinese bamboo flutes as well as tenor sax. His 1975 album, *Hells Angels*, was recorded with a big band on which he mainly played tenor and alto sax. After moving to Germany with his wife during the late 1970s, Downes released several further records, including an LP of solo flute improvisations (concert, alto and bass) aptly entitled *Solos*. These days he very rarely performs in public, since he no longer enjoys travelling, preferring instead to live in almost total isolation surrounded by vistas of forests and countryside. However, he remains a working composer, continually beavering away daily in his home studio, and still intent on discovering new ways of stretching himself musically.

Dave Richmond — took on session work for TV and films in addition to playing bass guitar with both Joe Loss and Bert Kaempfert bands. There seemed no limit to his adaptability given that his talent was called upon to accompany so many recordings, including those of Dusty Springfield, Cliff Richard and Cilla Black; among many, many others, notable inputs were made to Jane Birkin/Serge Gainsbourg's 'Je T'Aime' (just like Dougie Wright), Labi Siffre's 'It Must Be Love' and Elton John's debut hit, 'Your Song'. This ex-JB7 recruit even became a member of The Shadows for a brief period, contributing to two albums and co-writing the track, 'The Honourable Puff Puff'. He also recorded with Henry Mancini for a five-album Reader's Digest box set project, and played on the much-loved title and end songs book-ending *Only Fools & Horses*, even appearing in an episode entitled 'The Jolly Boys Outing'. One job lasting 24 years was his fretless bass augmentations to BBC's long-running series *Last of the Summer Wine*, which was honoured by an appearance on a '30 years' special broadcast in 2003. His connection with the Bert Kaempfert Orchestra lasted several years, throughout which he was also a member of Chris Smith's String of Pearls Orchestra, Toby Cruse's Manhattan Swing and Manhattan Jazz plus the occasional Paul Holgate So Sinatra presentation – all this in addition to playing numerous freelance jazz gigs! During 2007, tuition work became his forte, when he was appointed visiting bass guitar teacher by Stowe School, Buckinghamshire, while he also enjoys coaching the Stowe Jazz Combo. Dave Richmond can be currently seen playing regularly with the Berkeley Square Society Band directed by Alan Gout, which plays for a tea dance at the prestigious Waldorf Hotel every month.

Mike O'Neill — left The JB7 in October 1964 to join The Division Two – an outfit specifically formed to back The Ivy League live so that they could capitalise on a string of hit singles, a similar function that they subsequently undertook on behalf of The Flowerpot Men for the same reason. On fulfilling these duties, he then joined Poet and The One Man Band, which morphed into the country rock combo, Heads, Hands and Feet. A prolific session musician, O'Neill played with The Beatles, Jerry Lee Lewis, Dusty Springfield, Shirley Bassey, Deep Purple and Chuck Berry. He even jammed with Jimi Hendrix (who reportedly considered recruiting him permanently as his pianist); played on Donovan's double album, *A Gift from a Flower to a Garden*; toured with Joe Cocker and allegedly even gave Dire Straits their name. He picked up on the nostalgia circuit between 1991 and 2005 by reforming Nero and The Gladiators and found himself reunited with several of his sixties' contemporaries in a collective they called 'Pioneers of Rock 'n' Roll', a band that also included Big Jim Sullivan, Frank Farley, and Brian Gregg.

During the seventies, O'Neill drifted into theatre where he found a niche as musical director for the socialist-leaning 7:84 theatre company, working alongside playwright John McGrath and actors Colm Meaney and Alan Ford. This was where he first met his wife, actor Rachel Bell, whom he married in 1979. He later went on to work as a doorman at The Royal College of Art, forging a great friendship there with Eduardo Paolozzi, with whom he swapped sculptures and prints in return for back copies of *National Geographic*, which he lovingly rescued from many a London charity shop. Mike O'Neill died of cancer in 2013.

Terry Childs — remained a professional musician until 1980, which was the point at which he started working for the Musicians' Union with whom he remained until his retirement in 2006. Prior to this, he had worked in various ensembles: eighteen months with The Alan Price Set in addition to supplying backing on the road for many artists including Dusty Springfield, The Four Tops, Frankie Vaughan and Danny LaRue. He also secured residencies in Mecca and Top Rank Ballrooms and was hired as a peripatetic flute, clarinet and saxophone teacher by several local education authorities.

Alan Bown — formed The Alan Bown Set from the remnants of The JB7, which also included ex-Seven members Dave Green, Jeff Bannister, Stan Haldane and their final drummer, Vic Sweeney. After five singles with Pye, he changed names, labels and image in a re-branding exercise, and yet despite doing so and appearing on radio and television regularly, the all-important breakthrough hit remained elusive for the newly christened 'The Alan Bown!'. Always a popular live draw wherever they played, changes in personnel contributed to various changes in direction along the way and at one time the line-up included vocalists Jess Roden and Robert Palmer. After disbanding in the early seventies, Bown joined Jonesy, while also releasing a few records under his own name, namely versions of 'Moanin'' and 'The Rockford Files', before he finally gave up playing professionally to become an A&R manager with CBS Records, out of which he drifted into management to work for his old friend Keith Mansfield for many years. When son Julian – who had followed his dad into the music business as a drummer – married in 2006, the bassist in the jazz trio booked to play at his wedding reception was none other than Dave Richmond, who had been a colleague in The JB7 some 43 years previously. Small world! Sadly, Bown developed Alzheimer's disease at a relatively early age and died in 2014, aged 72.

Jeff Bannister — moved seamlessly into his role as lead singer/keyboard player for The Alan Bown Set alongside four of his JB7 colleagues, maintaining vocal duties until Jess Roden joined as frontman/lead singer. He toured extensively with each successive line-up, playing several Reading Festivals and appearing on all major TV shows at the time, including *Top of the Pops*, *Ready Steady Go!* and *Disco 2*, which was the precursor to *The Old Grey Whistle Test*. He appeared three times at The Royal Albert Hall on various shows with the band and made prominent contributions to the song writing on all five Alan Bown albums. In the mid-seventies, he joined A Band Called O, which over the course of time became internationally known as The O Band. As keyboard player/vocalist, he appeared on two of the band's most successful albums and wrote several of the songs. Subsequently, Bannister toured with various pick-up bands, including those backing Jack Green, Charlie Dore and Gerry Rafferty at the time when 'Baker Street' was riding high in the charts worldwide.

Bannister then designed and wrote *The Multichord for all Keyboards*, a tutorial published by Music Sales in both the UK and USA. In the 1990s, he joined blues band, The Breakers, led by ex-Ten Years After drummer, Rick Lee. His keyboard prowess was featured on several tracks of the band's debut album. As a member of the house band Rockin' Horse, he embarked on four major UK theatre tours (in 1996, 1997, 1999 and 2004 respectively) providing the backing for *The Solid Gold Rock 'n' Roll Show* that comprised of Marty Wilde, Joe Brown, Eden Kane, John Leyton, Craig Douglas, Freddie Cannon, and The Vernons. Each tour culminated with a performance at The London Palladium. In 2005, he added vocals to the soundtrack of *Virgin Warrior*, a musical about Joan of Arc, before devoting much of his time researching and writing Alan Bown's biography, *The Alan Bown Set – Before and Beyond*, published by Banland Publishing Ltd in 2007. From 2010 onwards, he became a permanent member of the renowned sixties group The Swinging Blue Jeans, regularly appearing in prestigious venues across the UK and Europe.

Stan Haldane — became a founder member of The Alan Bown Set with four of his JB7 colleagues, and remained part of its various formations until 1970. He worked in sales and promotions for Phonogram until he left the music business entirely in 1980.

Dave Green — was one of the quartet who followed Alan Bown into The Alan Bown Set, but left earlier than the others in 1966 when he decided that incessant touring was not what he wanted. Admired by his colleagues, both personally and professionally, they regret having lost touch with him.

Vic Sweeney — was another of the ex-JB7 entourage who fell in with Alan Bown's plans to form The Alan Bown Set. He was an integral part of the band in its various guises until it finished in 1972, after which he became resident drummer for the house band at The Hilton Hotel situated in London's Park Lane as well as playing with Kevin Coyne (from 1978 to 1980). By this time, he was already developing an interest in becoming a sound engineer, and with this in mind, set up Alvic Studios in Wimbledon (later based in West Kensington) with bassist friend, Al James. In fact, he engineered the demos for Ian Dury's critically acclaimed album, *New Boots and Panties* alongside numerous other punk/new wave-related recordings.

Although never actually members of the touring band, mention must also be made of the following three musicians who often augmented The JB7 on studio sessions:

John Scott — was a much requested session musician throughout the sixties as a flute and alto sax player. He could be heard on several film soundtracks associated with Henry Mancini and John Barry, in addition to a host of other 'pop'-oriented sessions including the one for The Beatles that spawned the memorable flute solo on 'You've Got to Hide Your Love Away'. He also arranged for the likes of The Hollies, and Freddie and The Dreamers. As a group leader himself, his own combos appeared regularly on such programmes as BBC TV's *Jazz 625* (billed as 'The Johnny Scott Quintet'), while he was often chosen to form part of a TV house band, for instance on *Around Seven* as a member of a group led by John Barry (that also featured Vic Flick). Following a jaw operation, which severely impeded his playing, he turned his attention towards arranging and composing, ostensibly for television and films, and now has more than a hundred titles to his name. A number of years ago, he formed his own record company, JOS Records, aimed at showcasing these works. He is still writing music, mainly for the concert hall.

Bob Rogers — played electric guitar on several of the early JB7 recordings including the *Beat Girl* soundtrack. A mainstay of The Ted Taylor Four for many years, he later fronted his own band, Sounds Bob Rogers. He also played on many recording sessions for other artists and made albums in his own name. Prior to all this, he was a member of Don Lang's Frantic Five, who appeared many times on BBC television and radio as well as the film version of *Six-Five Special* in which, coincidentally, The John Barry Seven also featured. During the late 1990s and early 2000s, he experienced somewhat of a renaissance on the small screen when he became a familiar face as one of The Skinnerettes, who were the house band on the Frank Skinner TV show.

Ted Taylor — was a multi-talented keyboard player who not only ran his own group, The Ted Taylor Four, but was also in demand for a variety of recording sessions. As previously noted, he was a specialist clavioline player, which was much in evidence not only on JB7 records but also some by Adam Faith. His band held residencies in various London nightclubs including one at The Jack of Clubs in Soho. Former JB7 drummer Dougie Wright joined the band in 1962. Taylor became best known for supplying the music for the long-running comedy series *The Benny Hill Show* throughout the seventies and eighties. He also appeared on screen in a few of these episodes, including one playing a wisecracking pianist in 'The Herd'. Other TV credits included *Studio E*, *Playbox*, *Tich and Quackers* and *Holiday Music*. He died in 1992.

— and as for 'The Guv'nor':

John Barry OBE — fulfilled his childhood dream of becoming a film composer and, in doing so, made a decent fist of it. He has often been feted since as Britain's finest exponent of the genre; justifiably so, it must be said. As it currently stands, he remains the only British citizen to have been awarded as many as five Academy Awards across the entire spectrum of categories.

Once his playing days as a member of The JB7 had finished, he continued as a musical director for EMI Records, before a brief stint saw him assume the role of musical overlord for the independent record label, Ember. At around the same time, he also conducted artists of the calibre of Shirley Bassey and Matt Monro on the concert platform before playing a significant part in the explosion of talent that put Britain at the forefront of the arts throughout the 1960s during which time his career as a film (and television) composer took off spectacularly.

His striking work on *Beat Girl* and *Never Let Go* attracted the attention of the producers of the then forthcoming first James Bond film, *Dr. No*. In shaping 007's musical DNA on that film, this led him to become the franchise's in-house composer. In fact, the resultant John Barry Seven and Orchestra's recording of 'The James Bond Theme' was to become, arguably, the most famous film theme in cinematic history.

Barry was also assisted into the film industry through a burgeoning relationship with actor/writer-turned-director Bryan Forbes, who asked him to write a couple of jazz numbers for use in a club scene in Forbes' 1962 film, *The L-Shaped Room*. From this very modest beginning, the couple went on to collaborate on five subsequent films, including the highly acclaimed *Séance on a Wet Afternoon*, *King Rat* and *The Whisperers*. Other highlights from the sixties included five more Bond films (resulting in a gold disc for sales of the *Goldfinger* LP), *Zulu*, *Born Free* (a double Oscar-winner), *The Lion In Winter* (another Oscar success) and *Midnight Cowboy*.

During the seventies, Barry scored the cult film *Walkabout*, *The Last Valley* and the Oscar-nominated *Mary, Queen Of Scots*; wrote the theme for TV's *The Persuaders*; a film musical version of *Alice's Adventures in Wonderland*; *The Tamarind Seed*, and with Don Black, the hit stage musical *Billy* (which launched Michael Crawford's stage musical career). He conducted concerts of his music in London, Los Angeles and throughout Japan during this time.

After relocating to the USA in 1975, Barry scored *Eleanor and Franklin*, *Robin and Marian* and *King Kong* in quick succession, but was to become less conspicuous as the decade wore on. However, the eighties saw him re-emerge impressively with a mix of larger-budget commissions of the calibre of *Body Heat*, *Jagged Edge*, *Out of Africa* (another Oscar winner) and *The Cotton Club*, in addition to smaller ones such as *Touched by Love* and *Svengali*. Other successes included *Somewhere In Time*, *Frances*, plus three more Bond outings, among them his last, *The Living Daylights*.

After recovering from a serious, life-threatening illness in the late eighties,

Barry returned with yet another Oscar success, this time winning Best Score for *Dances with Wolves* and he was also nominated for *Chaplin* in 1992. Subsequent commissions included *Indecent Proposal*, *My Life*, *Cry the Beloved Country*, during which time he also recorded the compilation albums *Moviola* and *Moviola II* as well as highly successful and well-received non-soundtrack albums, *The Beyondness of Things* and *Eternal Echoes*.

During the final years of the millennium, Barry made a staggeringly successful return to the live arena, by playing to sell-out audiences at The Royal Albert Hall, and was seen on numerous occasions making guest appearances at further concerts dedicated to his music when his health limited his ability to perform. He was awarded the OBE in the 1999 Queen's Birthday Honours List for his services to music, and was the subject of a BBC Omnibus special, *John Barry: Licence to Thrill*, in 2000. The following year he scored what turned out to be his last ever film score, *Enigma*. However, in 2004 he was re-united with Don Black in order to complete his fifth stage musical, *Brighton Rock*, which enjoyed a limited run at The Almeida Theatre in London.

On 30th January 2011, Barry died suddenly following a heart attack at his home in Oyster Bay, New York, aged 77. Heartfelt eulogies and tributes from all walks of life were to be found in every branch of the media on the announcement of his death. A sell-out memorial concert, held in June of that year at The Royal Albert Hall, was a fitting and moving occasion that illustrated precisely why John Barry's outstanding musical legacy will live on for generations to come.

GROUP MEMBERS INCLUDED

John Barry (vocals and trumpet), **Mike Cox** (tenor-sax), **Derek Myers** (alto-sax), **Ken Golder** (drums), **Don Martin** (drums), **Fred Kirk** (bass guitar), **Ken Richards** (lead guitar), **Keith Kelly** (rhythm guitar), **John E. Aris** (vibes), **Jimmy Stead** (baritone sax), **Mike Peters** (bass guitar), **Dennis King** (tenor sax), **Dougie Wright** (drums), **Jack Oliver** (guitar), **Vic Flick** (guitar), **Les Reed** (keyboards), **Bobby Carr** (trumpet), **Dick Harwood** (drums), **Brian Hazelby** (keyboards), **Andy White** (drums), **Ray Cooper** (drums), **Kenny Salmon** (keyboards), **Bobby Graham** (drums), **Ray Stiles** (bass guitar), **Tony Ashton** (keyboards), **Ray Russell** (lead guitar), **Terry Childs** (baritone sax), **Bob Downes** (tenor sax), **Alan Bown** (trumpet), **Dave Richmond** (bass guitar), **Ron Edgeworth** (keyboards), **Mike O'Neill** (vocals/keyboards), **Dave Green** (tenor sax), **Stan Haldane** (bass guitar), **Ernie Cox** (drums), **Ron Arghyrou** (lead guitar), **Jeff Bannister** (vocals/keyboards), **Dave Elvin** (drums), **Vic Sweeney** (drums).

AWARDS

New Musical Express Annual Popularity Poll
(Small group section)
The John Barry Seven – Runners-up (1959)
The John Barry Seven – Runners-up (1960)
The John Barry Seven – Runners-up (1961)

SELECTED DIARY OF EVENTS

1957

10th Mar: at The Rialto, York (unscheduled appearance during film show).

17th Mar: Mitchell Torok at The Rialto, York.

7th Apr: Johnnie Ray at The Rialto, York.

22nd Jul: for four weeks: Tommy Steele, The Ken-Tones, Desmond Lane, Reg Thompson at Blackpool Palace Theatre (afternoons).

19th Aug: for one week: Frankie Vaughan Show at The Winter Gardens, Bournemouth.

2nd Sep: for one week: Frankie Vaughan Show at Torquay.

8th Sep: Top 20 hit-parade all star show at The Royal Albert Hall.

7th – 22nd Dec: Paul Anka, Bob Cort Skiffle, Billie Anthony, Gitson Sisters, Dicky Dawson at The Regal, Edmonton, London.

31st Dec: S.O.S. Charity Ball at Grosvenor House, London.

1958

7th, 8th, 14th and 15th Jan: Six-Five Special Stage Show with Pete Murray, Jo Douglas, Freddie Mills, The Five Dallas Boys, Cab Kaye and His Quintet, Adam Faith, Kerry Martin, The Vernons Girls, Produced by Jack Good, script by Trevor Peacock, promoter: Harold Fielding.

14th – 26th Apr: Tommy Steele in Scandinavia.

22nd Jun: Sarah Vaughan, Johnny Duncan, at The Rialto, York. Music performed: Get Happy, Wonderful Time Up There, Rodeo, Blue Moon, Pancho, Every Which Way, You've Gotta Way, Hideaway, Festival, Up Above My Head.

2nd Jun – 1st Sep: Jackie Dennis, The Ken-Tones, Desmond Lane, Reg Thompson, Des O'Connor, Larry Grayson, Lena Martell, Liddell Triplets, one week each at Nottingham, Chiswick, Birmingham, Bournemouth, Margate, Sheffield, Manchester, Cardiff, Glasgow, Edinburgh, Newcastle.

20th Sep – 5th Oct: 'Extravaganza!' with Marty Wilde and Vince Eager at Burnt Oak, Clacton, Portsmouth, Loughborough, Southport, Birkenhead (Billy Fury debut), Stretford, Leicester.

27th Oct – 1st Dec: various weeks/one-nighters: Marty Wilde and His Wildcats, Nancy Whiskey, including at Chiswick, Norwich, Metropolitan, Edgware Road, Burnley, Scunthorpe, The Rialto, York, Sunderland, Cardiff.

1959

11th Jan: *NME* Poll Winners' Concert at The Royal Albert Hall, London.

7th – 20th Feb: Star cinema tour.

22nd Feb – 1st Mar: The King Brothers and Russ Conway at Worksop, Wombell, Scunthorpe, Dewsbury, Newark, Burnley, York, Pontefract.

22nd – 29th Mar: Granada tour with The Marino Marini Quartet, The Hedley Ward Trio, Des O'Connor.

18th Oct: 35th Annual Concert for Claxton Convalescent Homes with Adam Faith, Sylvia Sands, Jackie Dennis, Des Lane at Princes Theatre, London.

15th Nov: The Five Dallas Boys, Adam Faith, Lance Fortune, Morton Frazer's Harmonica Gang, at The Rialto, York – concert promoted by J. X. Prendergast.

1960

6th – 20th Feb: Adam Faith, Emile Ford, The Avons, Mike Preston, Julie Rayne at Sheffield, York, Worksop, Doncaster, Dewsbury, Halifax, Leeds, Bradford, Hull, Harrogate, Scunthorpe, Burnley, Newcastle, Manchester, Nottingham.

21st Feb: *NME* 1959-60 Annual Poll Winners' All-Star Concert at The Empire Pool, Wembley. Adam Faith, Bert Weedon, Billy Fury, Bob Miller and The Millermen, Cliff Richard, Craig Douglas, The Dallas Boys, Eddie

Cochran, Emile Ford and The Checkmates, Gene Vincent, Lonnie Donegan and His Skiffle Group, Marty Wilde, The Mudlarks, Pete Murray (compère), Russ Conway, Ted Heath and His Music.

21st – 28th Feb: Adam Faith, Little Tony, The Liddell Triplets, Julie Rayne, Mike Martin (compère) at Kingston, Maidstone, Dartford, Bedford, Aylesbury, Kettering, Rugby, Harrow.

27th Mar: Adam Faith, Cliff Richard S.O.S. Concert, The Empire Pool, Wembley.

3rd – 9th Apr: Adam Faith, Johnny Worth, The Honeys, Don Arrol at Slough, East Ham, Burnt Oak, Birmingham, Norwich, Grantham, Woolwich.

10th – 18th Apr: Adam Faith, Little Tony, The Honeys at Tooting, Greenford, Sutton, Tunbridge Wells, Liverpool.

12th Jun: Adam Faith, Emile Ford with The Checkmates, Morton Fraser's Harmonica Gang, The Lana Sisters, The Marie De Vere Dancers, Van Dam and His Orchestra, Don Arrol (compère).

24th Jun – 17th Sep: Adam Faith, Emile Ford and as above at Blackpool Hippodrome.

18th Sep: Printers Passion Corporation Charity concert with Adam Faith, Cliff Richard at The Royal Albert Hall, London.

10th – 31st Oct: Adam Faith, John and Paul Sharratt, Larry Grayson, The Honeys, Johnny Worth at Birmingham, Exeter, Dover, Cambridge, Northampton, Lincoln, Cleethorpes, Carlisle, Leeds, Sheffield.

13th – 27th Nov: Adam Faith, Johnny Worth, The Honeys, Johnny Le Roy, Chris Carlsen (compère), at Stockport, Bury, Keighley, Huddersfield, Birkenhead, Loughborough, Cannock, Hayes, Colchester.

28th Nov – 10th Dec: Adam Faith, Gerry Dorsey, The Honeys at Banbury, Cheltenham, Taunton, Plymouth, Cardiff, Worcester, Southampton, Hanley, Chester, York, Purfleet, Mansfield.

14th Dec: The Cavern Club, Liverpool.

1961

5th Mar: *NME* Poll Winners' Concert at Wembley.

18th – 29th Mar: Adam Faith at Gloucester, Peterborough, Maidstone, East Ham, Chesterfield, Hull, Cambridge, Ipswich, Watford, Bedford, Southall.

26th Mar: Adam Faith, Russ Conway, etc. Annual Record Stars Show at Empire Pool.

11th Apr – 21st Apr: Tour of Ireland; venues included The Guildhall, Londonderry, Top Hat Ballroom, Portstewart, and Roseland Ballroom, Moate.

23rd Apr: Adam Faith at Our Friends the Stars – Victoria Palace London.

5th – 14th May: Adam Faith, The Honeys, Johnny Leroy, Gerry Dorsey, Dave Allen at Doncaster, Stockton, Derby, Manchester, Ayr, Dundee, Leith, Glasgow, Wishaw, Newcastle.

10th Sep: *NME* Big Show of Stars, The Empire Pool, Wembley.

17th Sep: Pop Prom for Printers at The Royal Albert Hall (JB's last official appearance).

18th Sep: Adam Faith in cabaret at Room at the Top, Ilford (JB7 rhythm section only) for 2 weeks.

1st – 15th Oct: Adam Faith and The Roulettes; supporting acts varied but included: David Macbeth, Desmond Lane, Johnny Le Roy, Dave Allen (compère), The Honeys, Gerry Dorsey, Chris Carlsen (compère), at Colchester, Dartford, Harrow, Huddersfield, Finsbury Park, Kingston, Walthamstow, Worcester, Gloucester, Wolverhampton, Taunton, Portsmouth, Bristol, Southall, Peterborough.

20th Nov: JB7 tour Scotland for 10 days.

1962

3rd – 25th Feb: Adam Faith, Des Lane, Brad Newman, Johnny LeRoy, Dave Reid (compère) at Slough, Ipswich, Cambridge, Aylesbury, Bedford, Sutton, Rugby, Derby, Maidstone, Kettering, Grantham, Mansfield,

Woolwich, Tunbridge Wells, Carlisle, Preston, Bradford, Romford, Guildford, Exeter.

25th Mar: Adam Faith, Des Lane at S.O.S. Record Star Show, The Empire Pool, Wembley.

20th and 21st Apr: at Leeds – Silver Blades Ice Rink Opening.

22nd Apr – 6th May: Tour of Ireland.

2nd Aug: Shepperton Studios – *The Cool Mikado* filming.

27th Oct: Ossett Town Hall.

25th Nov: Grosvenor House – The Annual Ball of the Grand Order of Water Rats.

23rd Dec: Dundee Ritz Ballroom.

28th and 29th Dec: Streatham – Silver Blades Ice Rink.

1963

24th Jun: Balliol College Oxford – 700th anniversary ball.

28th Jun: The Barn, Chatteris, Cambridge.

27th Jul: Great Stukeley.

8th Sep: Danny Williams at Princess Theatre, Torquay (last appearance of Vic Flick-led line-up).

4th Oct: Locarno Ballroom, Coventry (first appearance of Bobby Graham-led line-up).

1964

26th Jun: Merton College Oxford – 700th Anniversary Ball, with The Applejacks, Joe Loss, The Crickets.

Oct 1964: The J.M. Ballroom, Dundee – two-week residency.

3rd Nov 1964: Brenda Lee at The Paris Olympia, Paris (2 shows).

? Nov 1964: The Star Club, Hamburg (without Brenda Lee).

? Nov 1964: Brenda Lee at an American airbase, Bielefeld, Germany.

14th Nov – 12th Dec: Brenda Lee, Marty Wilde *etc.* at Finsbury Park, Chelmsford, Guildford, Handsworth, Dunstable, Tooting, Maidstone, Belfast, Dublin, Boston, Birmingham, Sheffield, Bristol, Norwich, Wakefield, The Royal Albert Hall, London, Bedford, Kettering, Walthamstow, Slough, Blackpool.[1]

1965

First Billy Fury tour: 'The All-Round Family Show'
Billy Fury, The Gamblers, The John Barry Seven and Orchestra, The Kestrels, Bobby Pattinson, Promoter: Larry Parnes.

2nd – 21st Mar: Billy Fury, The Gamblers, The Kestrels, Bobby Pattinson, Larry Parnes (Promoter) at Romford, Dublin Adelphi, Belfast, Blackpool, Chesterfield, Chester, Wigan, Manchester, Wakefield, Cleethorpes, Lincoln, Cambridge, Bexleyheath, Ipswich, Leicester.

Second Billy Fury tour: 'Get Ready, Steady – Go, Go, Go!'
Billy Fury, Pretty Things, Dave Berry and The Cruisers, Brian Poole and The Tremeloes, The Zephyrs, The Gamblers, The Kestrels, John Barry 7, Bobby Pattinson (compère), Promoter: Larry Parnes.

24th Apr – 9th May: Billy Fury, The Pretty Things, Dave Berry and The Cruisers, Brian Poole and The Tremeloes, The Zephyrs, The Gamblers, The Kestrels, Bobby Pattinson (compère), Larry Parnes (Promoter) at Gloucester, Northampton, Plymouth, Exeter, Southampton, Croydon, Dover, Harrow, Hull, Stockton, Edinburgh, Carlisle, Bristol.

---

1 The supporting cast varied but included Marty Wilde, Manfred Mann, Johnny Kidd and The Pirates, Wayne Fontana and The Mindbenders, Heinz, Bern Elliott and The Fenmen, The Flee-Rekkers and The Bobby Patrick Big Six.

SELECTED TV AND RADIO APPEARANCES

The John Barry Seven, or variations of it, appeared in the following TV and radio programmes. The other musical acts in each show are listed wherever possible, along with the titles played by The JB7.

ATV – *Jack Hylton's Music Box*

30th Aug 1957:

BBC – *Six Five Special*

21st Sep 1957: Elvis Presley – *Loving You* film clip, Ted Heath and His Music, Dennis Lotis, Patti Lewis.
Music played: We All Love to Rock, Every Which Way.

23rd Nov 1957: Ronnie Aldrich and The Squadronaires, Chris Barber And His Jazz Band, Sister Rosetta Tharpe, Jim Dale, Sheila Buxton, The Gaunt Brothers, The Demijeans, Don Lang and His Frantic Five, Six-Five All Star Buskers.
Music played: Three Little Fishes and accompanied The Gaunt Brothers on I'm Satisfied with my Girl.

11th Jan 1958: Don Lang and His Frantic Five, Rosemary Squires, The Tony Kinsey Quintet, Marty Wilde and His Wildcats, Kerry Martin.
Music played: Every Which Way, You've Gotta Way.

5th Apr 1958: Max Bygraves, Marion Ryan, The Four Buddies, Don Lang and His Frantic Five, Harry Gold and His New Beat Band, Dickie Valentine.
Music played: Rodeo, C'Mon Get Happy.

31st May 1958: Marion Ryan, The Dallas Boys, The Mudlarks, The Cockatoos, Eric Delaney and His Band, The Frantic Five.
Music played: Blue Moon, Festival (c. Barry).

ABC – *Oh Boy!*

15th Jun 1958: (Pilot show) The Dallas Boys, Lord Rockingham's XI, Ronnie Carroll, Bertice Reading, Marty Wilde, Cherry Wainer, Red Price,

Neville Taylor and The Cutters, Dudley Heslop, Kerry Martin, The Vernons Girls.

29th Jun 1958: (Pilot show) The Dallas Boys, Jackie Dennis, Lord Rockingham's XI, Bertice Reading, Marty Wilde, Cherry Wainer, Red Price, Neville Taylor and The Cutters, The Vernons Girls.

13th Sep 1958: Bertice Reading, Marty Wilde, Ronnie Carroll, The Dallas Boys, Cherry Wainer, Lord Rockingham's XI, Neville Taylor and The Cutters, The Vernons Girls, Red Price, Cliff Richard and the Drifters.

27th Sep 1958: Jimmy Henney (compère), Lord Rockingham's XI, Red Price, The Dallas Boys, Neville Taylor and The Cutters, Cherry Wainer, The Vernons Girls, Lorie Mann, Marty Wilde, Ronnie Carroll.

18th Oct 1958: Tony Hall (compère), Marty Wilde, Ronnie Carroll, Terry Dene, Neville Taylor and The Cutters, Dudley Heslop, Cherry Wainer, Lord Rockingham's XI, The Vernons Girls, Red Price.

1st Nov 1958: Tony Hall (compère), Cliff Richard and The Drifters, Tommy Steele, Marty Wilde, Peter Elliott, Bill Forbes, Cherry Wainer, Red Price, Lord Rockingham's XI, The Vernons Girls.

15th Nov 1958: Tony Hall (compère), Cuddly Dudley, Cherry Wainer, Cliff Richard and the Drifters, The Dallas Boys, Neville Taylor and The Cutters, Peter Elliott, Red Price, Pat Laurence, Lord Rockingham's XI, The Two Vernons Girls, Bill Forbes.
Music played: Farrago.

29th Nov 1958: Tony Hall (compère), Lord Rockingham's XI, Red Price, Neville Taylor and The Cutters, Cherry Wainer, The Vernons Girls, 'Cuddly' Dudley., Emile Ford, Peter Elliott.

6th Dec 1958: Jimmy Henney (compère), Lord Rockingham's XI, Red Price, The Dallas Boys, Neville Taylor and The Cutters, Cherry Wainer, The Vernons Girls, Cliff Richard and The Drifters, 'Cuddly' Dudley, Michael Holliday, Peter Elliott.

ATV – *The Jack Jackson Show*

17th Dec 1958: Dickie Valentine, Russ Hamilton.
Music played: Farrago.

4th Mar 1959: Cliff Richard, The Lana Sisters.

ABC – *Music Shop*

8th Feb 1959: Lorne Lesley.

18th Oct 1959: Ray Ellington, Jo Shelton.

BBC TV – *Drumbeat*

4th Apr 1959: Bob Miller and The Millermen, Vince Eager, Sylvia Sands, Adam Faith, Gus Goodwin, The Three Barry Sisters, The Kingpins, Dennis Lotis.
Music played: Long John, When the Saints Go Marching In, Jumping with Symphony Sid (with The Millermen).

11th Apr 1959: Bob Miller and The Millermen, Vince Eager, Sylvia Sands, Adam Faith, Gus Goodwin (compère), The Three Barry Sisters, The Kingpins, Roy Young, Billy Fury, Petula Clark, Ronnie Carroll.
Music played: Mad Mab, Long John.

18th Apr 1959: Bob Miller and The Millermen, Vince Eager, Sylvia Sands, Adam Faith, Gus Goodwin (compère), The Three Barry Sisters, The Kingpins, Roy Young, Billy Fury, Lita Rosa.
Music played: Rebel Rouser, Long John.

25th Apr 1959: Bob Miller and The Millermen, Vince Eager, Sylvia Sands, Adam Faith, Gus Goodwin (compère), Roy Young, The Lana Sisters, The Raindrops, The Mudlarks, Terry Dene, Anthony Newley.
Music played: Farrago, Bee's Knees.

2nd May 1959: Bob Miller and The Millermen, Vince Eager, Sylvia Sands, Adam Faith, Gus Goodwin (compère), The Lana Sisters, The Raindrops, Billy Fury, Charlie Drake, Roy Young, Malcolm Vaughan.
Music played: Trollin', Tequila.

9th May 1959: Bob Miller and The Millermen, Vince Eager, Sylvia Sands, Adam Faith, Gus Goodwin (compère), The Lana Sisters, The Raindrops, Terry Dene, Cliff Richard and The Drifters, Roy Young, Sheila Buxton.
Music played: Roulette, Little John.

16th May 1959: Bob Miller and The Millermen, Vince Eager, Sylvia Sands, Adam Faith, Trevor Peacock (compère), The Three Barry Sisters, The

Kingpins, Roy Young, The King Brothers, Lonnie Donegan and Group.
Music played: Long John, Toots.

23rd May 1959: Bob Miller and The Millermen, Vince Eager, Sylvia
Sands, Adam Faith, Trevor Peacock (compère), The Three Barry Sisters, The
Kingpins, Roy Young, Danny Williams, Russ Conway, Paul Anka.
Music played: The Rumble, Long John.

30th May 1959: Bob Miller and The Millermen, Vince Eager, Sylvia
Sands, Adam Faith, Trevor Peacock (compère), The Three Barry Sisters, The
Kingpins, Roy Young, Dickie Valentine, Danny Williams.
Music played: Guitar Boogie Shuffle, Black Bottom.

6th Jun 1959: Bob Miller and The Millermen, Vince Eager, Sylvia
Sands, Adam Faith, Trevor Peacock (compère), The Three Barry Sisters, The
Kingpins, Roy Young, Marty Wilde, Danny Williams.
Music played: Trollin', Flippin'.

13th Jun 1959: Bob Miller and The Millermen, Vince Eager, Sylvia
Sands, Adam Faith, Trevor Peacock (compère), The Three Barry Sisters, The
Kingpins, Roy Young, Marty Wilde, Danny Williams, Don Lang.
Music played: Pancho, The Rumble.

20th Jun 1959: Bob Miller and The Millermen, Vince Eager, Sylvia Sands,
Adam Faith, Trevor Peacock (compère), Dennis Lotis, The Three Barry
Sisters, The Kingpins, Roy Young, Danny Williams.
Music played: Little John.

27th Jun 1959: Bob Miller and The Millermen, Vince Eager, Sylvia Sands,
Adam Faith, Trevor Peacock (compère), The Raindrops, The Jean-Ettes, Roy
Young, Danny Williams, Cliff Richard and The Drifters.
Music played: Guitar Boogie Shuffle, Flippin'.

4th Jul 1959: Bob Miller and The Millermen, Vince Eager, Sylvia Sands,
Adam Faith, Trevor Peacock (compère), The Raindrops, The Jean-Ettes,
Danny Williams, Cliff Richard and The Drifters, Marty Wilde, Duffy Power.
Music played: Juke Box Fury, For Pete's Sake.

11th Jul 1959: Bob Miller and The Millermen, Vince Eager, Sylvia Sands,
Adam Faith, Trevor Peacock (compère), The Raindrops, The Jean-Ettes,
Danny Williams, The Poni-Tails.
Music played: Bongo Rock, Little John.

18th Jul 1959: (recorded on 16th Jul) Bob Miller and The Millermen, Vince Eager, Sylvia Sands, Adam Faith, Trevor Peacock (compère), The Raindrops, Danny Williams, Poni-Tails, Derry Hart.
Music played: Teenage Guitar, Flippin' In.

25th Jul 1959: Bob Miller and The Millermen, Vince Eager, Sylvia Sands, Adam Faith, Trevor Peacock (compère), The Raindrops, Danny Williams, The Poni-Tails.
Music played: Farrago, Mason Dixon Line.

1st Aug 1959: Bob Miller and The Millermen, Vince Eager, Sylvia Sands, Adam Faith, Trevor Peacock (compère), The Raindrops, Danny Williams, Poni-Tails, Don Lang.
Music played: Little John, Festival.

8th Aug 1959: Bob Miller and The Millermen, Vince Eager, Sylvia Sands, Adam Faith, Trevor Peacock (compère), Joe Bundy, The Raindrops, Danny Williams, The Poni-Tails.
Music played: What is This Thing Called Love?, Flippin'.

15th Aug 1959: Bob Miller and The Millermen, Vince Eager, Sylvia Sands, Adam Faith, Trevor Peacock (compère), The Raindrops, Danny Williams, The Poni-Tails.
Music played: Peter Gunn, Flippin' In, Topsy (with The Millermen).

22nd Aug 1959: Bob Miller and The Millermen, Vince Eager, Sylvia Sands, Adam Faith, Trevor Peacock (compère), The Raindrops, Danny Williams, The Poni-Tails.
Music played: China Tea, Cerveza.

29th Aug 1959: Bob Miller and The Millermen, Vince Eager, Sylvia Sands, Adam Faith, Trevor Peacock (compère), The Raindrops, Danny Williams, The Poni-Tails, Jackie Dennis, Don Lang.
Music played: Bee's Knees (with The Millermen), Twelfth Street Rag, Peter Gunn.

2nd May 1959: BBC – *The Ted Ray Show*
Music played: Bee's Knees (intro only) and Long John.

ABC – *Sunday Break*

29th Nov 1959: Rev Charles Smith, The Singing Hills, Mike Preston.

30th Jul 1961: Danny Williams.

ITV – *The Melody Dances*

15th Mar 1960: Emile Ford and The Checkmates, Benny Tolmeyer, Cyril Stapleton and his Band, Julie Dawn, Ray Merrell, Sylvia Sylve.

ATV – *Val Parnell's Sunday Night at The London Palladium*

17th Apr 1960: Adam Faith.
Music played: Hit and Miss.

ATV – *Royal Variety Performance* (Victoria Palace)

22nd May 1960: Cliff Richard and The Shadows, Adam Faith, The Vernon's Girls, Lonnie Donegan, Russ Conway, Nat 'King' Cole, Sammy Davis, Jr.
Accompanied Adam Faith only.

ATV – *The Tin Pan Alley Show*

25th Jun 1960: Pete Murray, Jack Parnell, The Kaye Sisters, Emile Ford, Lionel Bart.

ATV – *Val Parnell's Star Time*

27th Jul 1960: Excerpts from the Blackpool show 'Seeing Stars', with Adam Faith, Emile Ford, The Lana Sisters.

ATV – *Bernard Delfont's Sunday Show from Prince of Wales Theatre*

18th Dec 1960: Accompanied Adam Faith only.

BBC TV – *Girl on a Roof*

16th Feb 1961: Ray Brooks, Johnny De Little.
Music played: see page 184 for full details.

BBC TV – *Juke Box Jury*

Whereas The JB7 didn't physically appear on *Juke Box Jury*, their records were played and voted on, on four occasions.

6th Feb 1960, 6-6.30 p.m.
Chairman: David Jacobs
Panel: Michael Craig, Wolf Mankowitz, Nancy Spain, Henrietta Tiarks
Producer: Russell Turner
I Love a Violin – Petula Clark (Pye)
Youthful Years – Danny Williams (HMV)
The Happy Muleteer – Mike Desmond (Top Rank)
Hit and Miss – The John Barry Seven Plus Four (Columbia)
He'll Have to Go – Jim Reeves (RCA)
Oh Judy – Jimmy Isle (Top Rank)
Time and the River – Nat King Cole (Capitol)

9th Apr 1960, 6-6.30 p.m.
Chairman; Digby Wolfe
Panel: Paul Carpenter, Hattie Jacques, Nancy Spain, Eric Sykes
Producer: Russell Turner
Someone Else's Baby – Adam Faith (Parlophone)
Beat for Beatniks – John Barry (Columbia)
Teenage Sonata – Kenny Day (Top Rank)
The Old Payola Roll Blues – Stan Freberg (Capitol)
The Piper of Love – Al Saxon (Fontana)
Green Fields – Beverley Sisters (Columbia)
A Girl Like You – Mike Preston (Decca)
Tall Oak Tree – Cy Grant (Columbia)

25th Nov 1961, 6-6.30 p.m.
Chairman: David Jacobs
Panel: Morey Amsterdam, Carole Carr, Jack Jackson + 1 other.
Producer: Johnnie Stewart
So Long Baby – Del Shannon (London)
Tennessee Flat Top Box – Johnny Cash (Philips)
Image, Part 1 – Hank Levine (HMV)
Rockabye Your Baby with a Dixie Melody – Aretha Franklin (Fontana)
The Charleston – Temperance Seven (Parlophone)
The Baby Boy – Harry Belafonte (RCA)
Watch Your Step – The John Barry Seven (Columbia)
Johnny Will - Pat Boone (London)

31st Mar 1962, 6-6.30 p.m.
Chairman: David Jacobs
Panel: Jane Asher, Alan Dell, Jimmy Henney, Jean Metcalfe
Producer: Harry Carlisle
Everybody's Twistin' – Frank Sinatra (Reprise) – voted a miss
A Girl Has to Know – G-Clefs (London) – voted a miss
Shout, Shout – Ernie Maresca (London) – voted a miss
The Wonderful World of the Young – Danny Williams (HMV) – voted a hit
Cutty Sark – The John Barry Seven (Columbia) – voted a hit
Clown Shoes – Johnny Burnette (Liberty) – voted a miss
Nicola – Steve Race (Parlophone) – voted a miss
Sweet Thursday – Johnny Mathis (Fontana) – voted a miss
When the Cats Come Twistin' In – Mike Pedicin Quintet (HMV) – voted a hit
What Now My Love – Jane Morgan (London) – voted a miss

ABC – *Big Night Out*

25th Mar 1961: The *NME* Pollwinners' Show, The Empire Pool, Wembley, London.
Presenter: David Jacobs, Cliff Richard, Adam Faith, Connie Francis, Lonnie Donegan, The King Brothers, Emile Ford and the Checkmates, The Shadows, Lyn Cornell, Ted Heath and His Music, Bob Miller and the Millermen.

ABC – *Thank Your Lucky Stars*

6th May 1961: Host: Brian Matthew, Adam Faith, Matt Monro, Gerry Dorsey, Susan Grey, Ken Jones.
Music played: The Magnificent Seven.

25th Nov 1961: Host: Brian Matthew, Joe (Mister Piano) Henderson, Ricky Stevens, Paul Raven, The McGuire Sisters, Guest DJ: Denny Piercy.
Music played: Watch Your Step.

14th Apr 1962: Gene Vincent, The Brook Brothers, Chas McDevitt and Shirley Douglas, Susan Maughan, Johnny Worth, Danny Rivers, guest DJ Jimmy Henney.
Music played: Cutty Sark.

30th Mar 1963: Billy Fury, Mike Preston, Bobby Rydell, Marcie Blaine, Lionel Blair Dancers.
Music played: The Human Jungle.

ATV – *Falling In Love*

31st May 1961: Music composed by John Barry and played by The John Barry Seven.

ATV – *All That Jazz*

19th Jan 1962: Chris Barber's Jazz-band, Ottilie Patterson, The Dallas Boys, Gary Lane, Jack Parnell and his Orchestra.

2nd Feb 1962: Chris Barber with Ottilie Patterson, The Dallas Boys, Sheila Southern, Jack Parnell and his Orchestra.

BBC TV: *Extended Juke Box Jury pilot show*

1st Nov 1962: Bobby Vee and 19-piece John Barry Orchestra, which may have included entire JB7.

BBC Radio – *Saturday Club*

3rd Oct 1959: Music played: Twelfth Street Rag, Peter Gunn, When The Saints Go Marching In, Little John, Bee's Knees.

21st Nov 1959: Music played: Copperknob, Red River Rock, The Stripper and Beat Girl.

16th Jan 1960: Adam Faith, The Lana Sisters, Al Saxon, Mike Shaun, Elaine Delmar, The Mike McKenzie Quartet, The Ken Jones Five, The Malcolm Mitchell Trio.
Music played: Juke Box Fury, Lindon Home Rock, Trollin', Bongo Rock.

30th Jan 1960: (BBC Jazz and Rock Night – Royal Albert Hall) Music played: Saturday Jump Theme, Juke Box Fury, Peter Gunn, Time Out, Beat Girl, Little John, Saturday Jump (and company), The Saints (and company).

12th Apr 1960: (Big Beat Concert – Royal Albert Hall) Adam Faith, Craig Douglas.

21st May 1960: Maureen Evans, Janet Richmond, Tommy Bruce, The Ken Jones Five, The Mike McKenzie Quartet with Scott Peters, Mr. Acker Bilk's Paramount Jazz Band (Les Reed absent – getting married!).
Music played: Beat Girl, Cerveza.

16th Jul 1960: Adam Faith, Lance Fortune, The Zodiacs, The Bert Weedon Quartet, Bill Bailey's Hop County Boys, Mr. Acker Bilk's Paramount Jazz Band.
Music played: Shazam, Never Let Go, Blueberry Hill, Easy Beat.

22nd Oct 1960: Adam Faith, Red Price Quintet, Johnny Wade, Bell-Tones, Dean Webb, Bill Bailey's Hop County Boys, The Ken Jones Five.
Music played: Beat Girl, Blueberry Hill, Hit and Miss, Walk Don't Run, I'm Moving On.

24th Dec 1960: Adam Faith, Lorrie Mann, The Brooks Brothers, The Trebletones, Arthur Greenslade and The Gee Men, Mick Mulligan and His band, George Melly.
Music played: Cannonball, Navajo Trail, Black Stockings, Gurney Slade, Walk Don't Run.

4th Feb 1961: Johnny De Little; The Rabin Band; Quintetto Italian; Riddell, Frazer and Hayes.
Music played: Black Stockings, Tuxedo Junction, Lonesome Road.

29th Apr 1961: Adam Faith, The Brook Brothers, Dinah Kaye, Mike Shaun, Ricky Baron, Tommy Sanderson and The Sandmen, Arthur Greenslade and The Gee Men.
Music played: Saturday's Child, The Magnificent Seven, Lonesome Road, The Stripper, Tuxedo Junction.

5th Aug 1961: Adam Faith, Helen Shapiro, Keith Kelly, George and Alan, Tommy Sanderson and The Sandmen, Bob Wallis's Storyville Jazzmen.

3rd Feb 1962: Adam Faith, The Polka Dots, Ray Pilgrim, Joy and Dave, The Eric Delaney Band, Arthur Greenslade and The Gee Men.
Music played: It doesn't matter Any More, The Young Ones, Image, Watch Your Step.
JB7 also accompanied Adam Faith, who sang: You and Me and the Gang, The Time Has Come, As Long As You keep Loving Me, Lonesome, If I had a Hammer.

2nd Jan 1965: Wayne Fontana and The Mindbenders, Brian Poole and The Tremeloes, Susan Maughan, The Barron Knights with Duke D'Mond, Marty Wilde, The Brian Fahey Band.
Music played: The James Bond Theme. The JB7 also accompanied Marty Wilde on: Um, Um, Um, Um, Um, All My Sorrows, Twist and Shout, Baby What Do You Want Me to Do?, Mexican Boy.

30th Jan 1965: Acker Bilk and His Paramount Jazz Band, The Hollies, Billy J. Kramer and The Dakotas, The Spencer Davis Group, Danny Williams, The Marionettes. (episode cancelled because of Sir Winston Churchill's funeral).

BBC Radio – *Easy Beat*

9th Jan 1960: Maureen Evans, The Steve Benbow Folk Four.
Music played: Easy Beat, Flippin' In, Twelfth Street Rag, No Go, Easy Beat (full version).

16th Jan 1960: Maureen Evans, The Steve Benbow Folk Four.
Music played: Easy Beat, Cerveza, Peter Gunn, What is This Thing Called Love?, Easy Beat.

23rd Jan 1960: Maureen Evans, The Steve Benbow Folk Four.
Music played: Easy Beat, Rebel Rouser, I Remember You, The Off Beat (JB Sextet), Easy Beat.

30th Jan 1960: Maureen Evans, The Steve Benbow Folk Four.
Music played: Easy Beat, Guitar Boogie Shuffle, Easy to Love, Lindon Home Rock, Easy Beat.

6th Feb 1960: Maureen Evans, The Steve Benbow Folk Four.
Music played: Easy Beat, Kid's Stuff, Teenage Guitar, How High the Moon, Easy Beat.

13th Feb 1960: Maureen Evans, The Steve Benbow Folk Four.
Music played: Easy Beat, Trollin', Hit and Miss, Bee's Knees, Easy Beat.

20th Feb 1960: Maureen Evans, The Steve Benbow Folk Four.
Music played: Easy Beat, Bongo Rock, Chiquita Linda, Beat Girl, Easy Beat.

27th Feb 1960: Maureen Evans, The Steve Benbow Folk Four.
Music played: Easy Beat, Black Bottom, Rockin' Already, Farrago, Easy Beat.

5th Mar 1960: Maureen Evans, The Steve Benbow Folk Four.
Music played: Easy Beat, Hit and Miss, Mad Mab, How High the Moon, Easy Beat.

12th Mar 1960: Maureen Evans, The Steve Benbow Folk Four.
Music played: Easy Beat, Too Much Tequila, Bonnie Came Back, Cerveza, Easy Beat.

19th Mar 1960: Maureen Evans, The Steve Benbow Folk Four.
Music played: Easy Beat, Big Beat Boogie, Royal Event, Beatnik Fly, Easy Beat.

26th Mar 1960: Maureen Evans, The Steve Benbow Folk Four.
Music played: Easy Beat, Bonnie Came Back, Dumplings, Too Much Tequila, Easy Beat.

2nd Apr 1960: Maureen Evans, The Steve Benbow Folk Four.
Music played: Easy Beat, Mason Dixon Line, Big Beat Boogie, Beatnik Fly, Easy Beat.

10th Apr 1960: Maureen Evans, Dorita y Pepe and Steve Benbow.
Music played: Easy Beat (JB7 plus 4), Black Bottom, Theme From a Summer's Place (JB7 plus 4), Manhunt, Easy Beat (JB7 plus 4).

17th Apr 1960: Maureen Evans, The Joe Gordon Folk Four and Steve Benbow.
Music played: Easy Beat (JB7 plus 4), Two Way Stretch, Rockin' Already (JB7 plus 4), Like Young (JB7 plus 4), Easy Beat (JB7 plus 4).

24th Apr 1960: Maureen Evans, Paddy Edwards.
Music played: Easy Beat (JB7 plus 4), No Moon at All (JB7 plus 4), The Stripper, Young Man's Lament (JB7 plus 4), Easy Beat (JB7 plus 4).

1st May 1960: Maureen Evans, Robin Hall and Jimmie MacGregor.
Music played: Easy Beat (JB7 plus 4), My Old Man's a Dustman, On the Beach, Theme from a Summer's Place (JB7 plus 4), Easy Beat (JB7 plus 4).

8th May 1960: Maureen Evans, The Joe Gordon Folk Four.
Music played: Easy Beat (JB7 plus 4), Kid's Stuff, The Swingin' Preacher (JB7 plus 4), Manhunt (JB7 plus 4), Easy Beat (JB7 plus 4).

15th May 1960: Maureen Evans, Bob Cort.
Music played: Easy Beat (JB7 plus 4), Lindon Home Rock (JB7 plus 4), Rockin' Already (JB7 plus 4), Like Young (JB7 plus 4), Easy Beat (JB7 plus 4).

22nd May 1960: Maureen Evans, Wally Whyton.
Music played: Easy Beat (JB7 plus 4), The Swingin' Preacher (JB7 plus 4), How High the Moon, No Moon at All (JB7 plus 4), Easy Beat (JB7 plus 4)

29th May 1960: Maureen Evans, Chas McDevitt and Shirley Douglas. Music played: Easy Beat (JB7 plus 4), The Stripper, What is this thing called Love?, Young Man's Lament (JB7 plus 4), Easy Beat (JB7 plus 4).

5th Jun 1960: Maureen Evans, The Thames-side Four. Music played: Easy Beat (JB7 plus 4), Cerveza, Flippin In', Manhunt (JB7 plus 4), Easy Beat (JB7 plus 4).

12th Jun 1960: Maureen Evans, The Steve Benbow Folk Four with Nadia Cattouse. Music played: Easy Beat (JB7 plus 4), The Off Beat, Easy to Love, Like Young (JB7 plus 4), Easy Beat (JB7 plus 4).

19th Jun 1960: Maureen Evans, Clinton Ford. Music played: Easy Beat (JB7 plus 4), Shazam, The Swingin' Preacher (JB7 plus 4), Young Man's Lament (JB7 plus 4), Easy Beat (JB7 plus 4).

26th Jun 1960: Maureen Evans, Clinton Ford. Music played: Easy Beat (JB7 plus 4), Down Yonder, Blueberry Hill, Never Let Go (JB7 plus 4), Easy Beat (JB7 plus 4).

BBC Radio – *Music with a Beat*

1st Jun 1961: Kay McKinley, The Quartetto Italiano. Music played: Long John, The Menace, The Magnificent Seven, Tuxedo Junction, Trouble Shooter.

15th Jun 1961: Kay McKinley, The Ted Taylor Four. Music played: Cerveza, St. Louis Blues, The Menace, A Matter of WHO, Lonesome Road.

14th Sep 1961: Kay McKinley, The Karl Denver Trio. Music played: The Magnificent Seven, A Matter of WHO, Starfire, Route No. 1, Lonesome Road

BBC Radio – *Roundabout*

12th Sep 1964: Music played: The James Bond Theme, Twenty-Four Hours Ago, Seven Faces, You Can't Sit Down.

SELECTED DISCOGRAPHY

In addition to the original singles, EPs and LPs, The John Barry Seven's repertoire has been reissued on countless occasions through various CD albums and compilations. It isn't practical to include all the CDs here, but the major ones are listed.

(*) indicates a release on both 45 and 78 rpm.
(1) John Barry and The Seven
(2) The John Barry Seven
(3) The John Barry Seven Plus 4
(4) John Barry and His Orchestra
(5) The John Barry Seven and Orchestra
(6) Michael Angelo and His Orchestra

CATALOGUE NO	TITLES	COMPOSER(S)	RELEASE
Parlophone			
R 4363 (*)	Zip Zip (1)	(Kaye–Booros)	
	Three Little Fishes (1)	(Dowell)	Oct 1957
R 4394 (*)	Every Which Way (2)	(Torme)	
	You've Gotta Way (2)	(Barry)	Jan 1958
R 4418 (*)	Big Guitar (2)	(De Rosa–Genovese)	
	Rodeo (2)	(Barry)	Mar 1958
R 4453 (*)	Pancho (2)	(Barry)	
	Hideaway (2)	(Barry)	Jul 1958
	With Latin–American Rhythm Accompaniment		
R 4488 (*)	Farrago (2)	(White)	
	Bee's Knees (2)	(Barry)	Nov 1958
R 4530 (*)	Long John (2)	(White)	
	Snap 'N' Whistle (2)	(Barry)	Feb 1959
R 4560 (*)	Little John (2)	(Barry)	
	For Pete's Sake (2)	(Barry)	Jun 1959
R 4580	Twelfth Street Rag (2)	(Bowman)	
	Christella (2)	(Barry)	Sep 1959
Columbia			
DB 4414	Hit and Miss (3)	(Barry	
	Rockin' Already (3)	(Trad. Arranged: Barry)	Feb 1960
DB 4446	Beat for Beatniks (4)	(Barry)	
	Big Fella (4)	(Barry)	Apr 1960

Catalogue No	Titles	Composer(s)	Release
DB 4480	Blueberry Hill (4) Never Let Go (4)	(Lewis–Stock–Rose) (Barry)	Jun 1960
DB 4505	Walk Don't Run (2) I'm Movin' On (3)	(Smith) (Snow)	Sep 1960
DB 4554	Black Stockings (2) Get Lost Jack Frost (2)	(Barry) (Barry)	Dec 1960
DB 4598	Magnificent Seven (2) Skid Row (2)	(Bernstein) (Barry)	Feb 1961
DB 4659	The Menace (4) Rodeo (4)	(Barry) (Barry)	Jun 1961
DB 4699	Starfire (2) A Matter of Who (3)	(Lordan) (Russell)	Sep 1961
DB 4705	Rocco's Theme (6) Spinneree (6)	(Rota) (Barry)	Sep 1961
DB 4746	Watch Your Step (2) Twist It (2)	(Parker) (Barry)	Nov 1961
DB 4800	Theme from 'The Roman Spring Of Mrs Stone' (6) Tears (6)	(Addinsell) (Maxwell)	Mar 1962
DB 4806	Cutty Sark (5) Lost Patrol (5)	(Barry) (Maxwell)	Mar 1962
DB 4898	The James Bond Theme (5) The Blacksmith Blues (5)	(Norman) (Holmes)	Sep 1962
DB 4941	The Lolly Theme (5) March of the Mandarins (5)	(Barry) (Barry)	Nov 1962
DB 7003	The Human Jungle (5) Onward, Christian Spacemen (5)	(Ebbinghouse) (Barry)	Mar 1963
Db 7414	Twenty-Four Hours Ago (2) Seven Faces (2)	(Suede) (Bown–Mansfield)	Dec 1964

Ember

Catalogue No	Titles	Composer(s)	Release
EMB S 178	Kinky (5) Fancy Dance (5)	(Scott) (Barry)	Aug 1963
EMB S 181	007 (5) From Russia with Love (5)	(Barry) (Bart)	Oct 1963
EMB S 183	Elizabeth (5) The London Theme (5)	(Barry) (Barry)	Dec 1963
EMB S 185	Zulu Stamp (2) Monkey Feathers (2)	(Barry) (Barry)	Jan 1964

CATALOGUE NO	TITLES	COMPOSER(S)	RELEASE

EPs

Parlophone

GEP 8737	The Big Beat (2)		
	Farrago	(White)	
	Pancho*	(Barry)	
	Hideaway*	(Barry)	
	Rodeo	(Barry)	Jul 1958
	* With Latin–American Rhythm Accompaniment.		

Columbia

SEG 8069	The John Barry Sound (3) Except * – (2)		
	Hit and Miss	(Barry)	
	Rockin' Already	(Trad. Arranged: Barry)	
	Walk Don't Run *	(Smith)	
	I'm Movin' On	(Snow)	Feb 1961
SEG 8138	Beat Girl (Original Soundtrack)		
	I Did What You Told Me*	(Barry–Peacock)	
	The Stripper	(Barry)	
	Made You*	(Barry–Peacock)	
	Main Title – Beat Girl	(Barry)	Mar 1962
	* Vocals by Adam Faith		
SEG 8255	John Barry Theme Successes (5)		
	The Human Jungle	(Ebbinghouse)	
	Cutty Sark	(Barry)	
	The James Bond Theme	(Norman)	
	The Lolly Theme	(Barry)	Jul 1963

Ember

EMB EP 4551	James Bond Is Back		
	From Russia With Love (5)	(Bart)	
	007 (5)	(Barry)	
	Monkey Feathers (2)	(Barry)	
	Zulu Stamp (2)	(Barry)	Aug 1964

LABEL	TITLES	RELEASE
LPs		
Parlophone	Six–Five Special	1957
Parlophone	Oh Boy!	1958
Parlophone	Drumbeat	1959
Parlophone	Saturday Club	1960
Columbia	Beat Girl	1960
Columbia	Stringbeat	1961
Parlophone	The Cool Mikado	1963
EMI	The Best of John Barry Seven and Orchestra	1979
Charly	Hit and Miss	1982
Cherry Red	Stringbeat (Insert and different artwork)	1983
C5	Hit and Miss	1988
Simply Vinyl	Best of The EMI Years	2001
	Limited edition virgin vinyl pressing 2 LP Set with insert	
COMPACT DISCS		
C5	Hit and Miss	1988
Play It Again	Beat Girl/Stringbeat	1990
EMI	John Barry: The EMI Years Vol. 1 (1957–1960)	1993
EMI	John Barry: The EMI Years Vol. 2 (1961)	1993
EMI	John Barry: The EMI Years Vol. 3 (1962–1964)	1995
Music For Pleasure	Hit and Miss with John Barry	1997
Connoisseur	Beat for Beatniks and Beat Girls	1999
EMI	Best of the EMI Years	1999
HMV	John Barry Collection	1999
EMI	The Ultimate John Barry	2001
El	The Cool Mikado	2002
Silva Screen	Drumbeat	2010
EMI	John Barry – The Bee's Knees (box–set)	2011
Not Now Music	The Music of John Barry (double CD)	2015
Real Gone Music	Two Classic Albums Plus Singles 1957–1962	2016

SELECTED BIBLIOGRAPHY

Bannister, Jeff. *The Alan Bown Set – Before and Beyond*. Reading, England: Banland Publishing, 2007.

Burlingame, Jon. *The Music of James Bond*. New York, USA: Oxford University Press, 2012.

Costello, Elvis. *Unfaithful Music and Disappearing Ink*. London, England: Penguin Viking, 2015.

Double, Oliver. *Britain Had Talent: A History of Variety Theatre*. Basingstoke, England: Palgrave Macmillan, 2012.

Eager, Vince. *Vince Eager's Rock 'n' Roll Files*. Radcliffe-On-Trent, England: Vipro, 2007.

Emerick, Geoff, and Howard Massey. *Here, There and Everywhere: My Life Recording the Music of The Beatles*. New York, USA: Gotham Books, 2006.

Evans, Jeff. *Rock and Pop on British TV*. London, England: Omnibus Press, 2016.

Faith, Adam. *Acts of Faith*. London, England: Bantam Press, 1996.

Faith, Adam. *Poor Me*. London, England: Four Square Books, 1961.

Faull, Trevor. *A Collector's Guide to 60's Brit-Pop Instrumentals*. London, England: Trev Faull, 1999.

Flick, Vic. *Vic Flick: Guitarman*. Albany, Ga., USA: Bear Manor Media, 2008.

Foster, Mo. *British Rock Guitar: The First 50 Years, the Musicians and their Stories*. Newcastle-Upon-Tyne, England: Northumbria Press, 2011.

Gambaccini, Paul, Jo Rice and Tim Rice. *The Guinness Book of British Hit Albums*. London, England: Guinness Publishing, 1988.

Hammond, Harry and Gered Mankowitz. *Hit Parade*. London, England: Plexus Publishing, 1984.

Harper, Colin. *Bathed in Lightning: John McLaughlin, the 60s and the Emerald Beyond*. London, England: Jawbone, 2014.

Harrington, Patrick and Bobby Graham. *The Session Man*. Raglan, Wales: Broom House Publishing, 2004.

Hudd, Roy and Philip Hindin. *Roy Hudd's Cavalcade of Variety Acts: A Who Was Who of Light Entertainment, 1945–60*. London, England: Robson Books, 1998.

Kynaston, David. *Modernity Britain: Opening the Box, 1957-59*. London, England: Bloomsbury Publishing, 2013.

Kynaston, David. *Modernity Britain: Book Two: A Shake of the Dice, 1959-62*. London, England: Bloomsbury Publishing, 2014.

Larkin, Colin. *The Guinness Who's Who of Fifties Music*. London, England: Guinness Publishing, 1993.

Lawrence, Alistair. *Abbey Road: The Best Studio in the World*. London, England: Bloomsbury Publishing, 2012.

Leonard, Geoff, Pete Walker and Gareth Bramley. *John Barry: A Life in Music*. Bristol, England: Sansom, 1998.

Leonard, Geoff, Pete Walker and Gareth Bramley. *John Barry: The Man with the Midas Touch*. Bristol, England: Redcliffe Press, 2008.

Lewisohn, Mark. *All These Years – Expanded Special Edition: Volume One: Tune In*. London, England: Little, Brown Book Group, 2013.

Martin, George and Jeremy Hornsby. *All You Need Is Ears*. London, England: Macmillan, 1979.

Martland, Peter. *Since Records Began: EMI – The First Hundred Years*. London, England: B.T. Batsford Ltd., 1997.

Massey, Howard. *The Great British Recording Studios*. Milwaukee, WI: Hal Leonard Books, 2015.

Matthew, Brian. *This is Where I Came In*. London, England: Constable, 1991.

Matthew, Brian. *Trad Mad*. London, England: Souvenir Press, 1962.

McAleer, Dave. *Hit Parade Heroes: British Beat Before The Beatles*. London, England: Hamlyn, 1993.

McDevitt, Chas. *Skiffle: The Definitive Inside Story*. London, England: Robson Books, 1997.

Read, Mike. *The Story of The Shadows*. London, England: Elm Tree Books, 1983.

Rice, Jonathan and Tim Rice. *The Guinness Book of British Hit Singles*. London, England: Guinness Publishing, 1991.

Sandbrook, Dominic. *Never Had It So Good: A History of Britain from Suez to The Beatles*. London, England: Abacus, 2006.

Scott, Ken and Bobby Owsinski. *Abbey Road to Ziggy Stardust*. LA, USA: Alfred Music Publishing, 2012.

Stanley, Bob. *Yeah! Yeah! Yeah!: The Story of Pop Music from Bill Haley to Beyonce*. London, England: Faber & Faber, 2013.

Southall, Brian, Peter Vince and Alan Rouse. *Abbey Road: The Story of the World's Most Famous Recording Studios*. London, England: Omnibus Press, 1997.

Swern, Phil. *Sounds of the Sixties*. Penryn, Cornwall: Red Planet Publishing, 2016.

Thompson, Gordon. *Please Please Me: Sixties British Pop, Inside Out*. Oxford, England: Oxford University Press, 2008.

Welch, Bruce. *Rock 'N' Roll – I Gave You the Best Years of My Life: A Life in 'The Shadows'*, London, England: Viking, 1989.

Wheen, Francis. *The Sixties*. London, England: Century Publishing, 1982.

Williams, John L. *Miss Shirley Bassey*. London, England: Quercus, 2010.

Wilson, Van. *Rhythm and Romance: An Oral History of Popular Music in York Volume 1*. York, England: York Oral History Society, 2002.

Wilson, Van. *Something in the Air: An Oral History of Popular Music in York Volume 2*. York, England: York Oral History Society, 2002.

Woodward, Chris. *The London Palladium: The Story of the Theatre and its Stars*. Huddersfield, England: Jeremy Mills Publishing, 2009.

INDEX

'007', 251, 339, 340

2 I's, The, 303

80,000 Suspects, 232

Abbey Road Studios, 32, 47, 60, 84, 93, 95, 96, 98, 99, 100, 113, 117, 125, 128, 132, 133, 155, 157, 164, 167, 173, 174, 175, 197, 202, 208, 217, 218, 219, 230, 231, 243, 288, 342, 343

Accordionaires, The, 249

Ackers, Zena, 242, 244, 279

Addey, Malcolm, 33, 175, 208, 209

Alan Bown Set, The, 283, 285, 287, 288, 313, 314, 342

All That Jazz, 177, 197, 237, 333

Allbritten, Dub, 275, 276, 277

Allen, Dave, 164, 170, 322

Amorous Prawn, The, 205, 217

Angelo, Michael and his Orchestra, 166, 167, 338

Anka, Paul, 33, 34, 65, 66, 247, 274, 319, 328

Arghyrou, Ron, 267, 268, 279, 283, 318

Aris, John, 27, 28, 30, 33, 302, 318

Aris, Vilma, 33

Arrol, Don, 118, 119, 124, 125, 261, 321

Ashton, Tony, 241, 246, 248, 260, 261, 308, 309, 318

Atkins, Stuart, 54, 55

ATV, 57, 87, 96, 98, 128, 134, 168, 177, 197, 308, 325, 326, 330, 333

Austin, Michael, 34

Baker, Stanley, 260

Balliol College Oxford, 233, 269, 323

Bannister, Jeff, 268, 272, 273, 274, 275, 276, 278, 282, 283, 284, 285, 313, 314, 318, 342

Barber, Chris, 33, 58, 63, 81, 97, 196, 197, 325, 333

Barry, Barbara, 86, 91, 212, 236

Bart, Lionel, 94, 128, 251, 260, 330, 339, 340

Bassey, Shirley, 118, 252, 260, 275, 307, 313, 316, 343

BBC Light Programme, 11, 13, 80, 97, 113, 134, 165, 176, 281, 307

BBC Playhouse Theatre, 111, 112, 236

Beaconsfield, 80, 98, 99

Bean, George and The Runners, 247

'Beat for Beatniks', 117, 120, 121, 124, 331, 338, 341

'Beat Girl', 60, 121, 203, 333, 334, 335, 340

Beat Girl, 80, 94, 98, 120, 121, 131, 155, 175, 197, 203, 204, 303, 315, 316, 340, 341

Beatles, The, 23, 49, 88, 97, 114, 134, 158, 162, 164, 172, 195, 214, 228, 229, 236, 252, 259, 264, 275, 281, 305, 308, 313, 315, 342, 343

'Bee's Knees', 60, 67, 87, 90, 93, 156, 269, 327, 329, 333, 335, 338, 341

Bell, Freddie and The Bell Boys, 16, 26, 27, 28

Bennett, Roger, 286, 287

Bernstein, Elmer, 120, 121, 155, 339

Berry, Dave & The Cruisers, 265, 287, 324

Beyondness of Things, The, 310, 317

'Big Fella', 117, 120, 121, 338

'Big Guitar', 48, 338

Big Night Out, 157, 332

Bill Marsden, 62, 63, 127

Billy Ternent Orchestra, The, 217, 218

'Black Stockings', 133, 153, 155, 156, 334, 339

Black, Don, 316, 317

Blackamore, The, 84

Blackpool, 23, 24, 25, 26, 27,112, 125, 126, 127, 128, 131, 132, 231, 246, 280, 319, 321, 324, 330

Blacksmith Blues', 'The, 213, 214, 339

Blue Mariners Band, The, 18, 26

'Blueberry Hill', 123, 124, 125, 157, 197, 334, 337, 339

Bob Cort Skiffle, The, 27, 34, 65, 66, 319, 336

Bobby Patrick Big Six, The, 274, 277, 280, 324

Boosey & Hawkes, 63, 249

Born Free, 288, 316

Bown, Alan, 13, 240, 241, 243, 245, 249, 259, 262, 264, 265, 267, 268, 270, 272, 275, 281, 283, 285, 287, 288, 313, 314, 318, 342

Boy Meets Girls, 96

Boys, The, 232

Brewer, Stacey, 21, 22, 23, 25

Brighton Rock, 317

Briscoe, "Colonel", 249

Bristol Evening Post, 280, 287

Brooks, Ray, 156, 330

Brown, Joe, 99, 198, 243, 250, 314

Brubeck, Dave, 171, 176, 202

Buchanan, Jack, 20

Burgess, John, 33, 46, 60, 96, 113, 133, 175, 197, 240

Butlin's Holiday Camp, 65, 84, 99, 168

Cadogan Square, 248, 265

Caiola, Al, 155

Cannon Records, 215, 216

Carr, Bobby, 169, 170, 171, 201, 207, 208, 228, 234, 240, 306, 307, 318

Cavern Club, The, 34, 134, 158, 159, 321

Chacksfield, Frank, 49

Chad and Jeremy, 238

Chaplin, 317

Chappell, 120

Childs, Terry, 241, 245, 246, 262, 267, 279, 283, 313, 318

Churchill, Sir Winston, 282, 335

Clarke, Les and his Musical Maniacs, 65

Claypole, Brendan, 266

Columbia Records, 60, 113, 115, 120, 121, 125, 129, 132, 163, 166, 175, 204, 208, 209, 232, 250, 270, 271, 331, 332, 338, 340, 341

Conway, Russ, 27, 82, 90, 92, 122, 157, 161, 311, 320, 321, 322, 328, 330

Cook, Roger, 286, 288

Cool for Cats, 49

Cool Mikado, The, 205, 210, 232, 323, 341

Cooper, Ray, 217, 218, 228, 308, 318

Cort, Bob, 27, 34, 65, 66, 319, 336

Cotton, Billy, 49, 123

Cox, Ernie, 267, 278, 283, 318

Cox, Mike, 17, 18, 19, 47, 50, 61, 302, 306, 318

Crawdaddies, The, 273

Crawford, Allan, 216

Crow, George and his Blue Mariners, 18, 26

CTS Studios, 208, 231, 250, 270

'Cutty Sark', 202, 203, 205, 211, 252, 263, 270, 332, 339, 340

Cy Laurie's Jazz Band, 24

Daily Express, The, 203

Daily Herald, *The*, 52

Dallas Boys, The, 51, 53, 57, 113, 119, 197, 319, 320, 325, 326, 333

Dateline London, 203

Davison, Harold, 25, 268, 277

De Grey Rooms, 18, 19

De Little, Johnny, 97, 154, 156, 166, 195, 330, 334

Deep Litter Club, 249

Dennis, Jackie, 50, 51, 53, 54, 57, 58, 64, 81, 98, 118, 320, 326, 329

Diamonds, The, 31

Disc Magazine, 84, 85, 95, 96, 115, 130, 155, 167, 177, 203, 207, 217, 230, 251, 271

Discs a Go-Go, 175

Division Two, The, 273, 312

Doctor Who, 251

Donegan, Lonnie, 20, 27, 47, 58, 66, 81, 95, 97, 116, 118, 122, 131, 157, 203, 321, 327, 330, 332

Dorsey, Gerry (aka Engelbert Humperdinck), 97, 154, 158, 162, 164, 165, 195, 321, 322, 332

Douglas, Josephine, 28, 47, 319

Downes, Bob, 240, 241, 244, 245, 246, 247, 248, 262, 265, 266, 311, 312, 318

Dr. No, 208, 214, 218, 316

Drumbeat, 83, 85, 87, 88, 89, 90, 91, 92, 93, 94, 95, 96, 97, 115, 162, 201, 276, 327, 341

Eager, Vince, 58, 90, 93, 320, 327, 328, 329, 342

Easy Beat, 111, 112, 124, 128, 134, 177, 201, 211, 216, 237, 276, 335

'Easy Beat', 334, 335, 336, 337

Eddy, Duane, 131, 176, 229, 240, 267

Eden, Anthony, 34

Edgeworth, Ron, 248, 260, 261, 262, 266, 267, 310, 311, 318

Elizabeth Taylor In London, 238, 251

'Elizabeth', 251

Elliott, Bern, 277, 324

Elvin, Dave, 279, 283, 285, 318

Embassy Records, 112, 169, 215, 216

Ember Records, 229, 232, 234, 235, 238, 241, 250, 251, 260, 270, 316, 339, 340

EMI, 30, 32, 47, 60, 61, 82, 93, 95, 96, 97, 98, 113, 117, 123, 128, 129, 130, 131, 132, 133, 154, 166, 168, 174, 175, 195, 197, 205, 208, 213, 214, 227, 229, 230, 231, 232, 235, 240, 250, 271, 310, 316, 341, 343

Eternal Echoes, 317

Evans, Maureen, 111, 112, 333, 335, 336, 337

'Every Which Way', 28, 29, 31, 32, 46, 319, 325, 338

Faith, Adam, 13, 48, 81, 89, 90, 93, 94, 95, 96,

97, 98, 99, 100, 111, 112, 113, 115, 116, 117, 118, 119, 120, 121, 122, 123, 124, 125, 126, 128, 129, 130, 131, 132, 133, 134, 153, 154, 156, 157, 158, 161, 162, 164, 165, 166, 167, 169, 170, 171, 173, 175, 176, 177, 196, 200, 201, 202, 203, 204, 205, 211, 213, 230, 237, 274, 315, 319, 320, 321, 322, 323, 327, 328, 329, 330, 331, 332, 333, 334, 340, 342

Falling In Love, 168, 333

'Fancy Dance', 250, 251, 339

'Farrago', 60, 68, 69, 82, 85, 87, 98, 168, 326, 327, 32, 335, 338, 340

Faye, Don, 284

Fielding, Harold, 24, 25, 26, 27, 28, 29, 30, 47, 49, 51, 319

Firman, Alec, 115, 304

Flee-Rekkers, The, 213, 237, 277, 324

Flick, Vic, 12, 13, 14, 34, 64, 65, 66, 67, 80, 83, 84, 85, 86, 87, 88, 89, 91, 92, 93, 95, 99, 100, 115, 118, 119, 120, 123, 124, 126, 127, 128, 129, 133, 134, 153, 154, 155, 158, 159, 160, 163, 164, 165, 168, 169, 172, 173, 177, 195, 196, 198, 199, 206, 208, 209, 212, 215, 216, 218, 219, 227, 228, 229, 230, 231, 234, 235, 236, 238, 239, 240, 241, 251, 260, 262, 264, 269, 272, 288, 305, 306, 315, 318, 323, 342

Flintstones, The, 267

Folkestone, 166, 231

Fontana, Wayne & The Mindbenders, 270, 277, 282, 324, 334

'For Pete's Sake', 93, 328, 338

Forbes, Bryan, 208, 284, 316

Ford, Eric, 129

Fordyce, Keith, 28, 95, 115, 133, 155, 162, 167, 238

Fortune, Lance, 128, 130, 320, 334

Freeman, Alan, 277

From Russia with Love, 238, 260

'From Russia with Love', 251, 263, 272, 339, 340

Fulford House, 14, 20

Fury, Billy, 57, 59, 157, 167, 196, 197, 229, 281, 284, 285, 286, 287, 320, 324, 327, 332

Gamblers, The, 284, 324

Geoff Laycock Orchestra, 17, 303

George Cooper Organisation, The, 280

'Get Lost Jack Frost', 133, 339

Gillespie, Rita, 197

Girl on a Roof, 156, 237, 330

Golder, Ken, 17, 18, 19, 20, 26, 28, 33, 50, 51, 58, 61, 62, 63, 303, 318

Goldfinger, 260, 270, 281, 283, 316

Good, Jack, 21, 25, 26, 27, 28, 47, 52, 57, 61, 62, 64, 87, 99, 115, 276, 319

Goodwin, Gus, 90, 327

Goodwin, Keith, 116, 157

Gordeno, Peter, 97, 195

Graham, Bobby, 212, 232, 240, 241, 242, 243, 245, 246, 249, 250, 259, 260, 264, 265, 267, 288, 309, 310, 318, 323, 342

Grant, Jimmy, 11, 30, 97, 200, 238, 272,

Grant, Keith, 260

Grayson, Larry, 58, 119, 124, 133, 320, 321

Great Stukeley, 234, 323

Green Howards, The, 15, 17

Green, Dave, 267, 283, 313, 314, 318

Green, Hughie, 95

Green, Isidore, 26

Greenaway, Roger, 286, 288

Hackney Empire, The, 53, 57

Haldane, Stan, 267, 268, 270, 274, 278, 280, 283, 313, 314, 318

Haley, Bill, 26, 343

Harris, Anita, 97, 166, 195

Harrison, George, 49, 134, 308

Hartnell, William, 251

Harwood, Dickie, 88, 212, 318

Haven, Alan, 250, 263

Hazelby, Brian, 198, 199, 200, 201, 207, 208, 210, 213, 304, 318

Hazlewood, Lee, 172

Heath, Ted, 16, 27, 68, 114, 157, 246, 321, 325, 332

Hefti, Neal, 172

Heinz, 277, 278, 324

Hellion, The, 95

'Hideaway', 51, 52, 53, 319, 338, 340

'Hit and Miss', 113, 114, 115, 117, 118, 120, 122, 124, 157, 167, 204, 250, 252, 270, 331, 334, 341

Holly, Buddy, 49, 131

Horricks, Roy, 197

Howes, Arthur, 158

Human Jungle, The, 218, 229

Human Jungle, The, 230, 332, 339, 340

Humperdinck, Engelbert, 97, 154, 304, 307, 311

Hurst, Mike, 249, 261, 308, 309

Hutchinson, Ray, 284

'I'm Movin' On', 129, 130, 339, 340
Impromptu, 263
Ivy League, The, 273, 312
J.B. Independent Record Productions, 271
Jack Jackson Show, The, 68, 87, 326
Jackson, Dr. Francis, 15, 20
Jacobs, David, 157, 203, 331, 332
Jamboree Seven, The, 161, 275
James Bond Theme', 'The, 60, 196, 208, 209, 213, 214, 217, 252, 272, 274, 275, 278, 280, 282, 285, 306, 334, 337, 339, 340
Joey, Shade and The Night Owls, 266
Johnson, Teddy, 87
Jolly Bad Fellow, A, 270
Jones, Tom, 262, 283, 307, 309, 311
Juke Box Jury, 96, 114, 157, 162, 215, 331, 333
Kallman, Dick, 97
Katz, Charlie, 115, 304
Keeler, Christine, 228
Kelly, Keith, 18, 19, 20, 24, 28, 31, 47, 51, 56, 66, 69, 82, 166, 303, 318, 334
Kennedy, President J. F., 134, 217, 252
Kenton, Stan, 15, 16, 20, 63, 65, 68, 121, 233, 242
Kentones, The, 27, 319, 320
Kestrels, The, 284, 285, 286, 287, 288, 324
Kidd, Johnny & The Pirates, 277, 280, 324
King Brothers, The, 27, 28, 82, 87, 157, 320, 327, 332
King, Dennis, 56, 61, 64, 66, 96, 154, 172, 212, 213, 228, 306, 318
Kingston, Bob, 85, 89
'Kinky', 250, 251, 339
Kirk, Fred, 17, 18, 19, 54, 56, 61, 302, 303, 318
Kruger, Jeffrey, 229, 235
Lana Sisters, The, 81, 87, 113, 121, 125, 126, 127, 128, 321, 326, 327, 330, 333
Lance, Major, 270
Landseer, 23
Lane, Desmond, 27, 81, 98, 118, 170, 200, 203, 319, 320, 322, 323
Lang, Don & His Frantic Five, 26, 27, 33, 48, 64, 315, 325, 328, 329
Lee, Brenda, 260, 274, 275, 276, 277, 279, 280, 285, 288, 323, 324
Lennon, John, 34
Levis, Carol , 247
Lewis, Tony, 166, 205, 237
Lewis, Vic, 24
'Little John', 91, 93, 327, 328, 329, 333, 338

'Living Doll', 94
Lloyd-Jones, June, 11, 14, 15, 22, 24
Lolly Theme', 'The, 208, 217, 218, 339, 340
London Theme', 'The, 251
'Long John', 64, 84, 85, 90, 93, 98, 327, 328, 329, 337, 338
Lord Rockingham's XI, 53, 57, 58, 62, 85, 87, 325, 326
Lordan, Jerry, 157, 167, 339
Losey, Joseph, 303
'Lost Patrol', 202, 203, 339
Love, Geoff, 166
L-Shaped Room, The, 205, 208, 316
Maclean, Donald, 30
Macmillan, Harold, 34, 86, 134, 228, 233
Magnificent Seven', 'The, 155, 157, 162, 165, 167, 168, 177, 230, 234, 249, 252, 269, 332, 337, 339
Magnificent Seven, The, 155
Mancini, Henry, 121, 270, 281, 312, 315
Man in the Middle, 270
Manfred Mann, 262, 277, 311, 324
Mankowitz, Gered, 259, 342
Mankowitz, Wolf, 331
Mansfield, Keith, 271, 313, 339
'March of the Mandarins', 174, 217, 339
Margo, Sid, 115
Marino Marini Quartet, The, 87, 320
Martin, Don, 26, 28, 318
Martin, Sir George, 113, 303
Martin, Terry, 232
Marvin, Hank B., 12, 132, 177, 216
Mason, Glen, 87
Matter of WHO, A, 156, 210
Matter of Who', 'A, 157, 165, 167, 337, 339
Matthew, Brian, 81, 97, 111, 112, 113, 121, 162, 165, 173, 196, 205, 332, 343
Mayfield, Curtis, 270
McCartney, Paul, 34
McGowan, Cathy, 238
McGrath, Nuggy, 206
McKinley, Kay, 165, 337
Meek, Joe, 232, 243, 266, 310
Melody Dances, The, 118, 330
Melody Maker, 121, 124, 201, 203, 214, 240, 247
Menace', 'The, 162, 163, 165, 167, 177, 337, 339
Merseybeat Sound, 229, 308
Merton College Oxford, 269, 323
Metropolitan, Edgware Road, 28, 64, 65, 66,

Miller, Bob and The Millermen, 90, 157, 158,
    165, 167, 201, 211, 215, 261, 320, 327, 328,
    329, 332
Mills, Freddie, 47, 319
Mills, Gordon, 262
Modernaires, The, 15, 17, 19
'Monkey Feathers', 260, 339, 340
Monro, Matt, 162, 251, 263, 316, 332
Monshin, Bernard, 115, 304
Moorhouse, Alan, 169, 215, 216
Morecambe, 166, 214, 231
Morris, Stewart, 83, 85, 89
Moss Empires, 25, 56, 61
Moviola, 317
Moviola II, 317
Murdoch, Wallace, 274
Murray, Pete, 47, 162, 167, 319, 321, 330
Music Box, 98, 325
Music Shop, 87, 327
Music While You Work, 231, 236
Music with a Beat, 165, 167, 337
Myers, Derek, 17, 18, 19, 54, 55, 61, 302, 318
National Service, 13, 15, 153, 203, 210, 244,
    245
Nero and The Gladiators, 268, 313
'Never Let Go', 123, 124, 125, 334, 337, 339
Never Let Go, 120, 303, 316
New Musical Express (NME), 25, 28, 30, 58,
    266, 318
New Record Mirror, 163, 166, 173, 203, 214,
    230
Newcomers, The, 250
Newell, Norman, 33, 46, 52, 60, 61, 93, 96,
    97, 113, 129, 175, 209, 230, 232,
Newley, Anthony, 99, 327
Oh Boy!, 53, 57, 58, 60, 61, 62, 64, 66, 87, 89,
    90, 93, 161, 197, 276, 325, 341
Oliver, Jack, 61, 64, 65, 318
Olympic Sound Studios, 95, 250, 260
O'Neill, Mike, 267, 268, 270, 271, 273, 312,
    313, 318
'Onward, Christian Spacemen', 174, 230, 339
Osborne, Tony, 114
Page, Lisa, 68, 82, 85, 87, 88, 303
'Pancho', 51, 52, 53, 61, 319, 328, 338, 340
Paris Olympia, 275, 276, 323
Parlophone, 31, 32, 48, 52, 58, 82, 84, 85, 93,
    96, 113, 125, 165, 166, 204, 210, 232, 266,
    303, 331, 332, 338, 340, 341

Parnell, Jack, 16, 17, 18, 55, 85, 128, 197, 330,
    333
Parnell, Val, 25, 122, 128, 330
Parnes, Larry, 54, 57, 59, 68, 284, 324
Party's Over, 'The, 217
Passion Flower Hotel, 270, 284
Pattinson, Bobby, 284, 324
Peacock, Trevor, 90, 284, 319, 327, 328, 329,
    340
Peters, Mike, 54, 56, 57, 60, 61, 62, 64, 66, 80,
    82, 86, 87, 88, 98, 100, 110, 132, 154, 156,
    166, 169, 176, 199, 208, 215, 219, 228, 235,
    305, 318
Pickard (Barry), Barbara, 18, 86, 91, 212, 236
Poole, Brian & the Tremeloes, 252, 282, 284,
    287, 324, 334
Prendergast, Jack, 14, 15, 20, 21, 23, 24, 25,
    26, 31, 67, 68, 241, 242, 320
Pretty Things, The, 284, 286, 287, 309, 324
Prince, Viv, 286, 287
Profumo Affair, 228
Race, Steve, 49, 332
Raindrops, The, 90, 96, 327, 328, 329
Ray, Johnnie, 24, 25, 51, 319
Rayne, Julie, 110, 117, 320, 321
Ready Steady Go!, 238, 262, 304, 314
Record and Show Mirror, 84, 98, 130
Record Mirror, The, 26, 28, 47, 52, 60, 82, 271
Reed, Les, 14, 83, 88, 89, 92, 93, 95, 96,117,
    120, 123, 124, 128, 133, 134, 154, 160, 163,
    164, 169, 171, 174, 175, 195, 197, 198, 199,
    201, 210, 232, 238, 239, 262, 286, 304,
    318, 333
Rialto, The, 14, 16, 18, 20, 21, 22, 23, 24, 25,
    26, 53, 67, 68, 116, 206, 233, 319, 320
Richard, Cliff, 57, 62, 87, 94, 100, 118, 122,
    128, 131, 132, 157, 167, 170, 196, 201, 204,
    209, 229, 249, 308, 311, 312, 320, 321, 326,
    327, 328, 330, 332
Richards, Ken, 17, 18, 19, 24, 61, 64, 303, 318
Riches, Charles, 17
Richmond, Dave, 248, 260, 261, 262, 266,
    267, 312, 313, 318
Robertson, Ker, 49
Robinson, Harry, 53, 87
'Rocco's Theme', 166, 339
Rock Around The Clock, 16, 22
'Rockin' Already', 115, 335, 336, 338, 340
'Rodeo', 46, 48, 49, 53, 87, 162, 163, 319, 325,
    338, 339, 340

Rodgers, Louis, 206, 207

Roulettes, The, 170, 200, 202, 205, 322

Roundabout, 272, 273, 282, 308, 337

Russell, Ray, 240, 241, 246, 247, 248, 249, 262, 263, 266, 267, 309, 310, 311, 318

Russo, Bill, 15, 20

Salmon, Kenny, 210, 211, 228, 236, 240, 241, 307, 308, 318

Sands, Sylvia, 85, 88, 90, 93, 98, 113, 320, 327, 328, 329

Saturday Club, 66, 97, 98, 111, 113, 121, 124, 128, 132, 133, 134, 154, 161, 166, 177, 200, 201, 216, 237, 238, 276, 277, 282, 303, 304, 333, 341

Scott, John, 120, 250, 315

Séance on a Wet Afternoon, 260, 270, 316

'Séance on a Wet Afternoon', 281

'Seven Faces', 271, 337, 339

Shadows, The, 12, 13, 23, 57, 60, 113, 122, 129, 131, 132, 133, 157, 167, 170, 171, 176, 196, 203, 204, 216, 229, 238, 239, 252, 278, 281, 311, 312, 330, 332, 343

Six-Five Special, 25, 27, 28, 30, 31, 33, 48, 49, 51, 52, 53, 57, 89, 93, 161, 201, 276

Six-Five Special (film), 47, 305

'Skid Row', 155, 156, 173, 339

Smith, Norman, 175

'Snap 'N' Whistle', 84, 85, 338

Sounds Incorporated, 237, 274

Spencer Davis Group, The, 282, 283, 307, 335

'Spinneree', 166, 339

Springfield, Dusty, 87, 262, 265, 309, 312, 313

Springfields, The, 249, 261

Stage, The, 27, 29, 34, 51, 54, 59, 67, 68, 119, 126, 127, 133, 157, 171, 203

Stapleford, Russ, 235

'Starfire', 157, 164, 165, 167, 175, 177, 337, 339

Stead, Jimmy, 17, 46, 54, 55, 56, 57, 58, 59, 60, 62, 63, 66, 86, 87, 88, 90, 92, 96, 116, 118, 122, 127, 134, 153, 154, 156, 160, 161, 176, 207, 208, 212, 215, 227, 228, 234, 236, 240, 306, 318

Steele, Tommy, 26, 27, 49, 50, 51, 53, 54, 249, 268, 287, 319, 326

Steppin' Out, 236

Stiles, Ray, 241, 246, 248, 249, 260, 261, 265, 267, 309, 310, 318

Stringbeat, 162, 163, 164, 165, 174, 175, 197, 250, 341

Suez, 19, 34, 122, 343

Sunday Break, 98, 166, 329

Sunday Mirror, 23

Sutton, Johnny, 15, 19, 20

Sweeney, Vic, 285, 287, 313, 314, 318

Taylor, Evelyn, 51, 81, 82, 86, 88, 93, 94, 95, 96, 113, 115, 117, 118, 126, 130, 132, 153, 158, 170, 201, 205, 237

Taylor, Ted, 60, 164, 166, 172, 201, 304, 315, 337

'Tears', 339

Telstar, 164, 216, 232

Terry-Thomas, 156

Thank Your Lucky Stars, 162, 173, 177, 205, 213, 276, 332

'Theme from 'The Roman Spring of Mrs. Stone'', 339

Thompson, Reg, 27, 319, 320

'Three Little Fishes', 28, 31, 325, 338

Tin Pan Alley, 128, 330

Toop, David, 46, 155, 175

Top of The Pops, 259, 307, 314

Topline, 166, 168, 205, 213, 237, 244

Tormé, Mel, 31, 338

Tornados, The, 164, 216, 237

Torok, Mitchell, 24, 319

Townsend, Ken, 32, 113

Tring, Eric, 234

Turner, Russell, 114, 331

'Twelfth Street Rag', 95, 163, 329, 333, 335, 338

'Twenty-Four Hours Ago', 271, 272, 273, 337, 339

'Twist It', 172, 173, 201, 339

Vaughan, Frankie, 27, 274, 313, 319

Vaughan, Sarah, 20, 53, 319

Vic Alan Quintet, 65, 84

Wadsworth, Derek, 284

Waghorn, Roger, 284

'Walk Don't Run', 129, 130, 133, 156, 157, 168, 173, 196, 204, 252, 270, 334, 339, 340

Walker, Francis, 17

Wallis, Bob, 166, 196, 334

Wallis, Peter, 234

Walton, Kent, 49, 175

'Watch Your Step', 172, 173, 201, 211, 331, 332, 339

Weedon, Bert, 112, 113, 121, 128, 157, 201, 320, 334

Welch, Bruce, 167, 177, 343

Western Daily Press, 280, 287

Weston-super-Mare, 166, 260, 281, 285

Wham!, 115

Whiskey, Nancy, 27, 28, 64, 66, 67, 320

White, Andy, 173, 211, 212, 213, 217, 305, 309, 318

White, Barry, 85

Wilde, Marty, 48, 53, 54, 57, 58, 59, 64, 66, 67, 196, 232, 266, 273, 274, 277, 278, 282, 314, 320, 321, 324, 325, 326, 328, 334

Williams, Cissie, 25

Williams, Danny, 90, 166, 235, 282, 323, 328, 329, 331, 332, 335

Willis Reed Group, The, 84

Willoughby, George, 94

Wilson, Harold, 274

Winner, Michael, 210

Winstone, Eric, 65, 169, 216

Winters, Mike and Bernie, 26, 51, 81, 210

Woolworth, 112, 169, 216

Worth, Johnny, 90, 96, 100, 117, 119, 124, 133, 206, 321, 332

Wright, Dougie, 62, 63, 64, 66, 80, 87, 88, 92, 93, 100, 119, 123, 129, 154, 159, 161, 173, 202, 211, 212, 213, 238, 239, 264, 304, 312, 315, 318

Young, Roy, 90, 92, 327, 328

'You've Gotta Way', 31, 53, 319, 325, 338

Zephyrs, The, 284, 324

'Zip Zip', 31, 32, 33, 63, 338

Zulu, 260, 316

'Zulu Stamp', 260, 262, 339, 340